Kitchen Princess

1

Natsumi Ando

Story by Miyuki Kobayashi

Translated by Satsuki Yamashita

Adapted by Nunzio DeFilippis and Christina Weir

Lettered by North Market Street Graphics

DEL REY

Ballantine Books · New York

Kitchen Princess volume 1 is a work of fiction. Names, characters, places, and incidents are the products of the author's imagination or are used fictitiously. Any resemblance to actual events, locales, or persons, living or dead, is entirely coincidental.

A Del Rey Books Trade Paperback Original

Published in the United States by Del Rey Books, an imprint of The Random House Publishing Group, a division of Random House, Inc., New York.

Del Rey is a registered trademark and the Del Rey colophon is a trademark of Random House, Inc.

Publication rights arranged through Kodansha Ltd.

First published in Japan in 2005 by Kodansha Ltd., Tokyo

ISBN 978-0-345-49620-1

Printed in the United States of America

www.delreymanga.com

9

Translator: Satsuki Yamashita
Adaptor: Nunzio DeFilippis and Christina Weir
Letterer: North Market Street Graphics
Original cover design by Akiko Omo

Contents

Honorifics Explained

Throughout the Del Rey Manga books, you will find Japanese honorifics left intact in the translations. For those not familiar with how the Japanese use honorifics and, more important, how they differ from American honorifics, we present this brief overview.

Politeness has always been a critical facet of Japanese culture. Ever since the feudal era, when Japan was a highly stratified society, use of honorifics—which can be defined as polite speech that indicates relationship or status—has played an essential role in the Japanese language. When addressing someone in Japanese, an honorific usually takes the form of a suffix attached to one's name (example: "Asuna-san"), as a title at the end of one's name, or in place of the name itself (example: "Negi-sensei," or simply "Sensei!").

Honorifics can be expressions of respect or endearment. In the context of manga and anime, honorifics give insight into the nature of the relationship between characters. Many translations into English leave out these important honorifics and therefore distort the "feel" of the original Japanese. Because Japanese honorifics contain nuances that English honorifics lack, it is our policy at Del Rey not to translate them. Here, instead, is a guide to some of the honorifics you may encounter in Del Rey Manga.

-*san*: This is the most common honorific and is equivalent to Mr., Miss, Ms., or Mrs. It is the all-purpose honorific and can be used in any situation where politeness is required.

-*sama*: This is one level higher than "-san." It is used to confer great respect.

-*dono*: This comes from the word "tono," which means "lord." It is an even higher level than "-sama" and confers utmost respect.

-*kun*: This suffix is used at the end of boys' names to express familiarity or endearment. It is also sometimes used by men among friends, or when addressing someone younger or of a lower station.

-chan: This is used to express endearment, mostly toward girls. It is also used for little boys, pets, and even among lovers. It gives a sense of childish cuteness.

Bozu: This is an informal way to refer to a boy, similar to the English terms "kid" and "squirt."

**Sempai/
Senpai:** This title suggests that the addressee is one's senior in a group or organization. It is most often used in a school setting, where underclassmen refer to their upperclassmen as "sempai." It can also be used in the workplace, such as when a newer employee addresses an employee who has seniority in the company.

Kohai: This is the opposite of "sempai" and is used toward underclassmen in school or newcomers in the workplace. It connotes that the addressee is of a lower station.

Sensei: Literally meaning "one who has come before," this title is used for teachers, doctors, or masters of any profession or art.

[blank]: This is usually forgotten in these lists, but perhaps the most significant difference between Japanese and English. The lack of honorific means that the speaker has permission to address the person in a very intimate way. Usually, only family, spouses, or very close friends have this kind of permission. Known as *yobisute*, it can be gratifying when someone who has earned the intimacy starts to call one by one's name without an honorific. But when that intimacy hasn't been earned, it can also be very insulting.

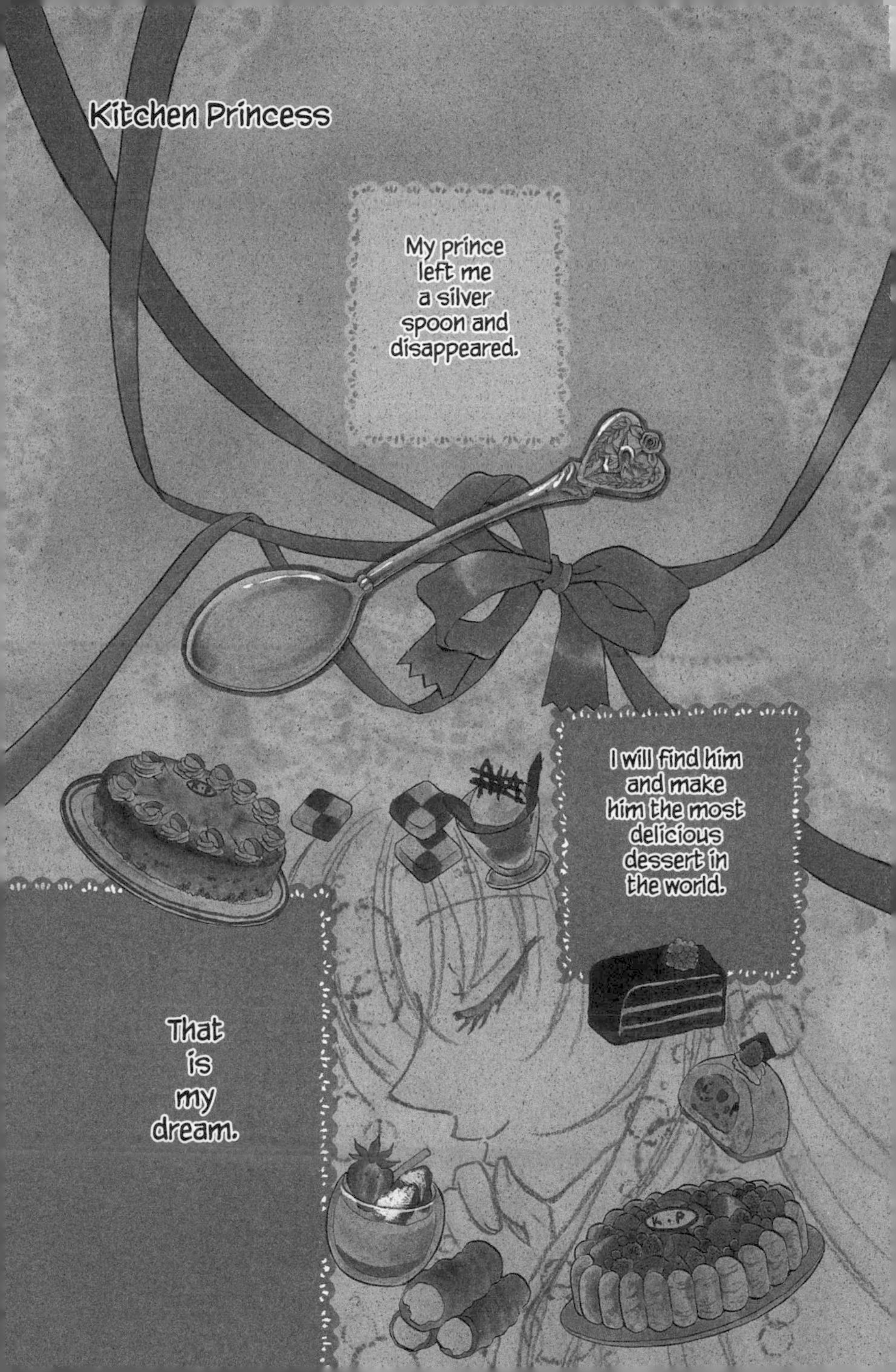
Kitchen Princess
My prince left me a silver spoon and disappeared.
I will find him and make him the most delicious dessert in the world.
That is my dream.

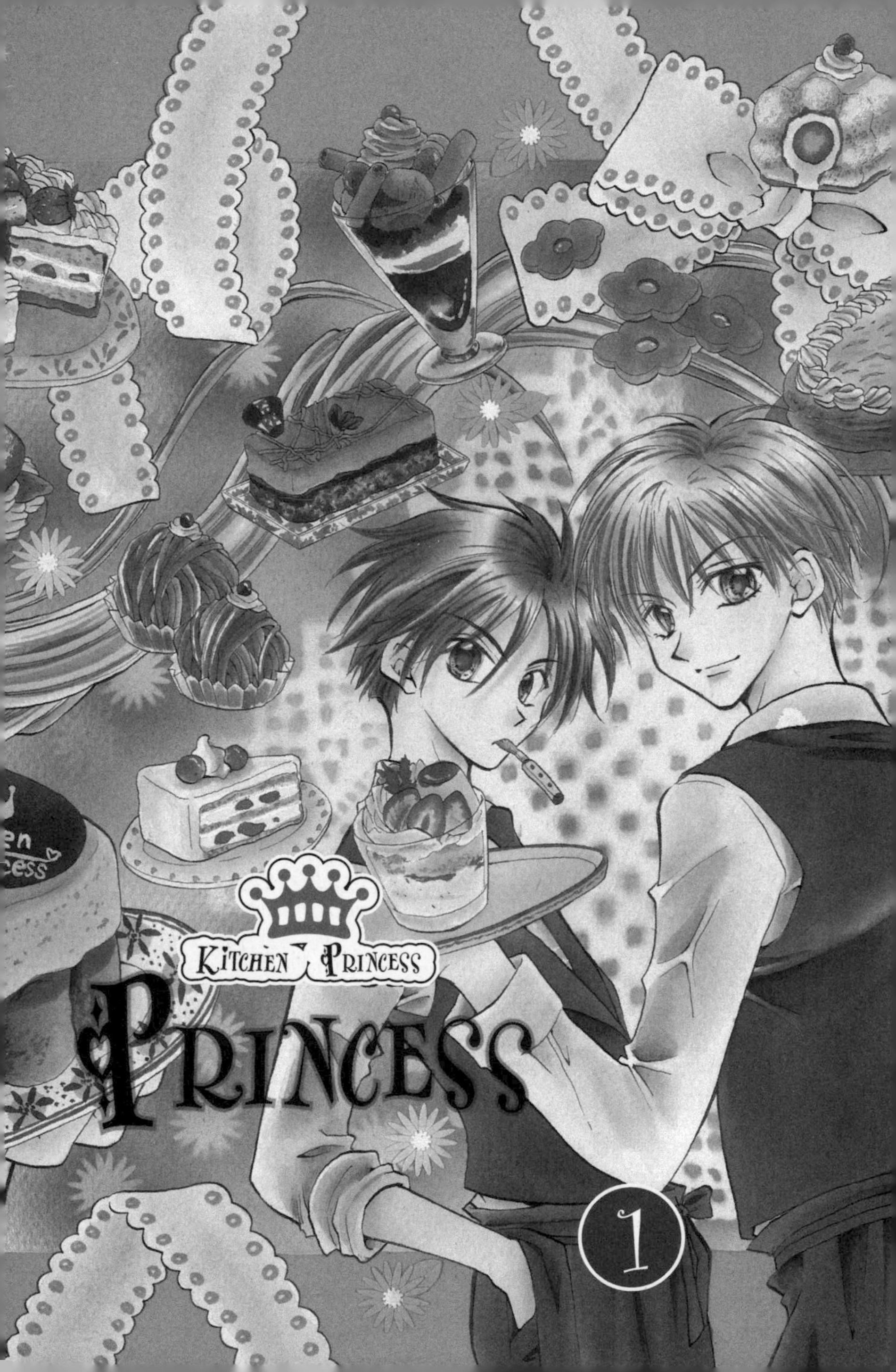
KITCHEN PRINCESS
PRINCESS
1

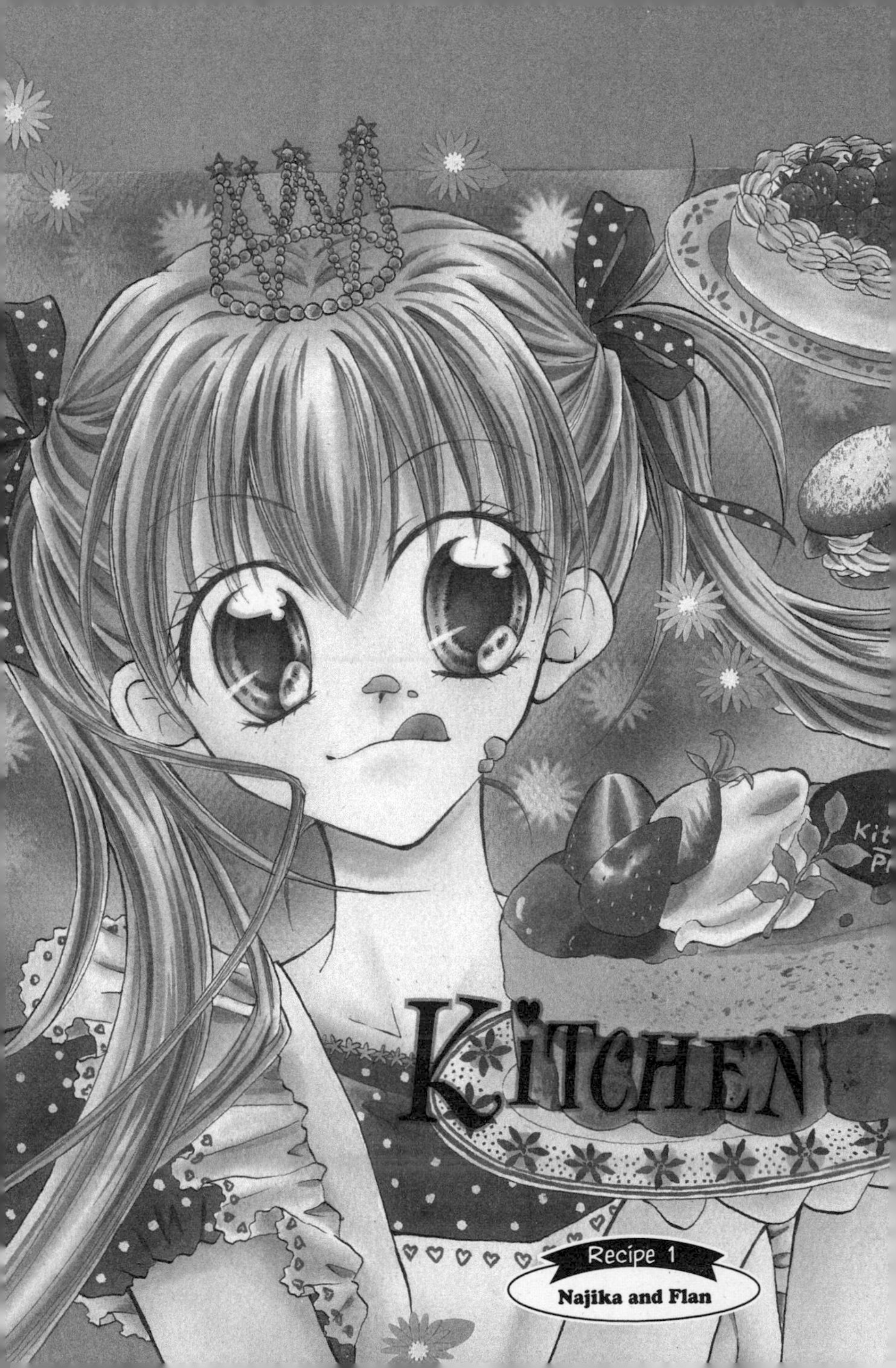
KITCHEN
Recipe 1
Najika and Flan

Kitchen Princess

Table of
Contents

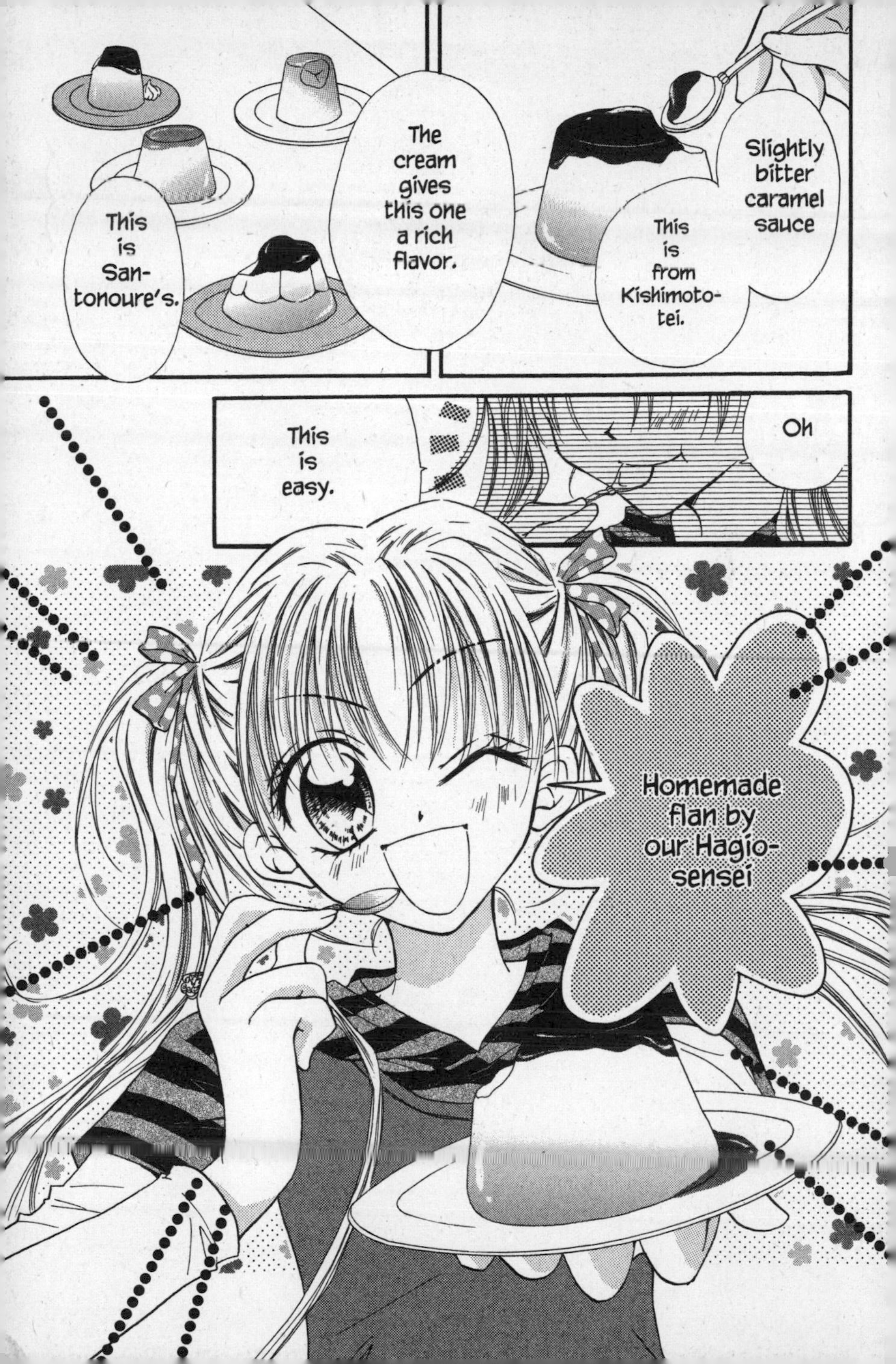
Slightly bitter caramel sauce
This is from Kishimoto-tei.
The cream gives this one a rich flavor.
This is San-tonoure's.
Oh
This is easy.
Homemade flan by our Hagio-sensei

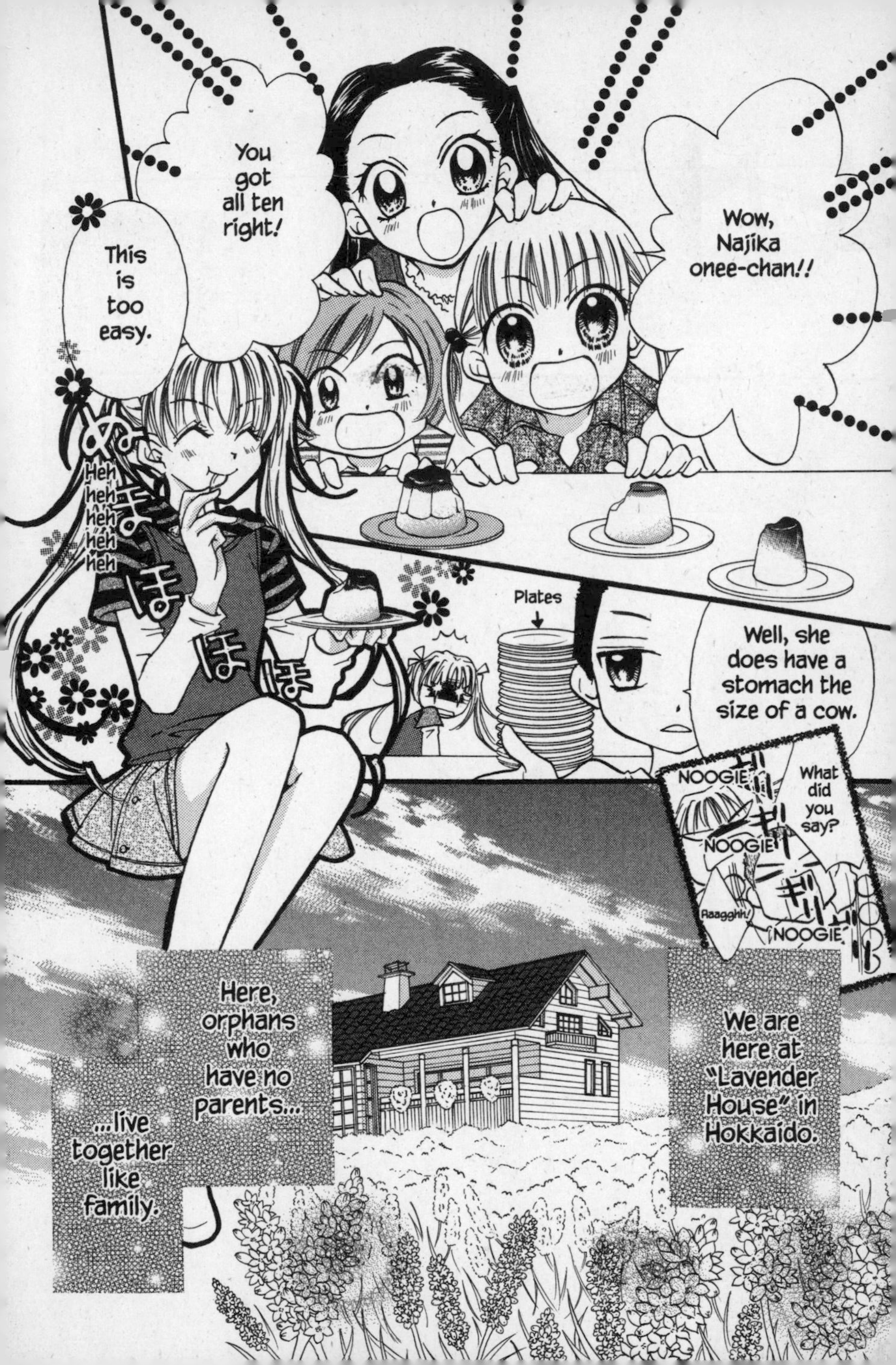
Wow, Najika onee-chan!!
You got all ten right!
This is too easy.
Heh heh heh heh heh
Well, she does have a stomach the size of a cow.
Plates
What did you say?
NOOGIE
NOOGIE
NOOGIE
Aaagghh!
We are here at "Lavender House" in Hokkaido.
Here, orphans who have no parents...
...live together like family.

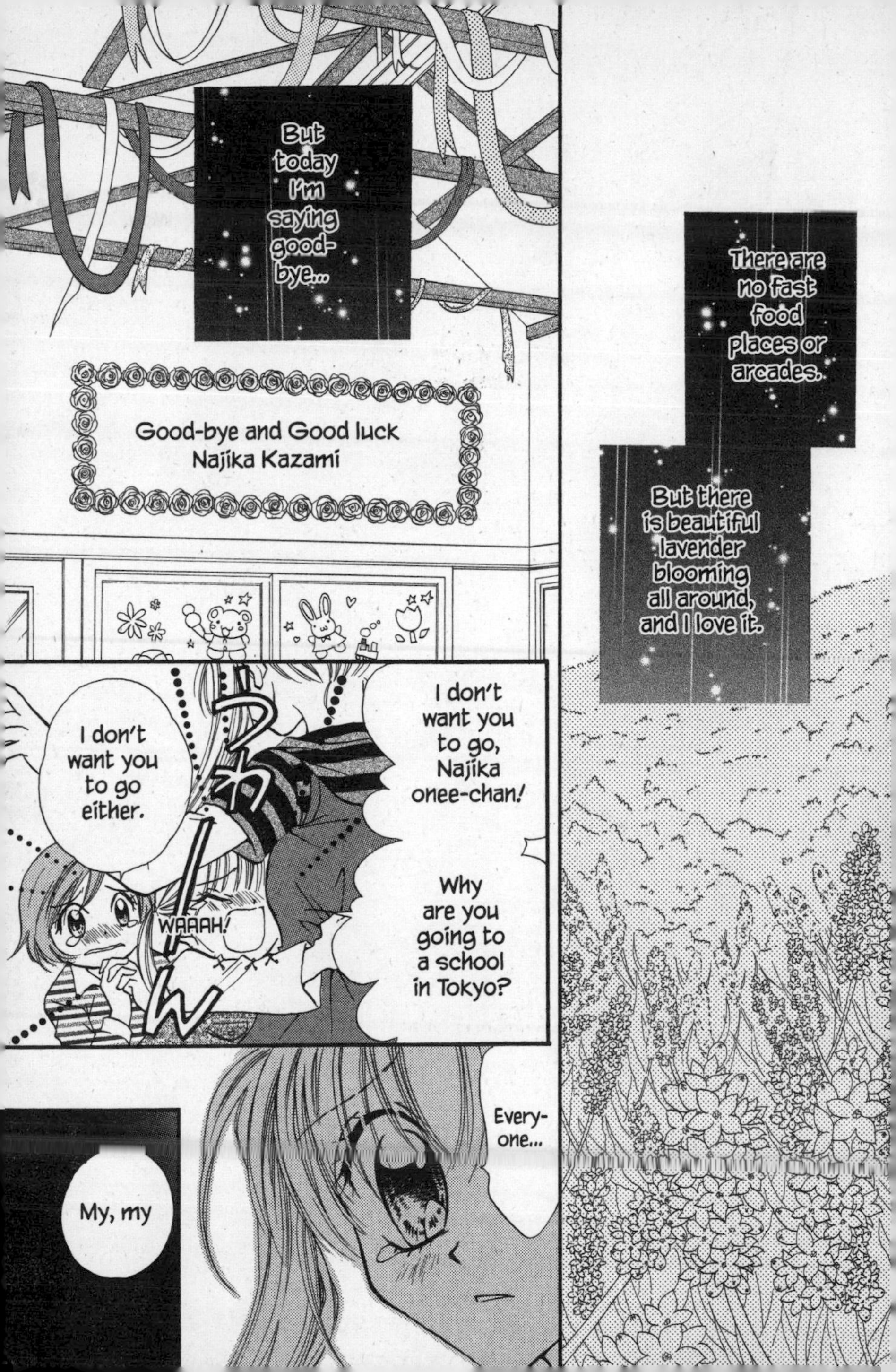
There are no fast food places or arcades.
But there is beautiful lavender blooming all around, and I love it.
But today I'm saying good-bye...
Good-bye and Good luck
Najika Kazami
I don't want you to go, Najika onee-chan!
Why are you going to a school in Tokyo?
WAAAH!
I don't want you to go either.
Every-one...
My, my

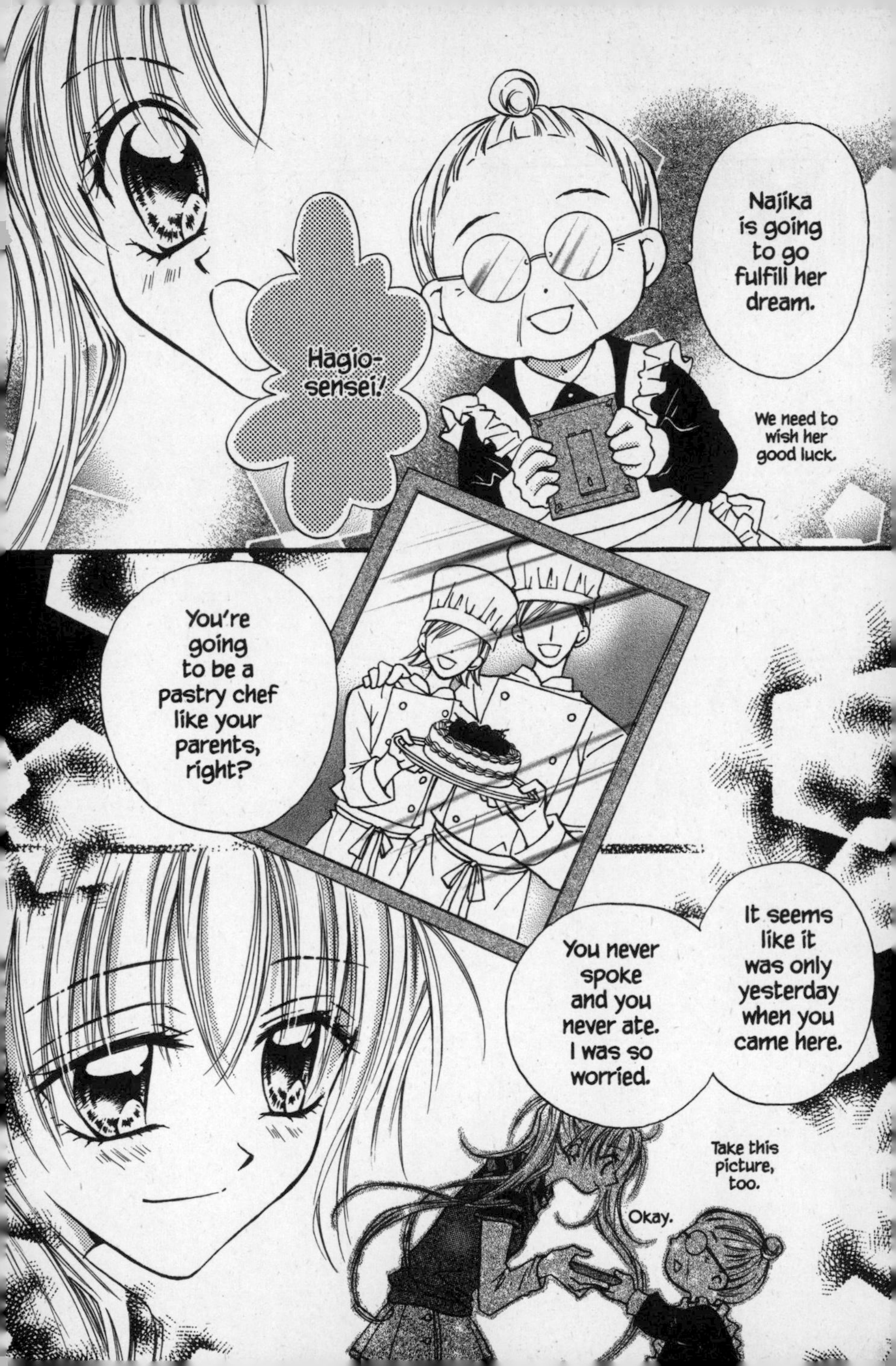
Najika is going to go fulfill her dream.
We need to wish her good luck.
Hagio-sensei!
You're going to be a pastry chef like your parents, right?
It seems like it was only yesterday when you came here.
You never spoke and you never ate. I was so worried.
Take this picture, too.
Okay.

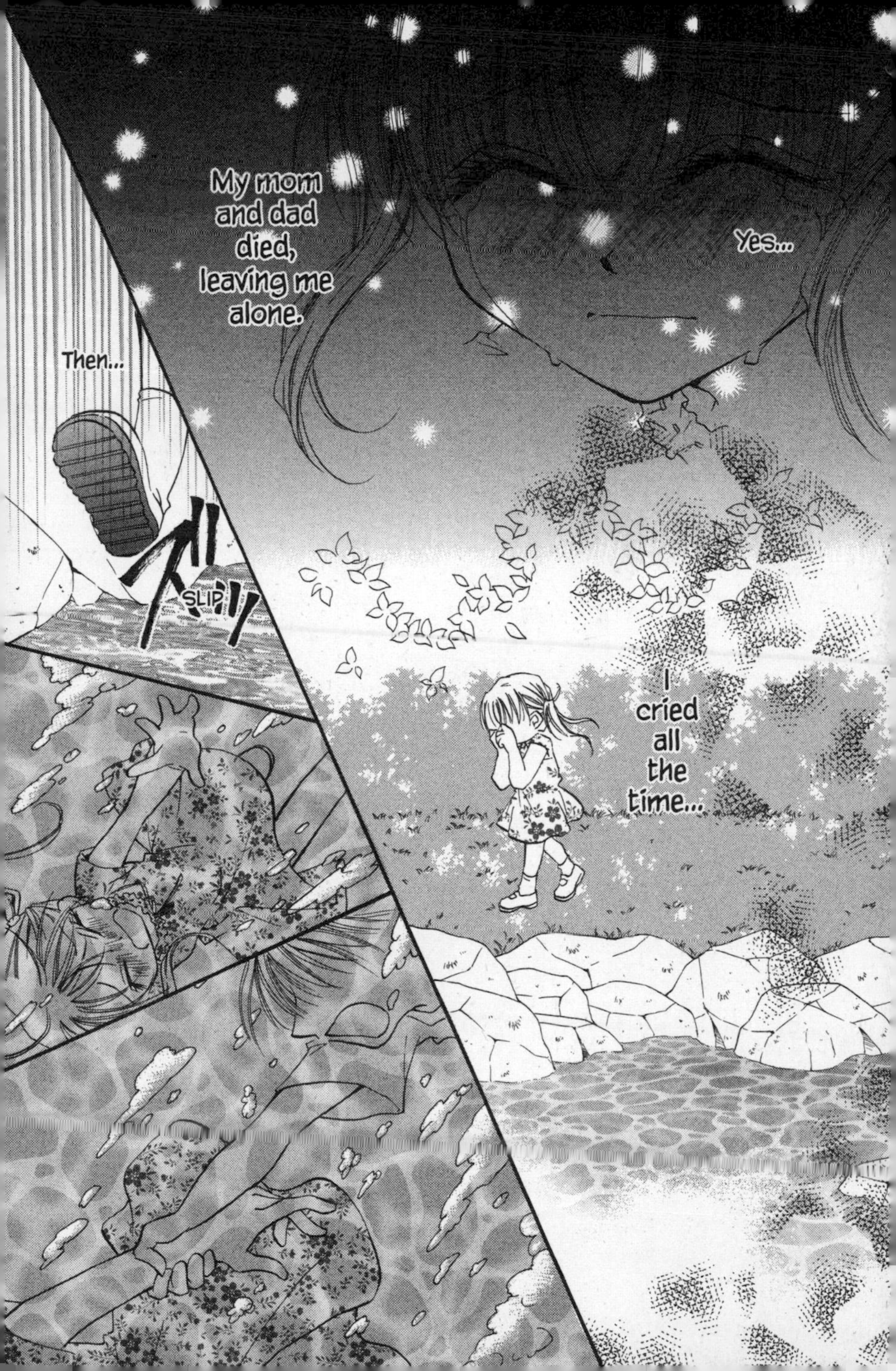

Yes...
My mom and dad died, leaving me alone.
I cried all the time...
Then...
SLIP

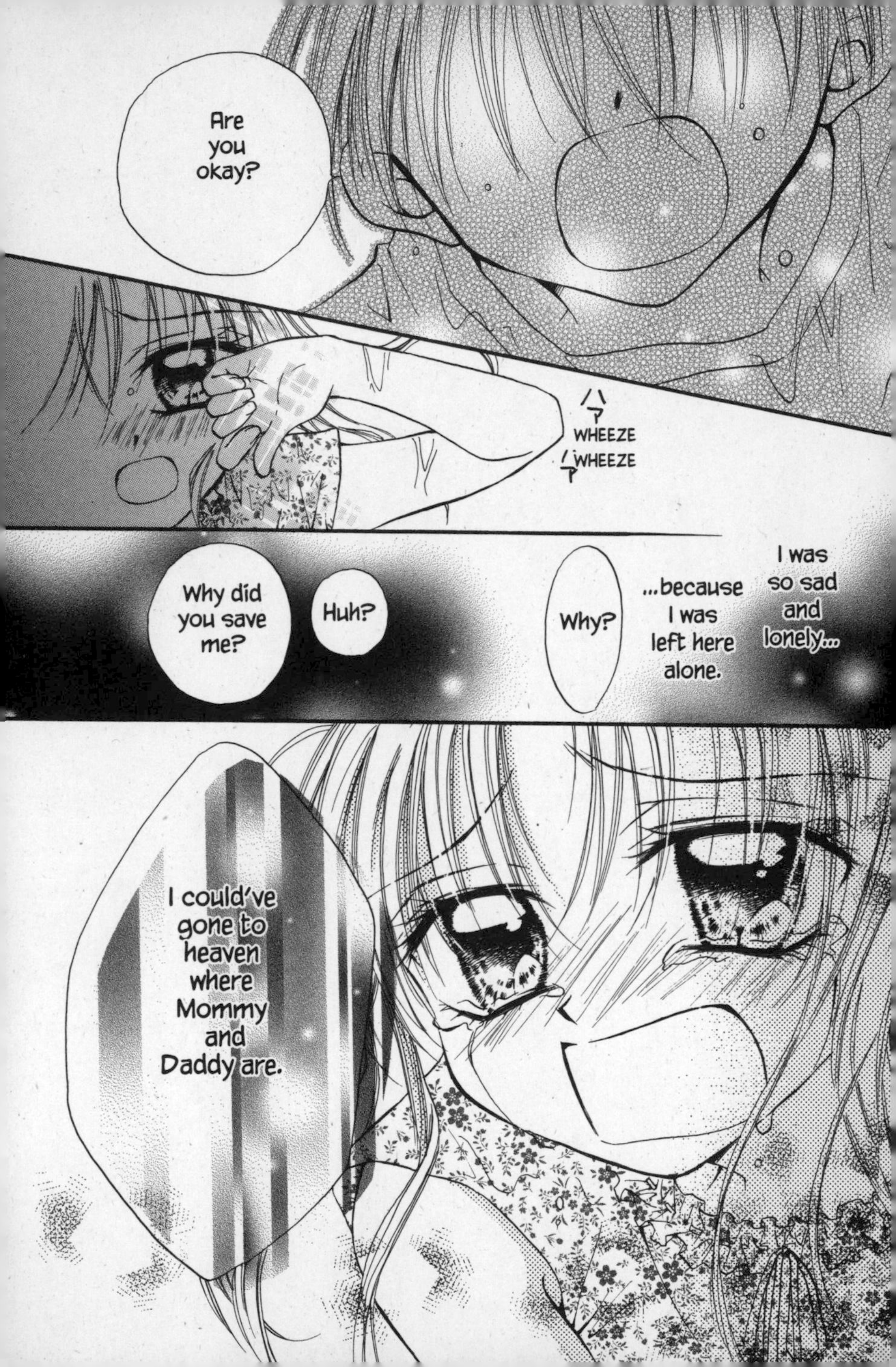
Are you okay?
WHEEZE
WHEEZE
I was so sad and lonely...
...because I was left here alone.
Why?
Huh?
Why did you save me?
I could've gone to heaven where Mommy and Daddy are.

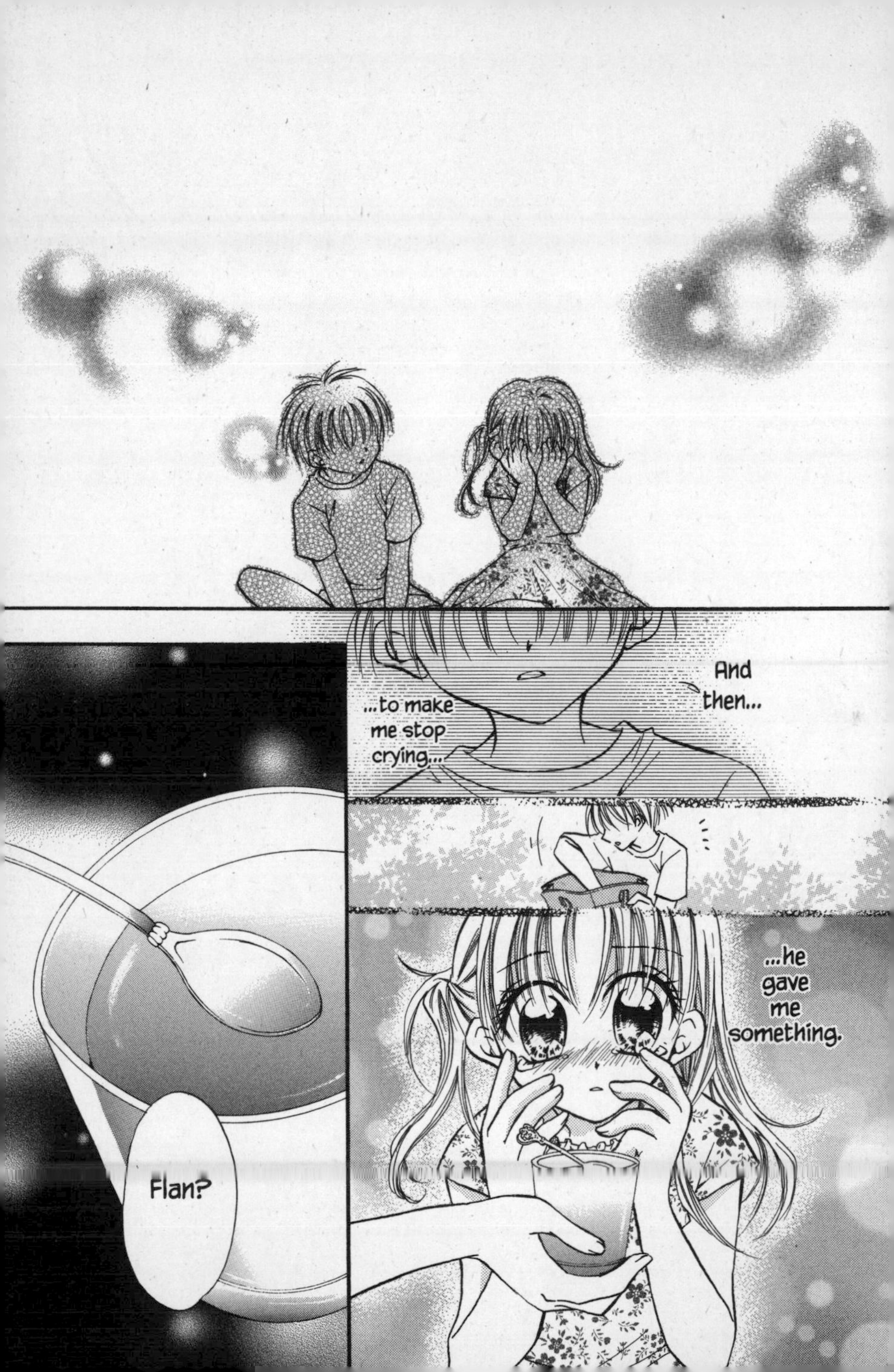
And then...
...to make me stop crying...
...he gave me something.
Flan?

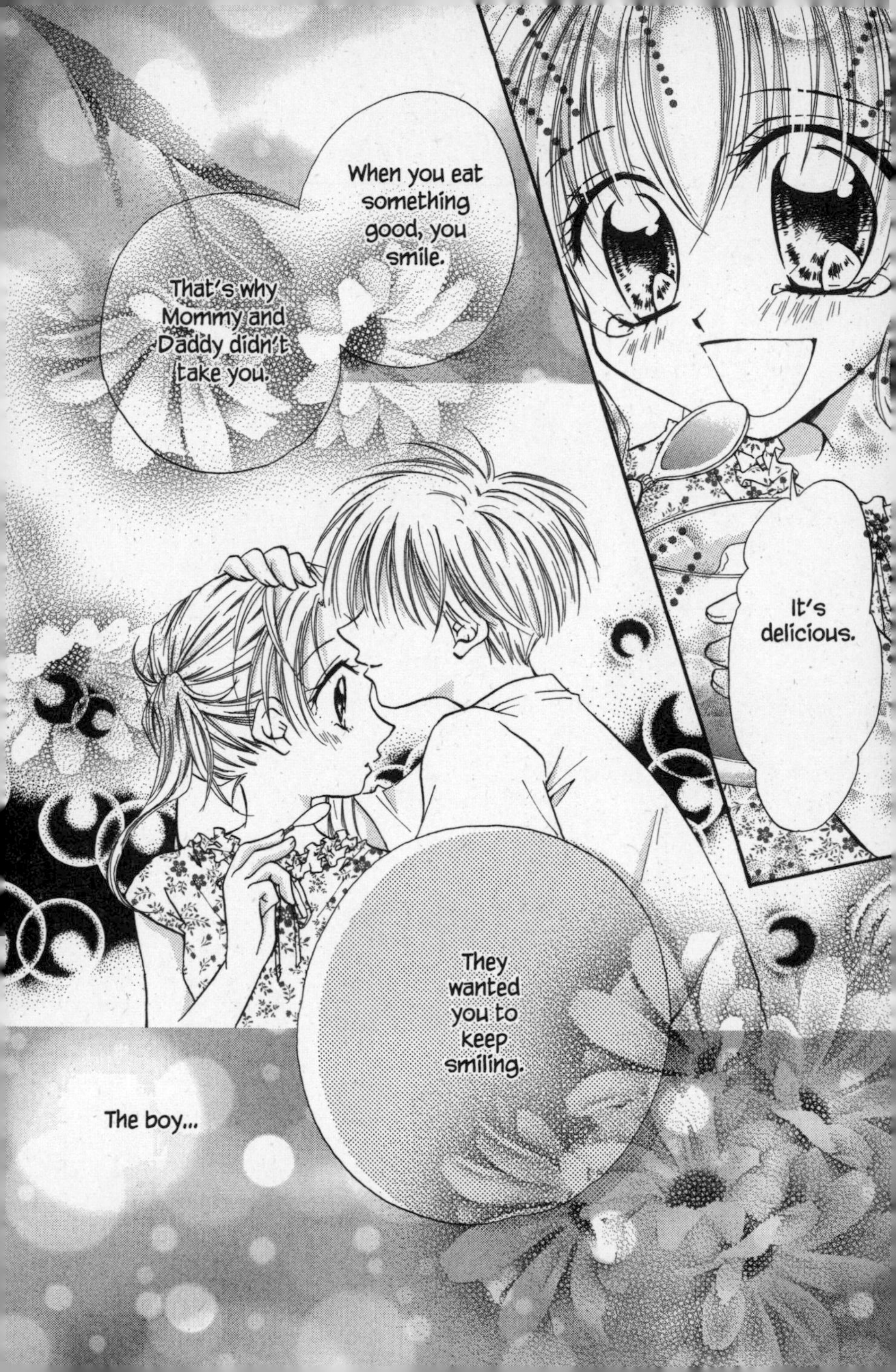
It's delicious.
When you eat something good, you smile.
That's why Mommy and Daddy didn't take you.
They wanted you to keep smiling.
The boy...

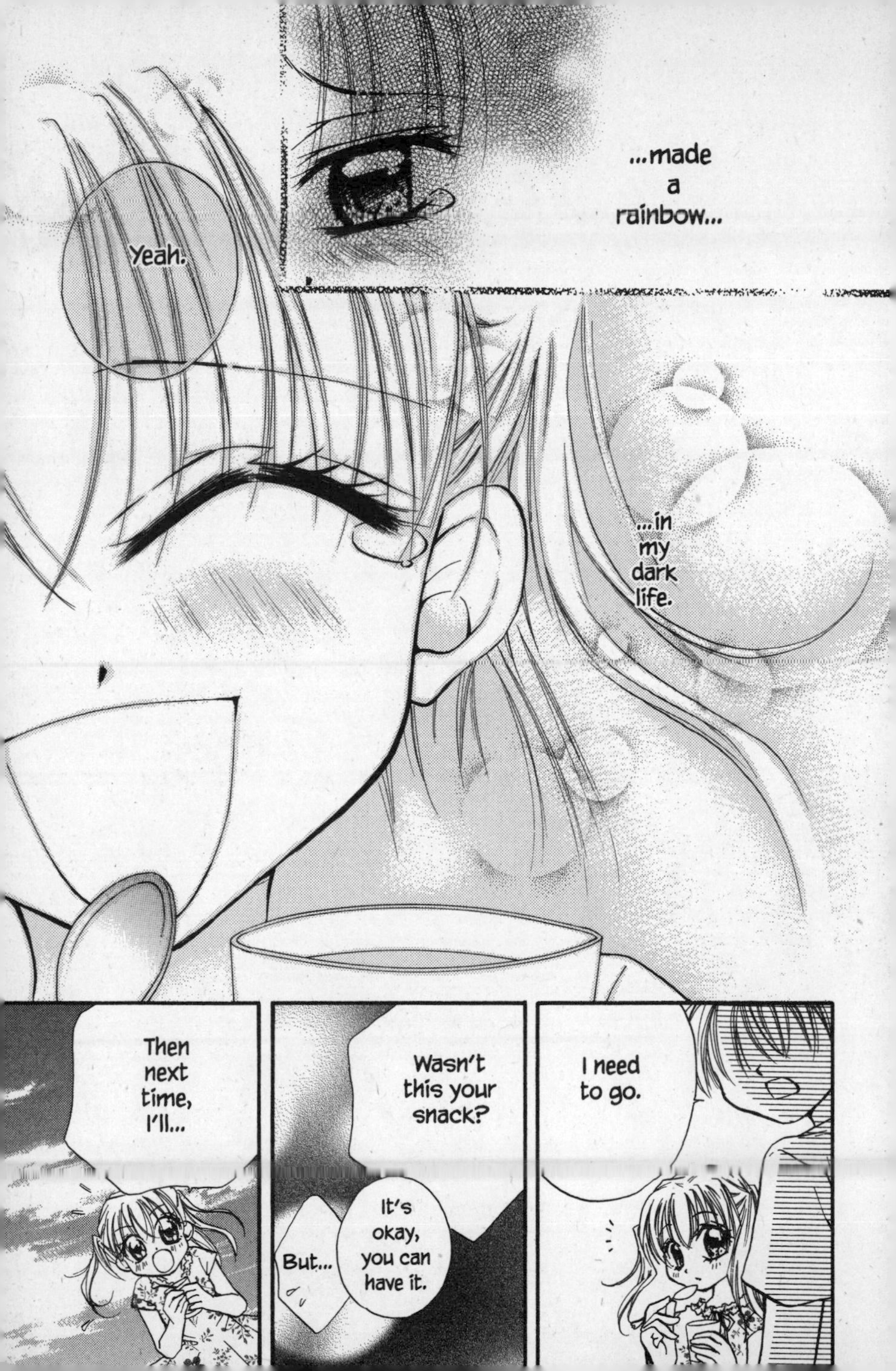
...made a rainbow...
...in my dark life.
Yeah.
I need to go.
Wasn't this your snack?
It's okay, you can have it.
But...
Then next time, I'll...

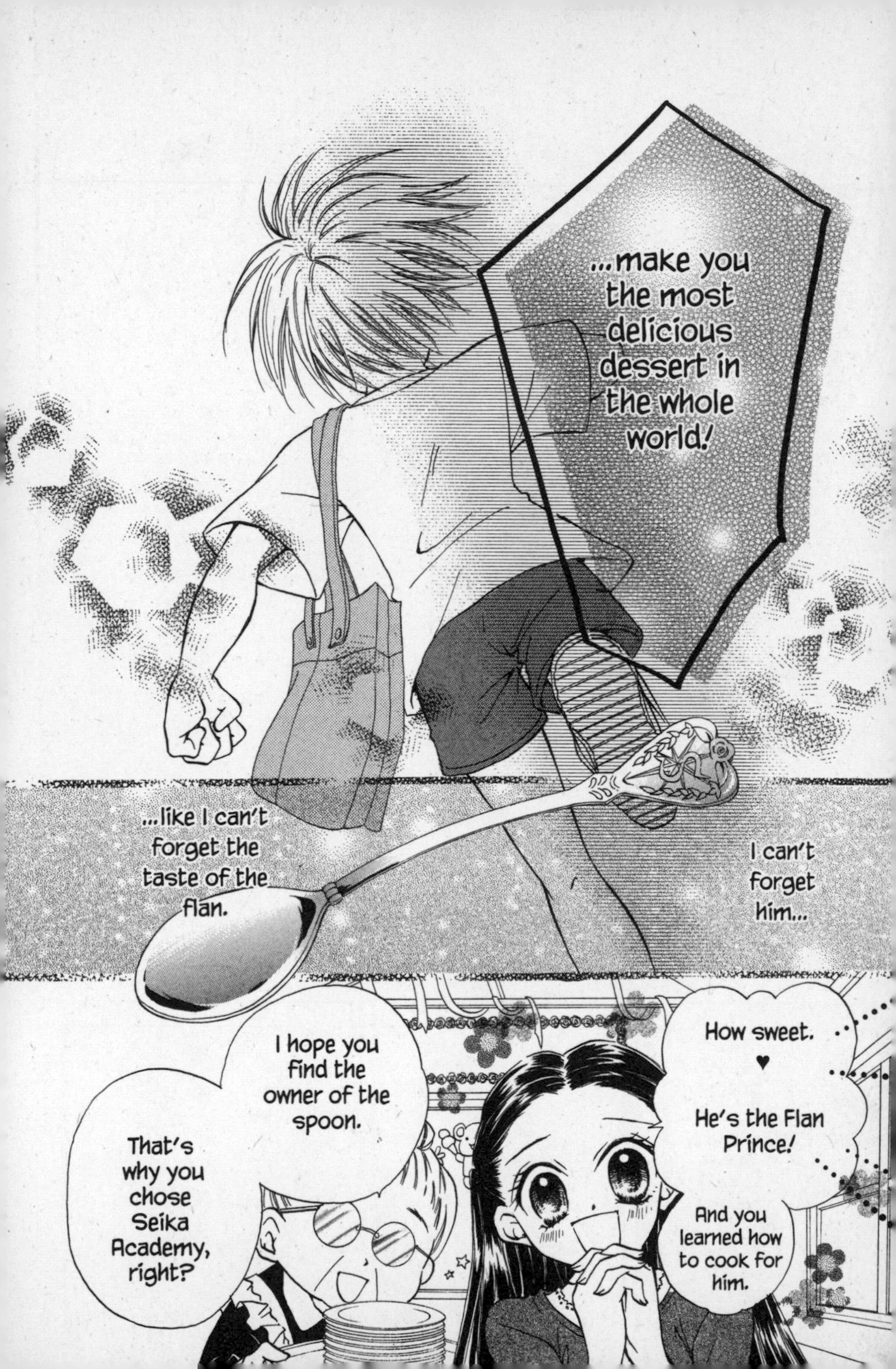
...make you the most delicious dessert in the whole world!
I can't forget him...
...like I can't forget the taste of the flan.
How sweet. ♥
He's the Flan Prince!
And you learned how to cook for him.
I hope you find the owner of the spoon.
That's why you chose Seika Academy, right?

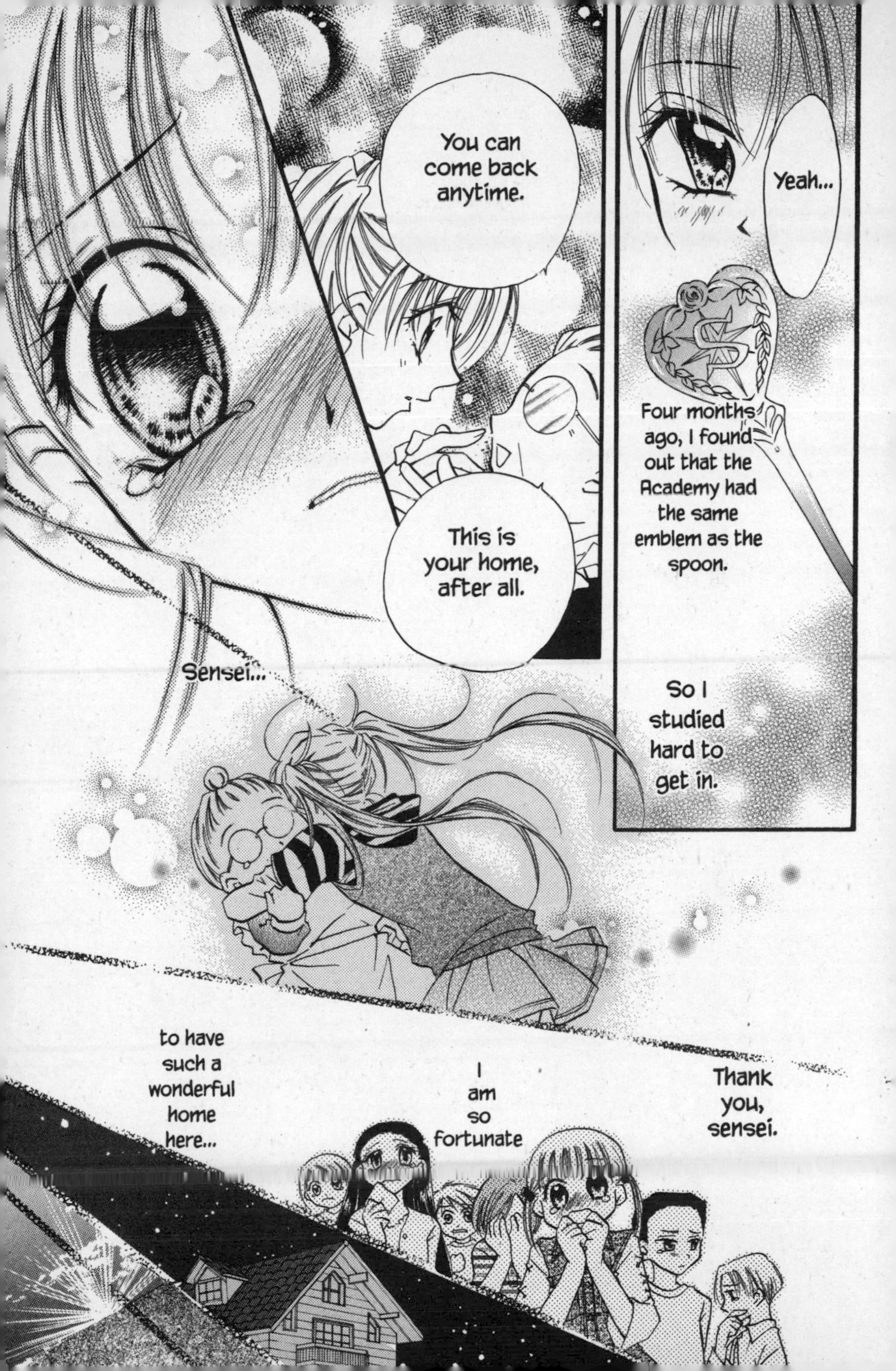

Yeah...
Four months ago, I found out that the Academy had the same emblem as the spoon.
So I studied hard to get in.
You can come back anytime.
This is your home, after all.
Sensei...
Thank you, sensei.
I am so fortunate
to have such a wonderful home here...

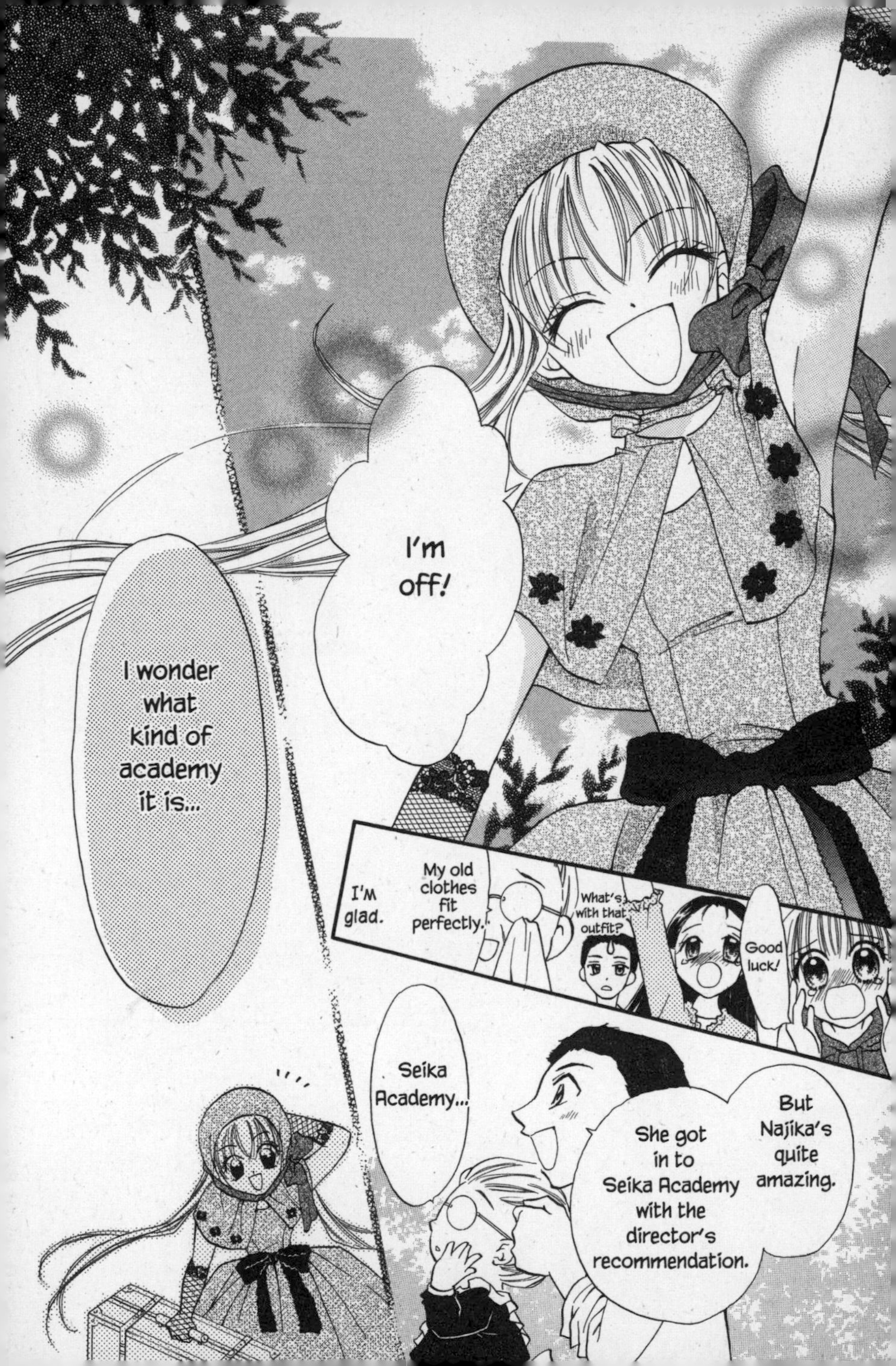
I'm off!
I wonder what kind of academy it is...
Good luck!
What's with that outfit?
My old clothes fit perfectly.
I'M glad.
But Najika's quite amazing.
She got in to Seika Academy with the director's recommendation.
Seika Academy...

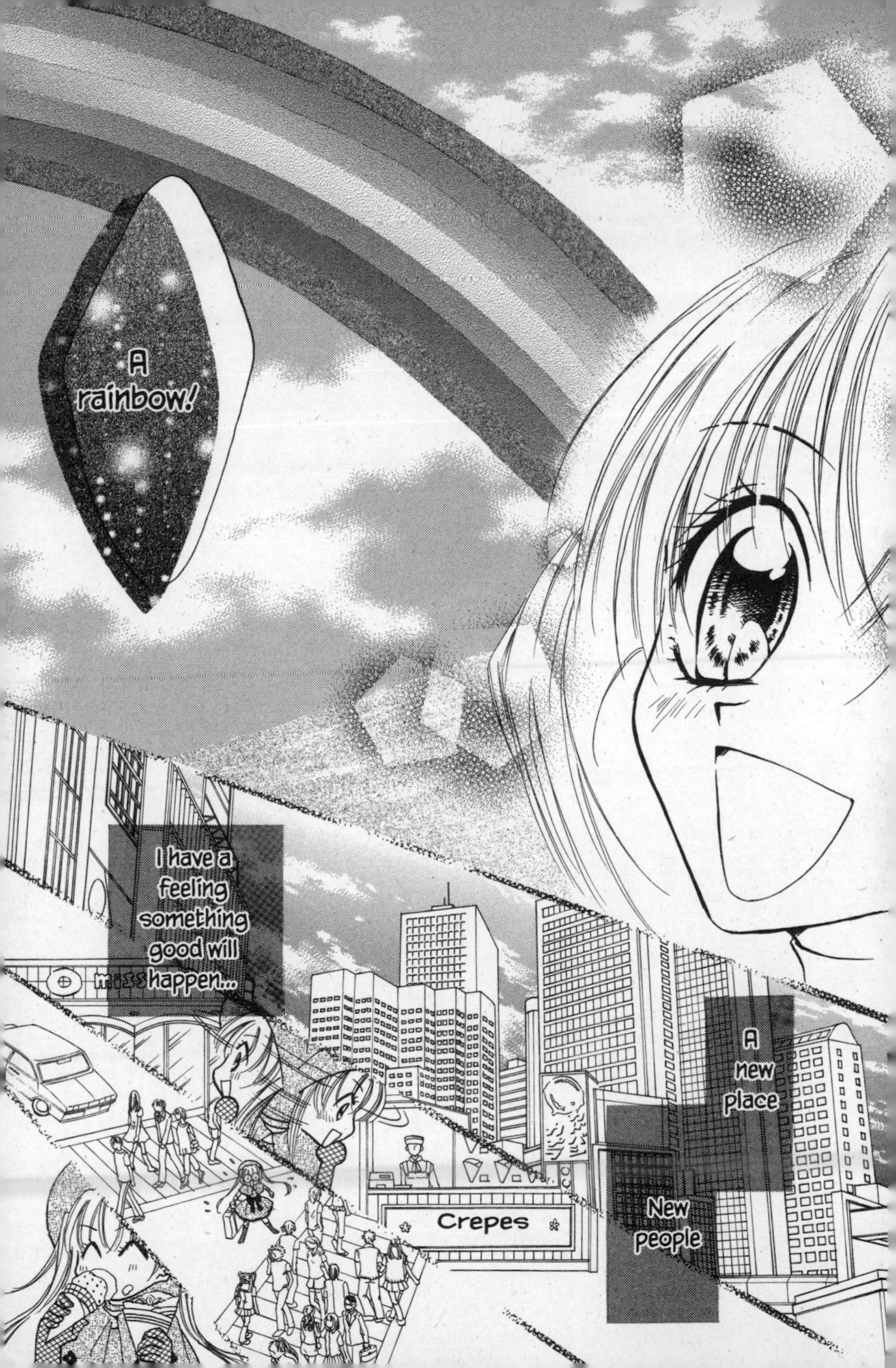
A rainbow!
A new place
New people
Crepes
I have a feeling something good will happen...

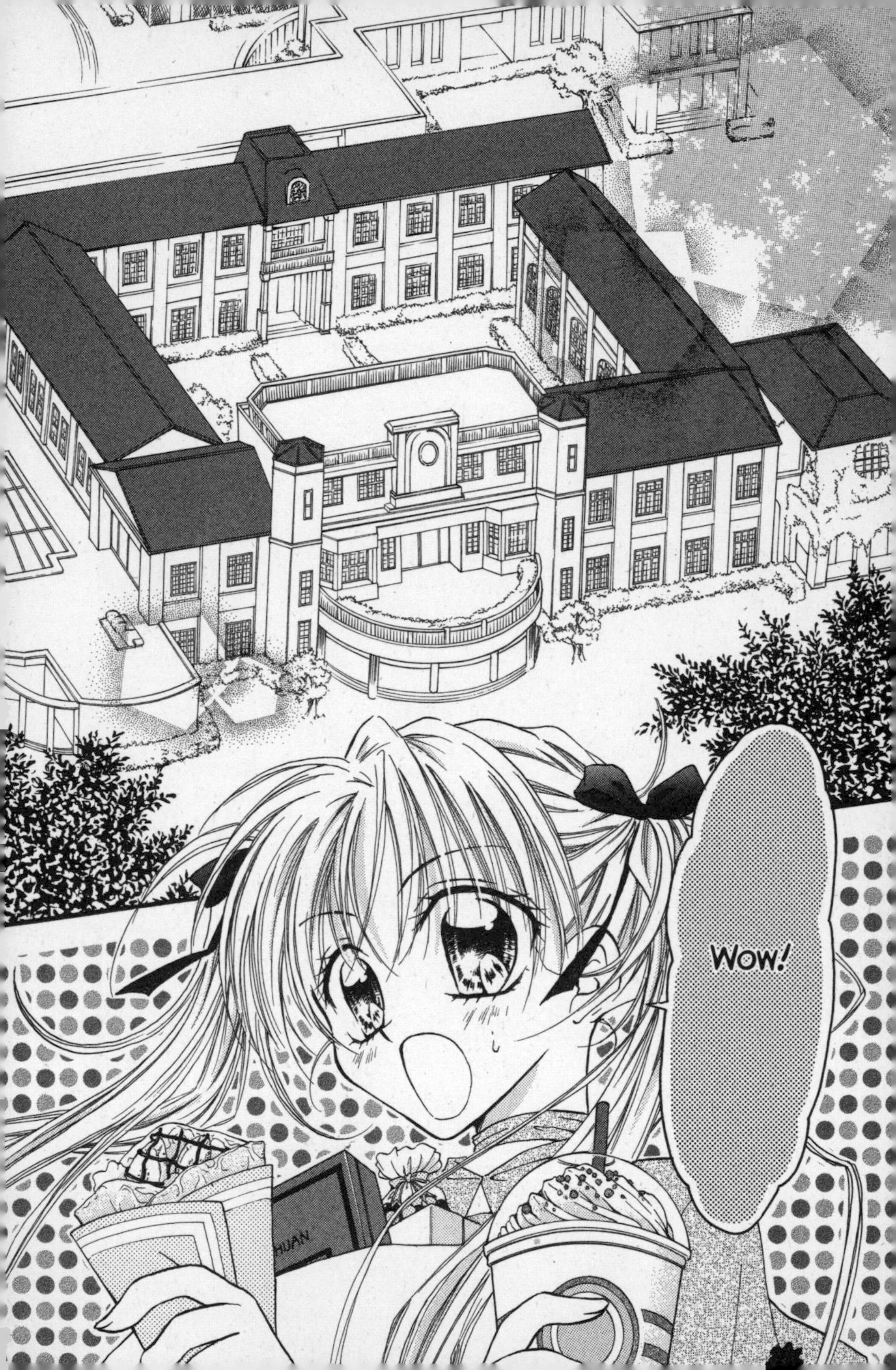
WOW!

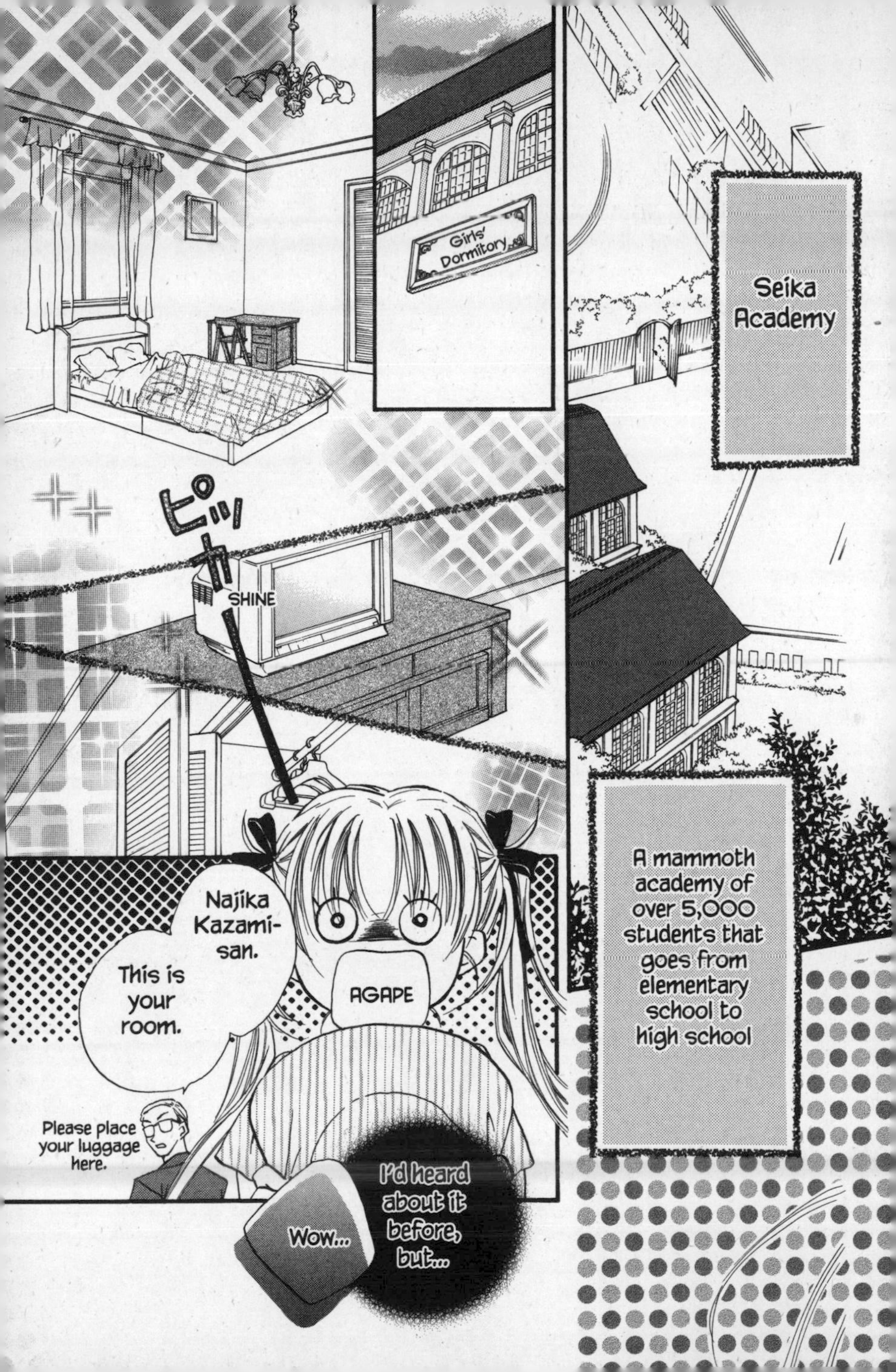
Seika Academy
A mammoth academy of over 5,000 students that goes from elementary school to high school
Girls' Dormitory
ピッカ
SHINE
Najika Kazami-san.
This is your room.
AGAPE
Please place your luggage here.
I'd heard about it before, but...
Wow...

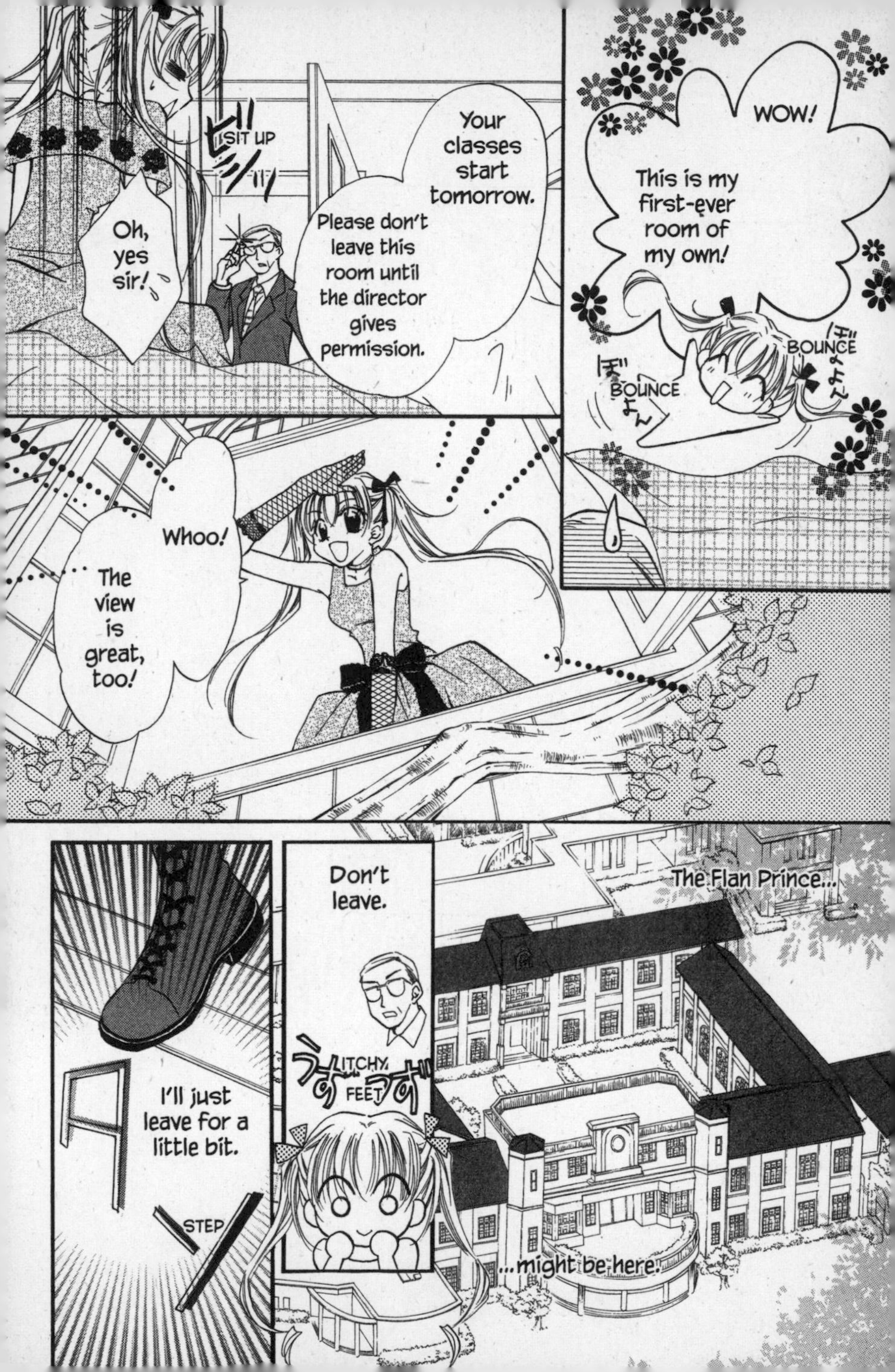
WOW!
This is my first-ever room of my own!
BOUNCE
ぼよん
BOUNCE
ぼよん
Your classes start tomorrow.
Please don't leave this room until the director gives permission.
SIT UP
Oh, yes sir!
Whoo!
The view is great, too!
The Flan Prince...
...might be here.
Don't leave.
ITCHY FEET
うずうず
I'll just leave for a little bit.
STEP

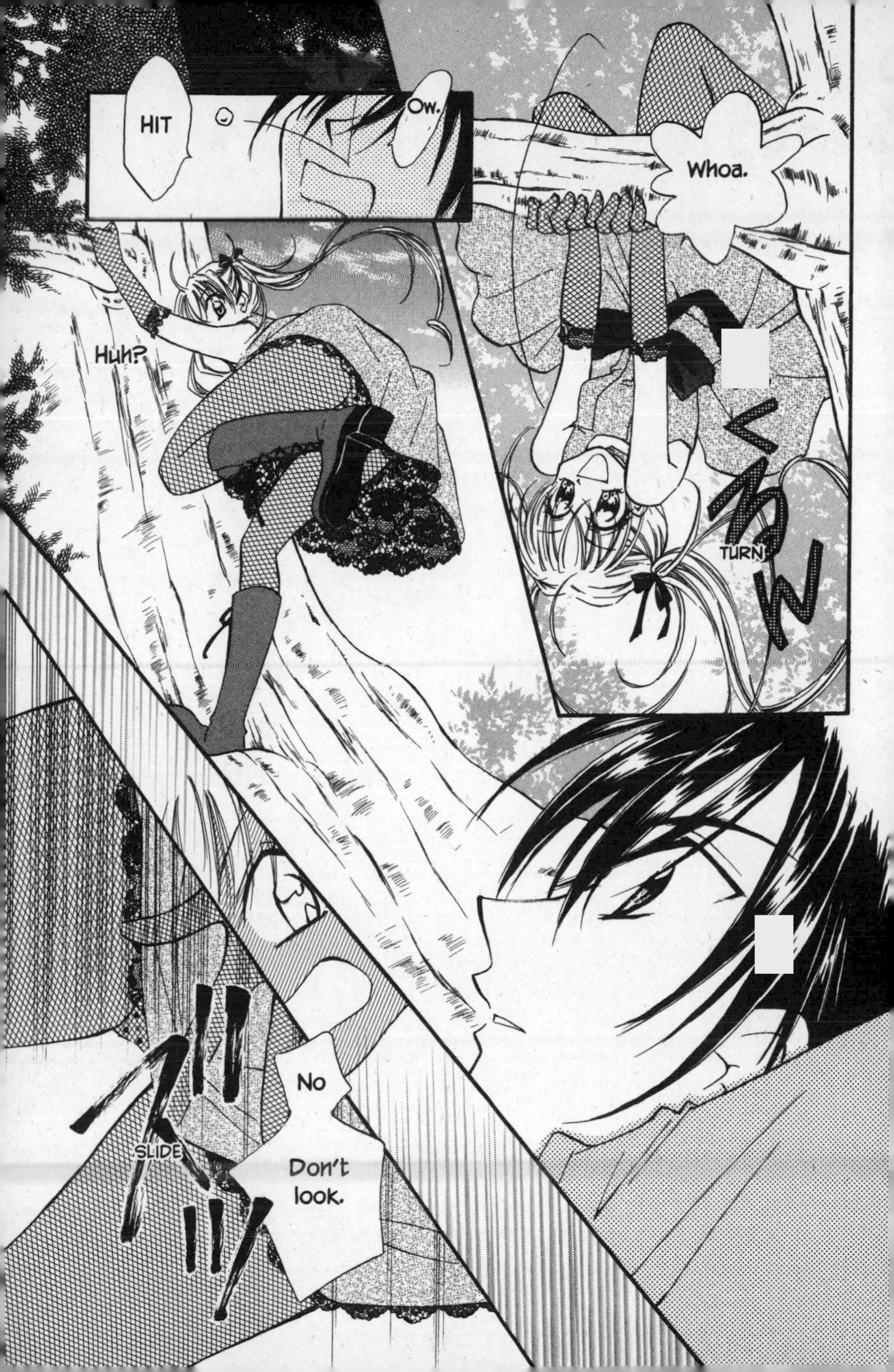
Whoa.
TURN
Ow.
HIT
Huh?
No
Don't look.
SLIDE

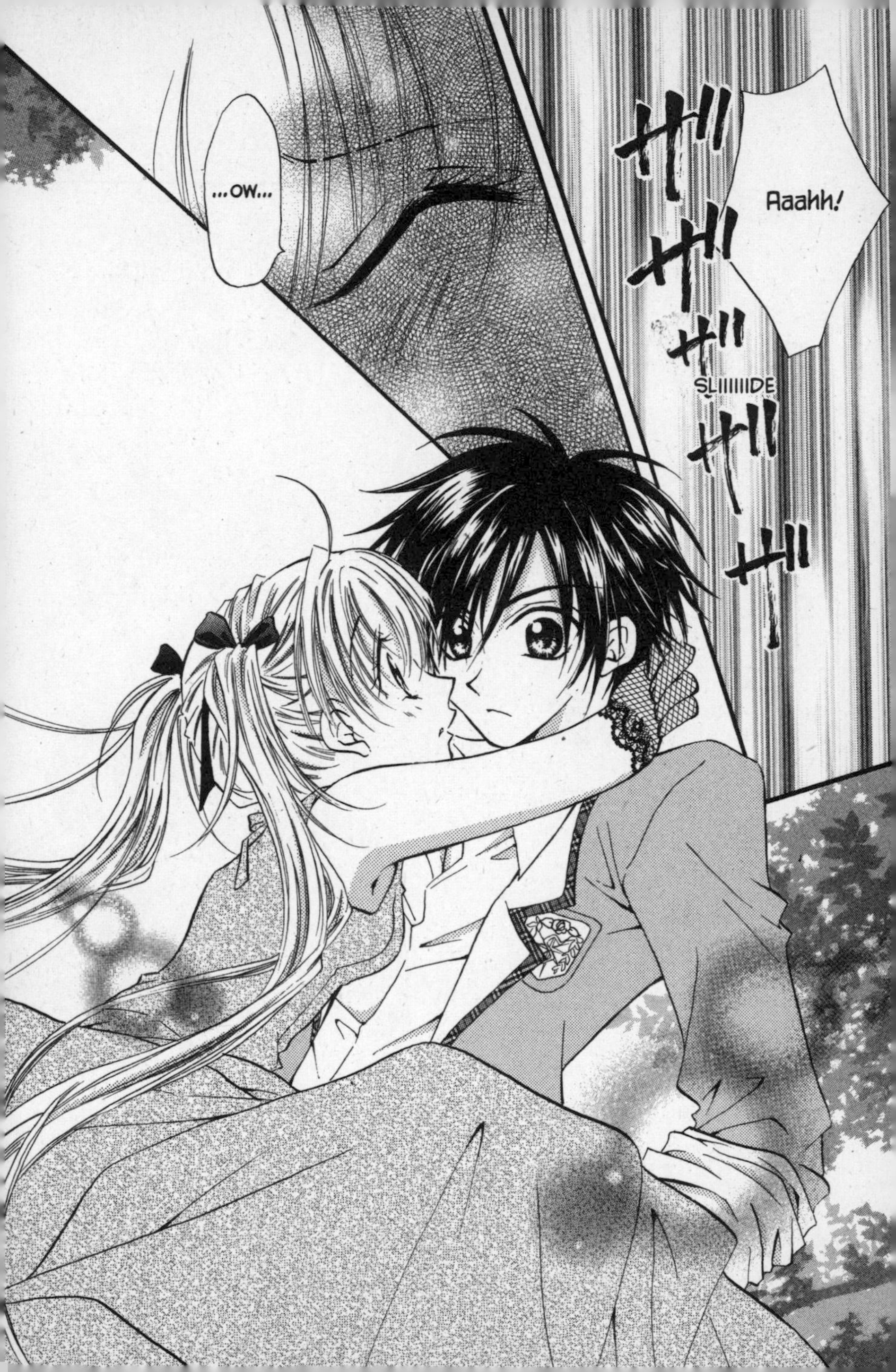
Aaahh!
ザザザザザザ
SLIIIIIIIDE
...OW...

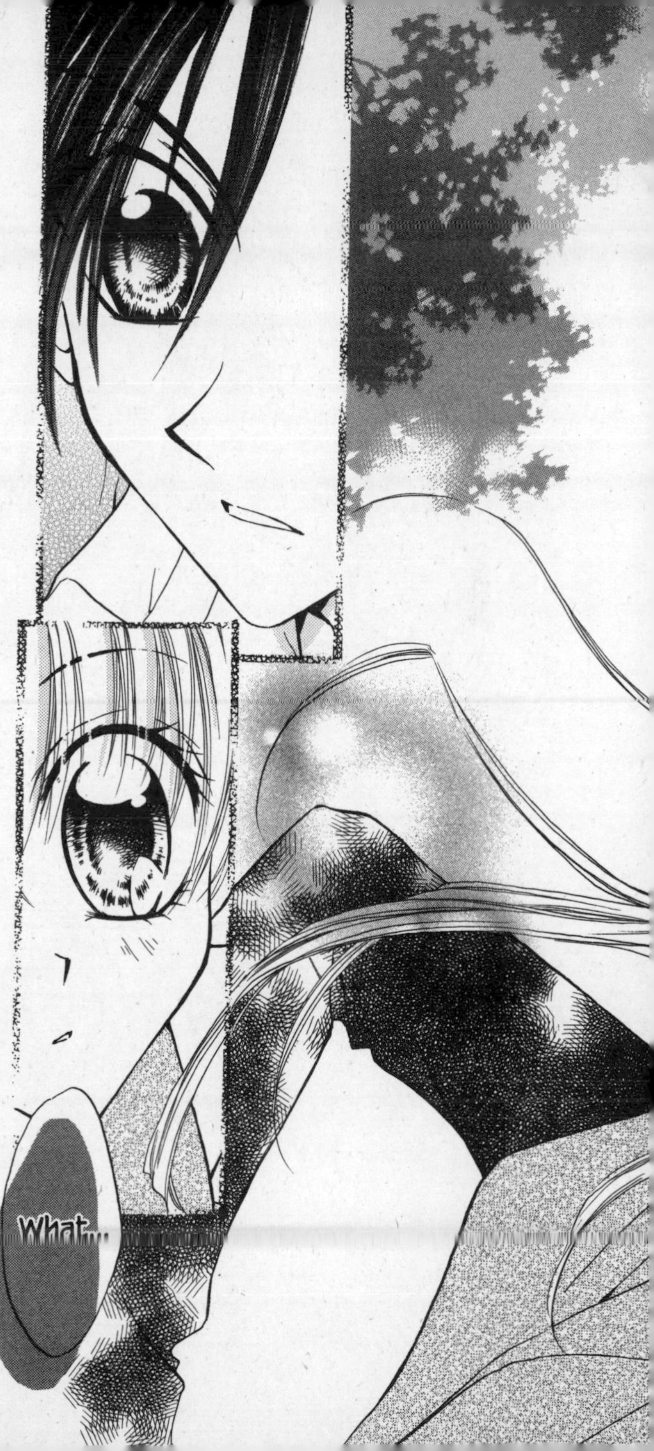
What...

Hello

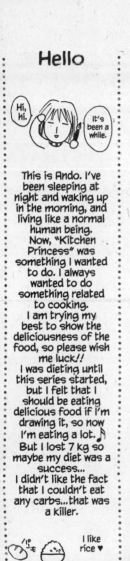

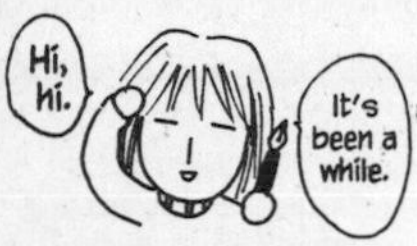
Hi, hi.
It's been a while.

This is Ando. I've been sleeping at night and waking up in the morning, and living like a normal human being.
Now, "Kitchen Princess" was something I wanted to do. I always wanted to do something related to cooking.
I am trying my best to show the deliciousness of the food, so please wish me luck!!
I was dieting until this series started, but I felt that I should be eating delicious food if I'm drawing it, so now I'm eating a lot.♪
But I lost 7 kg so maybe my diet was a success...
I didn't like the fact that I couldn't eat any carbs...that was a killer.

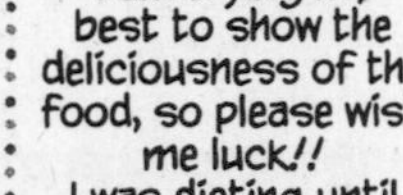
and bread.
I like rice ♥

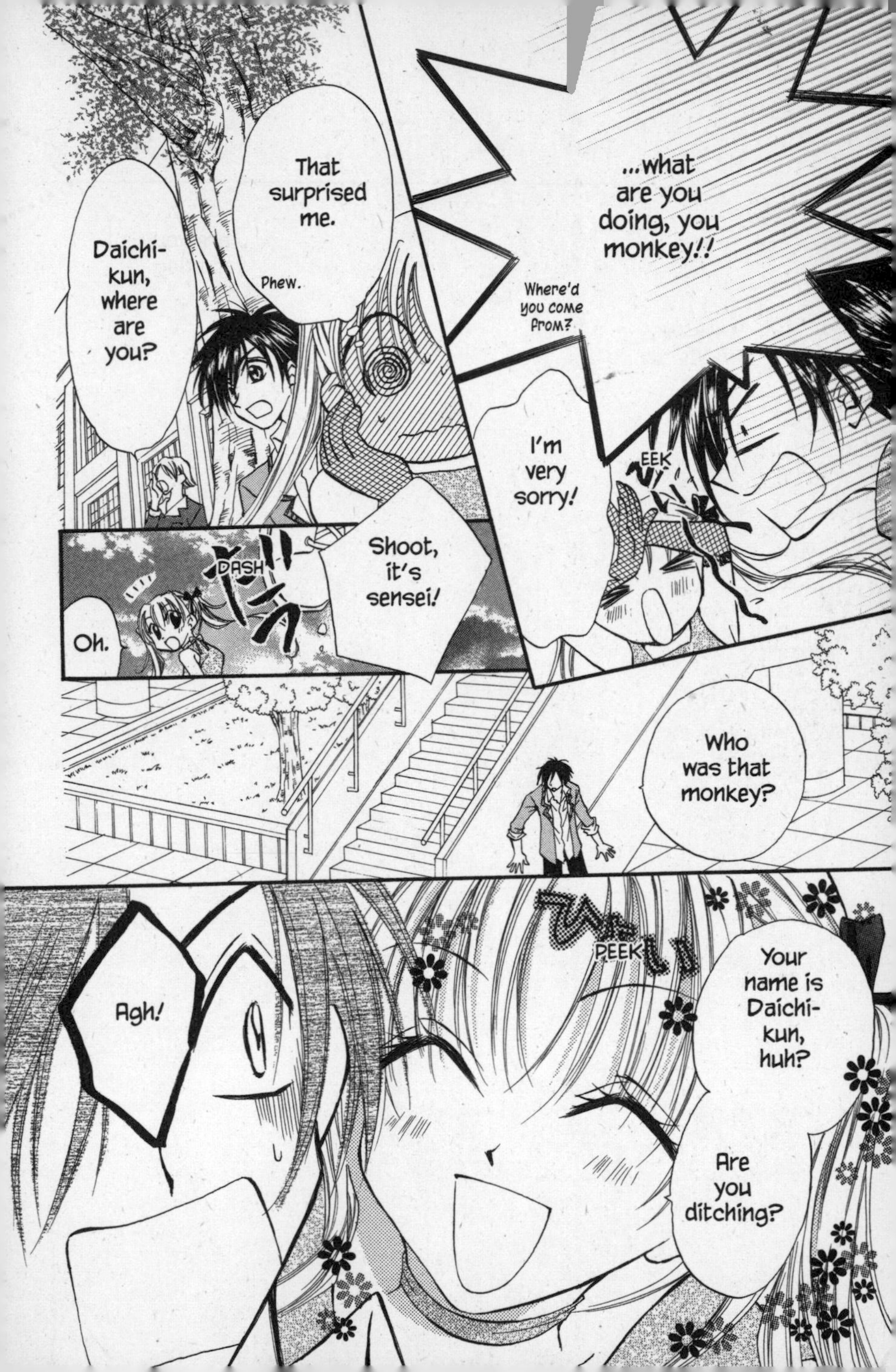

...what are you doing, you monkey!!
Where'd you come from?
EEK
I'm very sorry!
That surprised me.
Phew.
Daichi-kun, where are you?
Shoot, it's sensei!
DASH
Oh.
Who was that monkey?
PEEK
Your name is Daichi-kun, huh?
Are you ditching?
Agh!

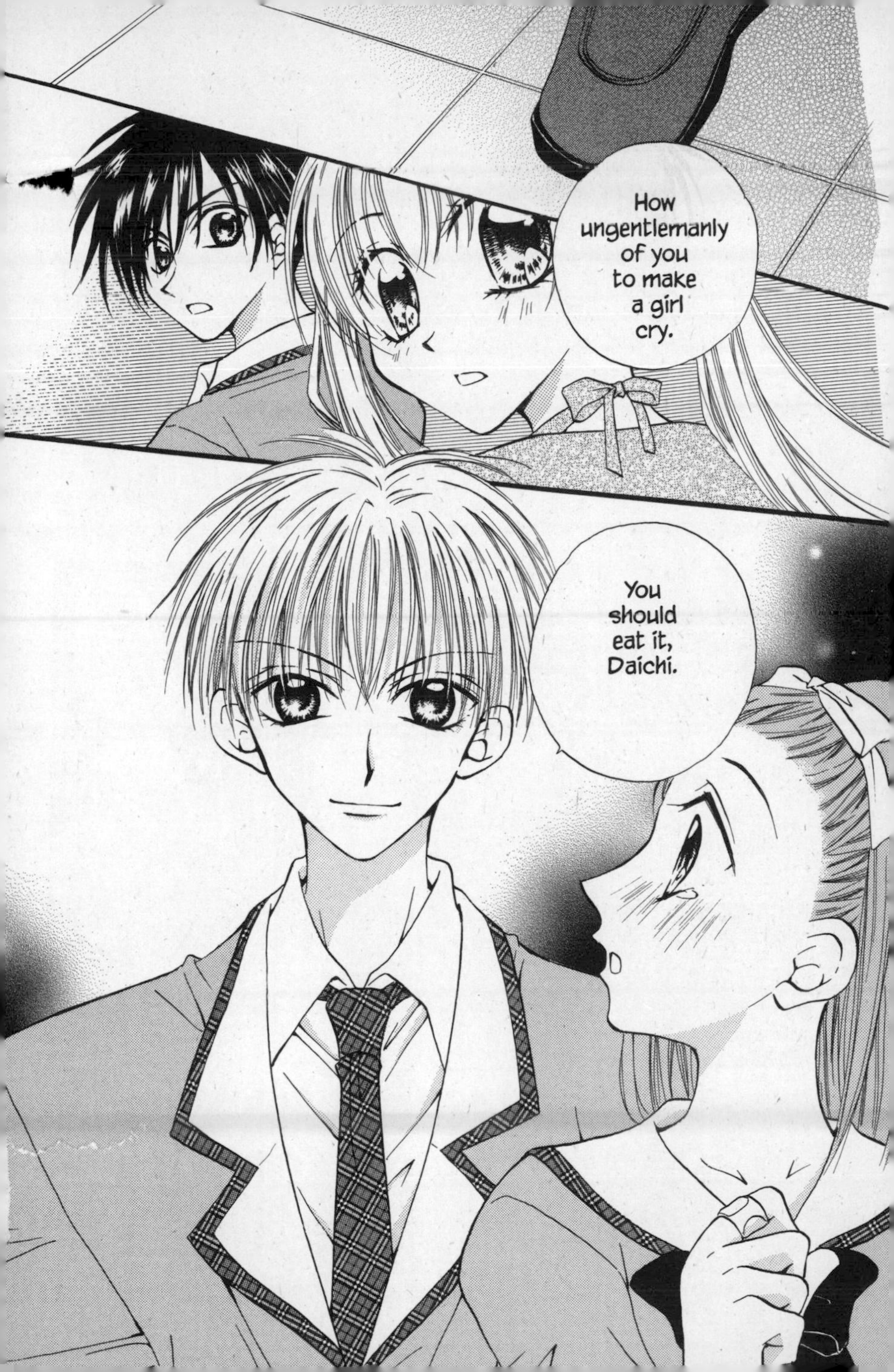
How ungentlemanly of you to make a girl cry.
You should eat it, Daichi.

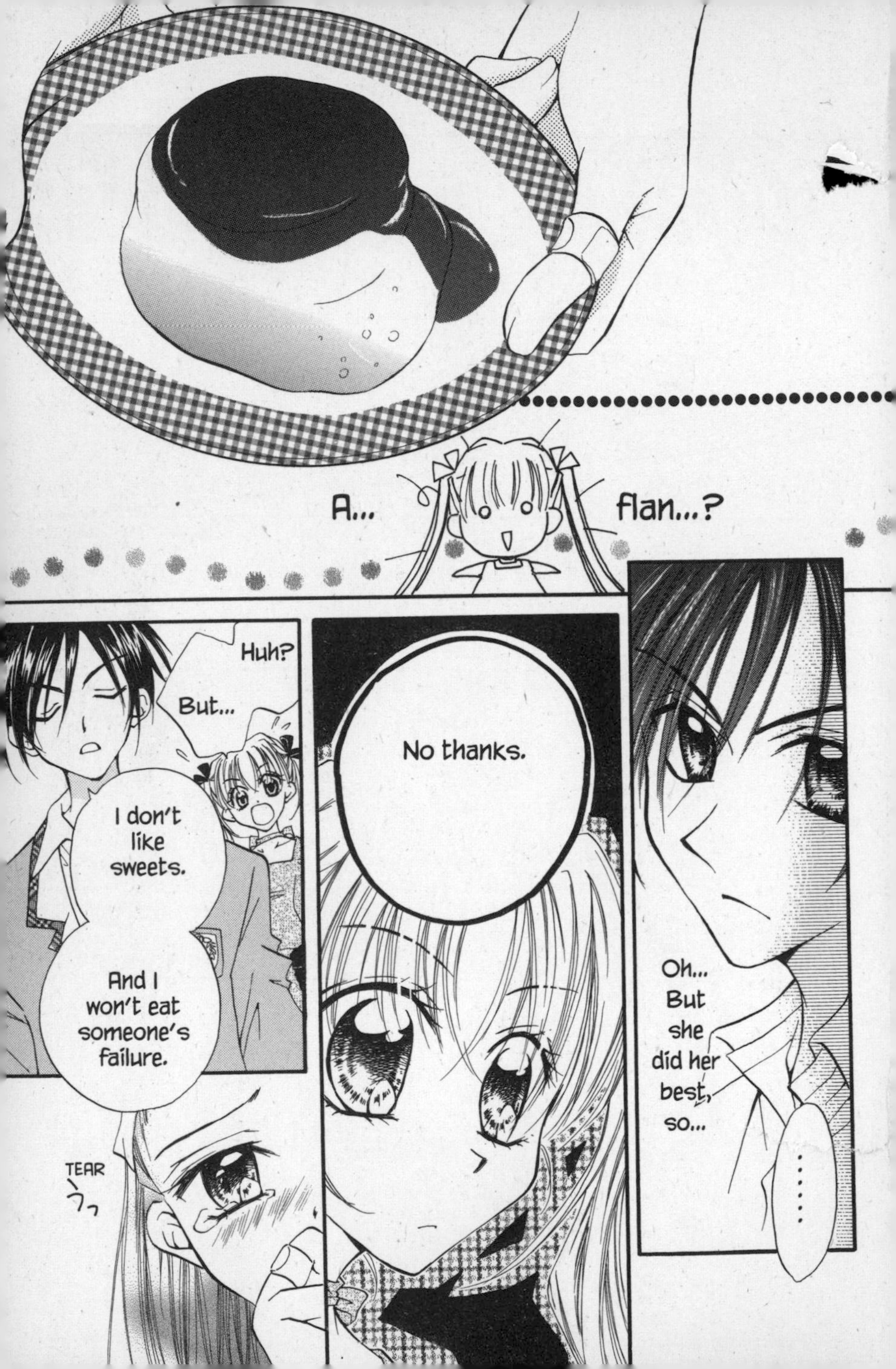
A...
flan...?
Oh... But she did her best, so...
......
No thanks.
Huh?
But...
I don't like sweets.
And I won't eat someone's failure.
TEAR

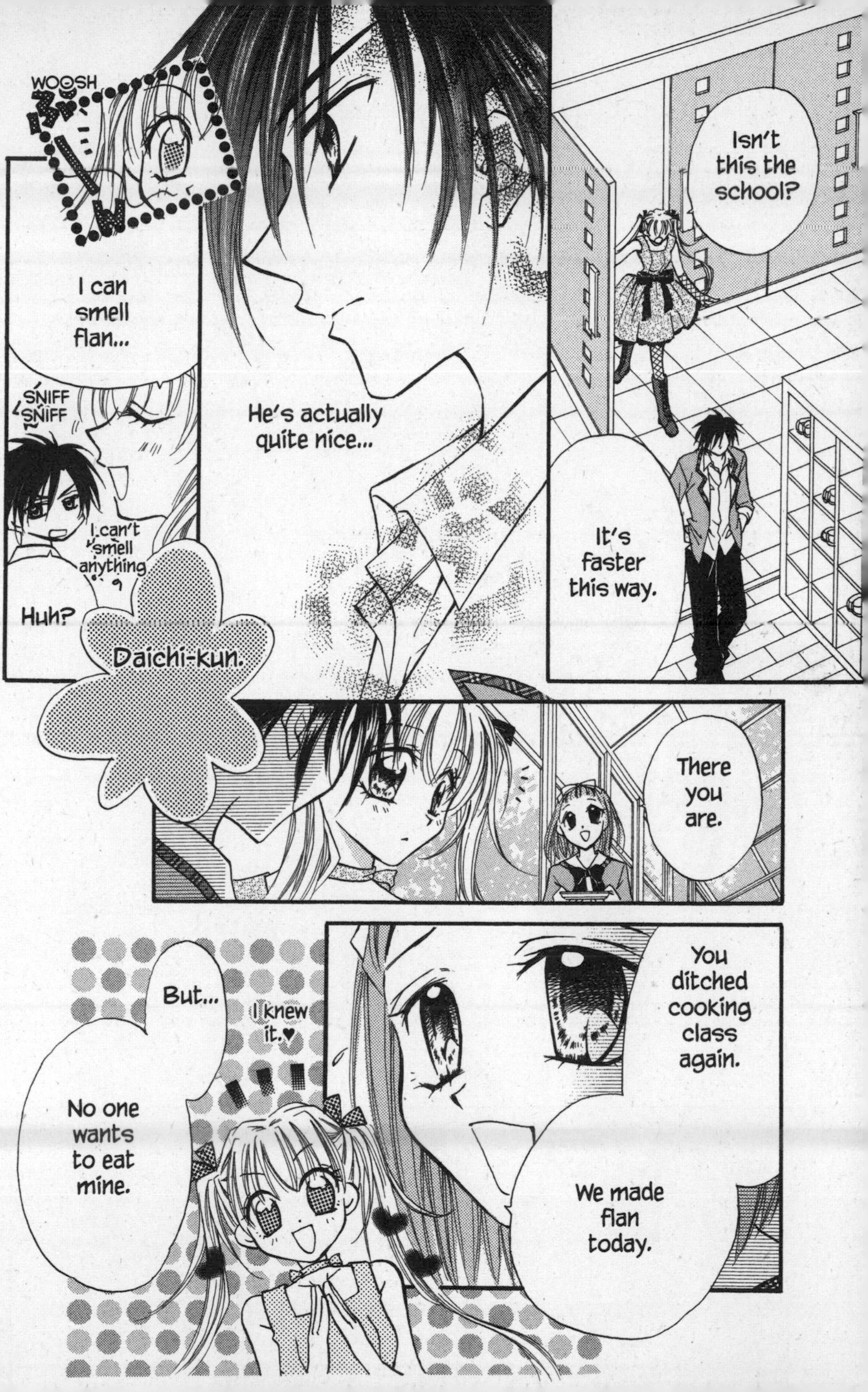
Isn't this the school?
It's faster this way.
He's actually quite nice...
WOOSH
I can smell flan...
SNIFF SNIFF
I can't smell anything
Huh?
Daichi-kun.
There you are.
You ditched cooking class again.
We made flan today.
But...
I knew it.♥
No one wants to eat mine.

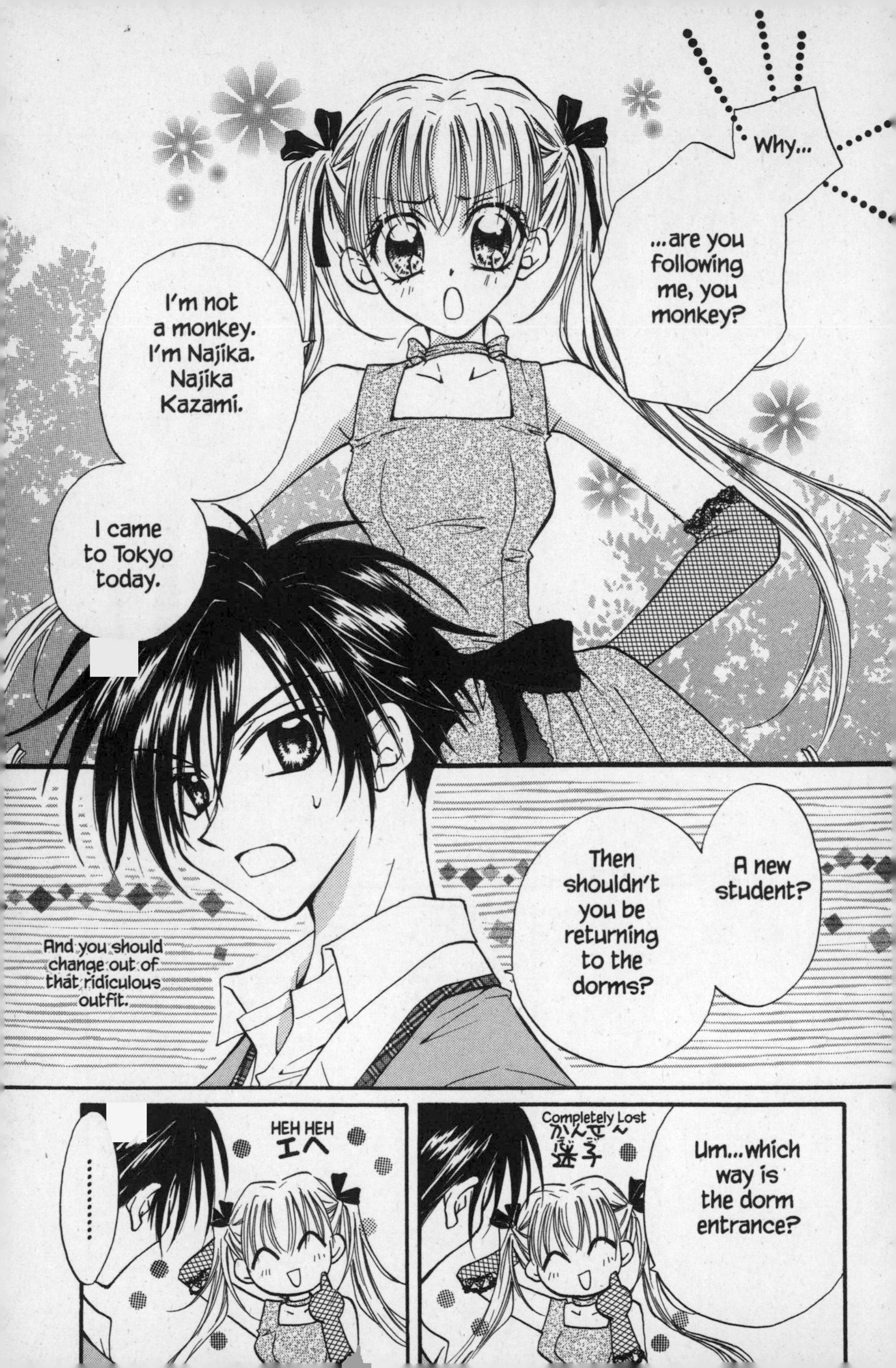
Why...
...are you following me, you monkey?
I'm not a monkey. I'm Najika. Najika Kazami.
I came to Tokyo today.
A new student?
Then shouldn't you be returning to the dorms?
And you should change out of that ridiculous outfit.
Um...which way is the dorm entrance?
Completely Lost
HEH HEH
エヘ
......

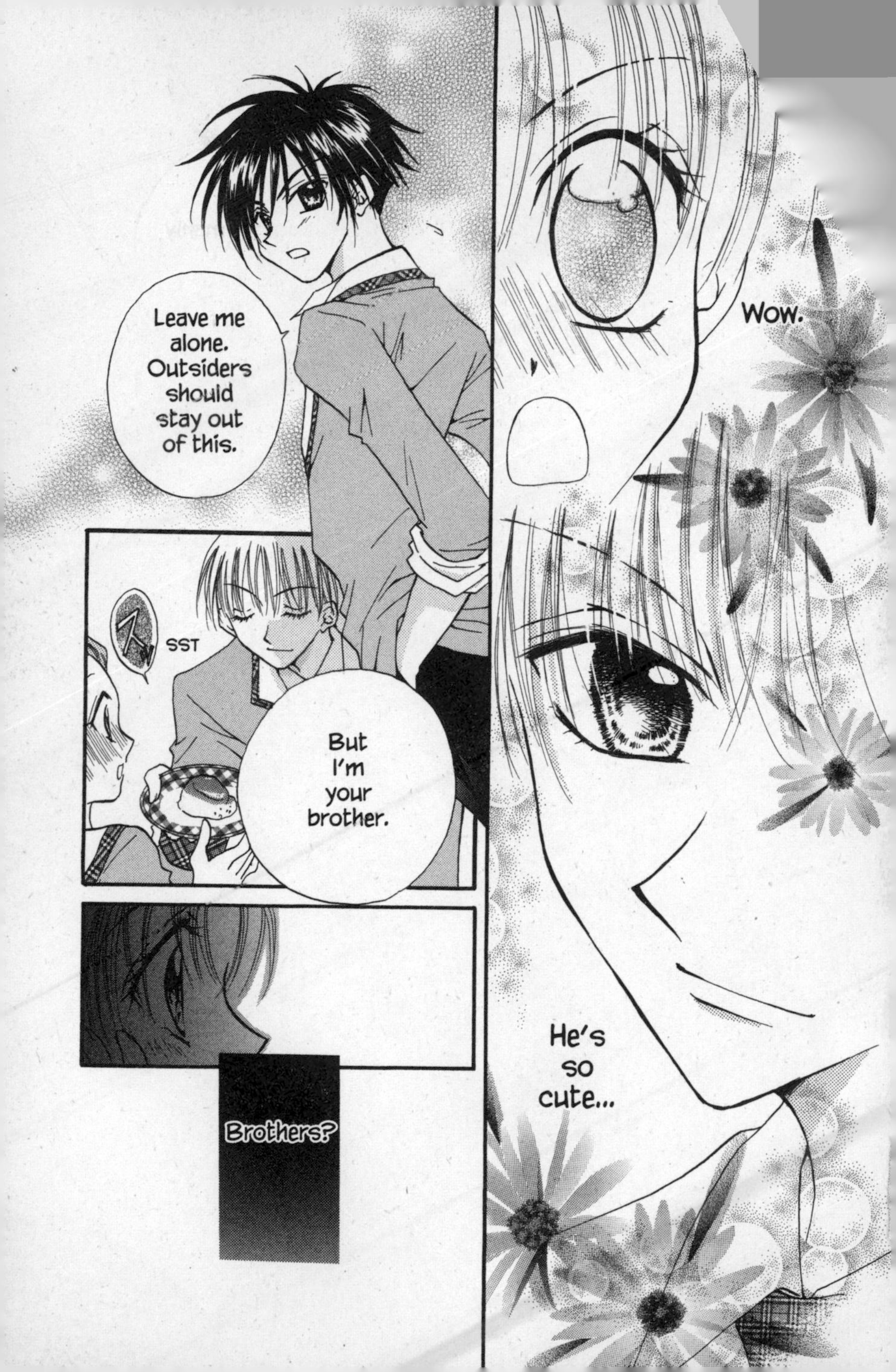
Wow.
He's so cute...
Leave me alone. Outsiders should stay out of this.
SST
But I'm your brother.
Brothers?

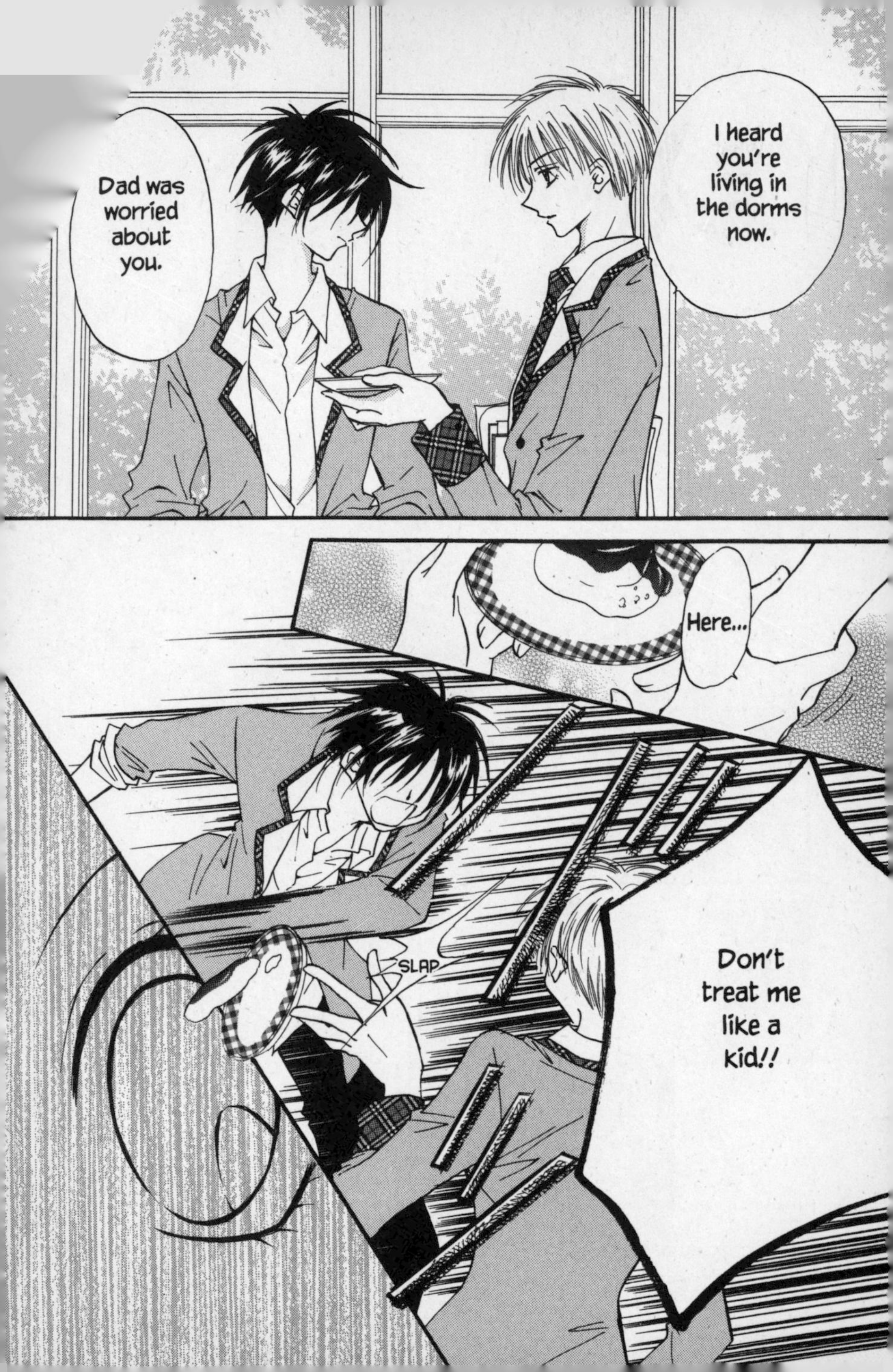
I heard you're living in the dorms now.
Dad was worried about you.
Here...
Don't treat me like a kid!!
SLAP

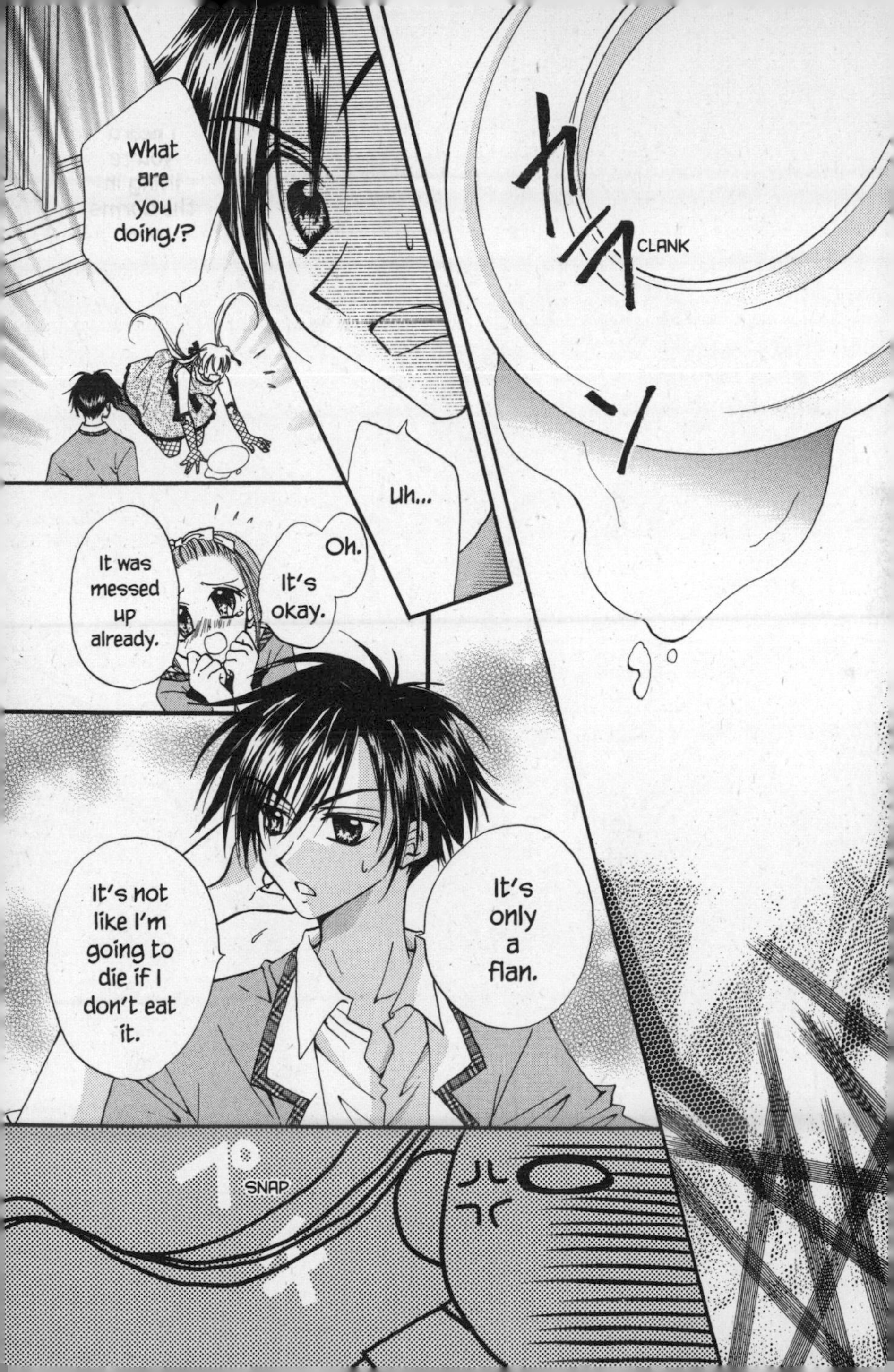
CLANK
What are you doing!?
Uh...
Oh.
It's okay.
It was messed up already.
It's only a flan.
It's not like I'm going to die if I don't eat it.
SNAP

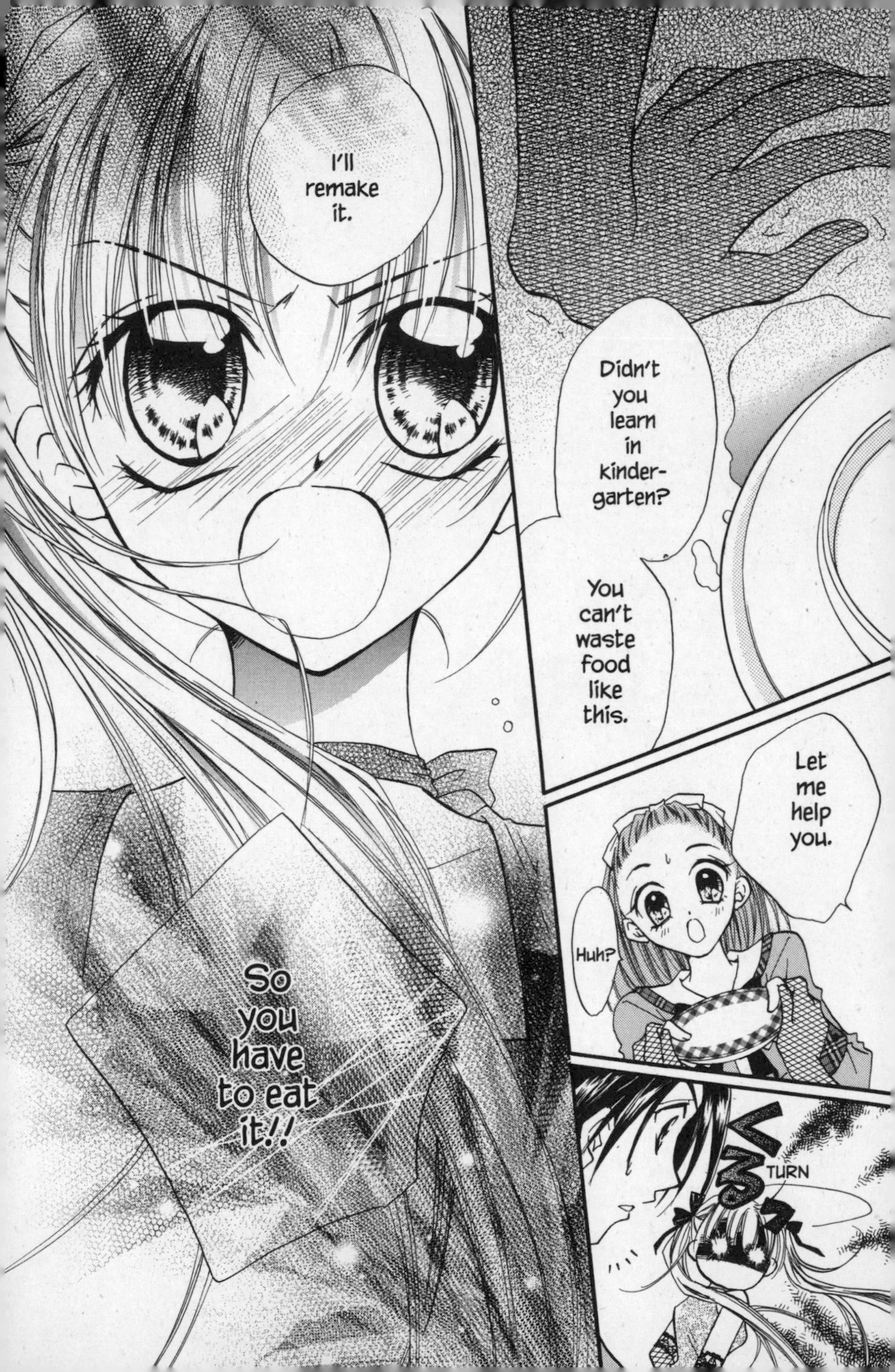
Didn't you learn in kinder-garten?
You can't waste food like this.
Let me help you.
Huh?
TURN
I'll remake it.
So you have to eat it!!

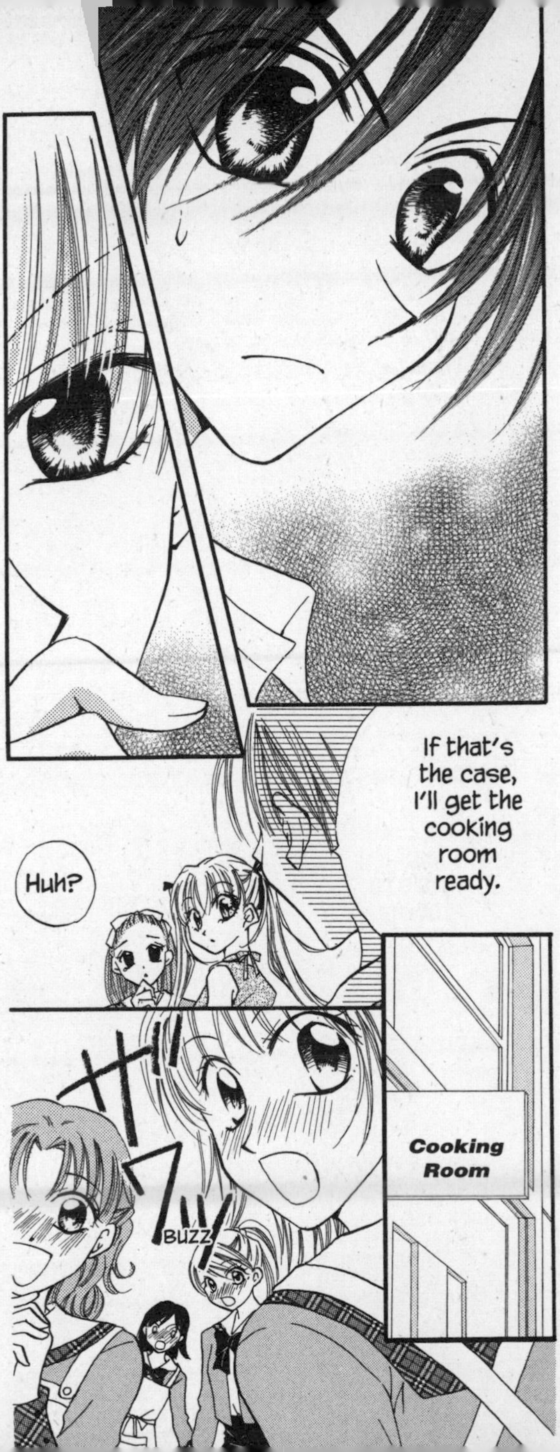
If that's the case, I'll get the cooking room ready.
Huh?
Cooking Room
BUZZ

Food

Since I'm doing a manga on food, I'll try to talk about my likes and dislikes. Not that anyone cares. ♪

- **Green Tea**

  I choose this flavor for everything—drinks, ice cream, cake, flan, you name it! I love it!! When a friend told me that I could make pancakes using the rice cooker, I made them green tea-flavored. ♪

- **Hacchou Miso**

  Since I'm from Nagoya, I love this taste. It's so sweet! I usually don't like pork cutlets, but if they're topped with hacchou miso, they become my favorite food. ♥

  For miso soup, I prefer red miso, too.

- **Seasoning**

  I usually don't use seasoning other than miso. I don't pour soy sauce on my fish, and I don't dip tempura in the tempura sauce.

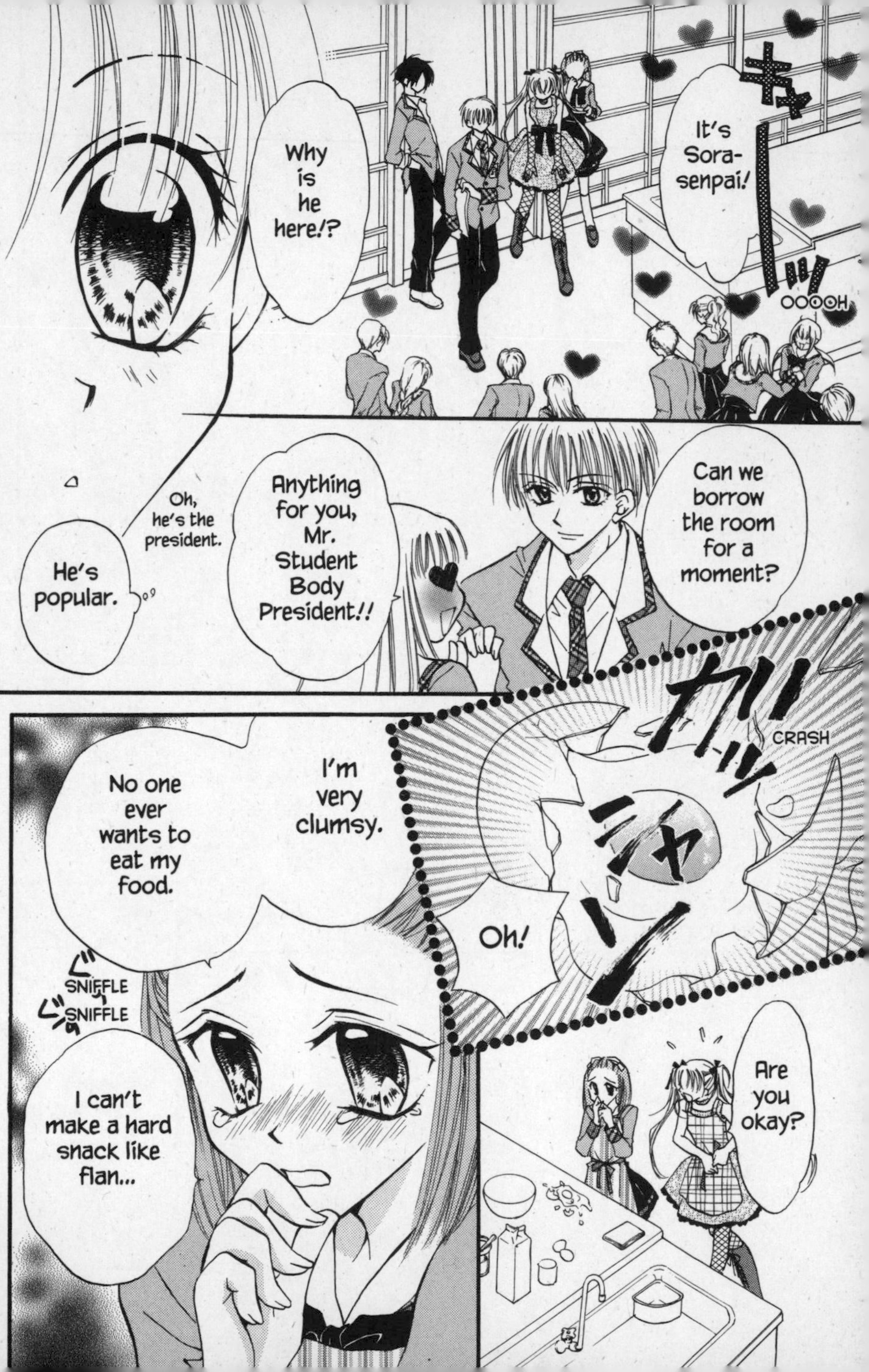
It's Sora-senpai!
OOOOH
Why is he here!?
Can we borrow the room for a moment?
Anything for you, Mr. Student Body President!!
Oh, he's the president.
He's popular.
CRASH
Oh!
Are you okay?
I'm very clumsy.
No one ever wants to eat my food.
SNIFFLE SNIFFLE
I can't make a hard snack like flan...

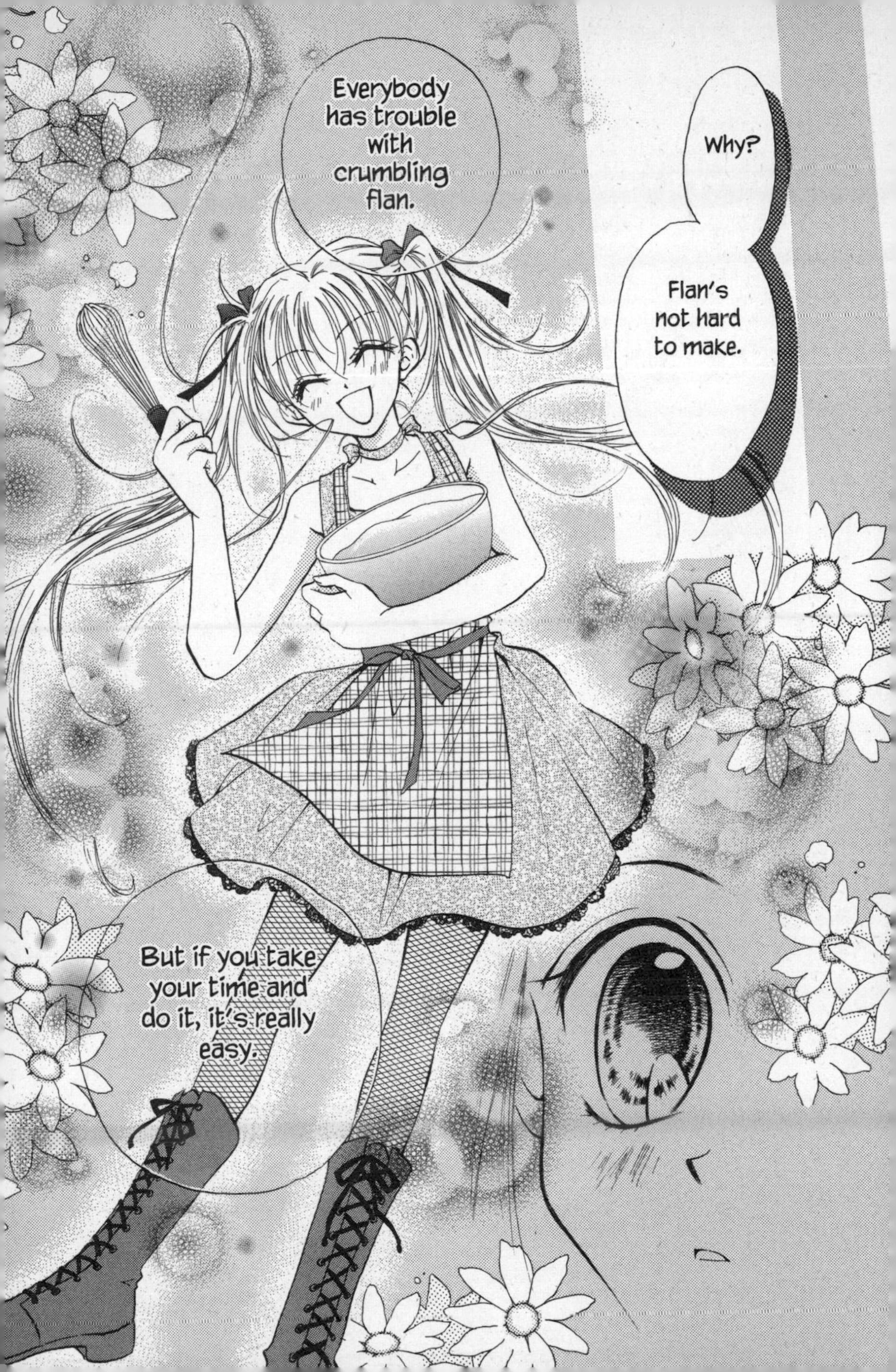
Why?
Flan's not hard to make.
Everybody has trouble with crumbling flan.
But if you take your time and do it, it's really easy.

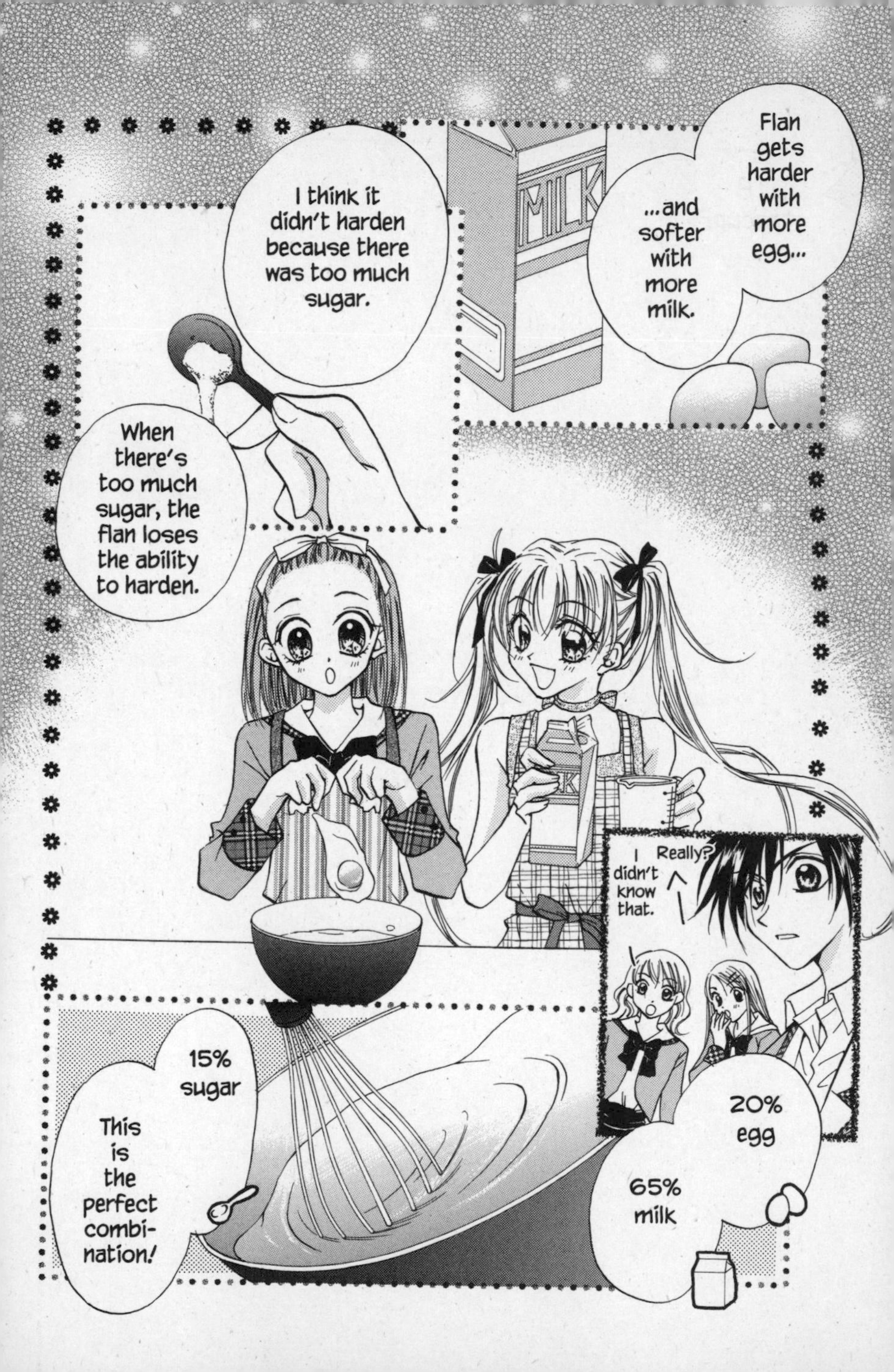
Flan gets harder with more egg...
...and softer with more milk.
I think it didn't harden because there was too much sugar.
When there's too much sugar, the flan loses the ability to harden.
Really?
I didn't know that.
20% egg
65% milk
15% sugar
This is the perfect combination!

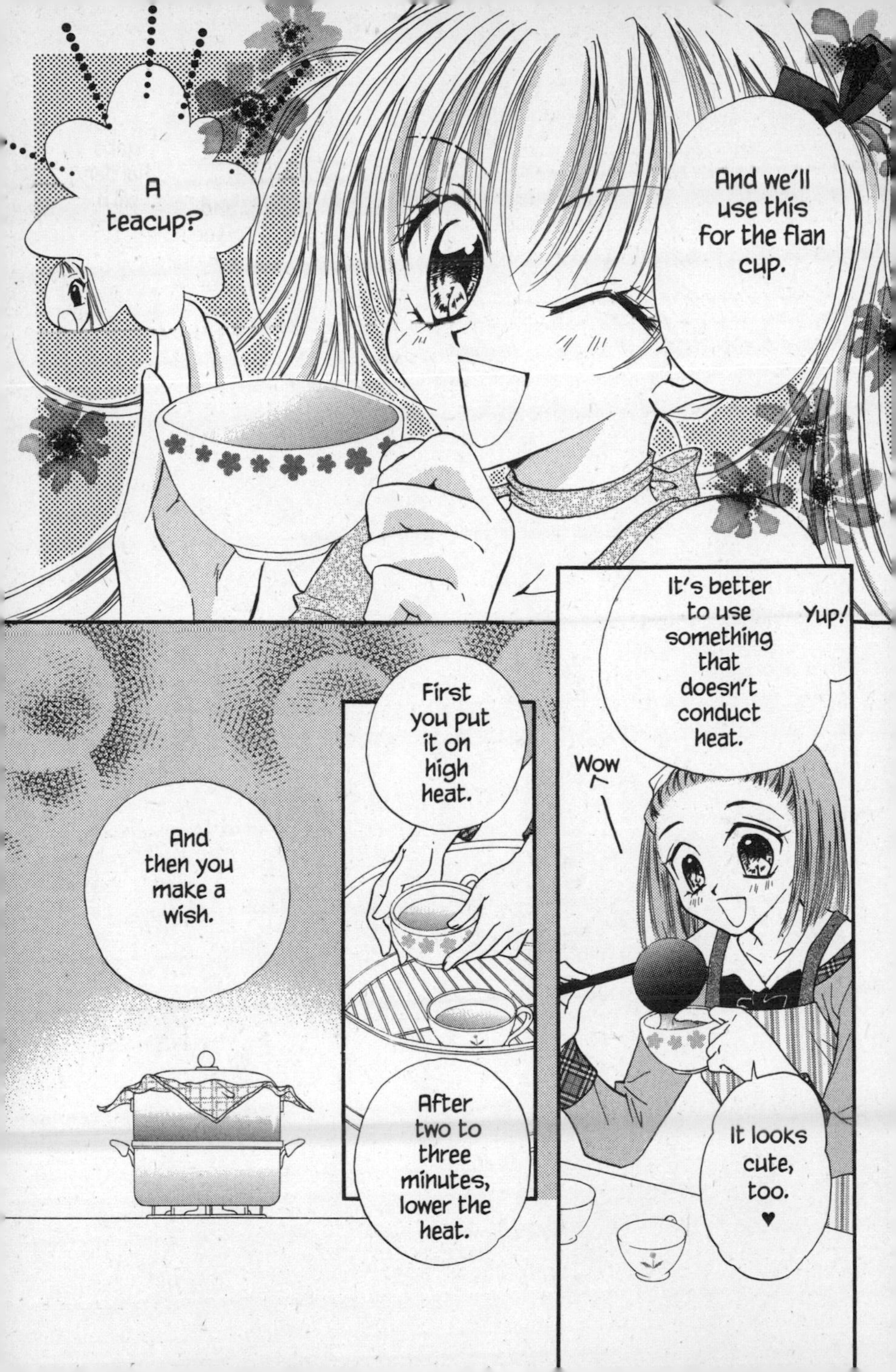
And we'll use this for the flan cup.
A teacup?
It's better to use something that doesn't conduct heat.
Yup!
Wow
It looks cute, too. ♥
First you put it on high heat.
After two to three minutes, lower the heat.
And then you make a wish.

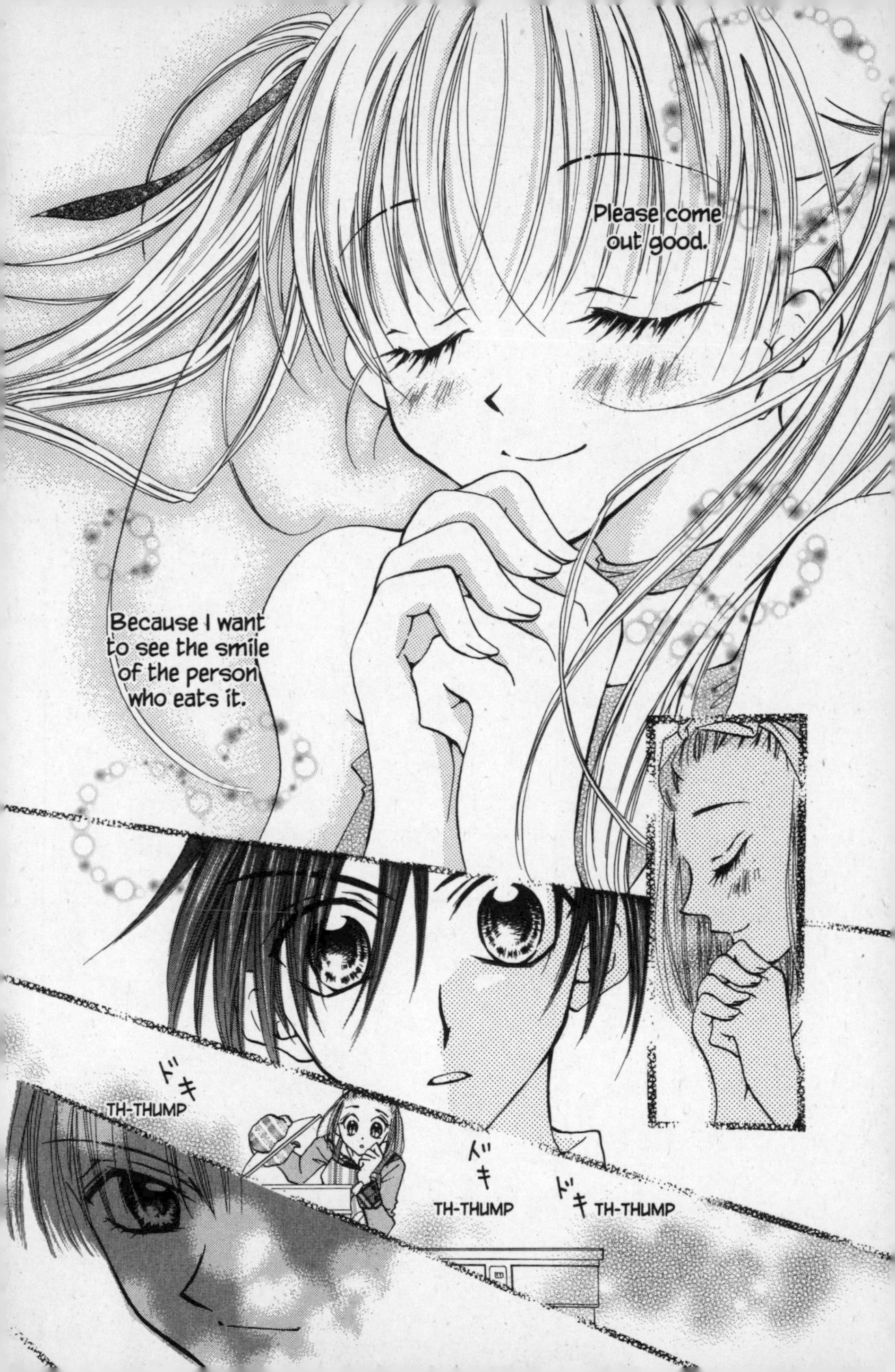
Please come out good.
Because I want to see the smile of the person who eats it.
ドキ
TH-THUMP
ドキ
TH-THUMP
ドキ
TH-THUMP

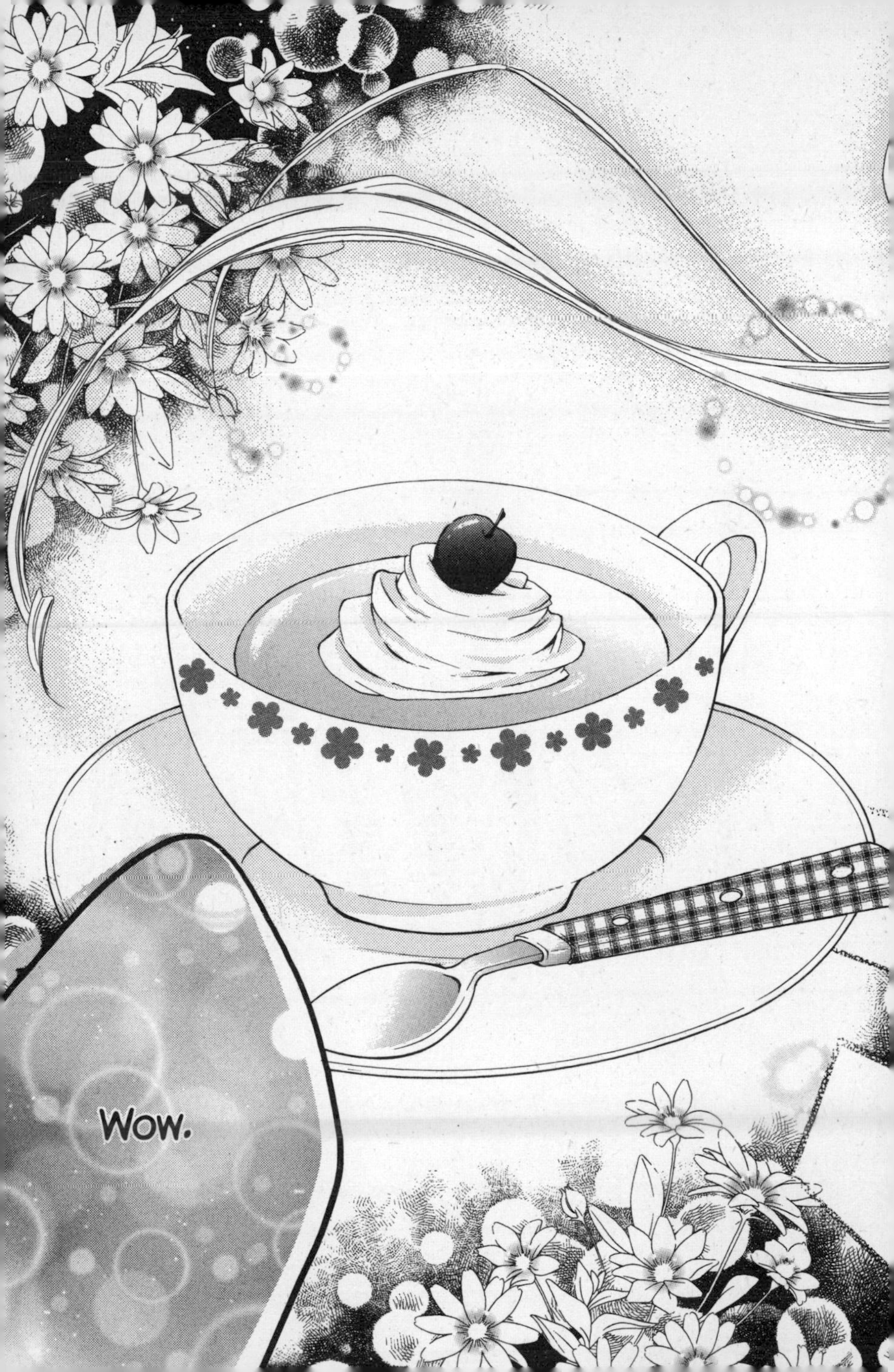
Wow.

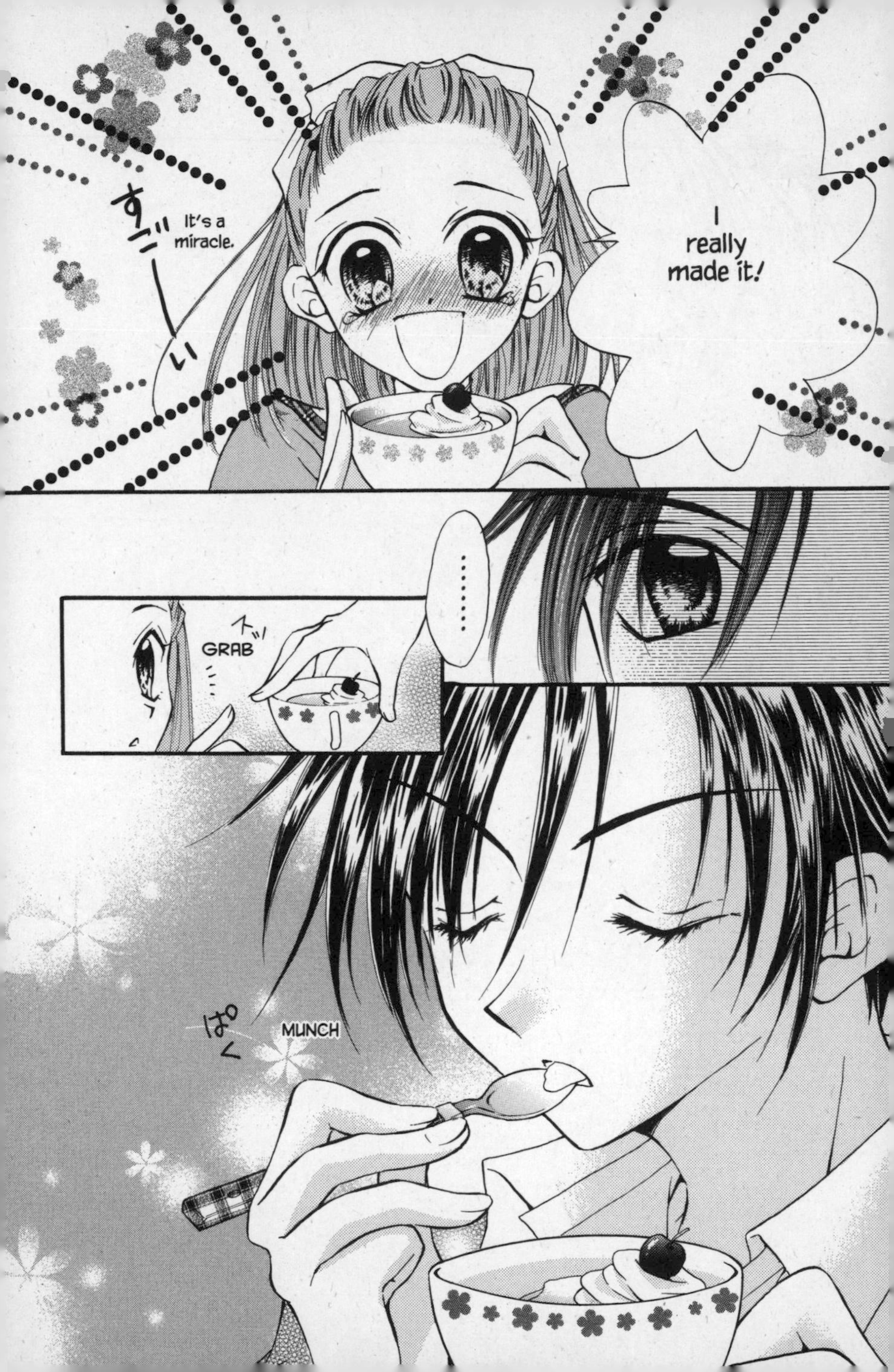
I really made it!
すごーい
It's a miracle.
......
ズッ
GRAB
ぱく
MUNCH

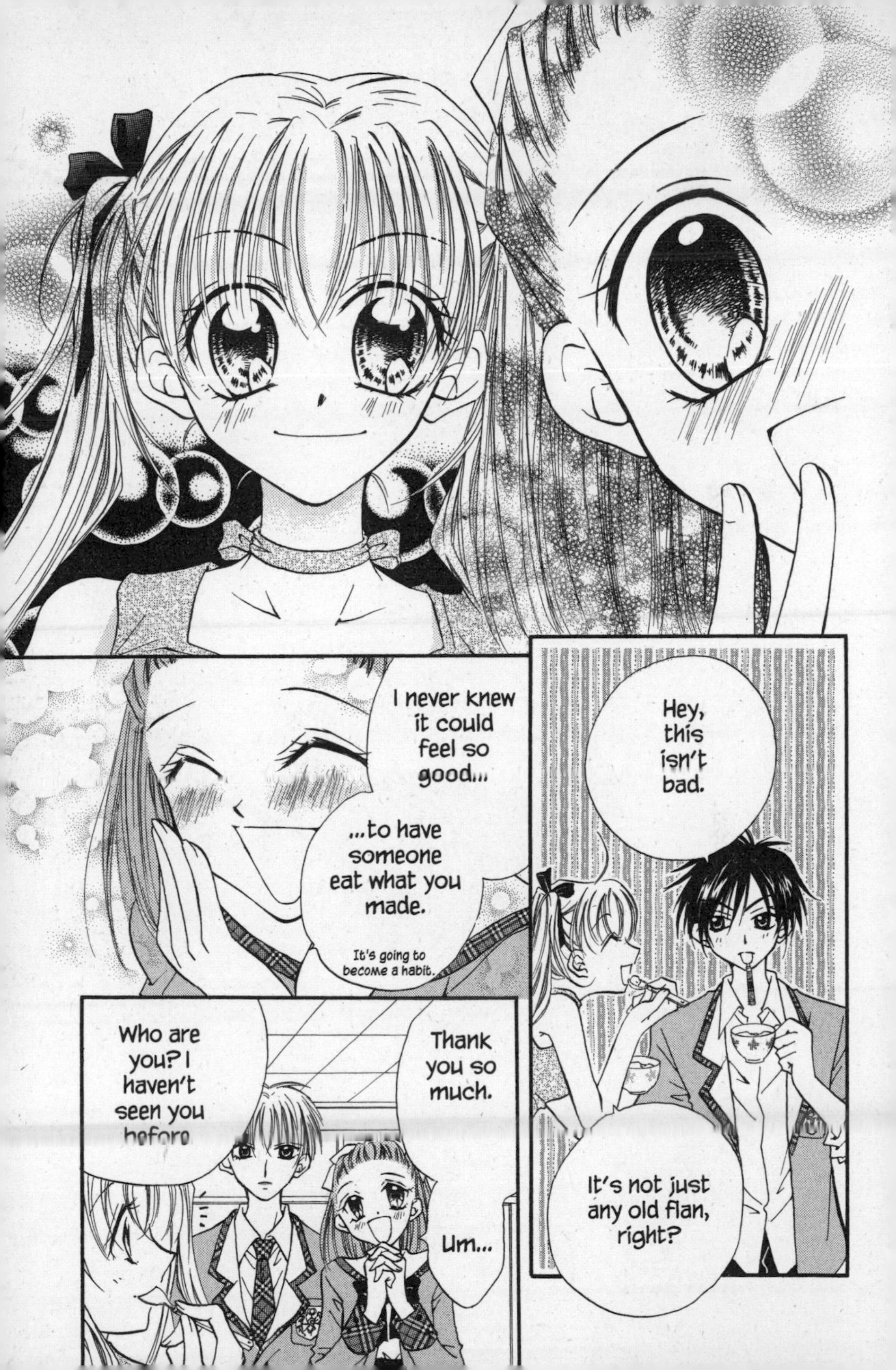
Hey, this isn't bad.
It's not just any old flan, right?
I never knew it could feel so good...
...to have someone eat what you made.
It's going to become a habit.
Thank you so much.
Who are you? I haven't seen you before
Um...

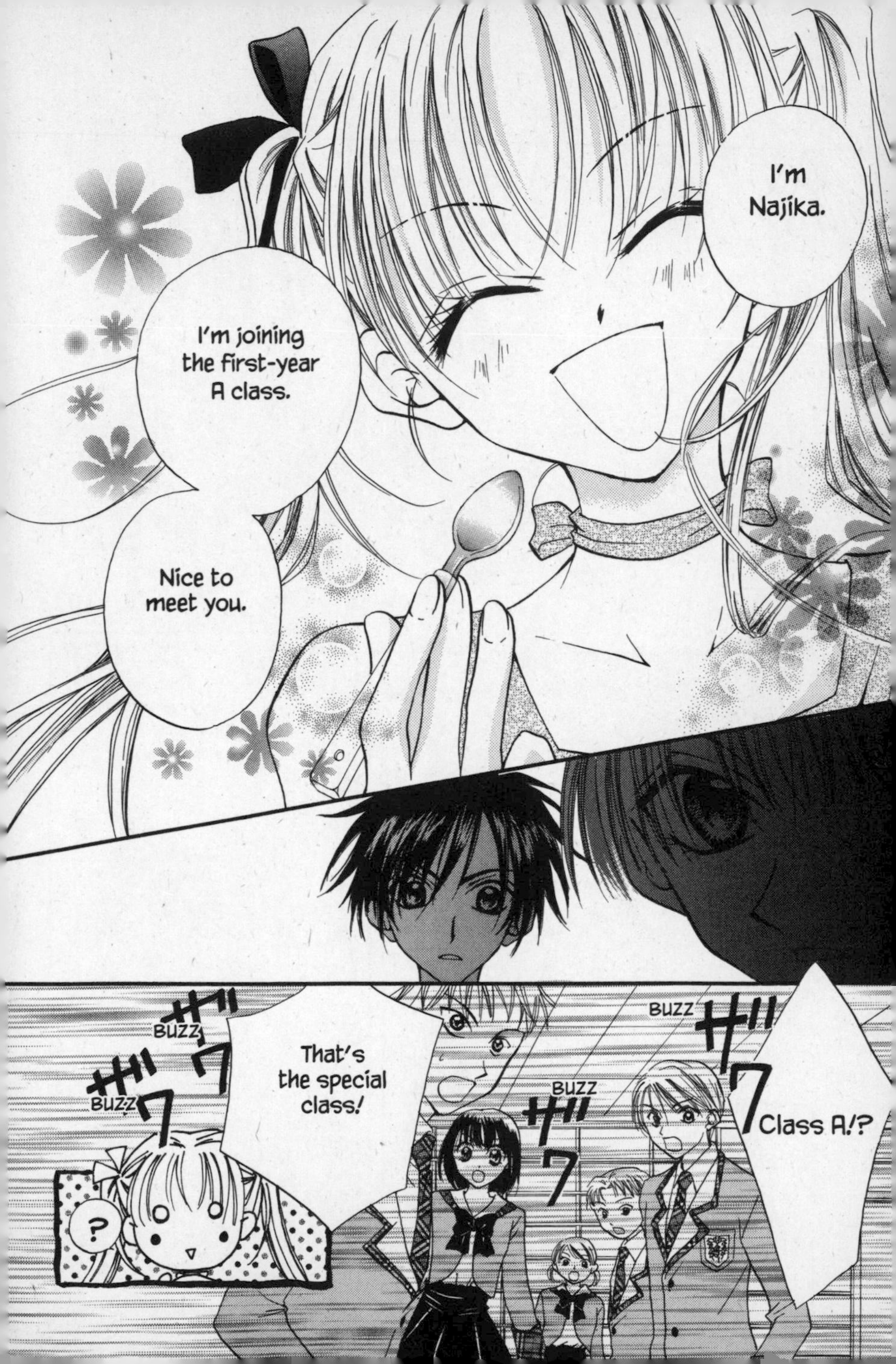
I'm Najika.
I'm joining the first-year A class.
Nice to meet you.
BUZZ
Class A!?
BUZZ
That's the special class!
BUZZ
BUZZ
?

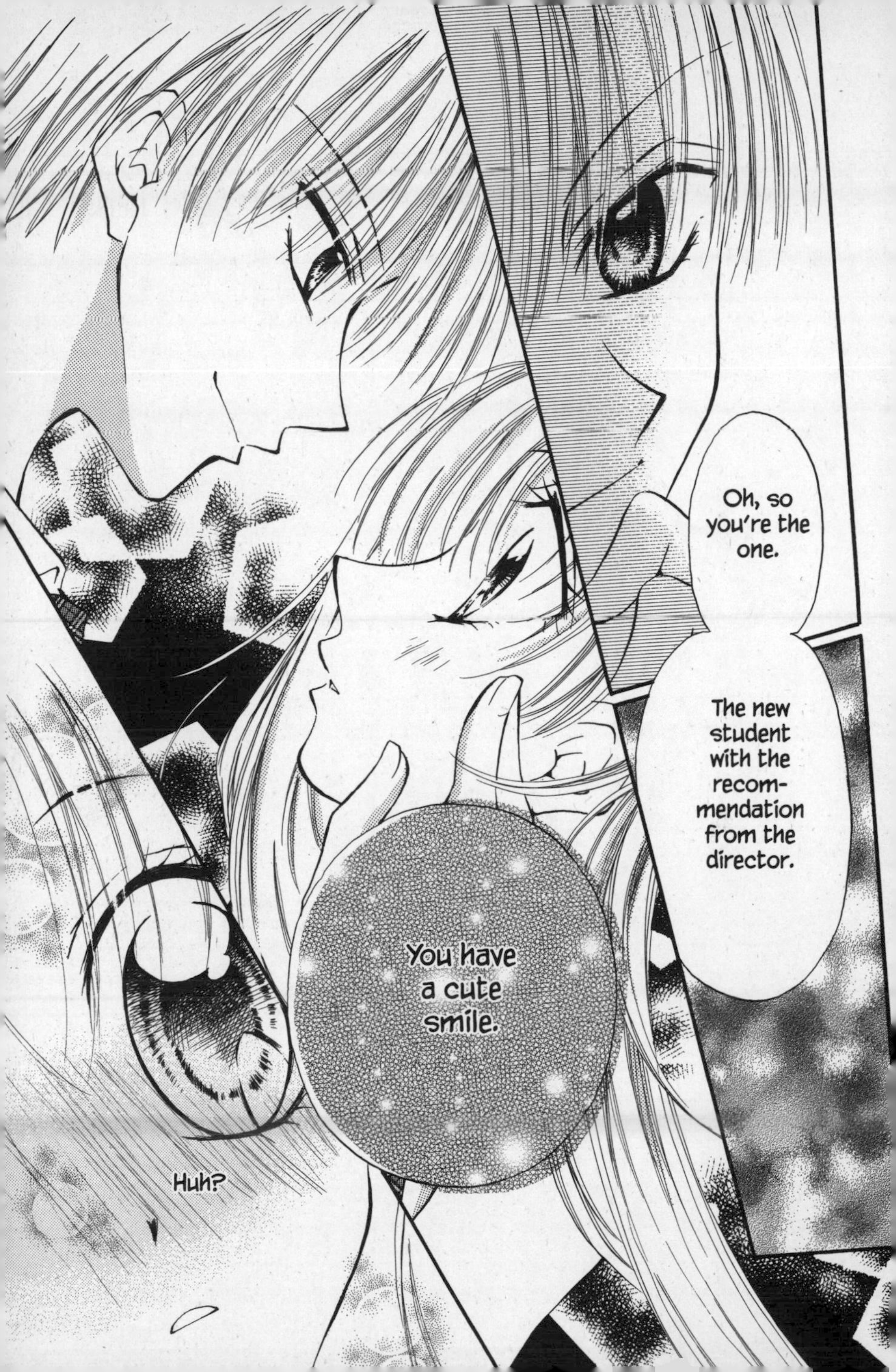
Oh, so you're the one.
The new student with the recom-mendation from the director.
You have a cute smile.
Huh?

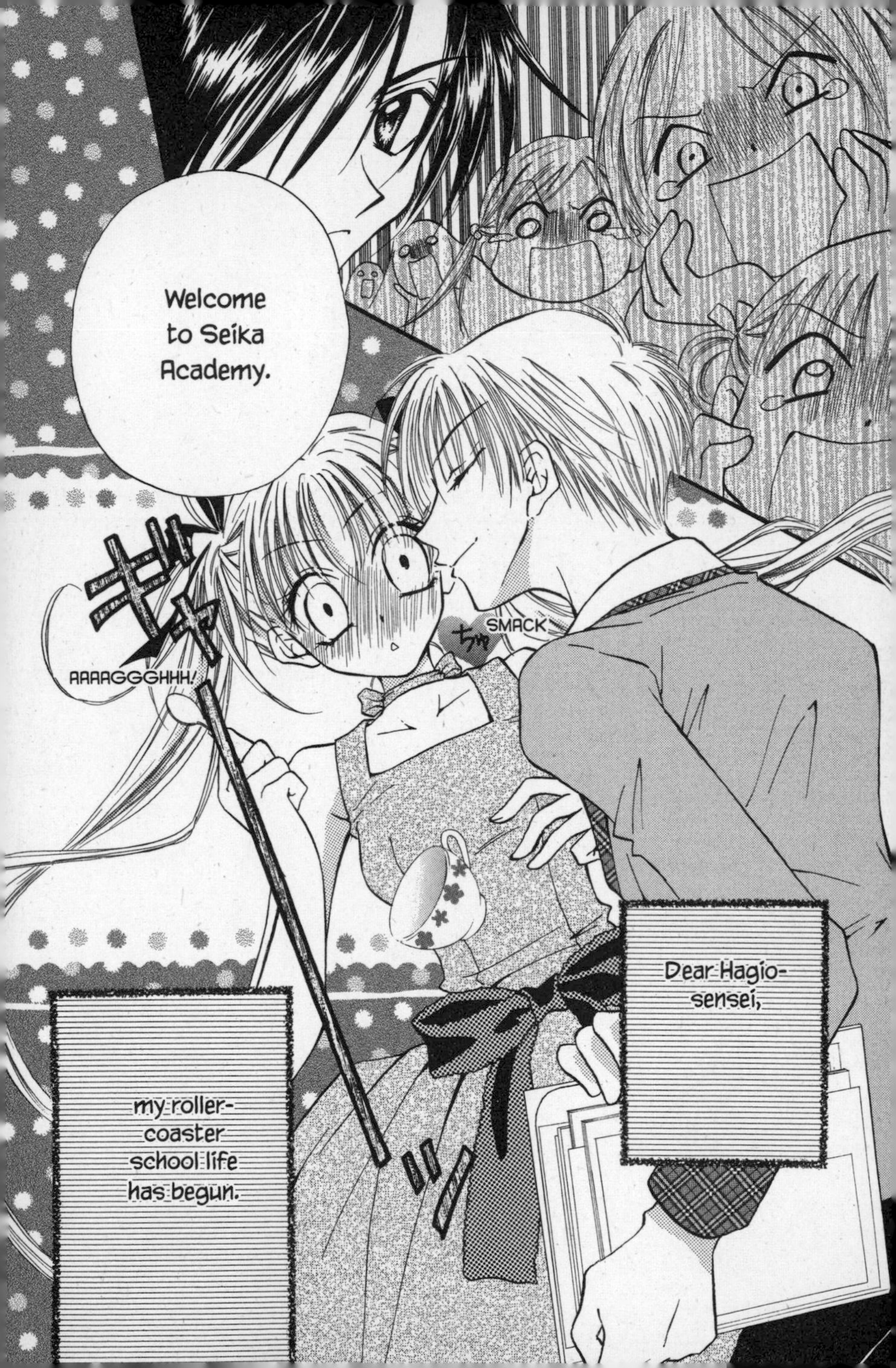
Welcome to Seika Academy.
SMACK
AAAAGGGHHH!
Dear Hagio-sensei,
my roller-coaster school life has begun.

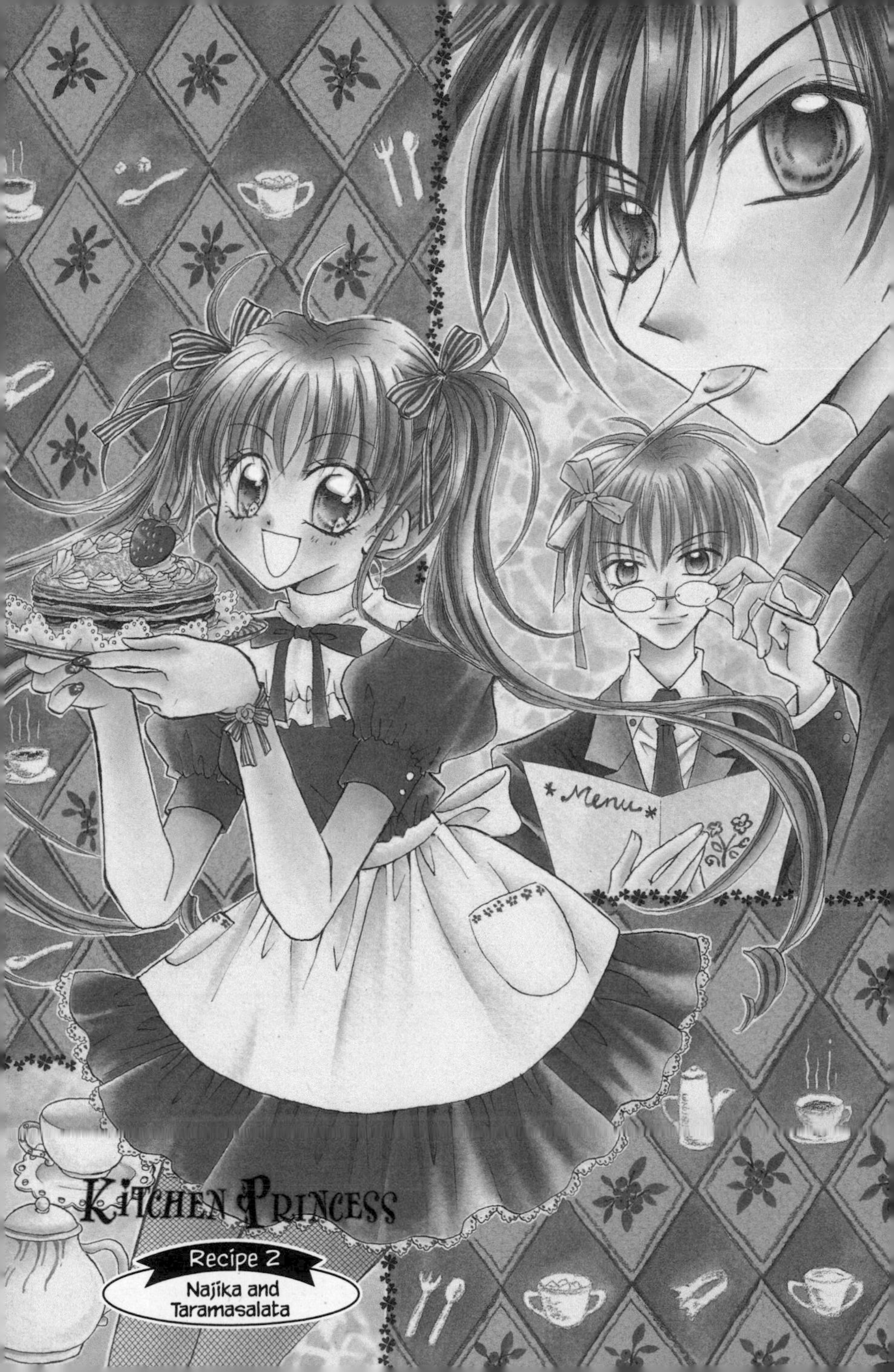
Menu
Kitchen Princess
Recipe 2
Najika and Taramasalata

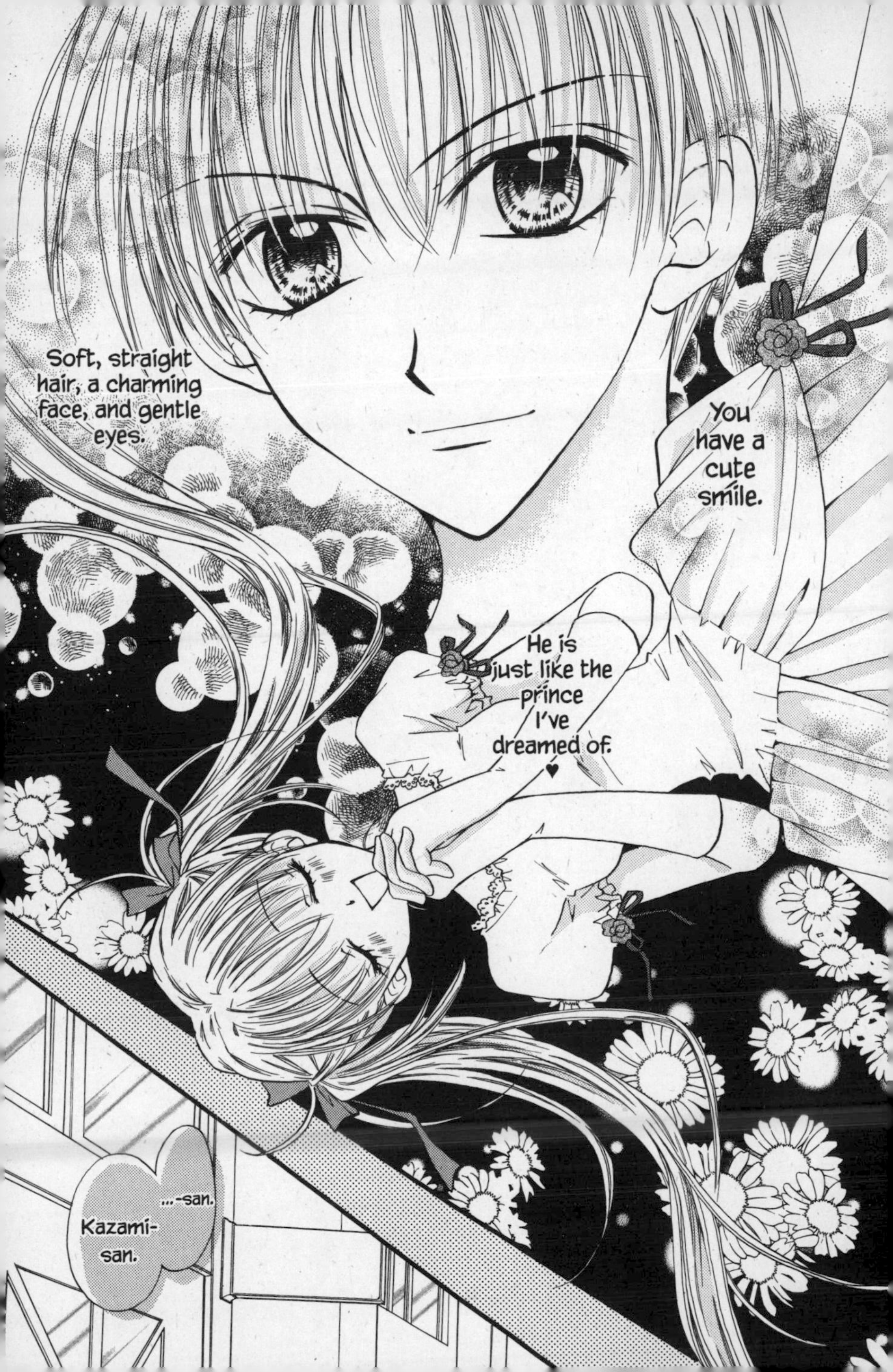

You have a cute smile.
Soft, straight hair, a charming face, and gentle eyes.
He is just like the prince I've dreamed of. ♥
...-san.
Kazami-san.

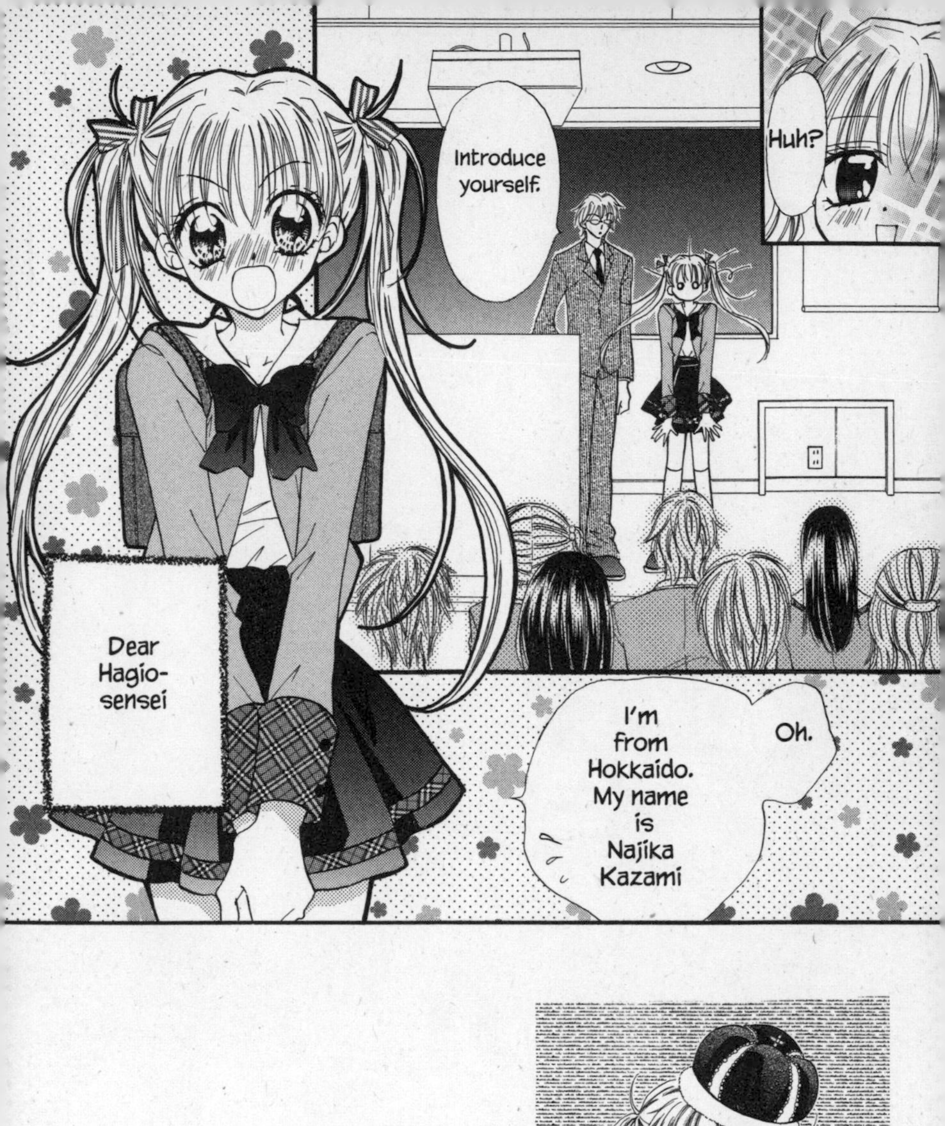
Huh?
Introduce yourself.
Oh.
I'm from Hokkaido. My name is Najika Kazami
Dear Hagio-sensei

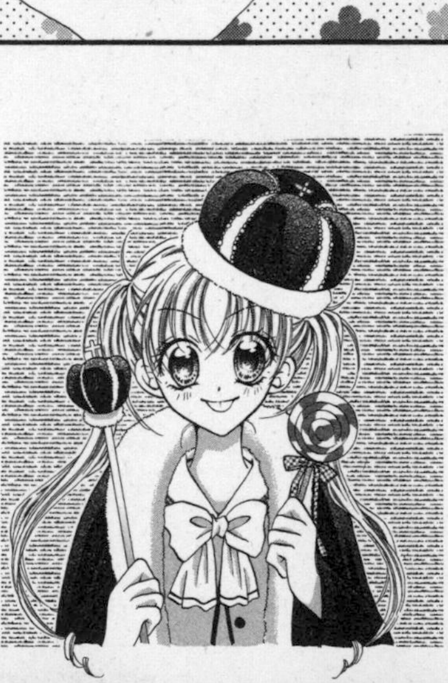

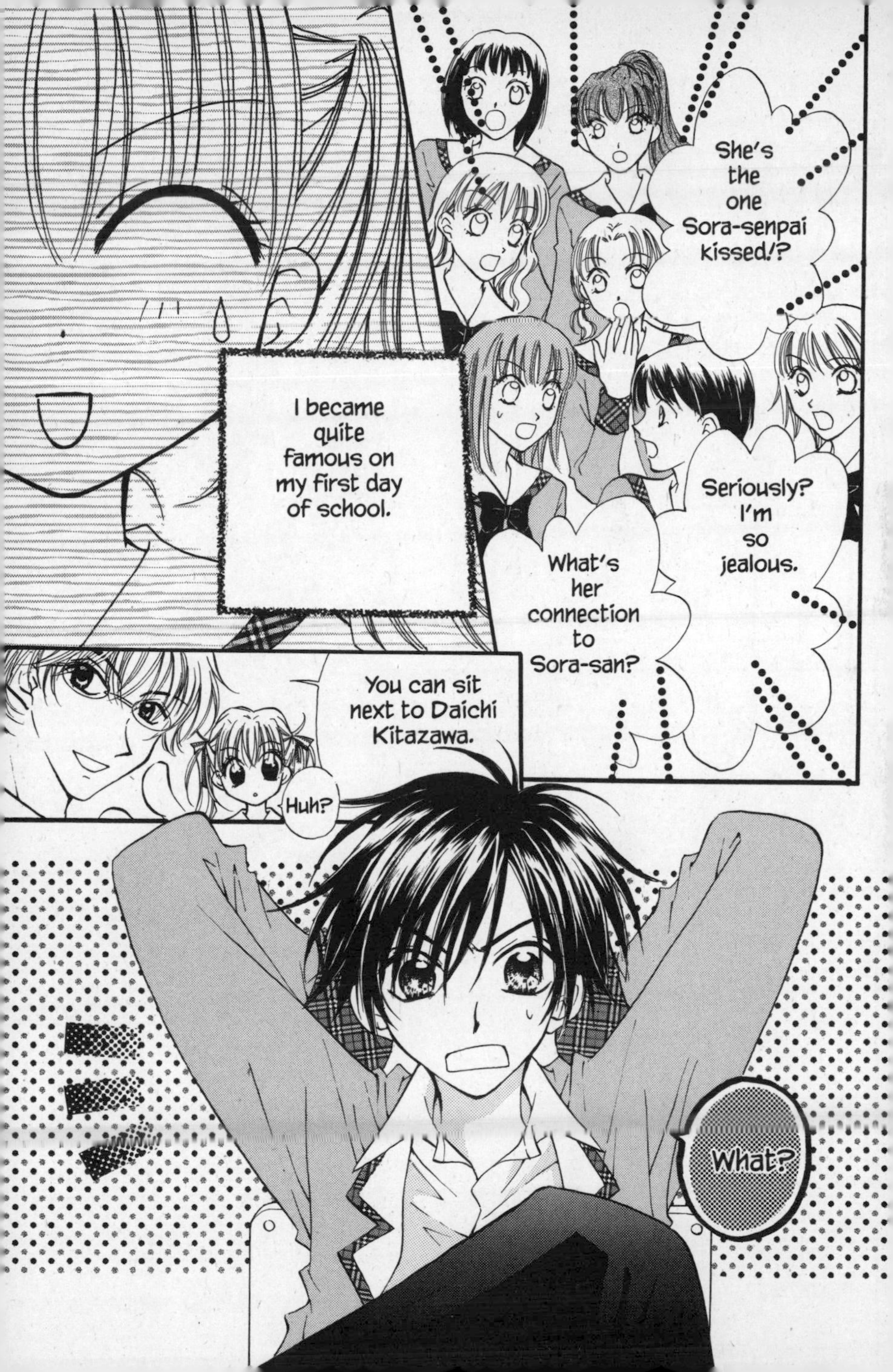
She's the one Sora-senpai kissed!?
Seriously? I'm so jealous.
What's her connection to Sora-san?
I became quite famous on my first day of school.
You can sit next to Daichi Kitazawa.
Huh?
What?

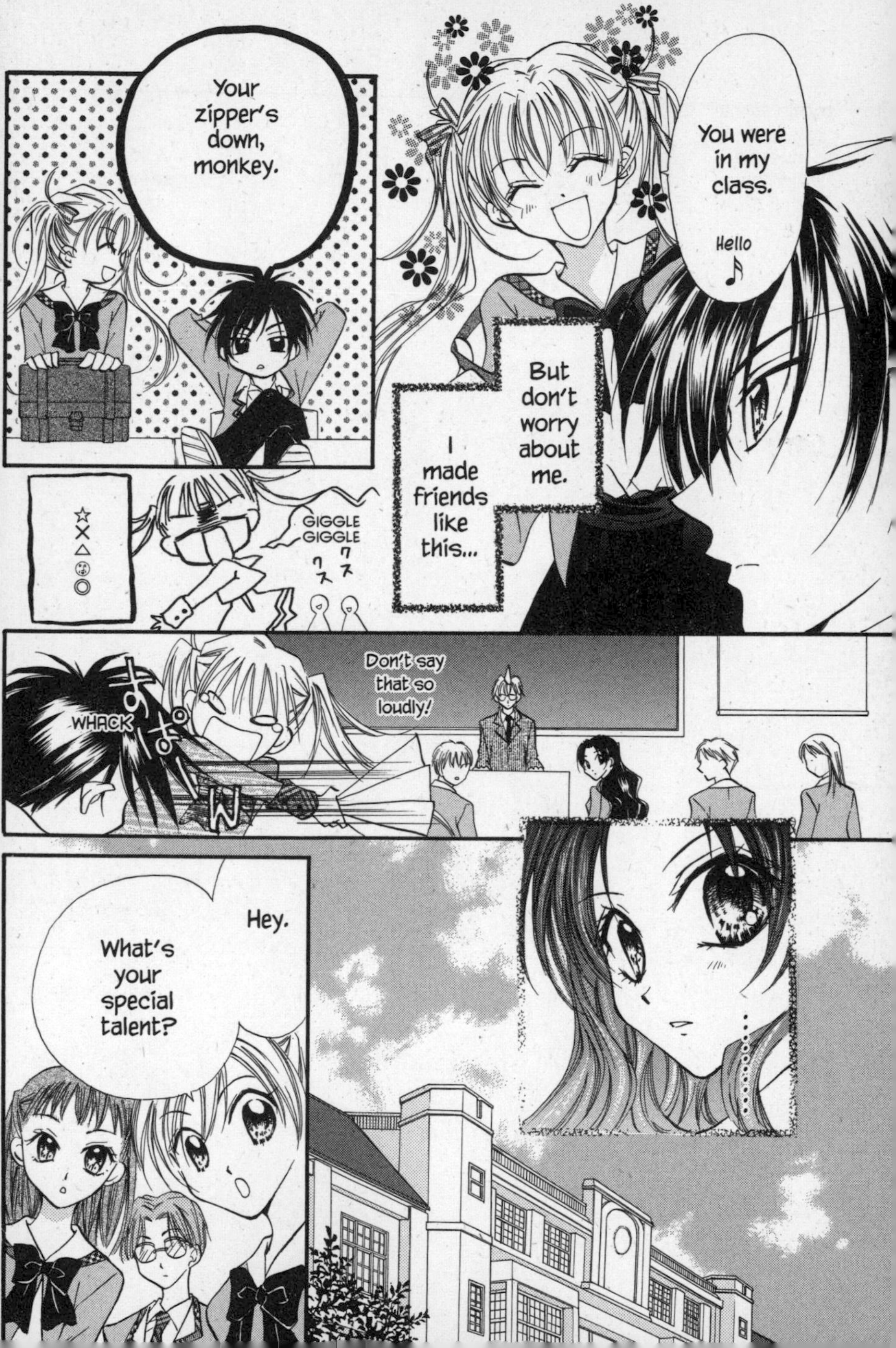
You were in my class.
Hello ♪
But don't worry about me.
I made friends like this...
Your zipper's down, monkey.
☆×△◎
GIGGLE GIGGLE
クス クス
Don't say that so loudly!
WHACK
Hey.
What's your special talent?

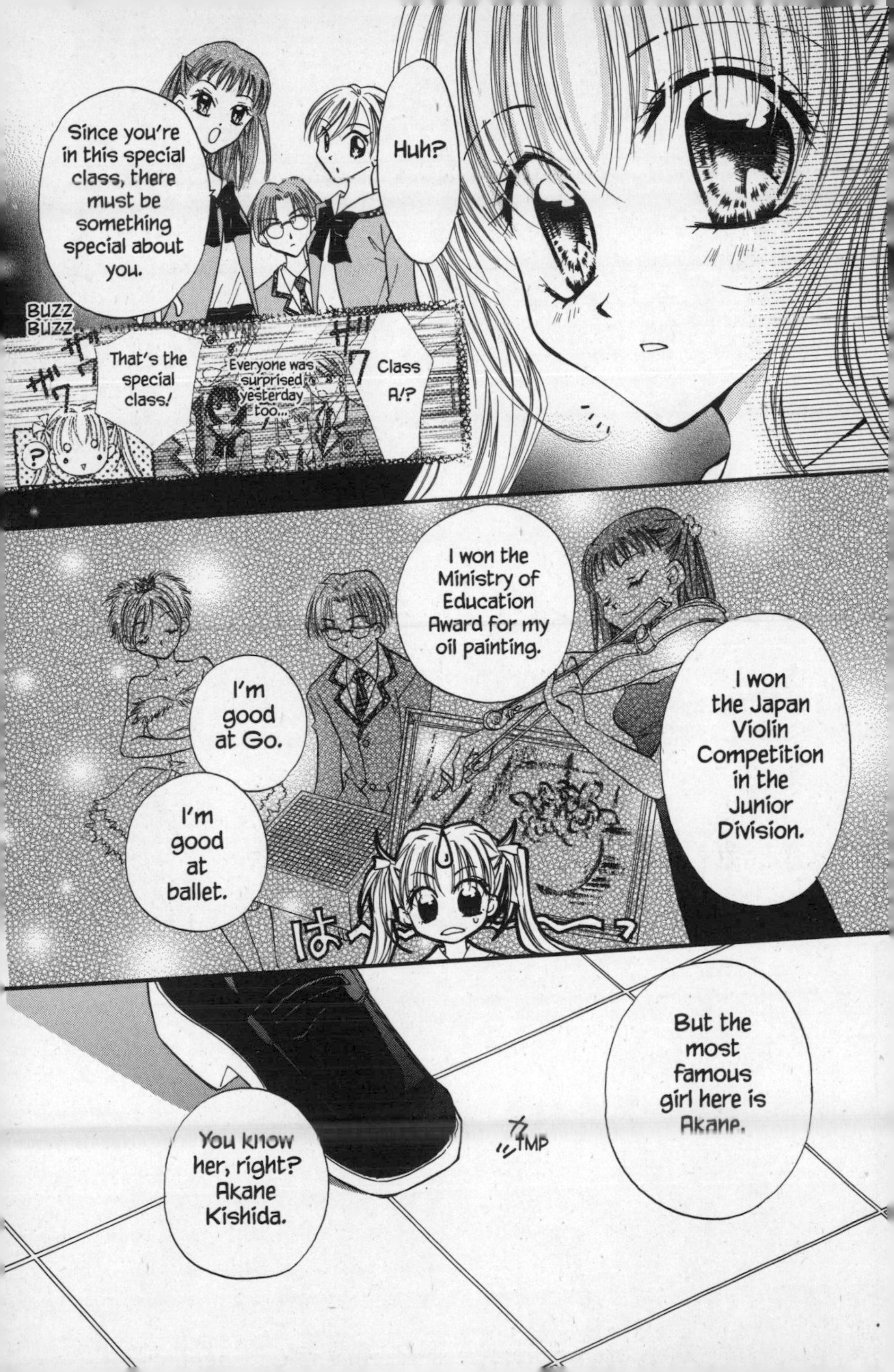
Since you're in this special class, there must be something special about you.
Huh?
BUZZ BUZZ
Class A!?
Everyone was surprised yesterday too...
That's the special class!
I won the Japan Violin Competition in the Junior Division.
I won the Ministry of Education Award for my oil painting.
I'm good at Go.
I'm good at ballet.
But the most famous girl here is Akane.
TMP
You know her, right? Akane Kishida.

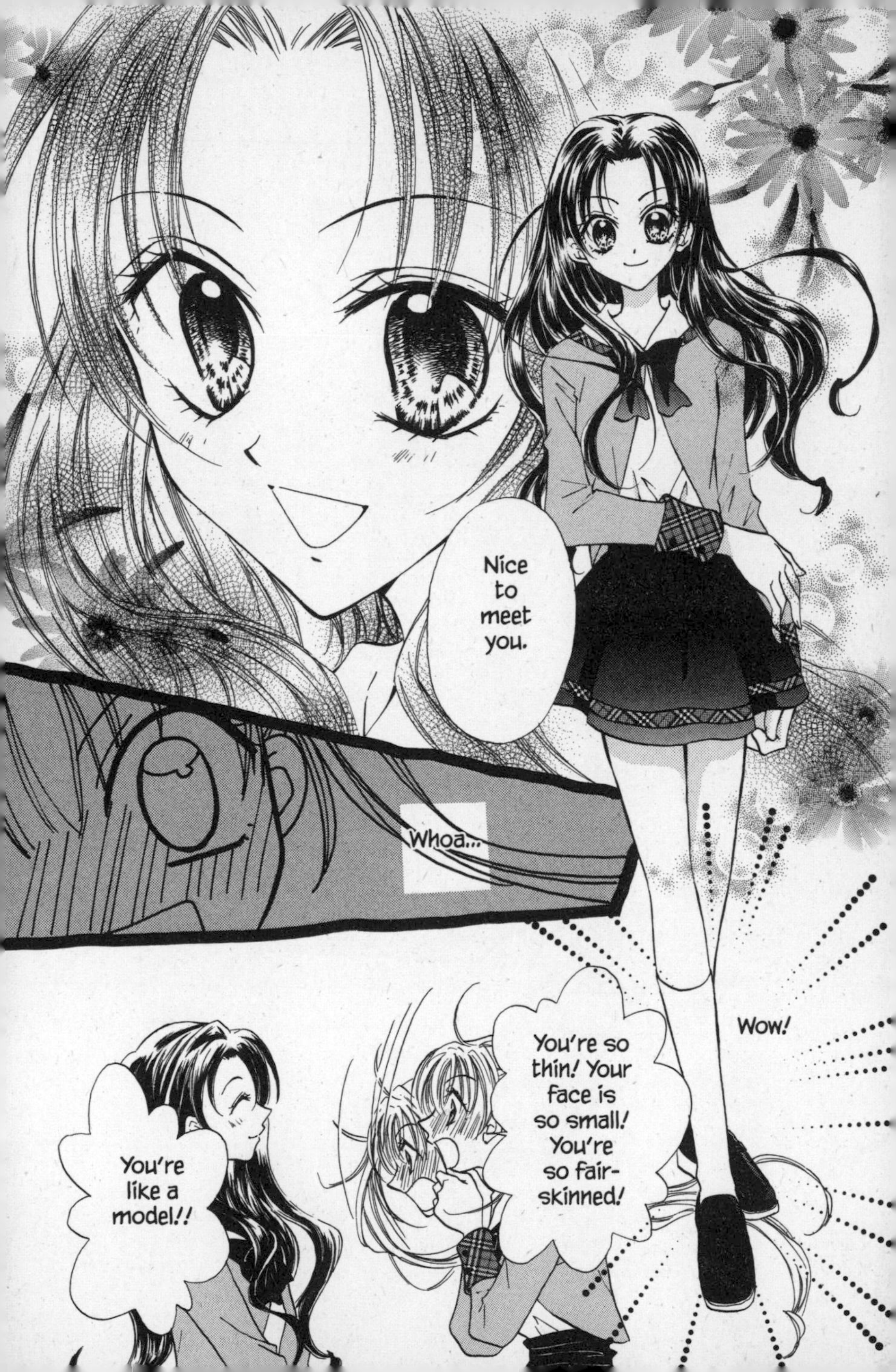
Nice to meet you.
Whoa...
Wow!
You're so thin! Your face is so small! You're so fair-skinned!
You're like a model!!

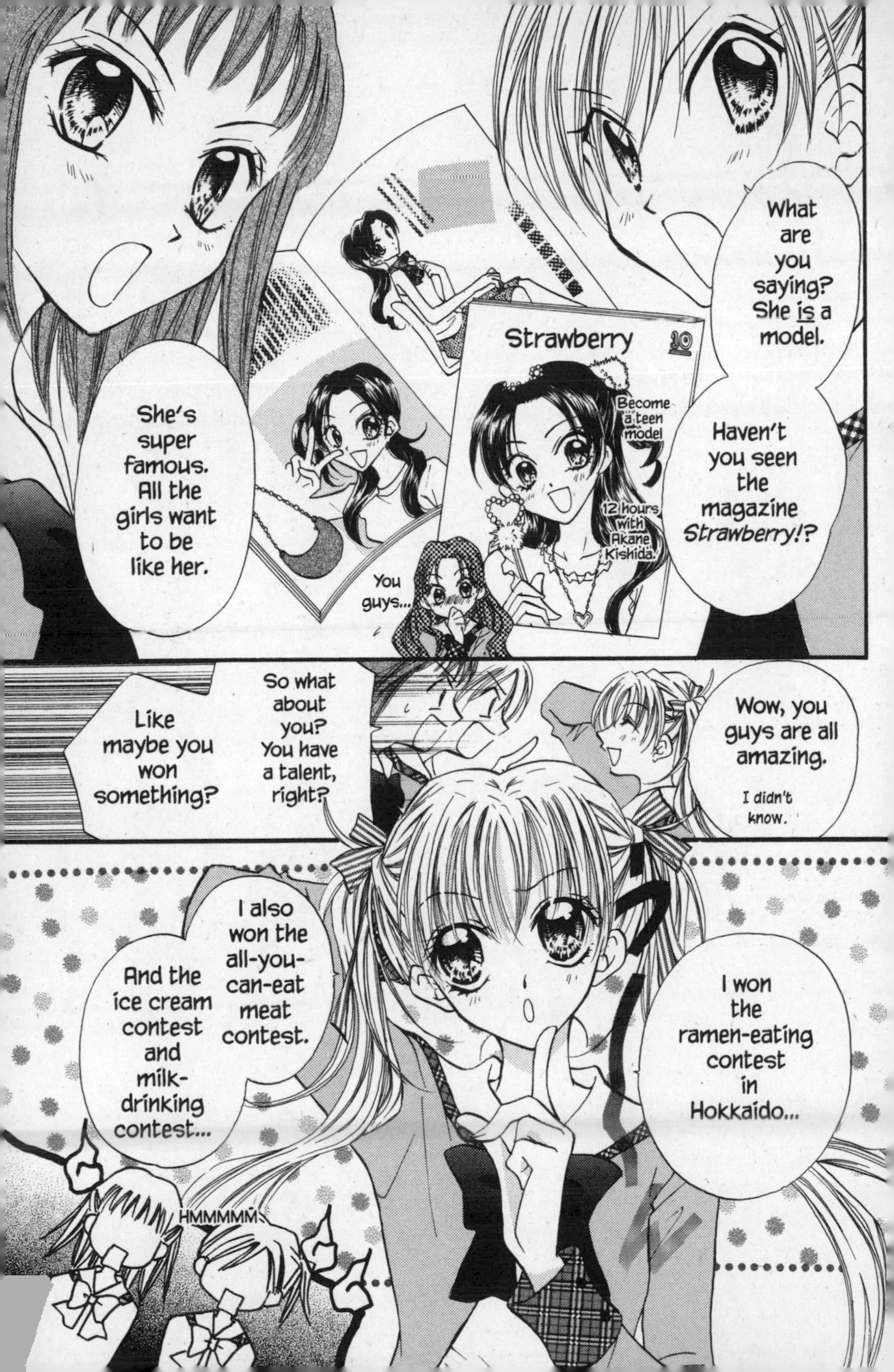
What are you saying? She is a model.
Haven't you seen the magazine Strawberry!?
Strawberry
10
Become a teen model
12 hours with Akane Kishida.
She's super famous. All the girls want to be like her.
You guys...
Wow, you guys are all amazing.
I didn't know.
So what about you? You have a talent, right?
Like maybe you won something?
I won the ramen-eating contest in Hokkaido...
I also won the all-you-can-eat meat contest.
And the ice cream contest and milk-drinking contest...
HMMMMM

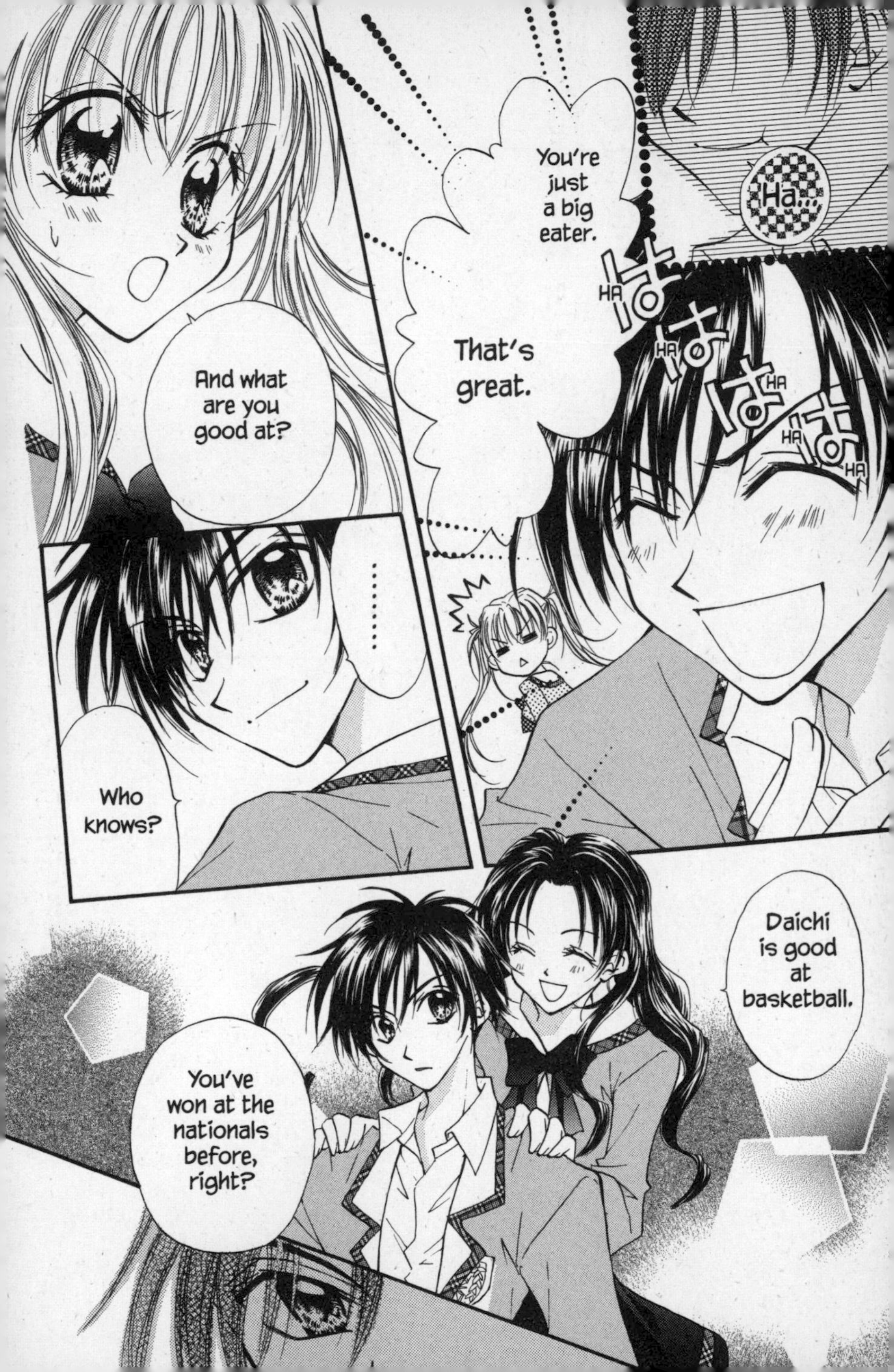
Ha...
HA HA HA HA HA
You're just a big eater.
That's great.
And what are you good at?
...
Who knows?
Daichi is good at basketball.
You've won at the nationals before, right?

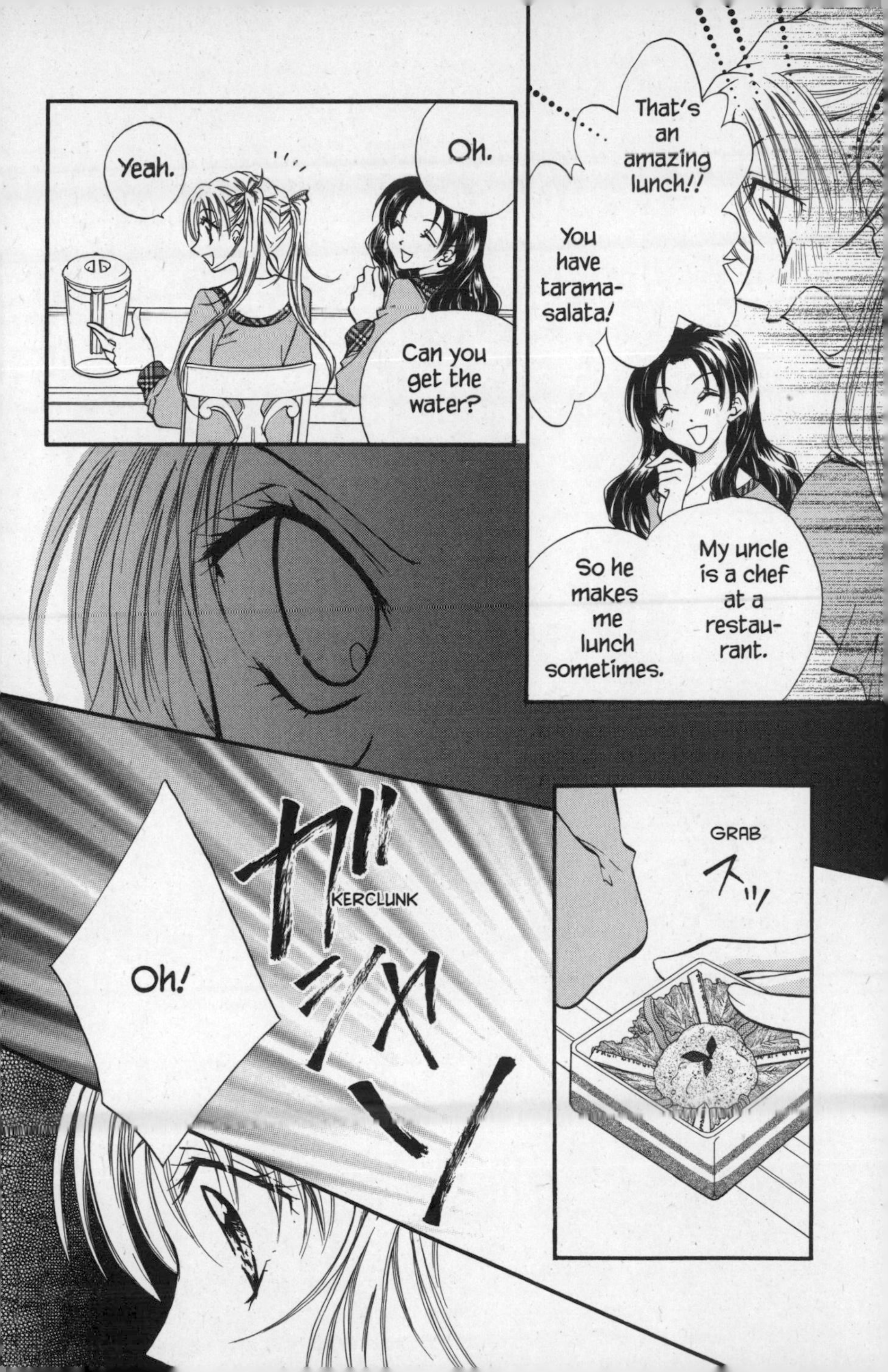
That's an amazing lunch!!
You have tarama-salata!
My uncle is a chef at a restau-rant.
So he makes me lunch sometimes.
Oh.
Can you get the water?
Yeah.
GRAB
KERCLUNK
Oh!

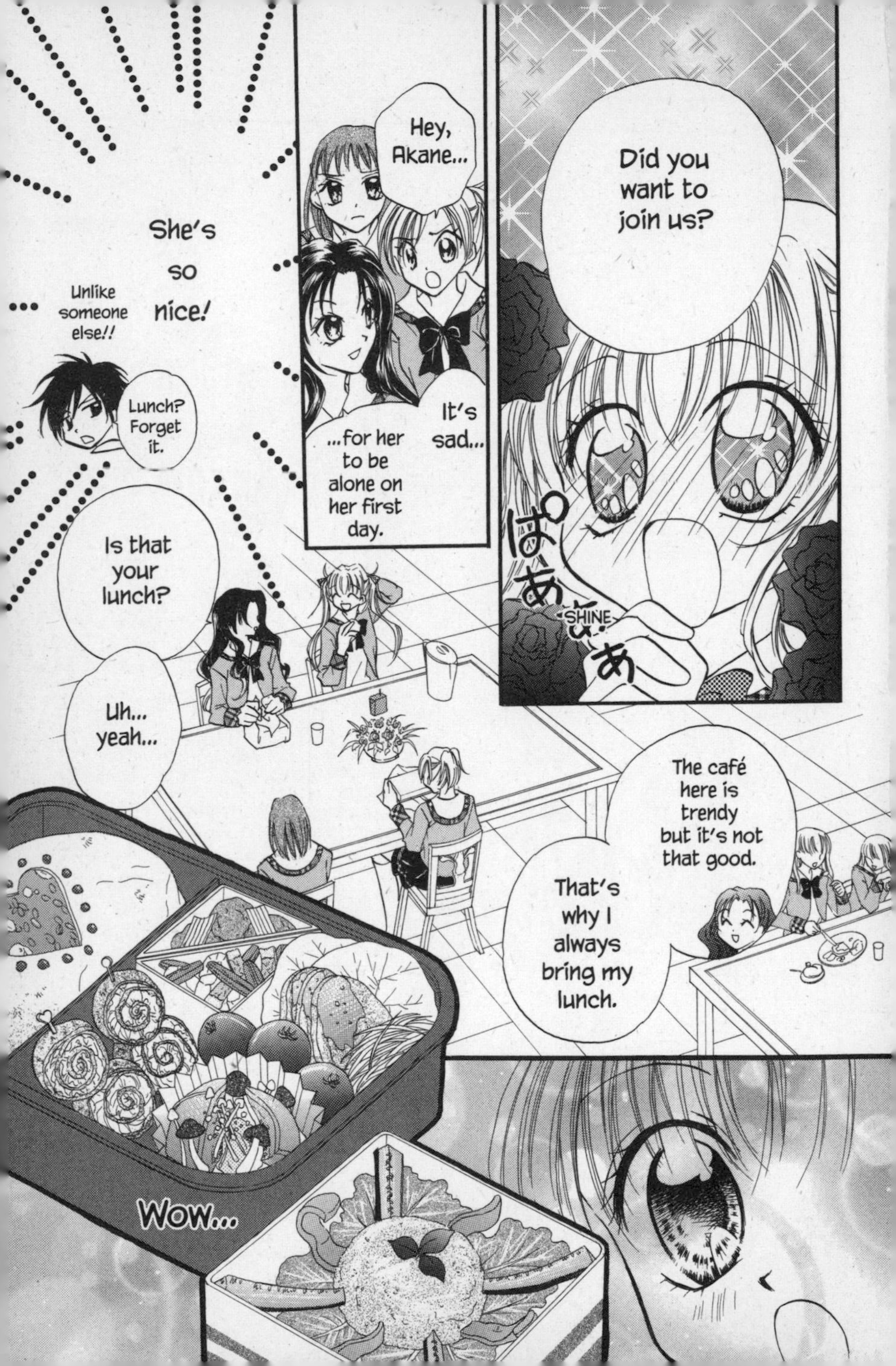
Did you want to join us?
ぱあぁあ
SHINE
Hey, Akane...
It's sad...
...for her to be alone on her first day.
She's so nice!
Unlike someone else!!
Lunch? Forget it.
The café here is trendy but it's not that good.
That's why I always bring my lunch.
Is that your lunch?
Uh... yeah...
Wow...

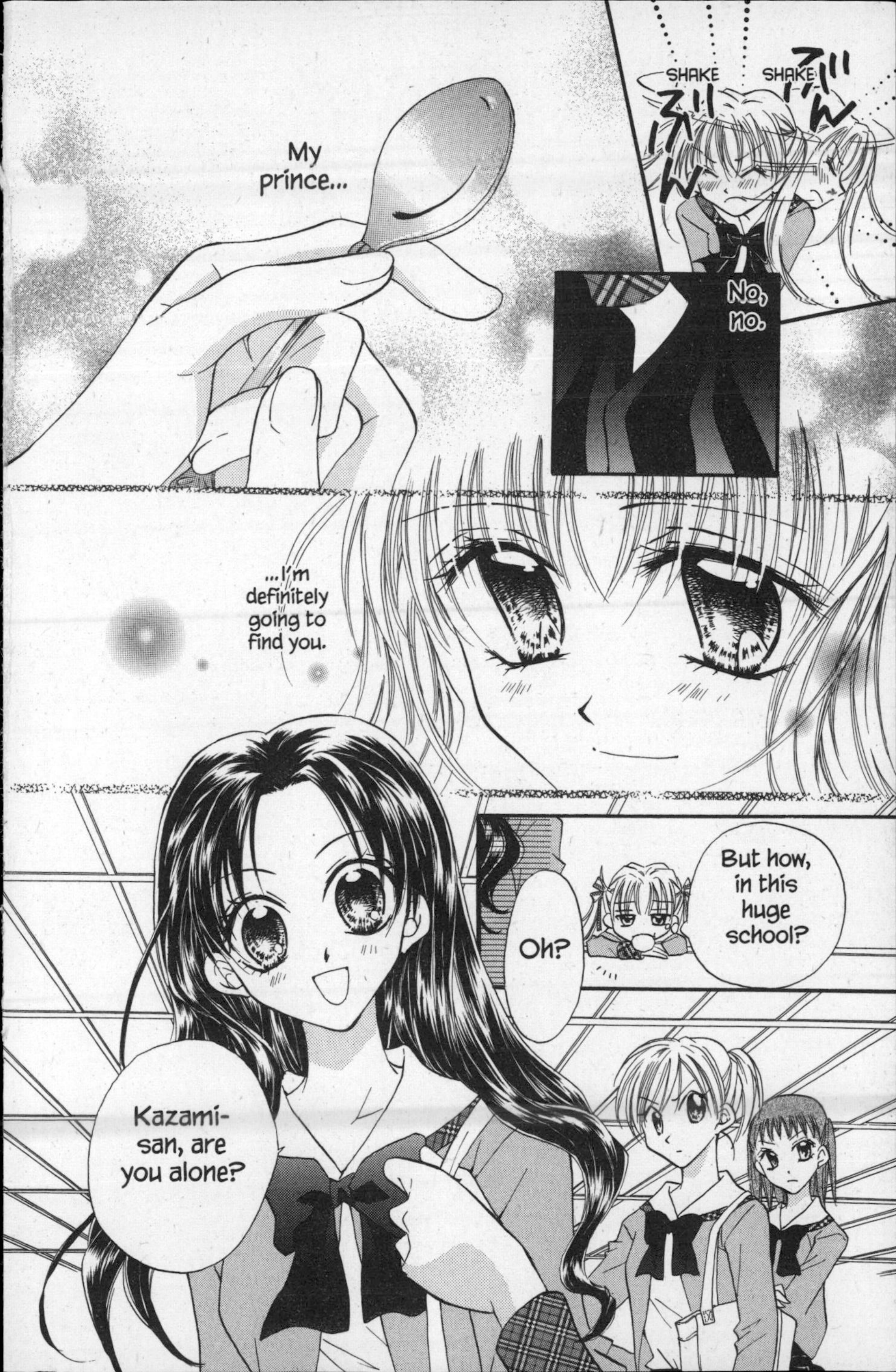
SHAKE
SHAKE
No, no.
My prince...
...I'm definitely going to find you.
But how, in this huge school?
Oh?
Kazami-san, are you alone?

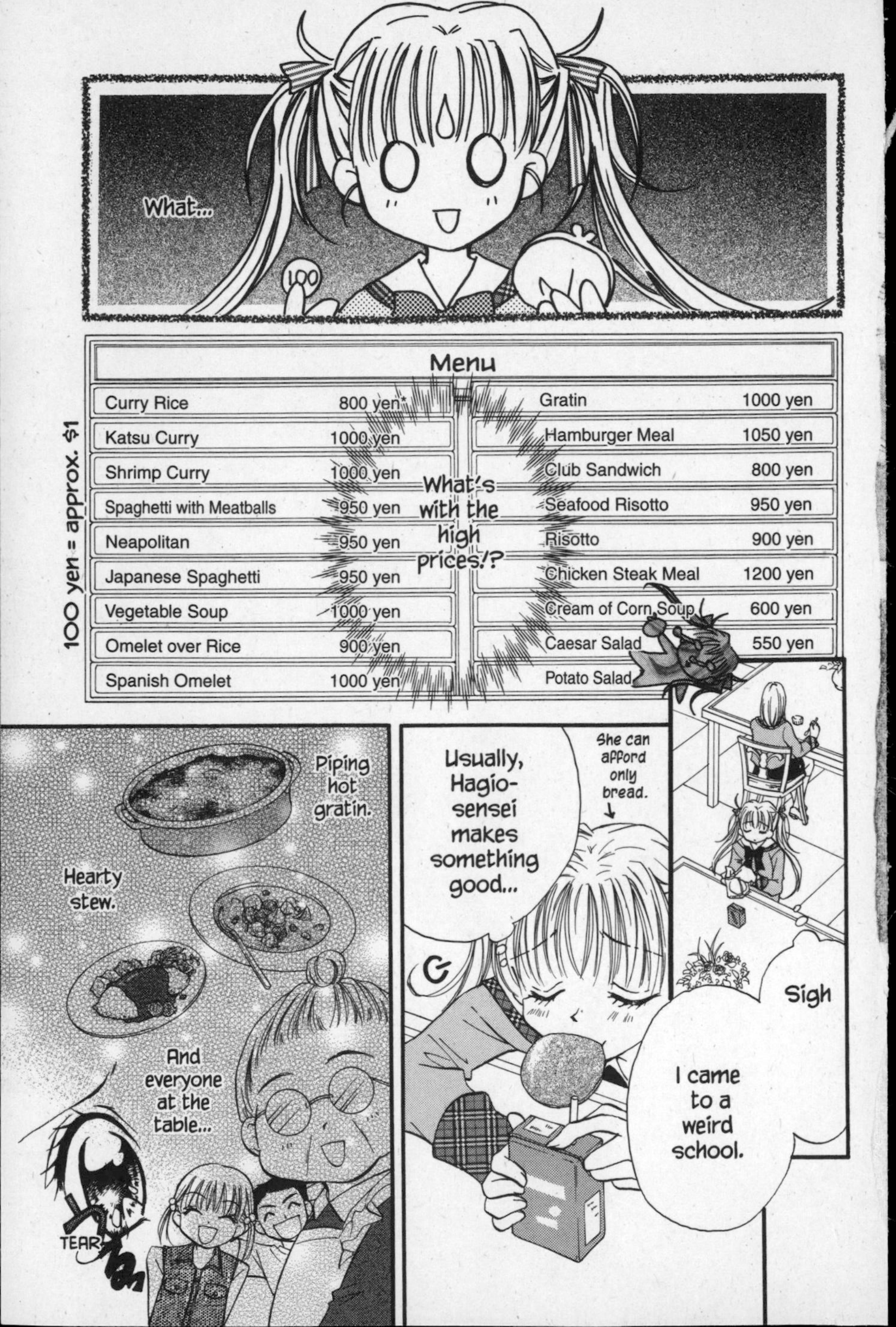
What...
100
Menu
Curry Rice 800 yen*
Katsu Curry 1000 yen
Shrimp Curry 1000 yen
Spaghetti with Meatballs 950 yen
Neapolitan 950 yen
Japanese Spaghetti 950 yen
Vegetable Soup 1000 yen
Omelet over Rice 900 yen
Spanish Omelet 1000 yen
Gratin 1000 yen
Hamburger Meal 1050 yen
Club Sandwich 800 yen
Seafood Risotto 950 yen
Risotto 900 yen
Chicken Steak Meal 1200 yen
Cream of Corn Soup 600 yen
Caesar Salad 550 yen
Potato Salad
What's with the high prices!?
*100 yen = approx. $1
Usually, Hagio-sensei makes something good...
She can afford only bread.
Sigh
I came to a weird school.
Piping hot gratin.
Hearty stew.
And everyone at the table...
TEAR

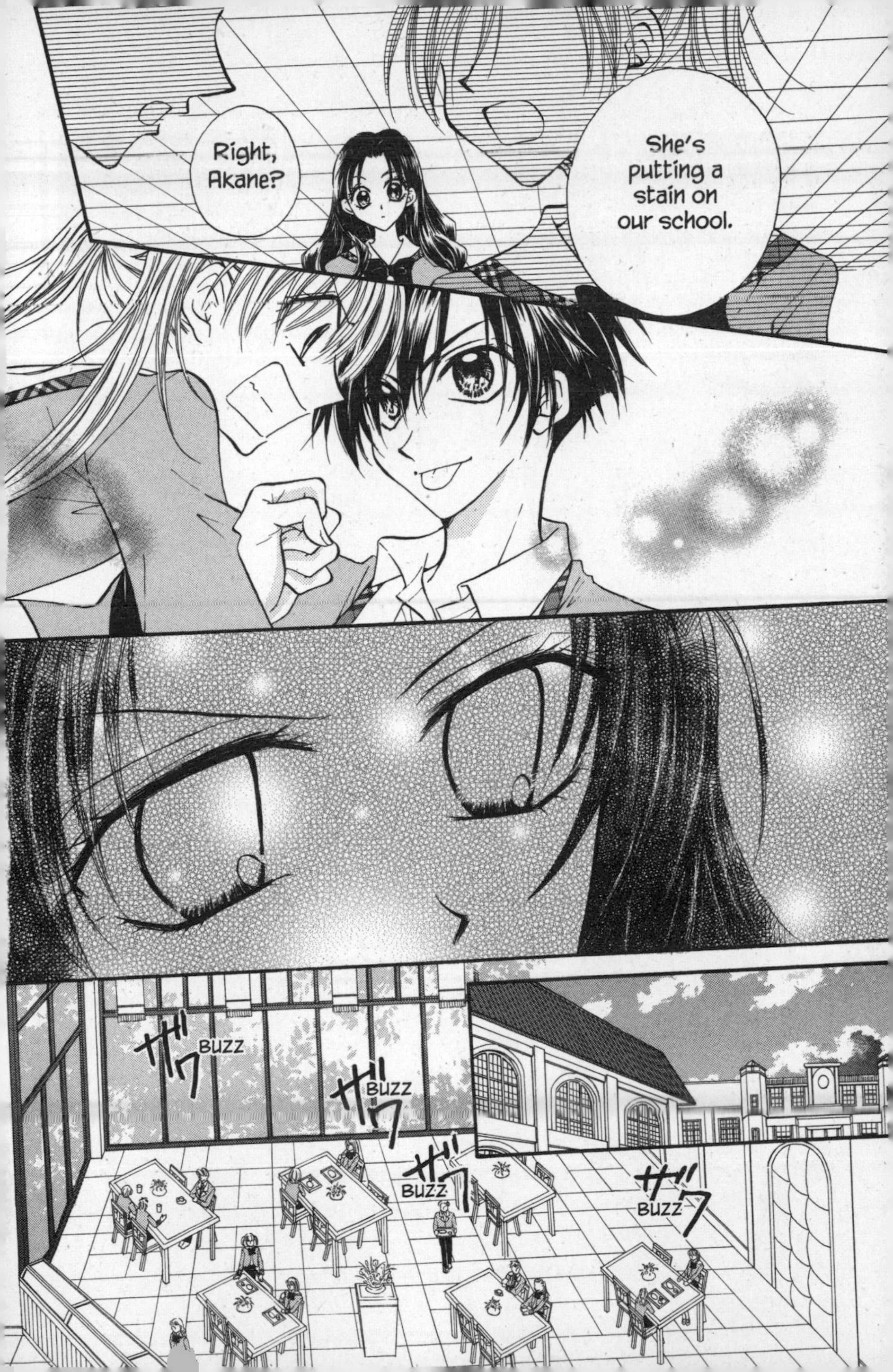
She's putting a stain on our school.
Right, Akane?
ザワ BUZZ
ザワ BUZZ
ザワ BUZZ
ザワ BUZZ

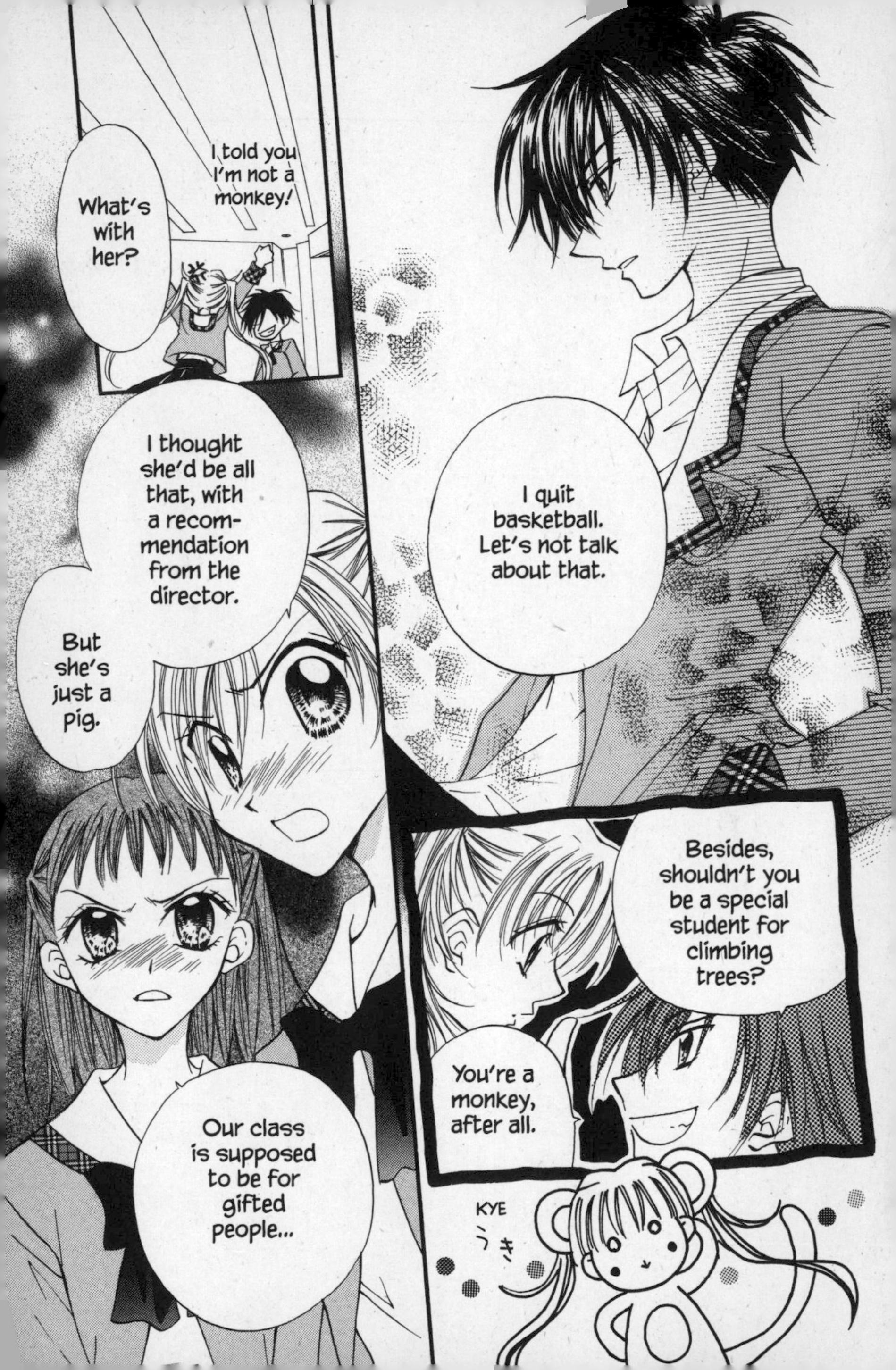
I quit basketball. Let's not talk about that.
Besides, shouldn't you be a special student for climbing trees?
You're a monkey, after all.
KYE
うき
I told you I'm not a monkey!
What's with her?
I thought she'd be all that, with a recommendation from the director.
But she's just a pig.
Our class is supposed to be for gifted people...

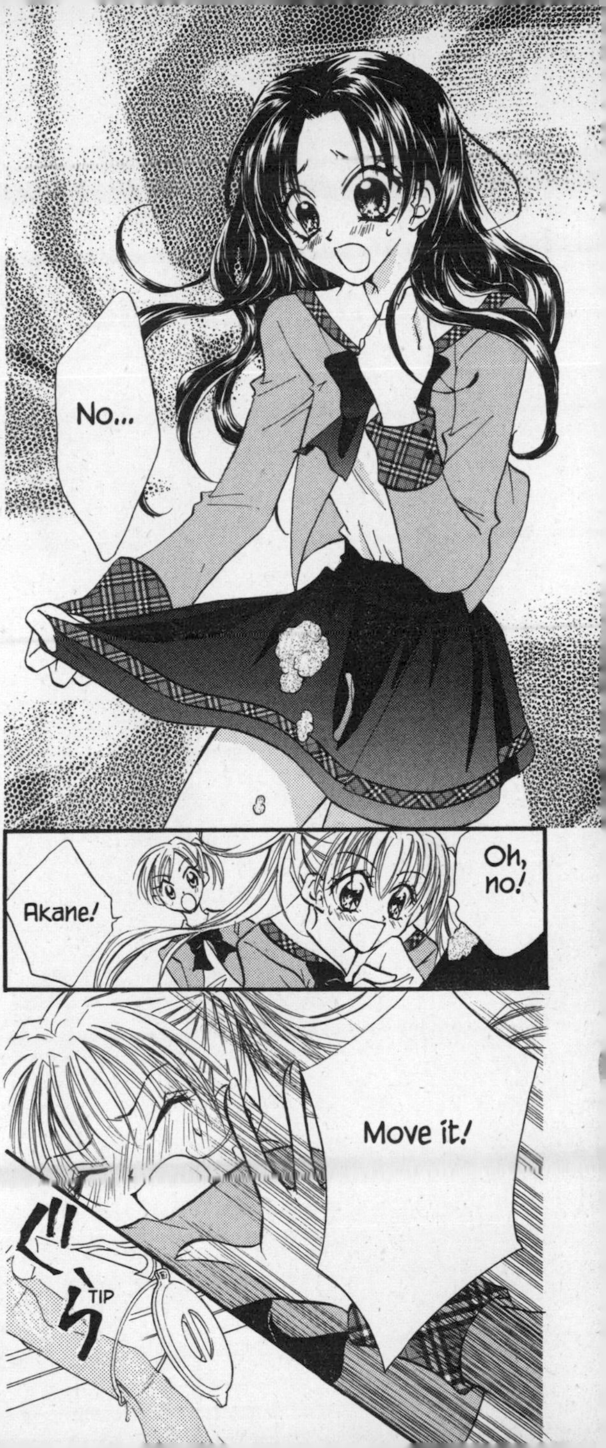
No...
Oh, no!
Akane!
Move it!
TIP

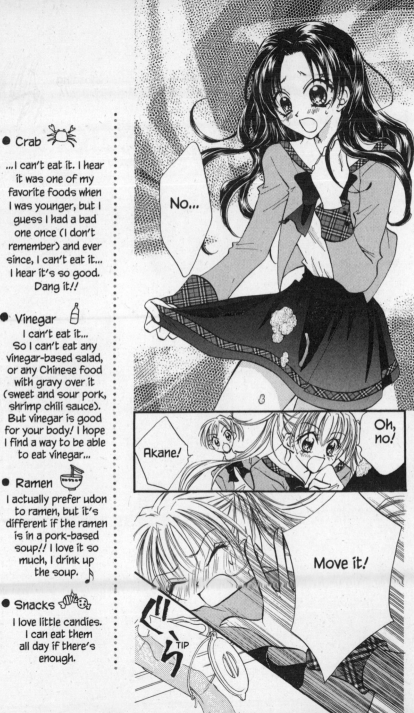

● Crab

...I can't eat it. I hear it was one of my favorite foods when I was younger, but I guess I had a bad one once (I don't remember) and ever since, I can't eat it... I hear it's so good. Dang it!!

● Vinegar

I can't eat it... So I can't eat any vinegar-based salad, or any Chinese food with gravy over it (sweet and sour pork, shrimp chili sauce). But vinegar is good for your body! I hope I find a way to be able to eat vinegar...

● Ramen

I actually prefer udon to ramen, but it's different if the ramen is in a pork-based soup!! I love it so much, I drink up the soup. ♪

● Snacks

I love little candies. I can eat them all day if there's enough.

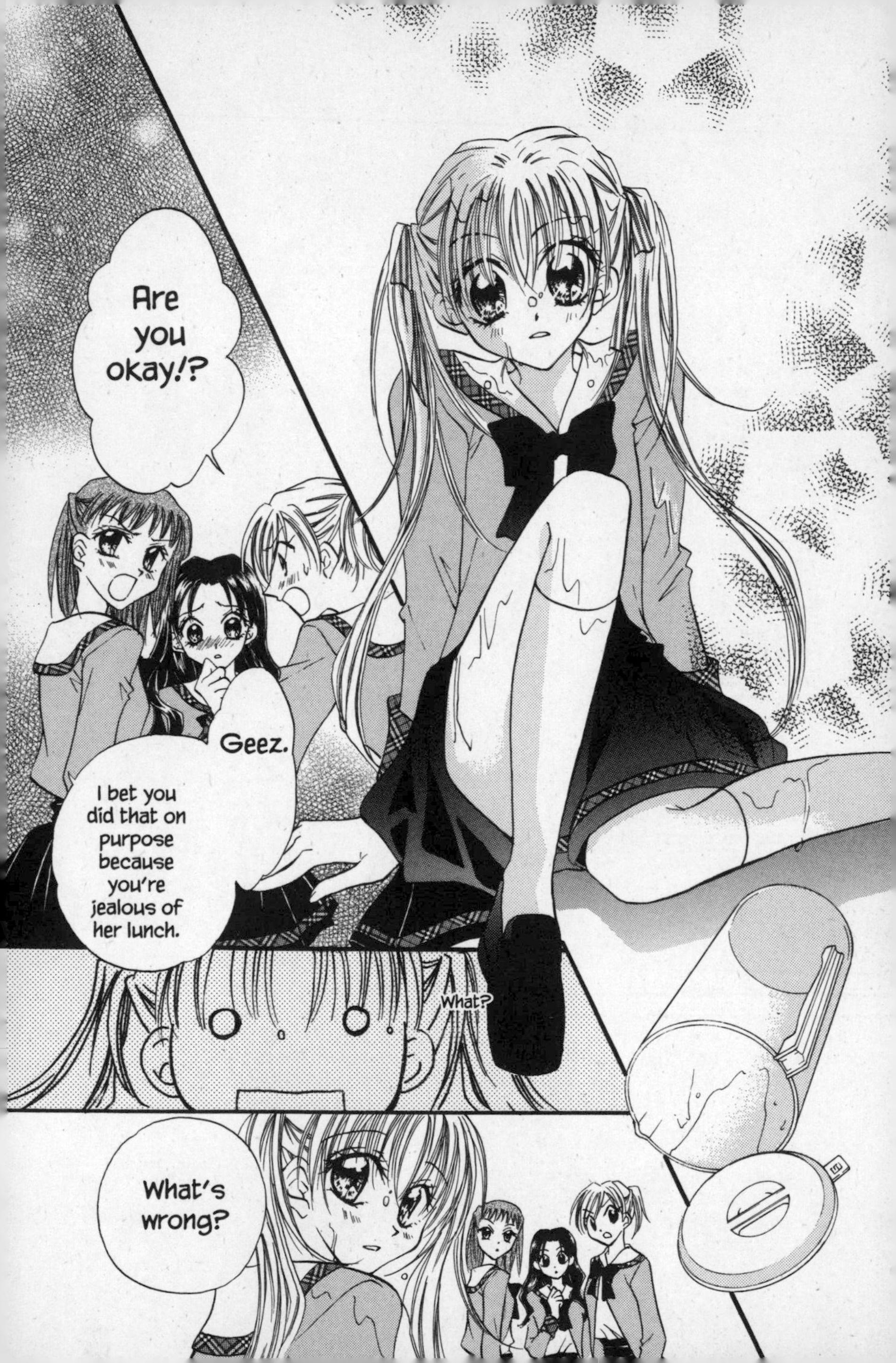
Are you okay!?
Geez.
I bet you did that on purpose because you're jealous of her lunch.
What?
What's wrong?

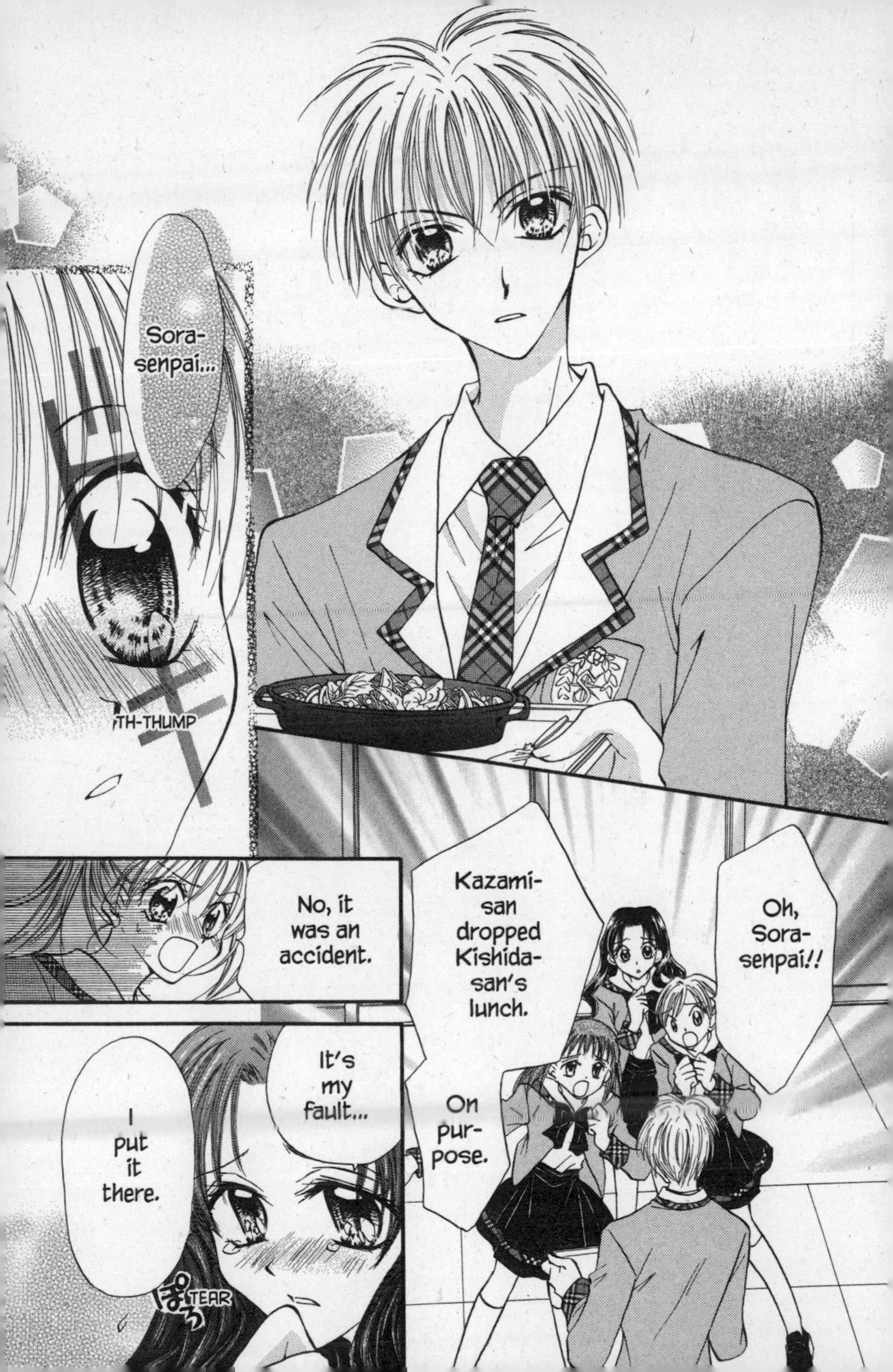
Sora-senpai...
TH-THUMP
Oh, Sora-senpai!!
Kazami-san dropped Kishida-san's lunch.
On purpose.
No, it was an accident.
It's my fault...
I put it there.
ぽろ TEAR

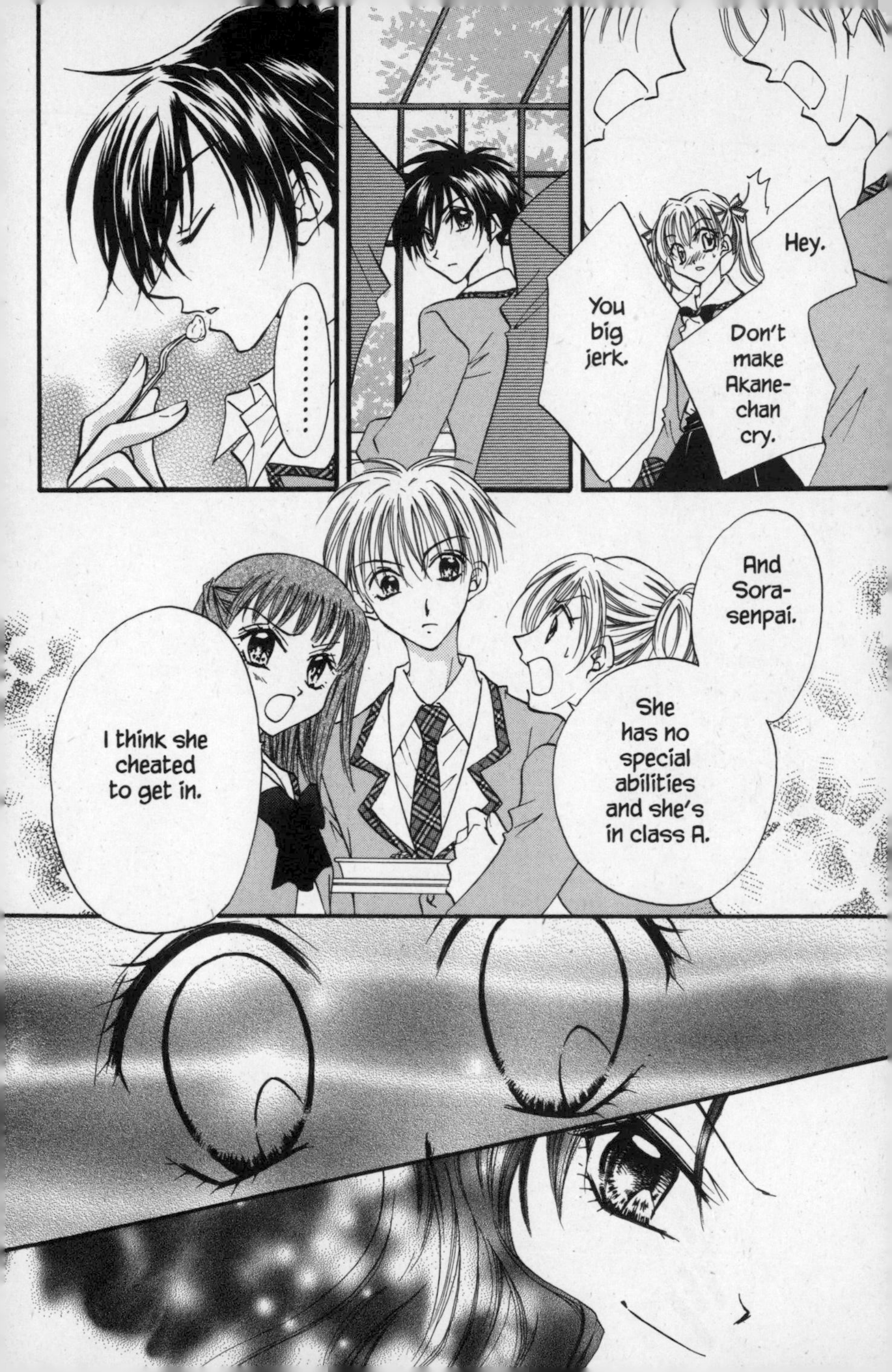
Hey.
Don't make Akane-chan cry.
You big jerk.
......
And Sora-senpai.
She has no special abilities and she's in class A.
I think she cheated to get in.

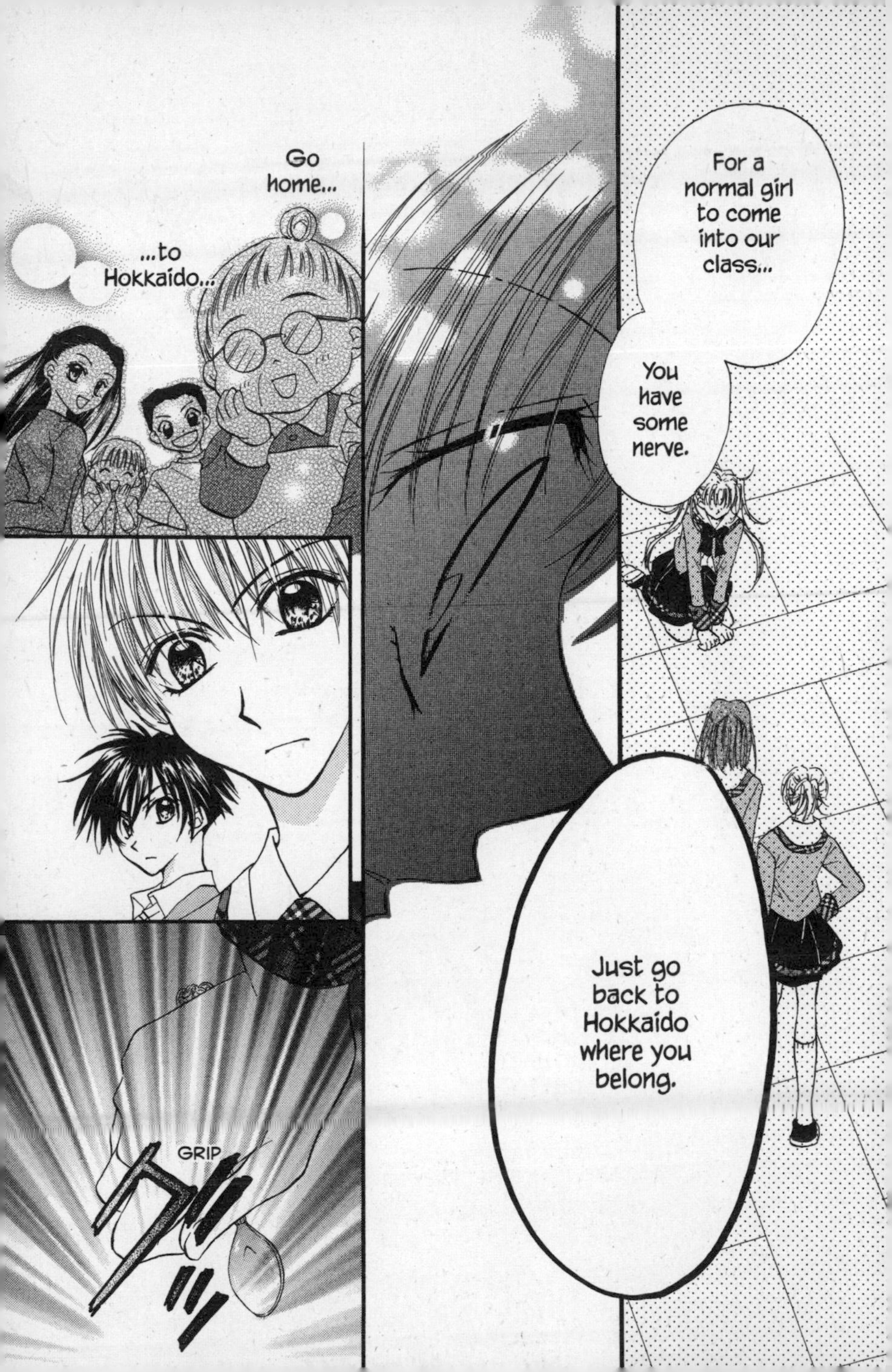

For a normal girl to come into our class...
You have some nerve.
Just go back to Hokkaido where you belong.
Go home...
...to Hokkaido...
GRIP

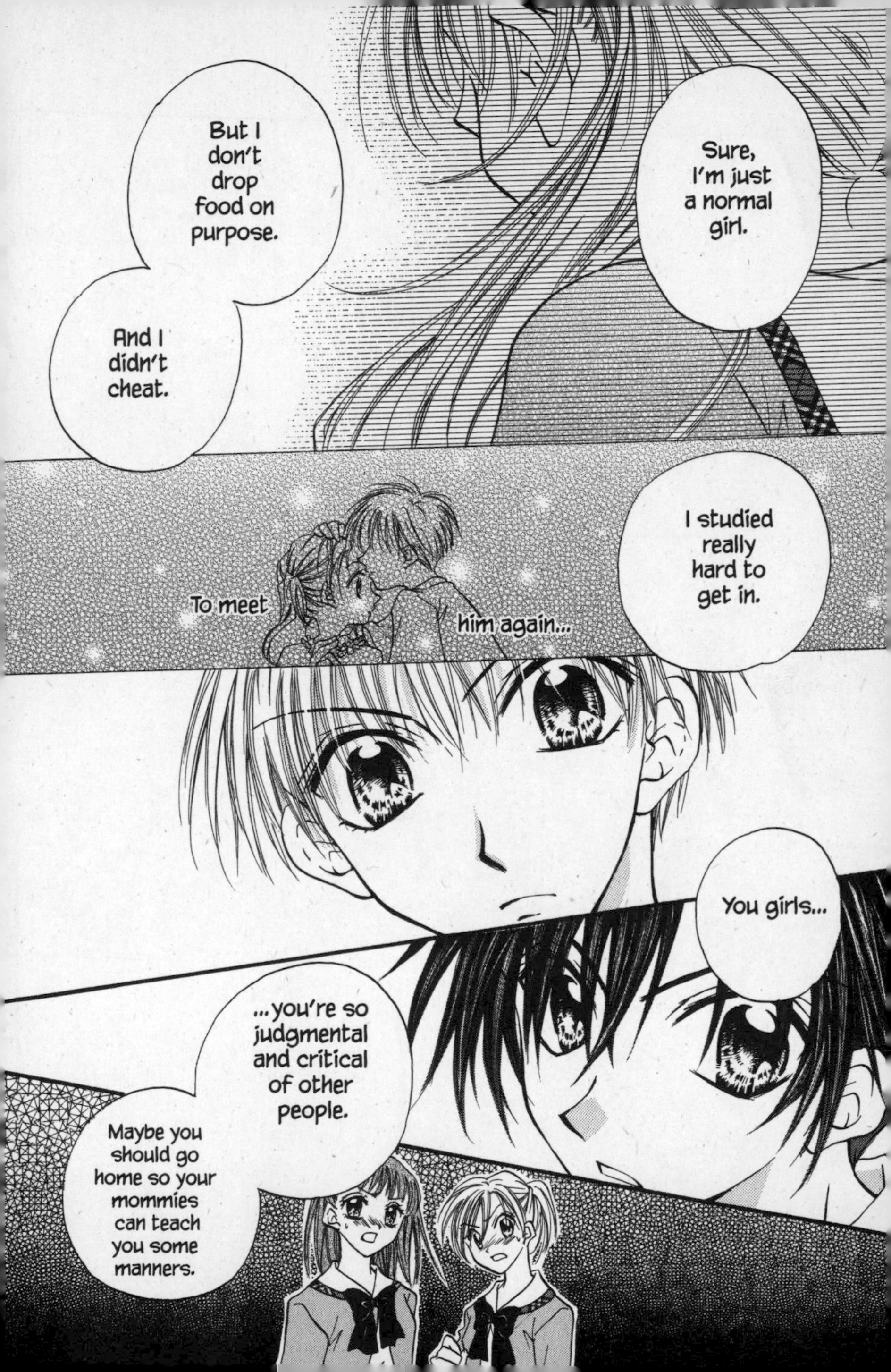

Sure, I'm just a normal girl.
But I don't drop food on purpose.
And I didn't cheat.
I studied really hard to get in.
To meet him again...
You girls...
...you're so judgmental and critical of other people.
Maybe you should go home so your mommies can teach you some manners.

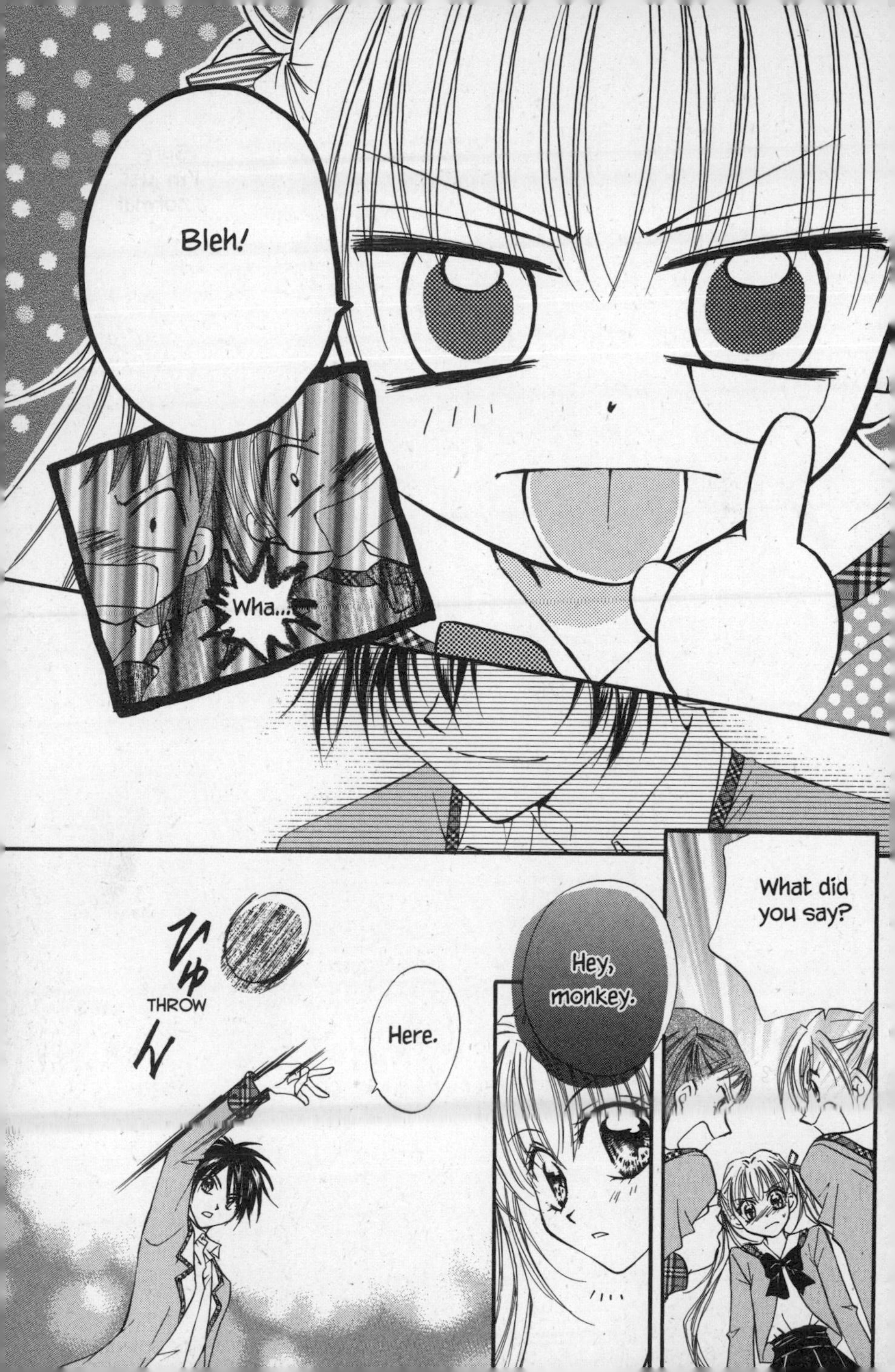
Bleh!
Wha...
What did you say?
Hey, monkey.
Here.
ひゅん
THROW

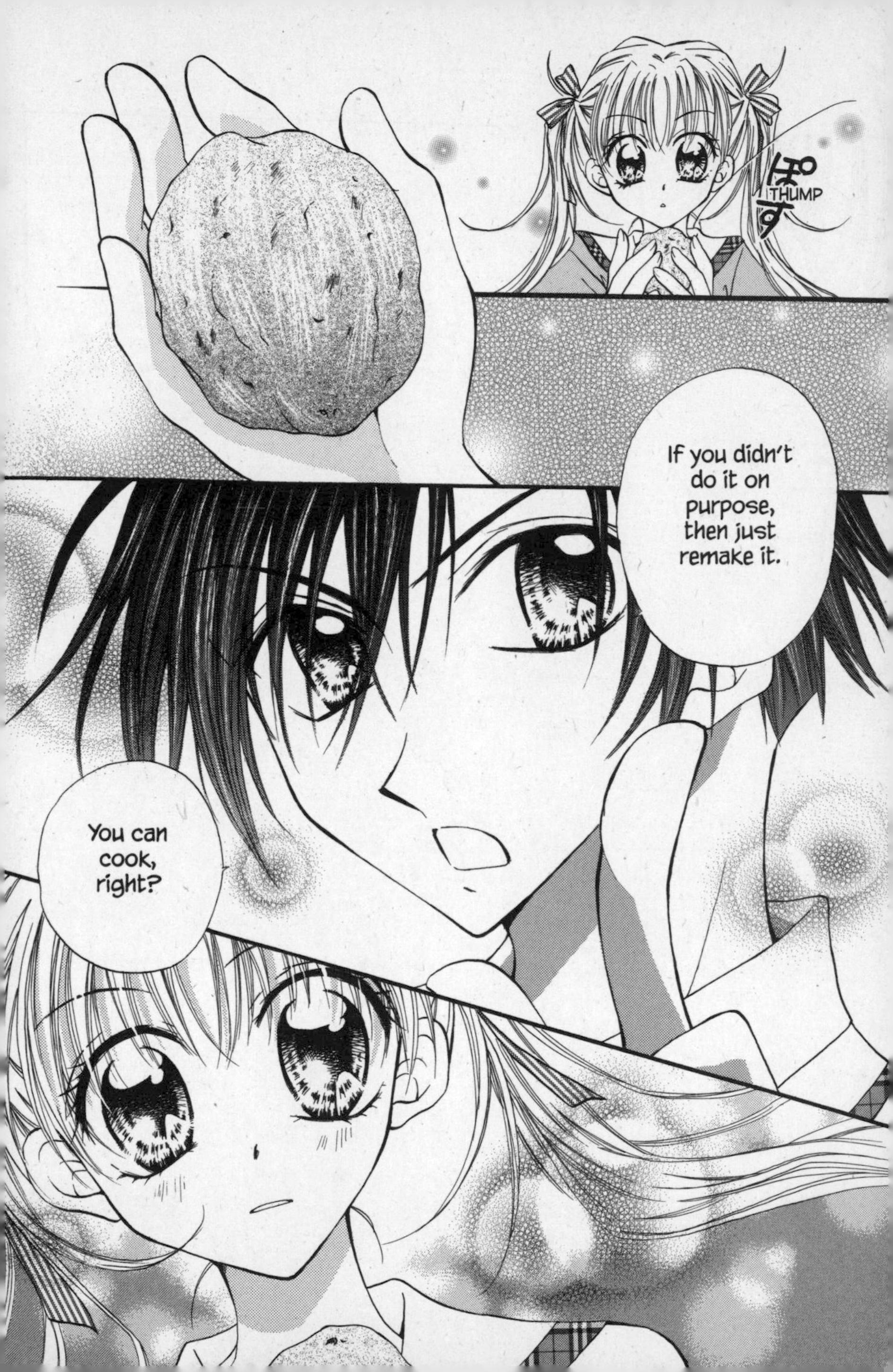
ぽす
THUMP
If you didn't do it on purpose, then just remake it.
You can cook, right?

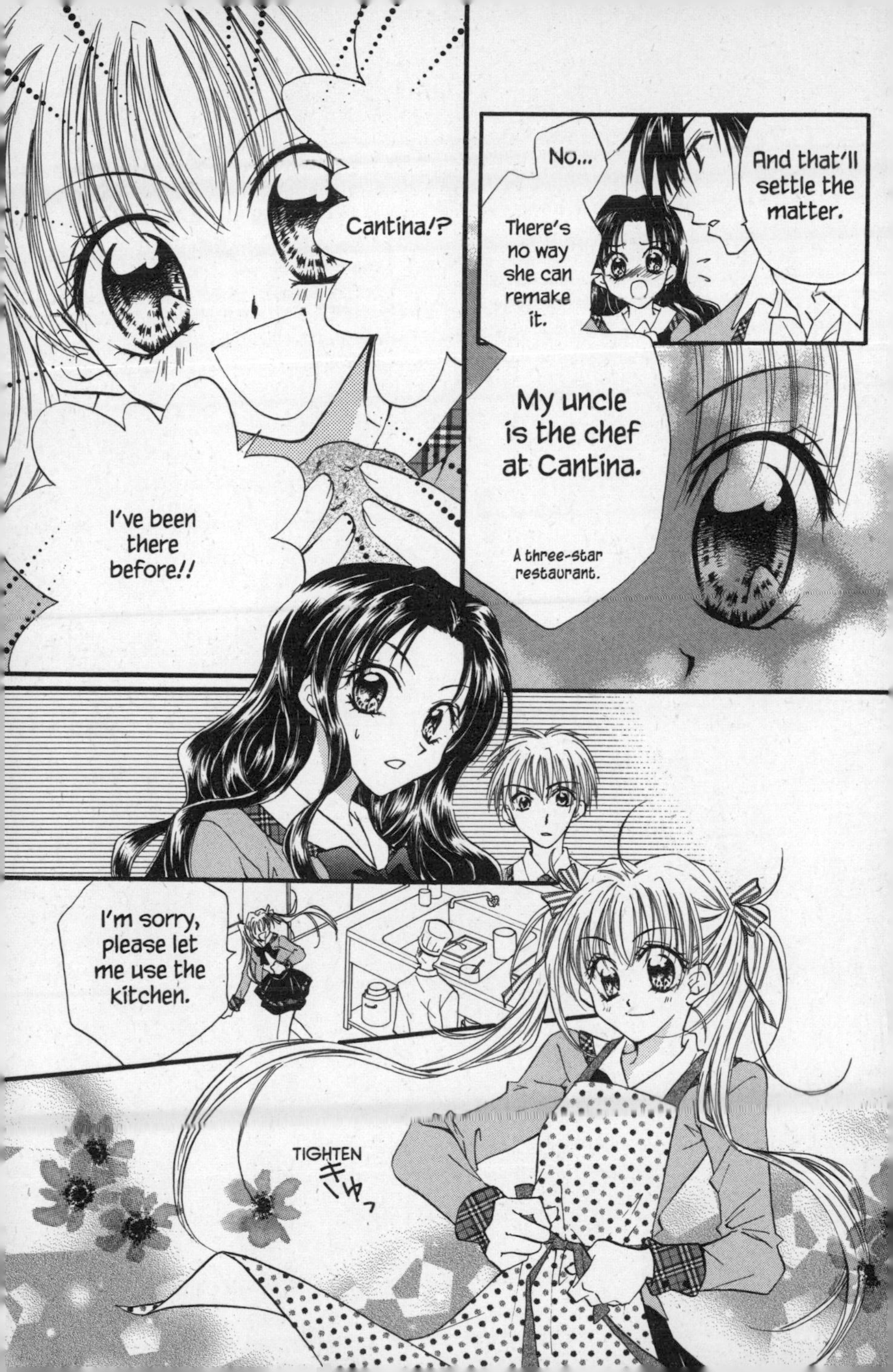

And that'll settle the matter.
No...
There's no way she can remake it.
My uncle is the chef at Cantina.
A three-star restaurant.
Cantina!?
I've been there before!!
I'm sorry, please let me use the kitchen.
TIGHTEN

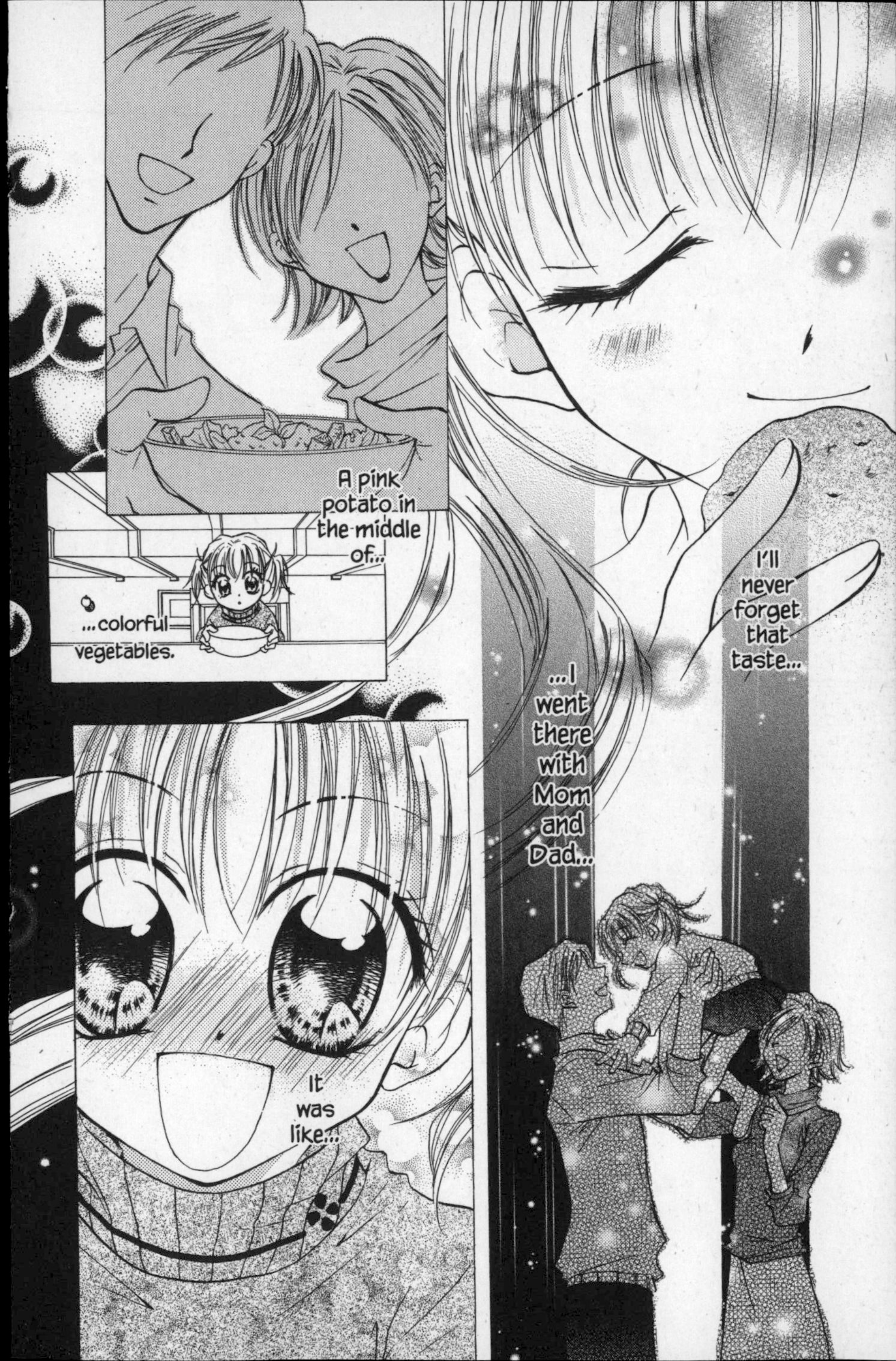
I'll never forget that taste...
...I went there with Mom and Dad...
A pink potato in the middle of...
...colorful vegetables.
It was like...

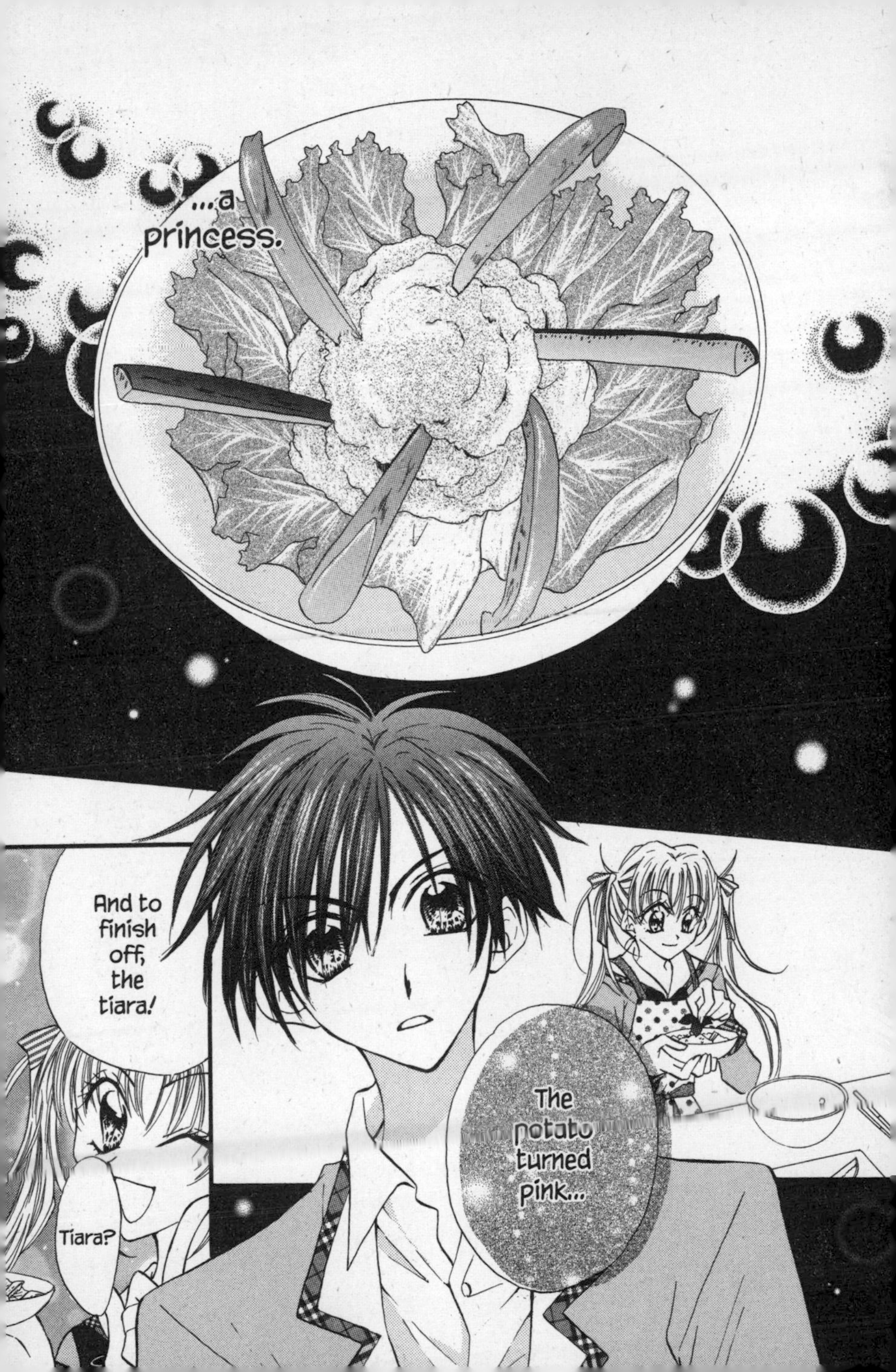
...a princess.
The potato turned pink...
And to finish off, the tiara!
Tiara?

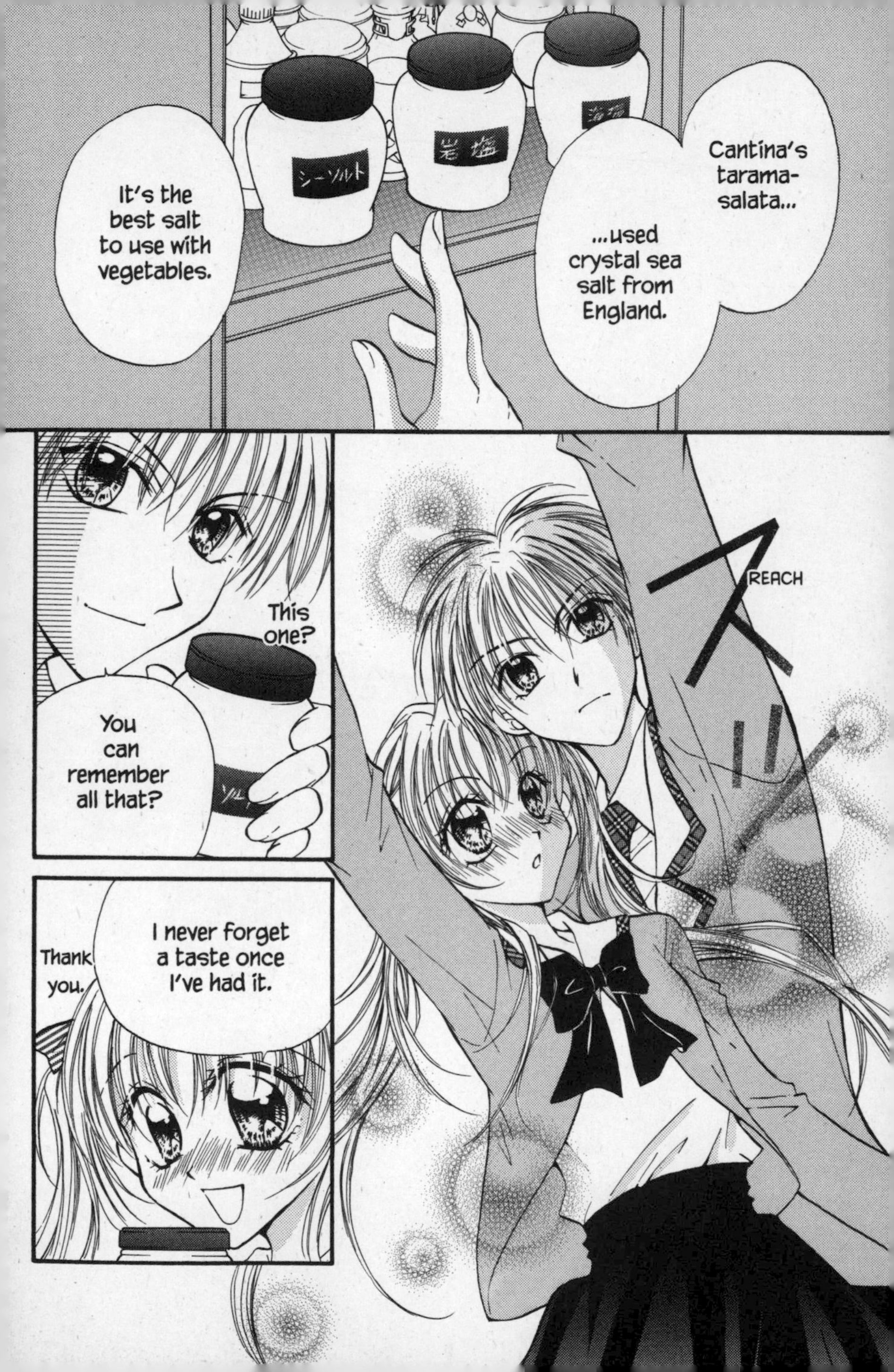

海塩
岩塩
シーソルト
Cantina's tarama-salata...
...used crystal sea salt from England.
It's the best salt to use with vegetables.
REACH
This one?
You can remember all that?
I never forget a taste once I've had it.
Thank you.

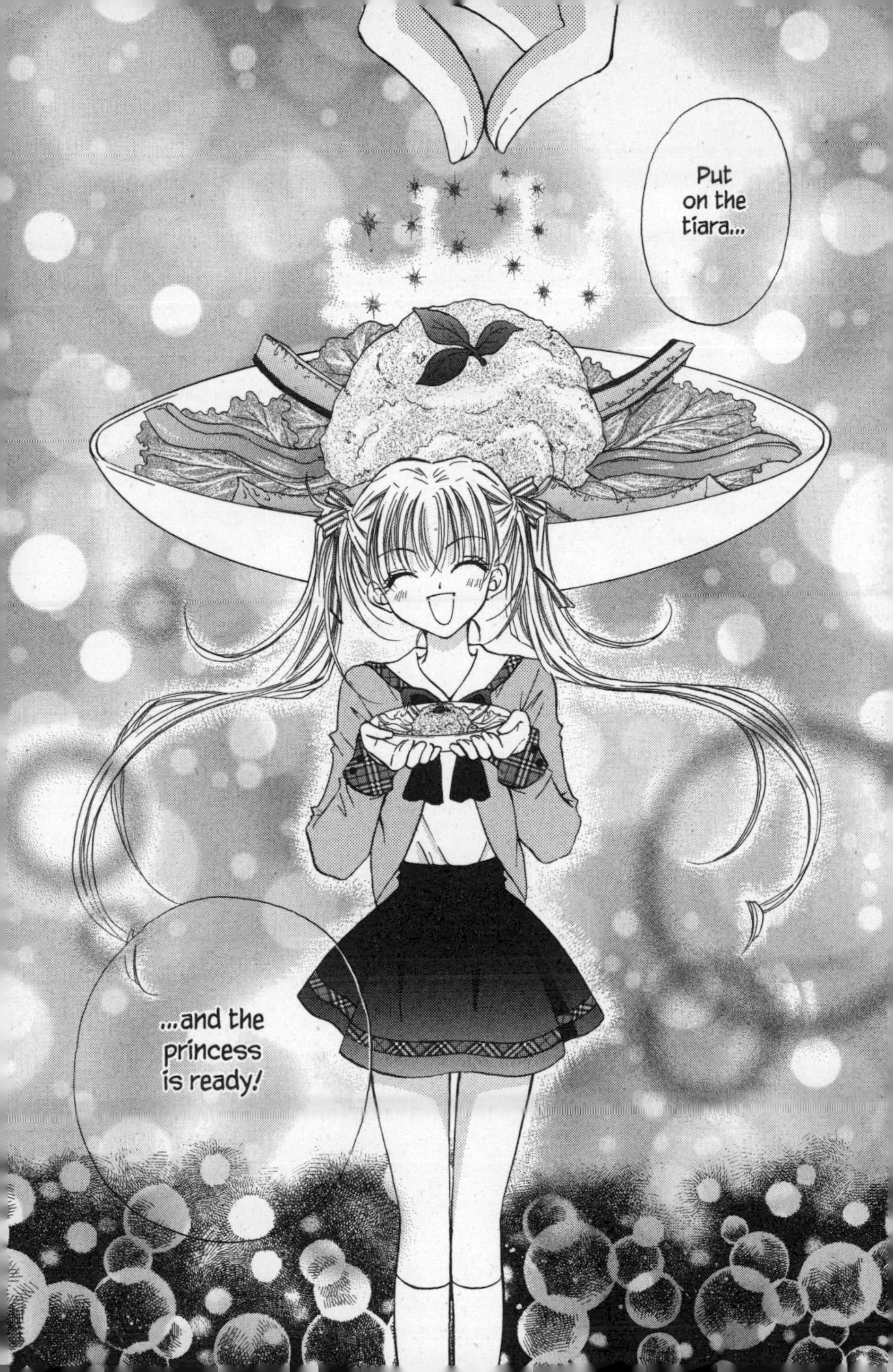
Put on the tiara...
...and the princess is ready!

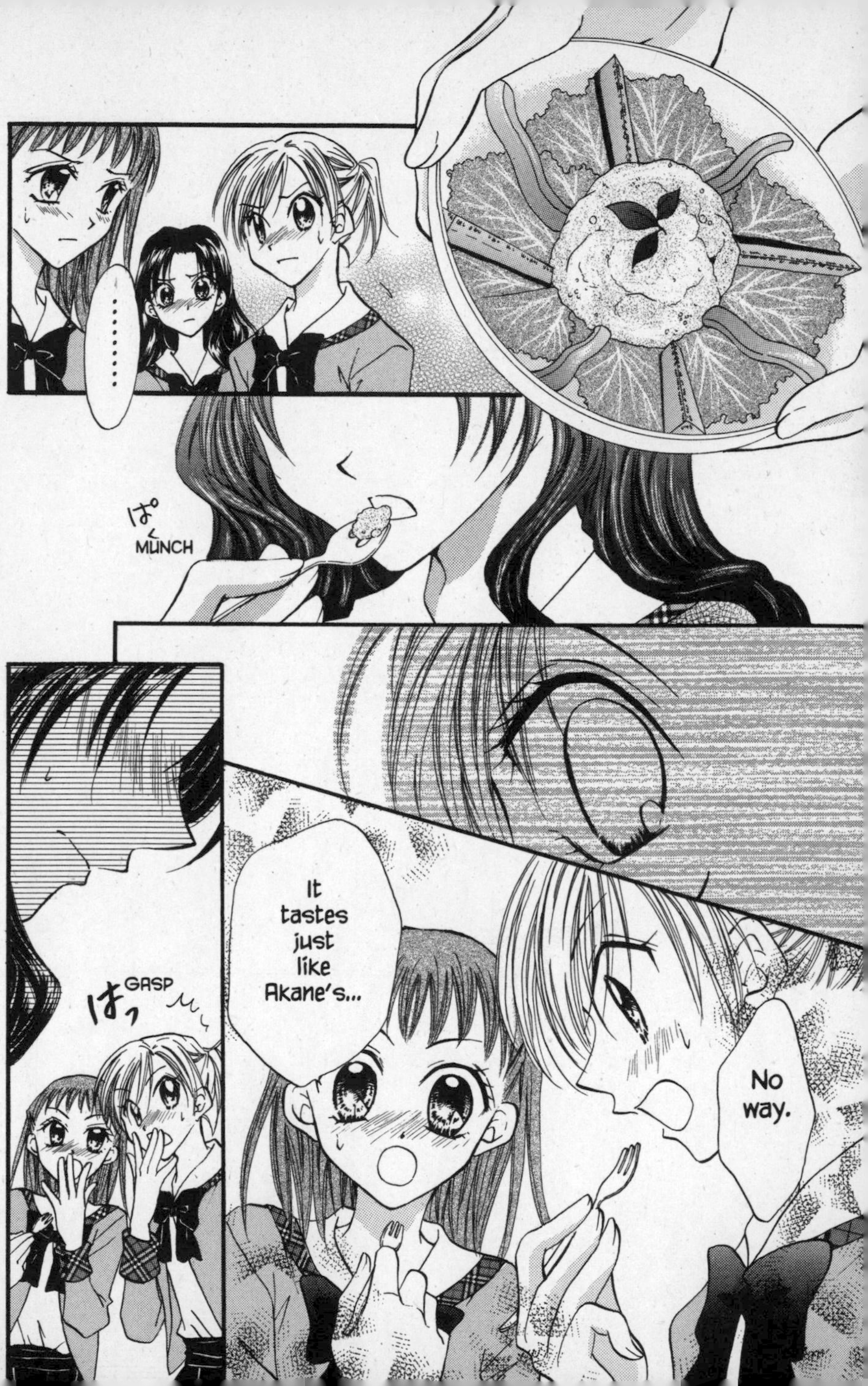
......
ぱく
MUNCH
It tastes just like Akane's...
No way.
はっ
GASP

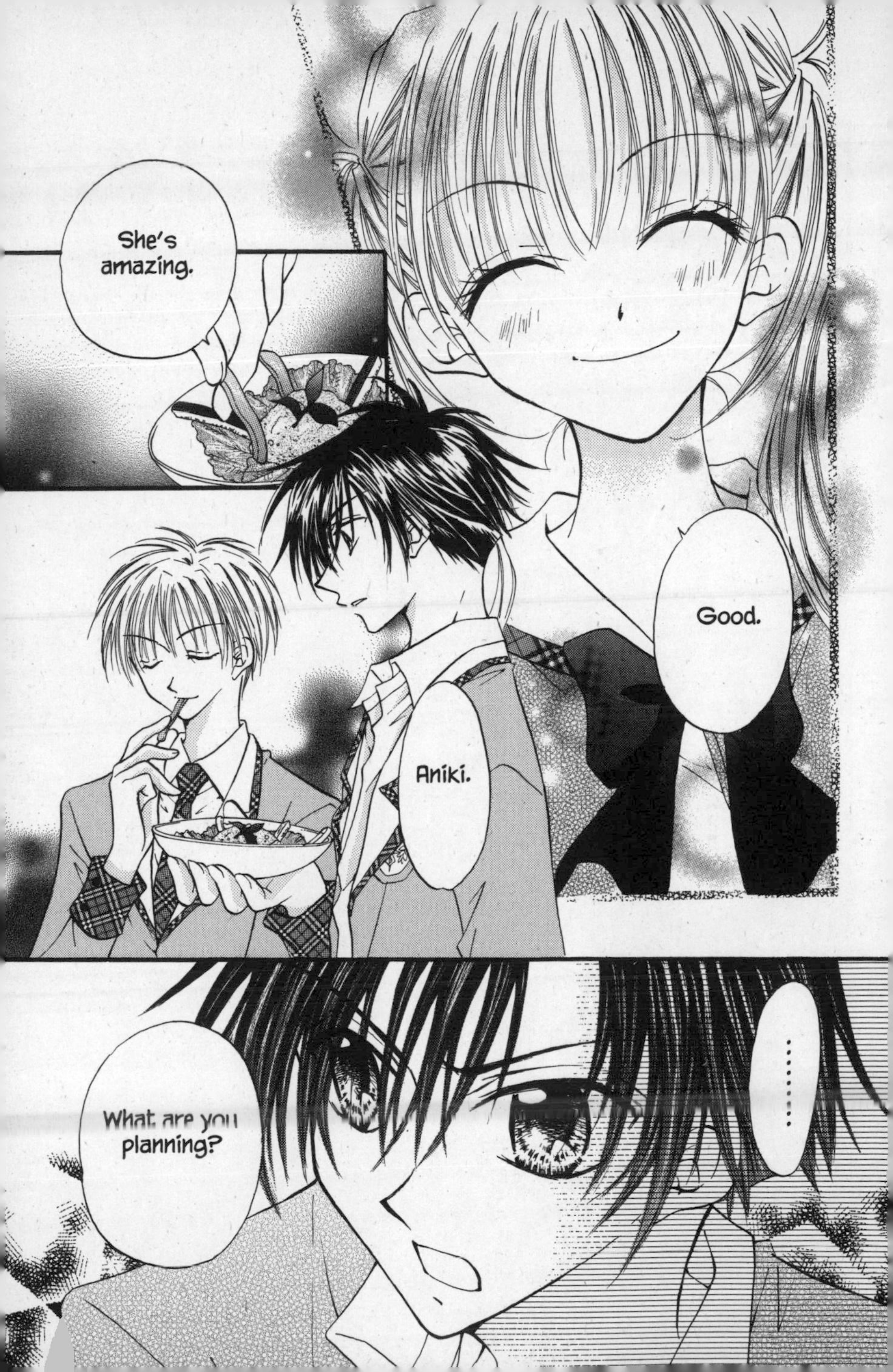
She's amazing.
Good.
Aniki.
……
What are you planning?

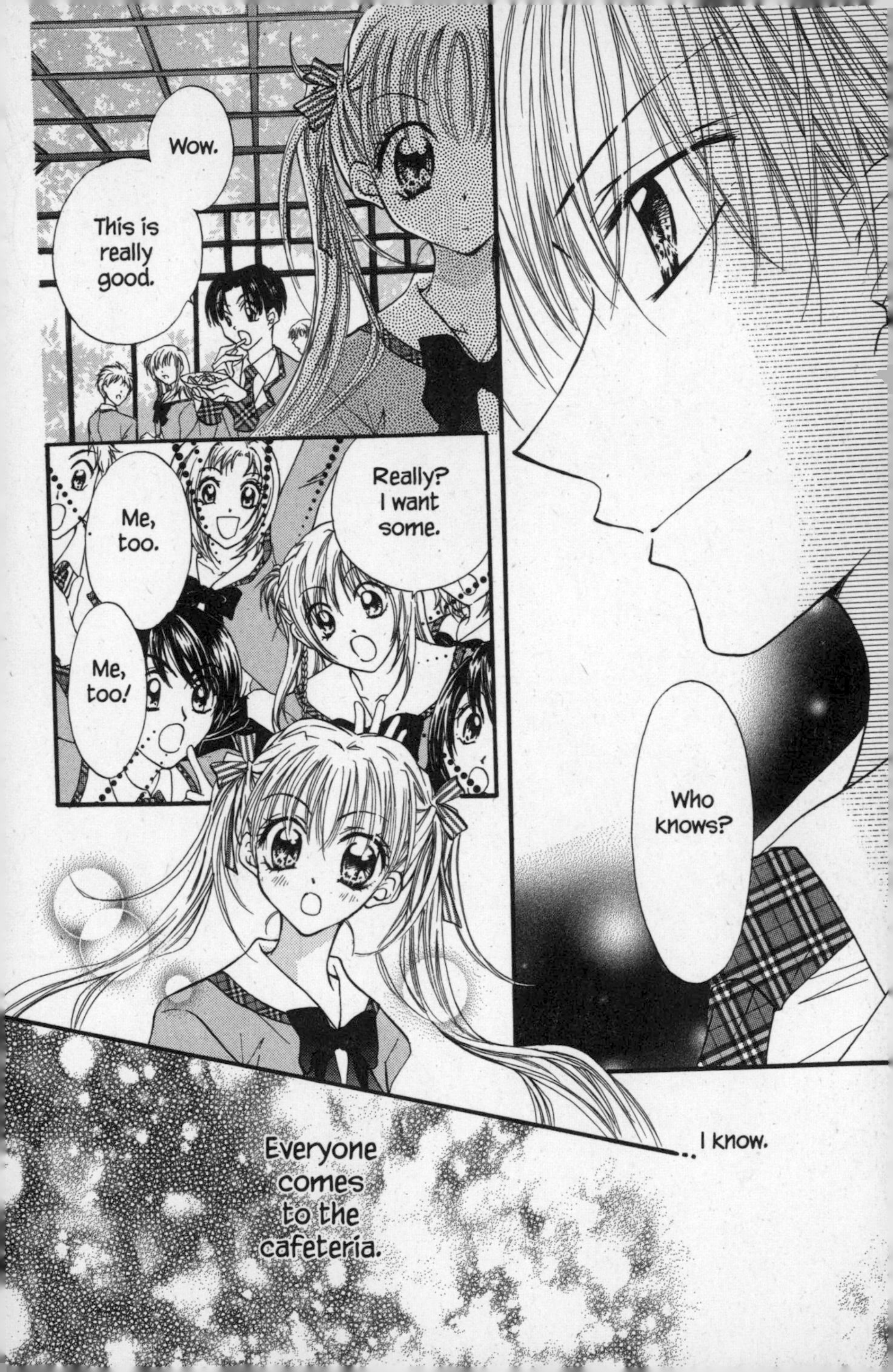
Who knows?
Wow.
This is really good.
Really? I want some.
Me, too.
Me, too!
...I know.
Everyone comes to the cafeteria.

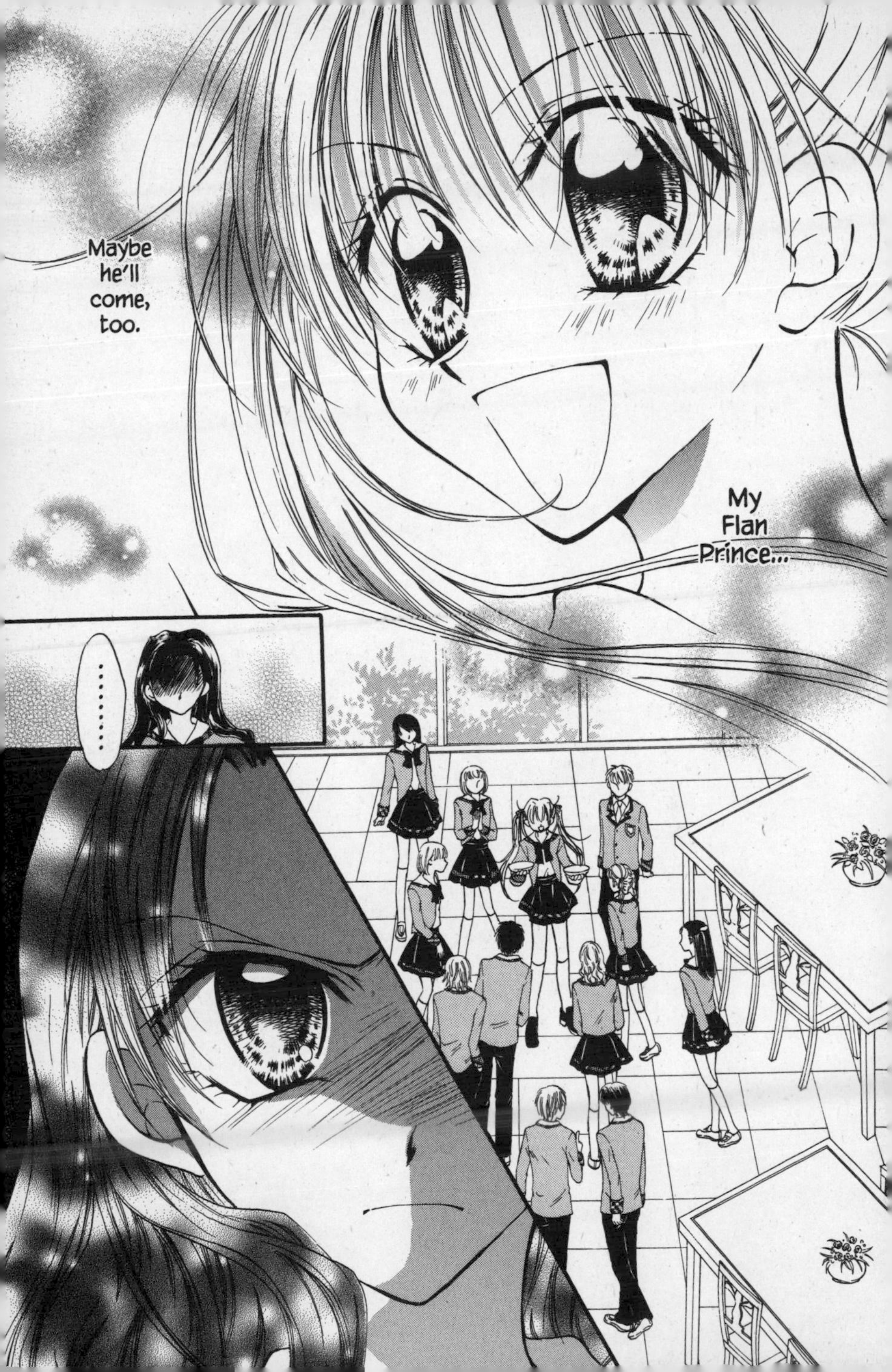
Maybe he'll come, too.
My Flan Prince...
......

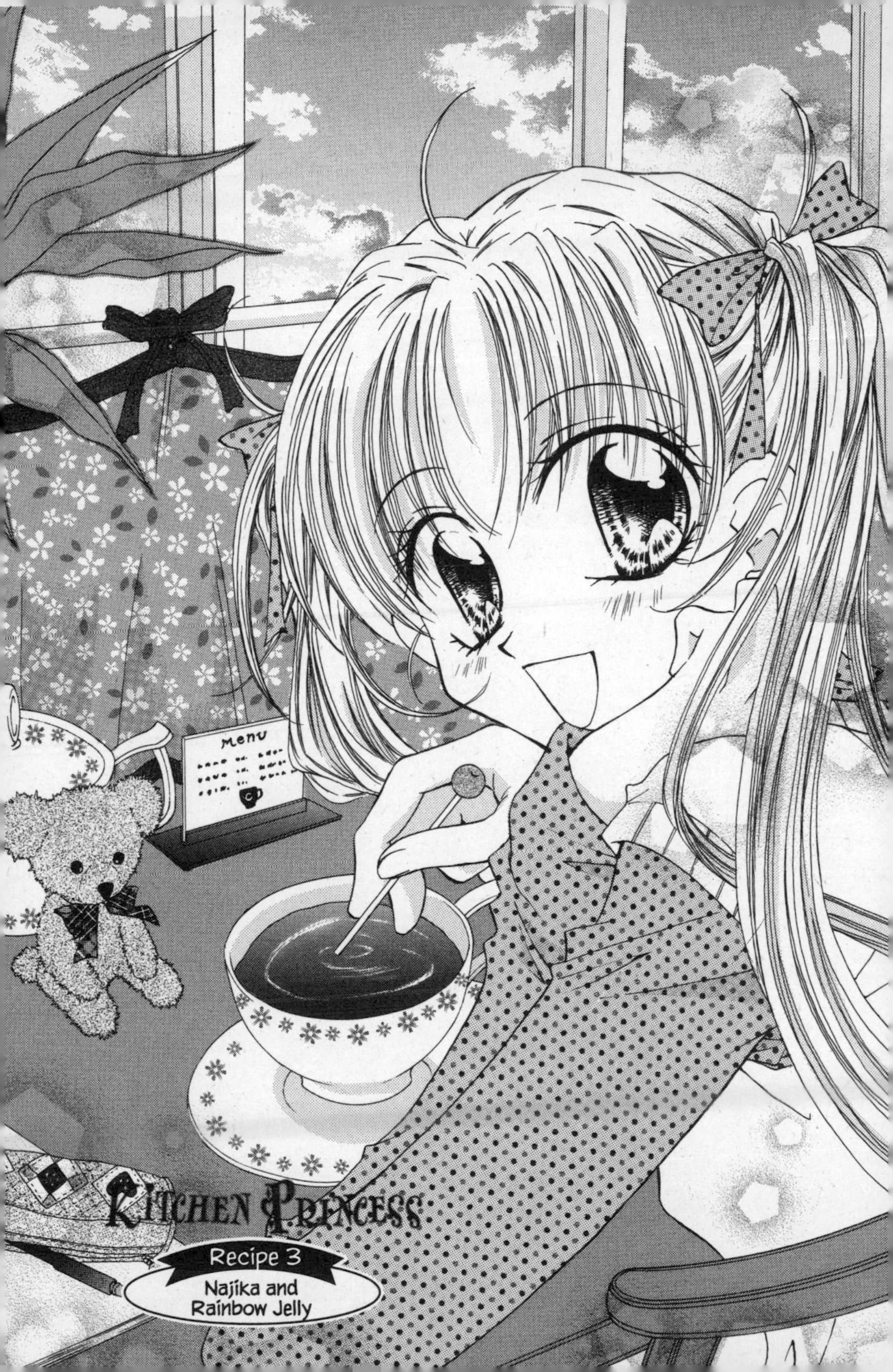
Menu
Kitchen Princess
Recipe 3
Najika and
Rainbow Jelly

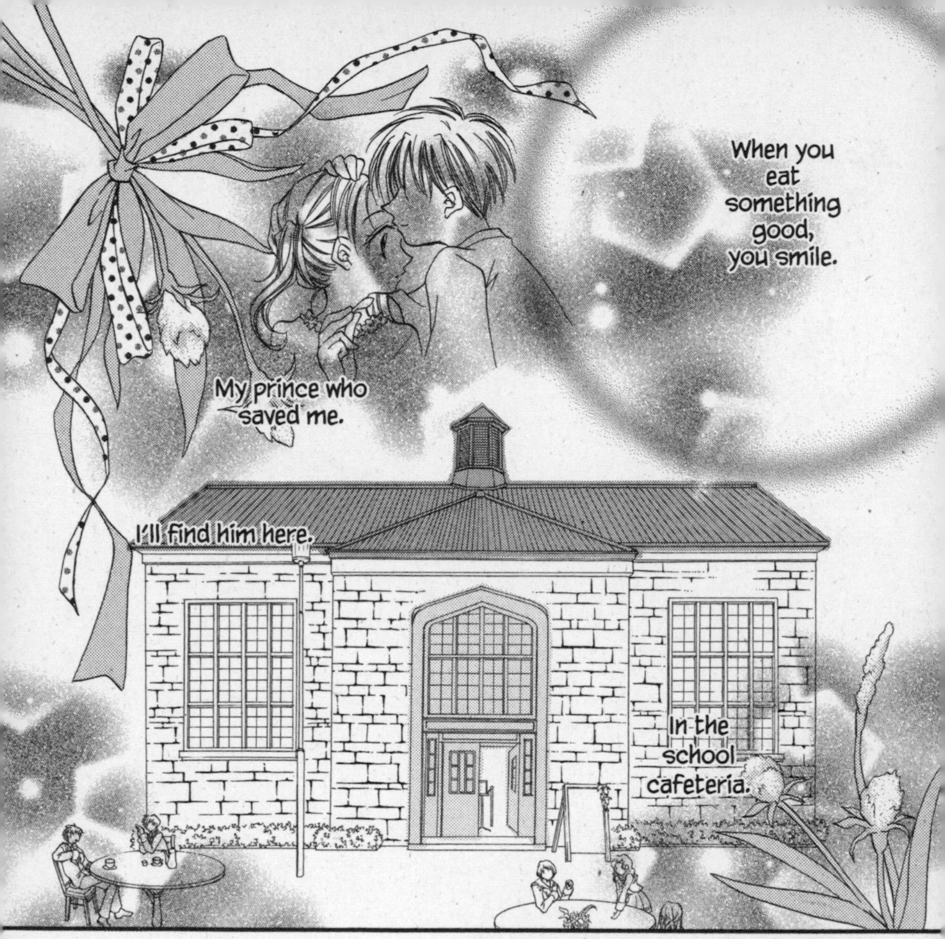
When you eat something good, you smile.
My prince who saved me.
I'll find him here.
In the school cafeteria.
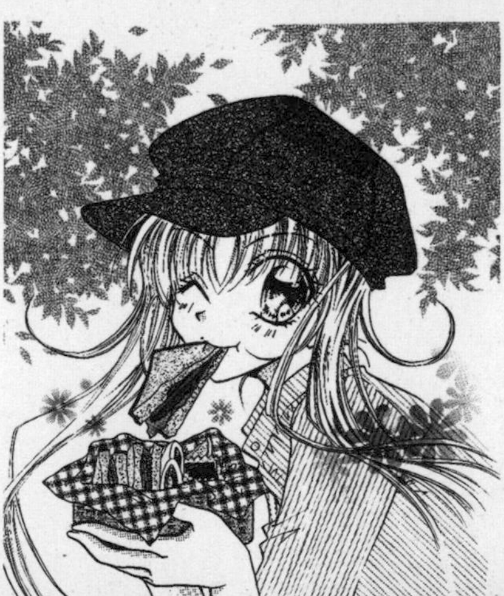

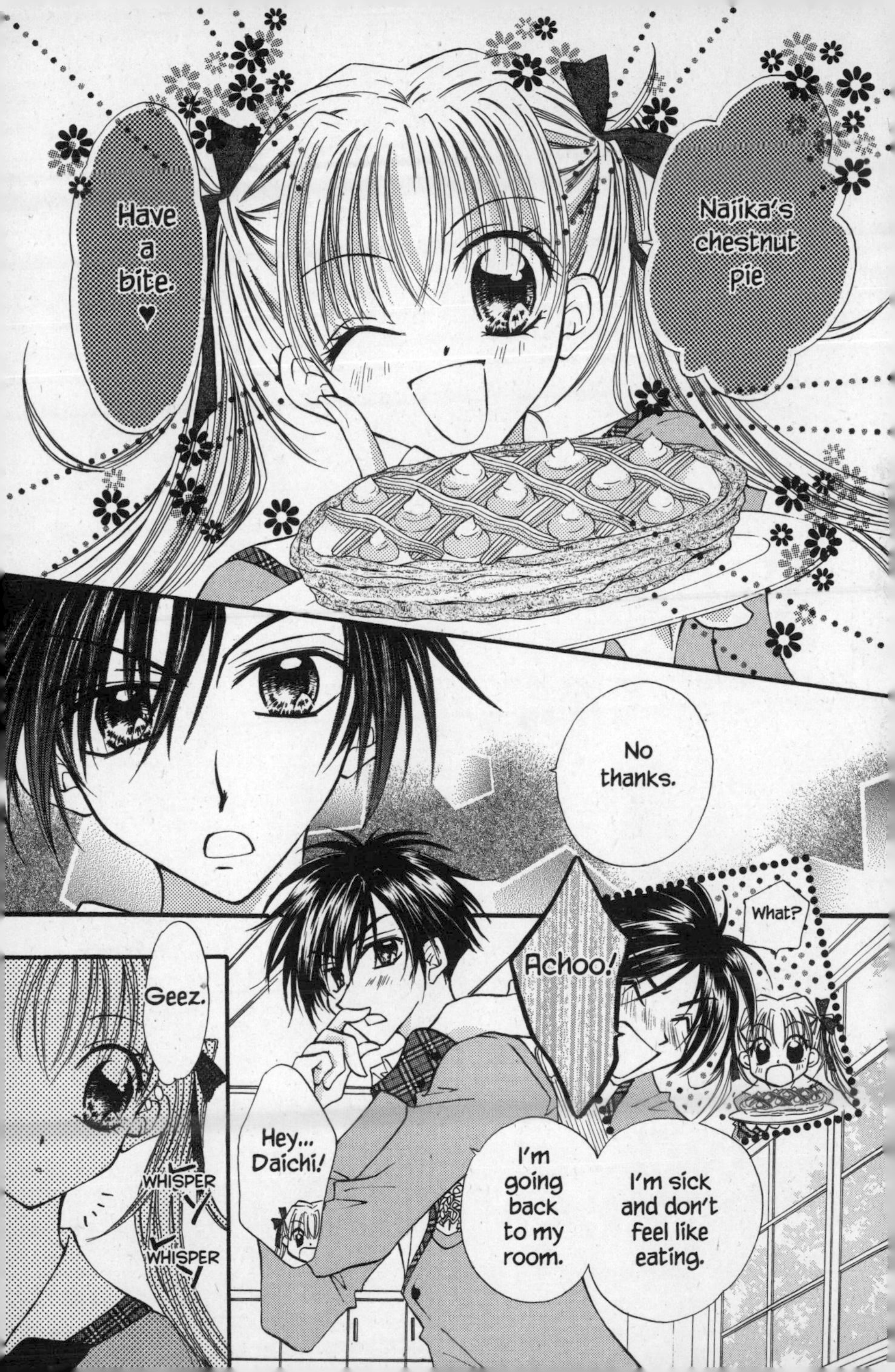
Najika's chestnut pie
Have a bite. ♥
No thanks.
What?
Achoo!
I'm sick and don't feel like eating.
I'm going back to my room.
Hey... Daichi!
Geez.
WHISPER
WHISPER

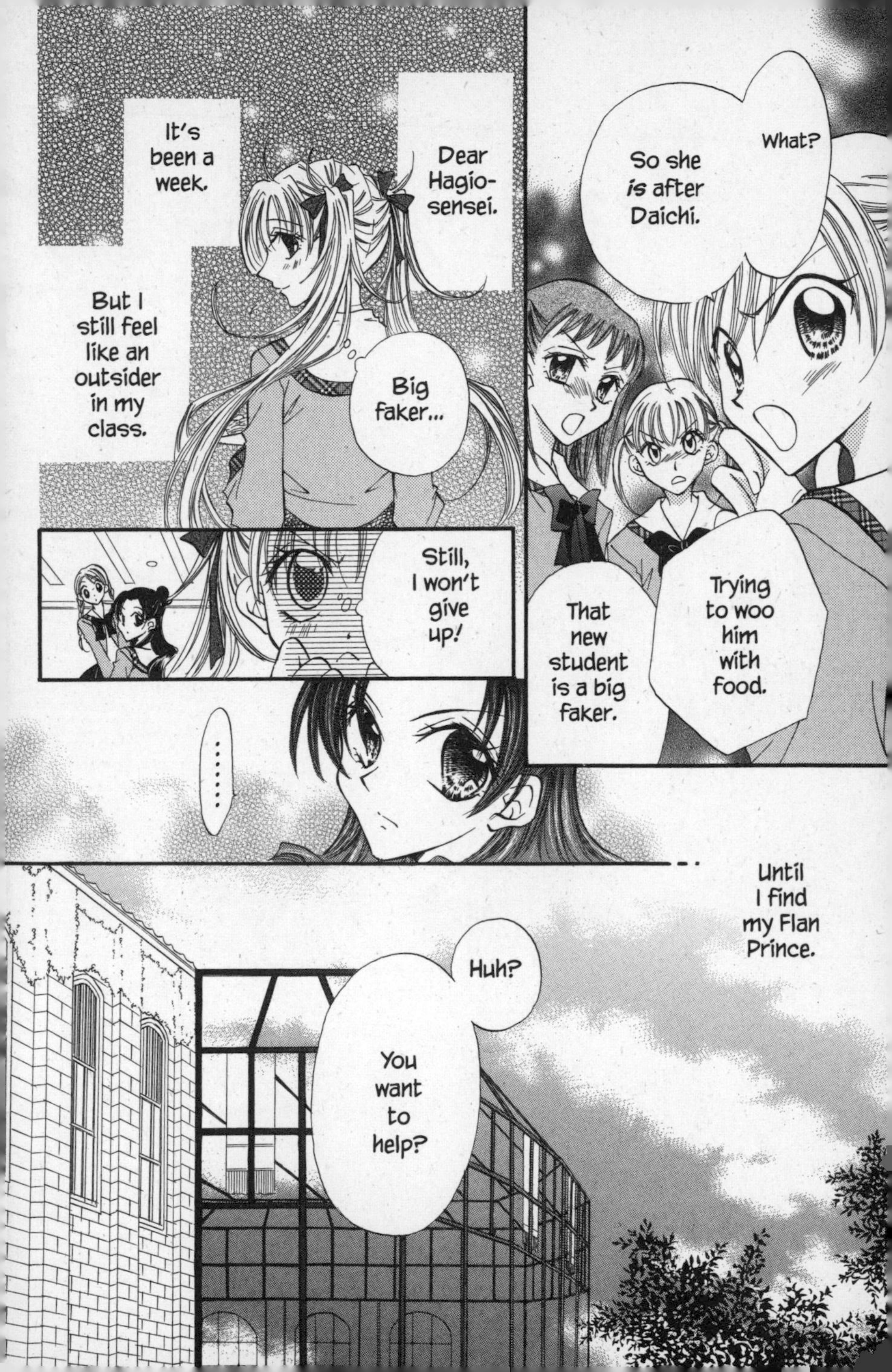

What?
So she *is* after Daichi.
Trying to woo him with food.
That new student is a big faker.
Dear Hagio-sensei.
It's been a week.
But I still feel like an outsider in my class.
Big faker...
Still, I won't give up!
......
Until I find my Flan Prince.
Huh?
You want to help?

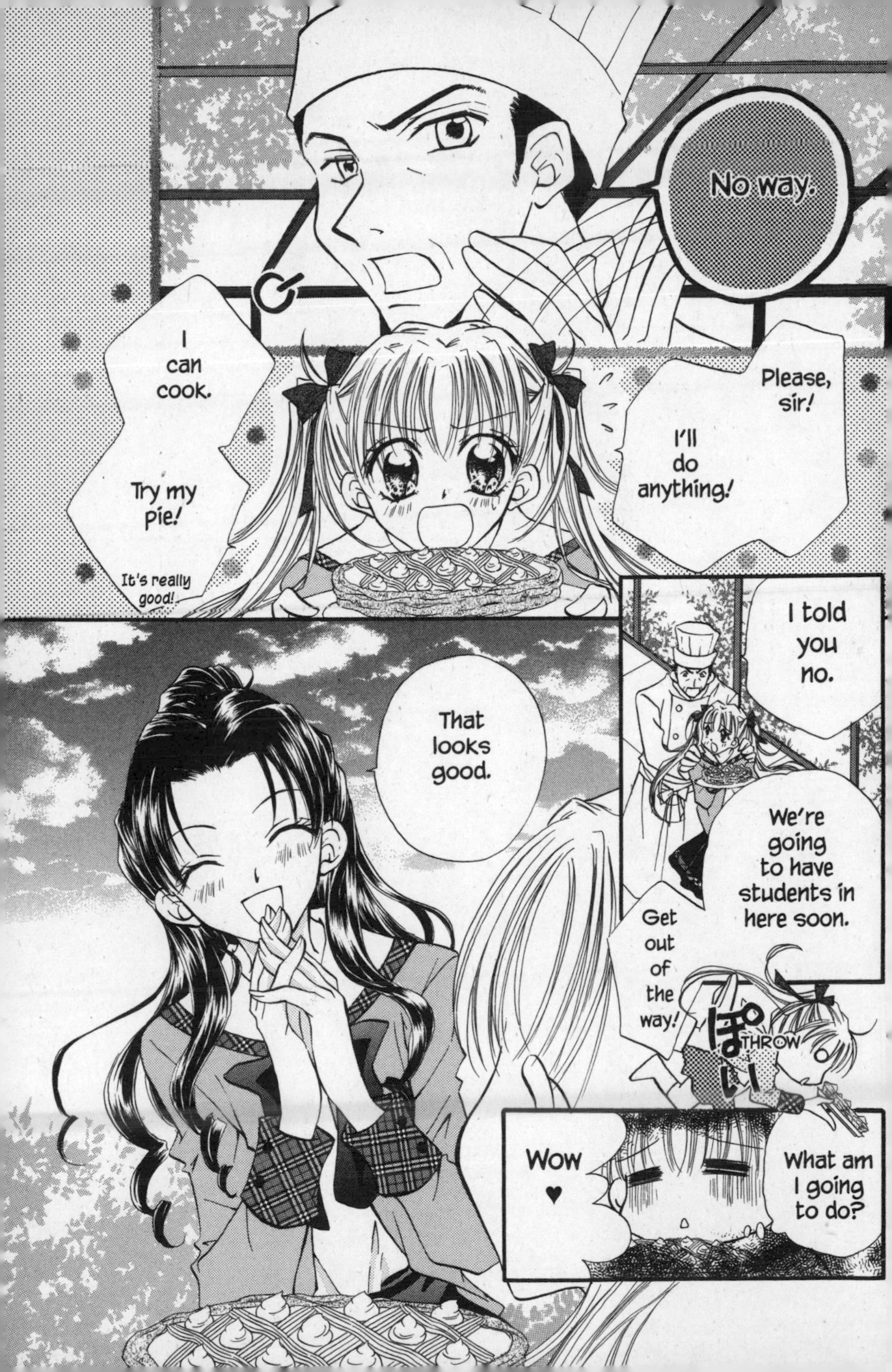

No way.
Please, sir!
I'll do anything!
I can cook.
Try my pie!
It's really good!
I told you no.
We're going to have students in here soon.
Get out of the way!
ぽい
THROW
What am I going to do?
Wow ♥
That looks good.

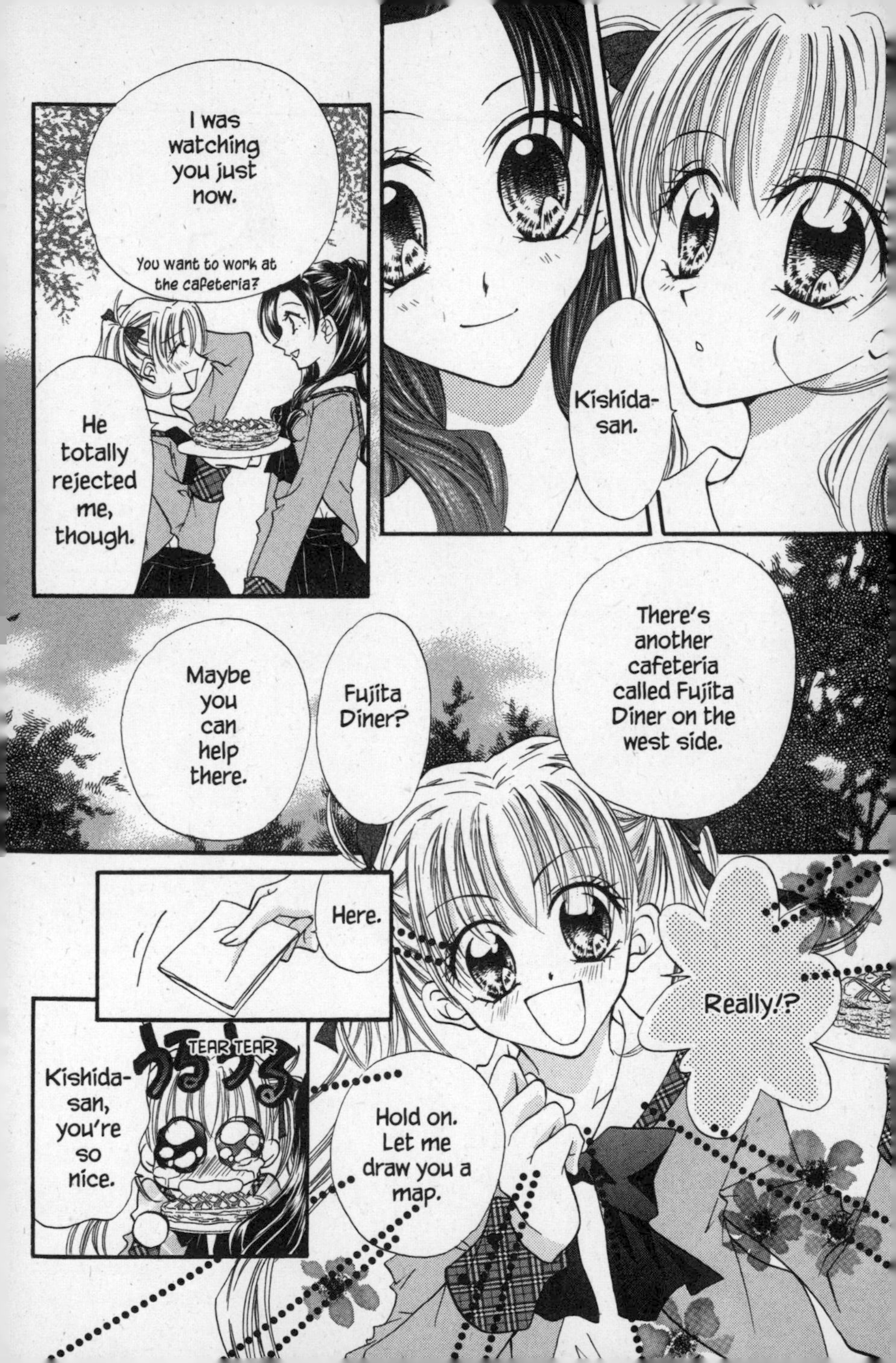
Kishida-san.
I was watching you just now.
You want to work at the cafeteria?
He totally rejected me, though.
There's another cafeteria called Fujita Diner on the west side.
Fujita Diner?
Maybe you can help there.
Really!?
Hold on. Let me draw you a map.
Here.
うるうる
TEAR TEAR
Kishida-san, you're so nice.

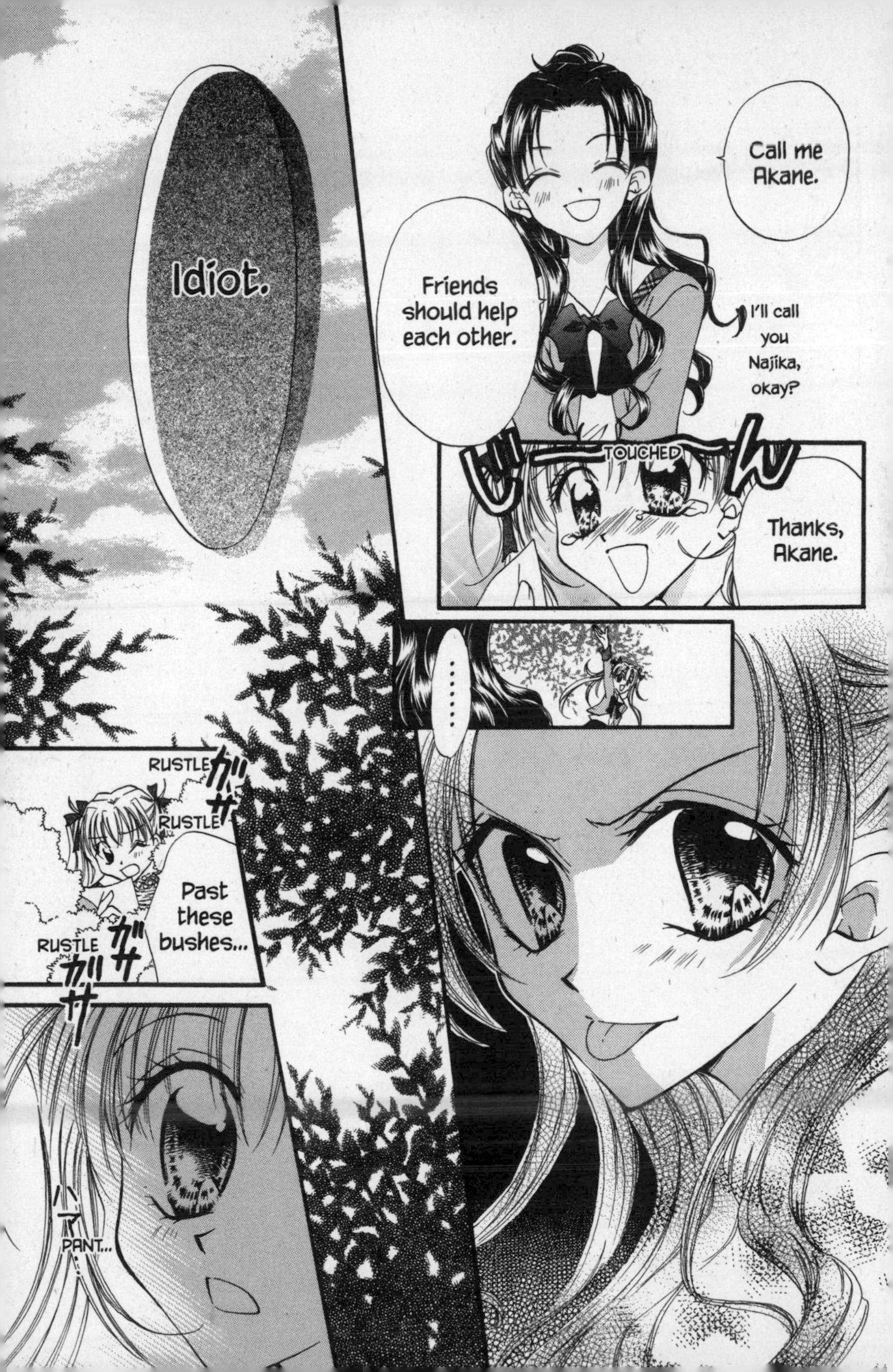

Call me Akane.
Friends should help each other.
I'll call you Najika, okay?
TOUCHED
Thanks, Akane.
Idiot.
......
RUSTLE
RUSTLE
Past these bushes...
RUSTLE
PANT...

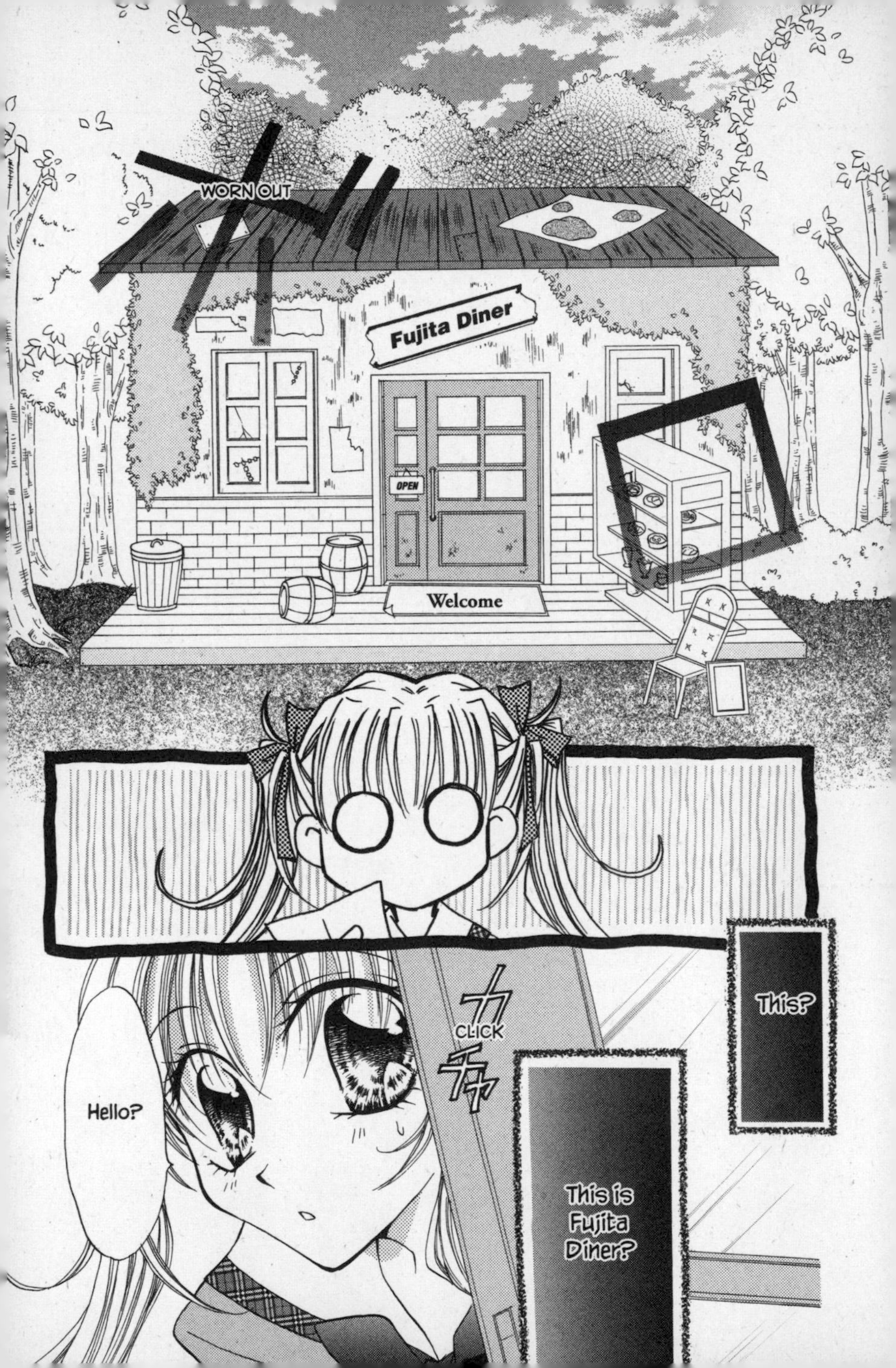
WORN OUT
Fujita Diner
OPEN
Welcome
This?
This is Fujita Diner?
CLICK
Hello?

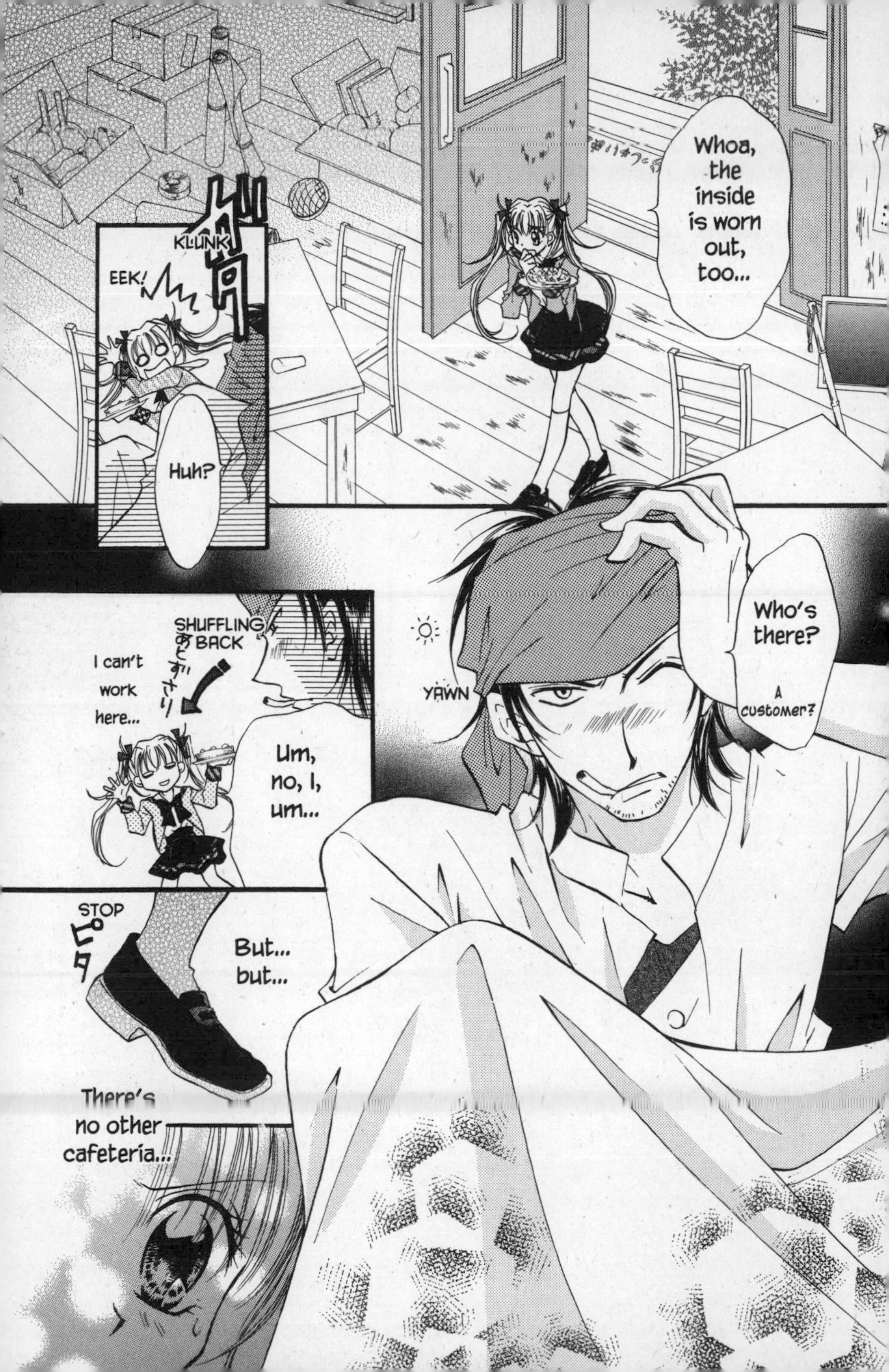
Whoa, the inside is worn out, too...
KLUNK
EEK!
Huh?
Who's there?
A customer?
YAWN
SHUFFLING BACK
あとずさり
I can't work here...
Um, no, I, um...
STOP
ピタ
But... but...
There's no other cafeteria...

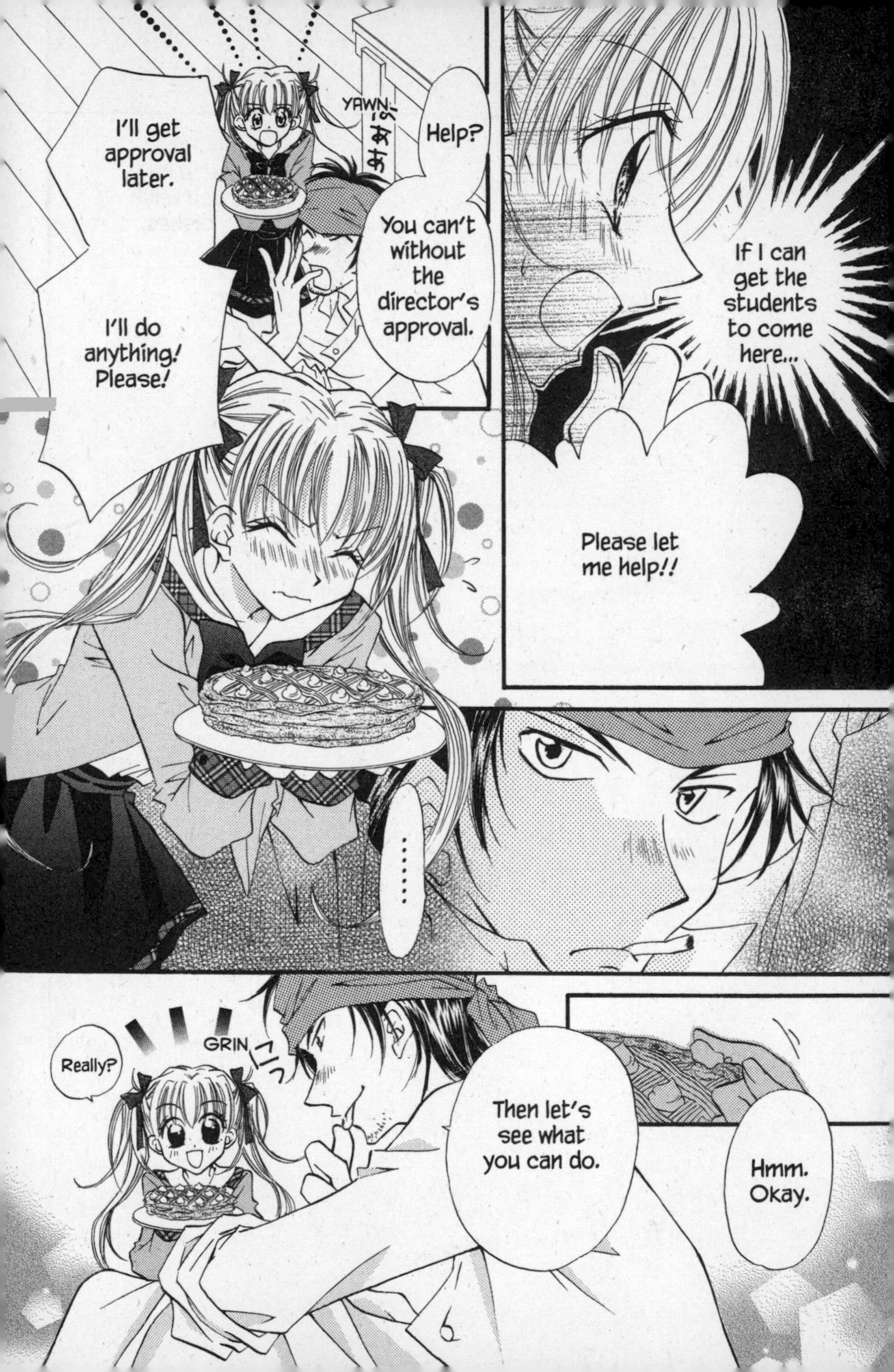

If I can get the students to come here...
Please let me help!!
Help?
YAWN
You can't without the director's approval.
I'll get approval later.
I'll do anything! Please!
......
Hmm. Okay.
Then let's see what you can do.
GRIN
Really?

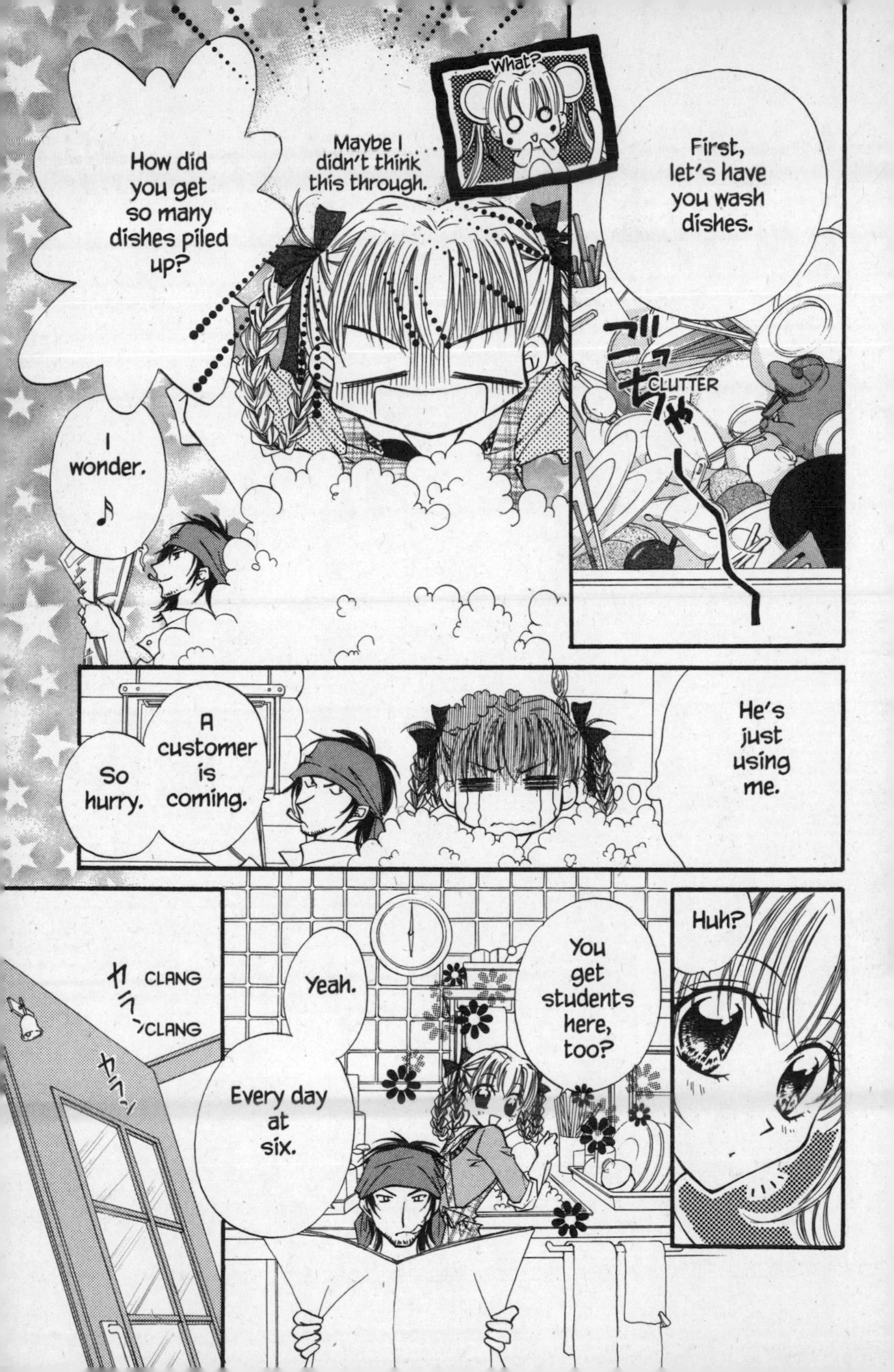

First, let's have you wash dishes.
ごちゃ
CLUTTER
What?
Maybe I didn't think this through.
How did you get so many dishes piled up?
I wonder. ♪
He's just using me.
A customer is coming.
So hurry.
Huh?
You get students here, too?
Yeah.
Every day at six.
CLANG
CLANG

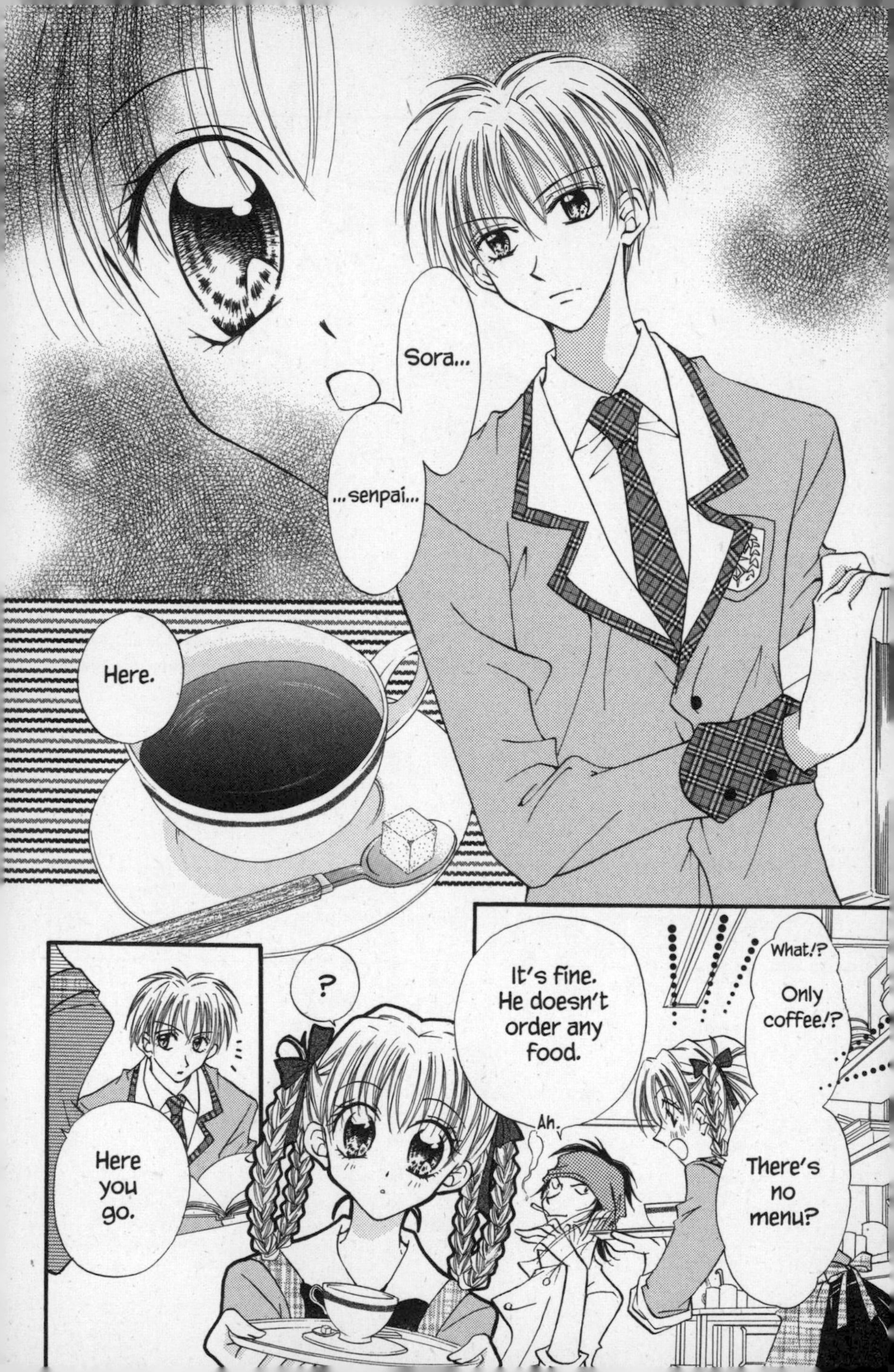
Sora...
...senpai...
Here.
What!?
Only coffee!?
It's fine. He doesn't order any food.
There's no menu?
Ah.
?
Here you go.

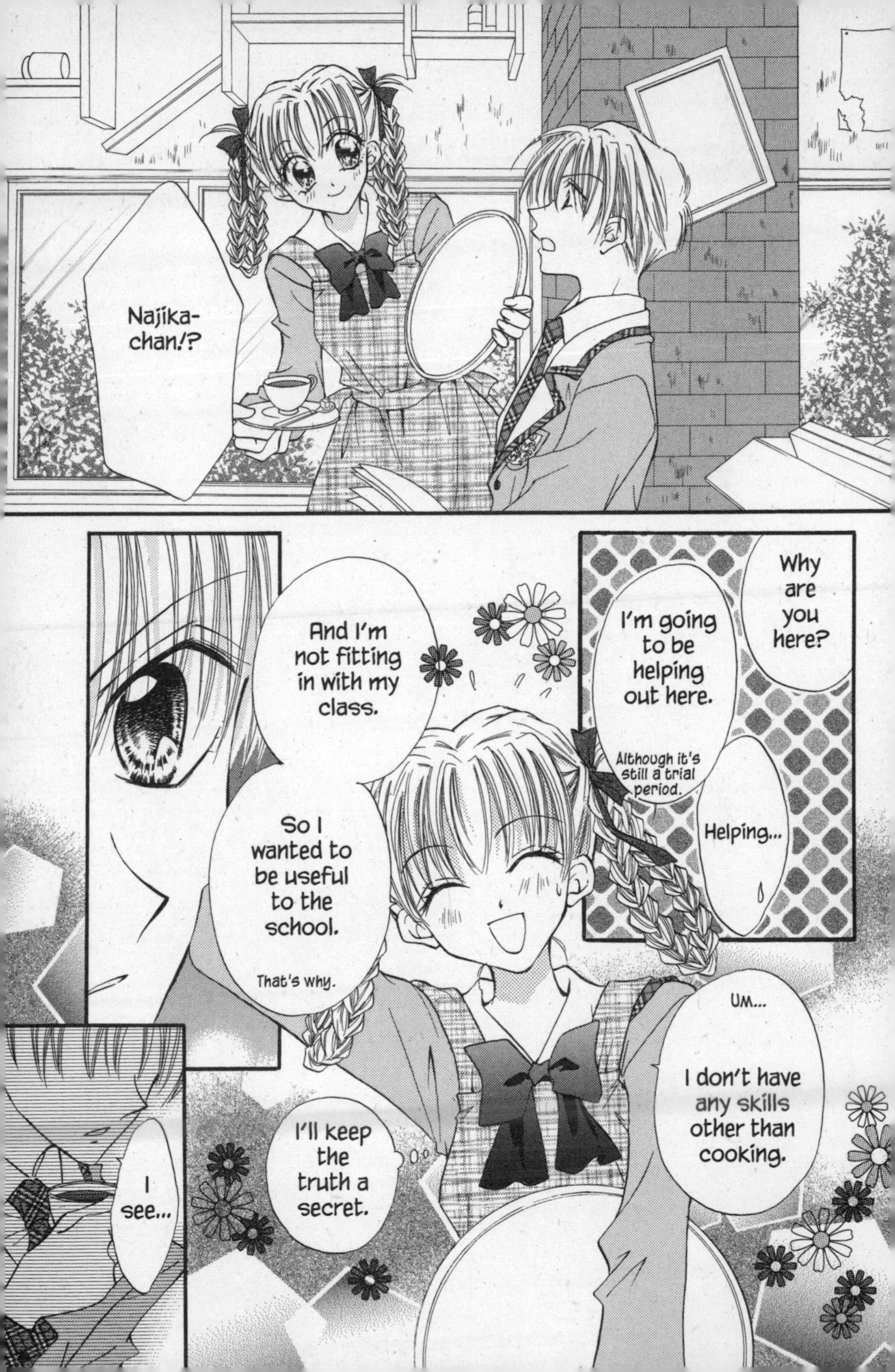

Najika-chan!?
Why are you here?
I'm going to be helping out here.
Although it's still a trial period.
Helping...
Um...
I don't have any skills other than cooking.
And I'm not fitting in with my class.
So I wanted to be useful to the school.
That's why.
I'll keep the truth a secret.
I see...

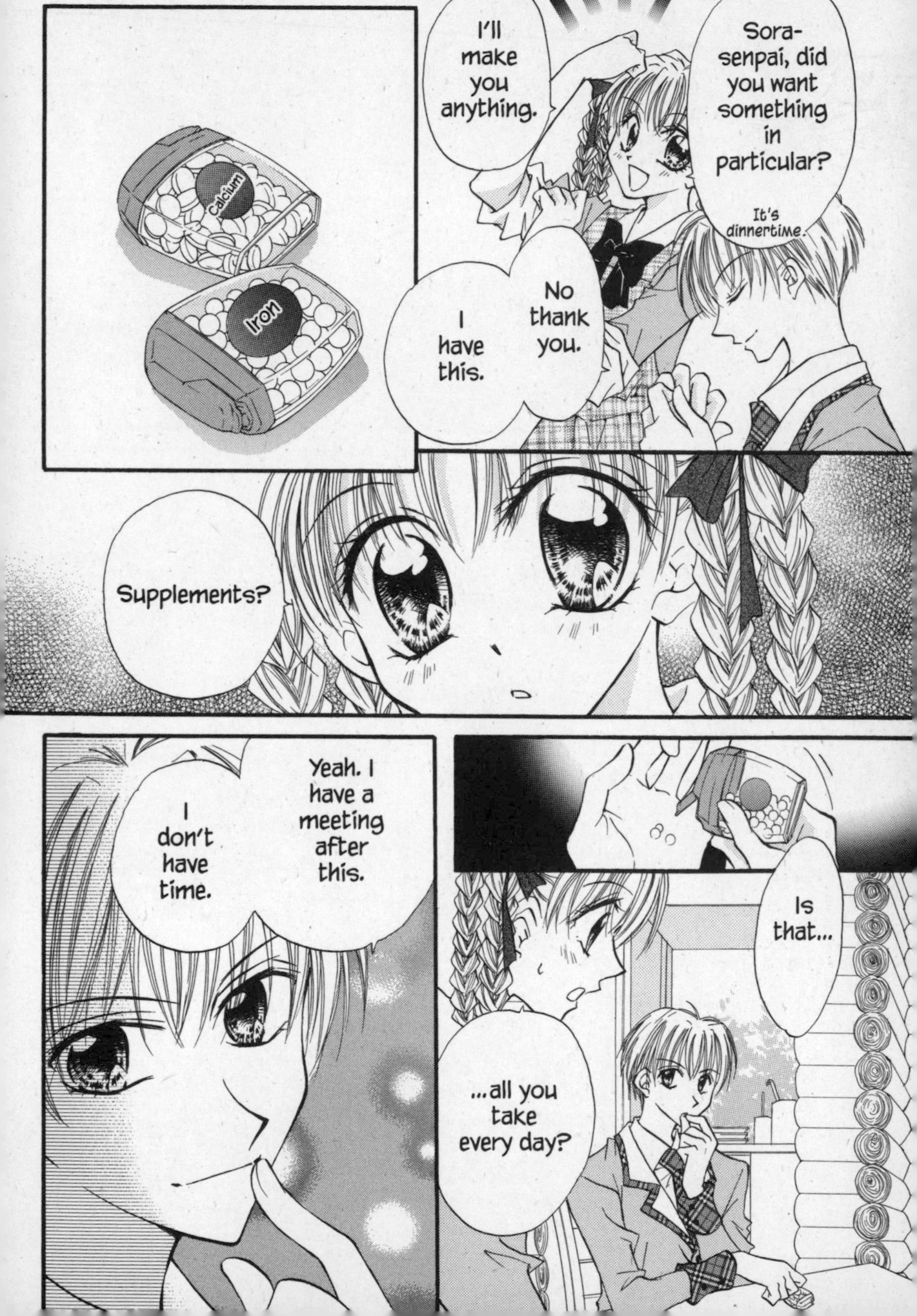
Sora-senpai, did you want something in particular?
It's dinnertime.
I'll make you anything.
No thank you.
I have this.
Calcium
Iron
Supplements?
Is that...
...all you take every day?
Yeah. I have a meeting after this.
I don't have time.

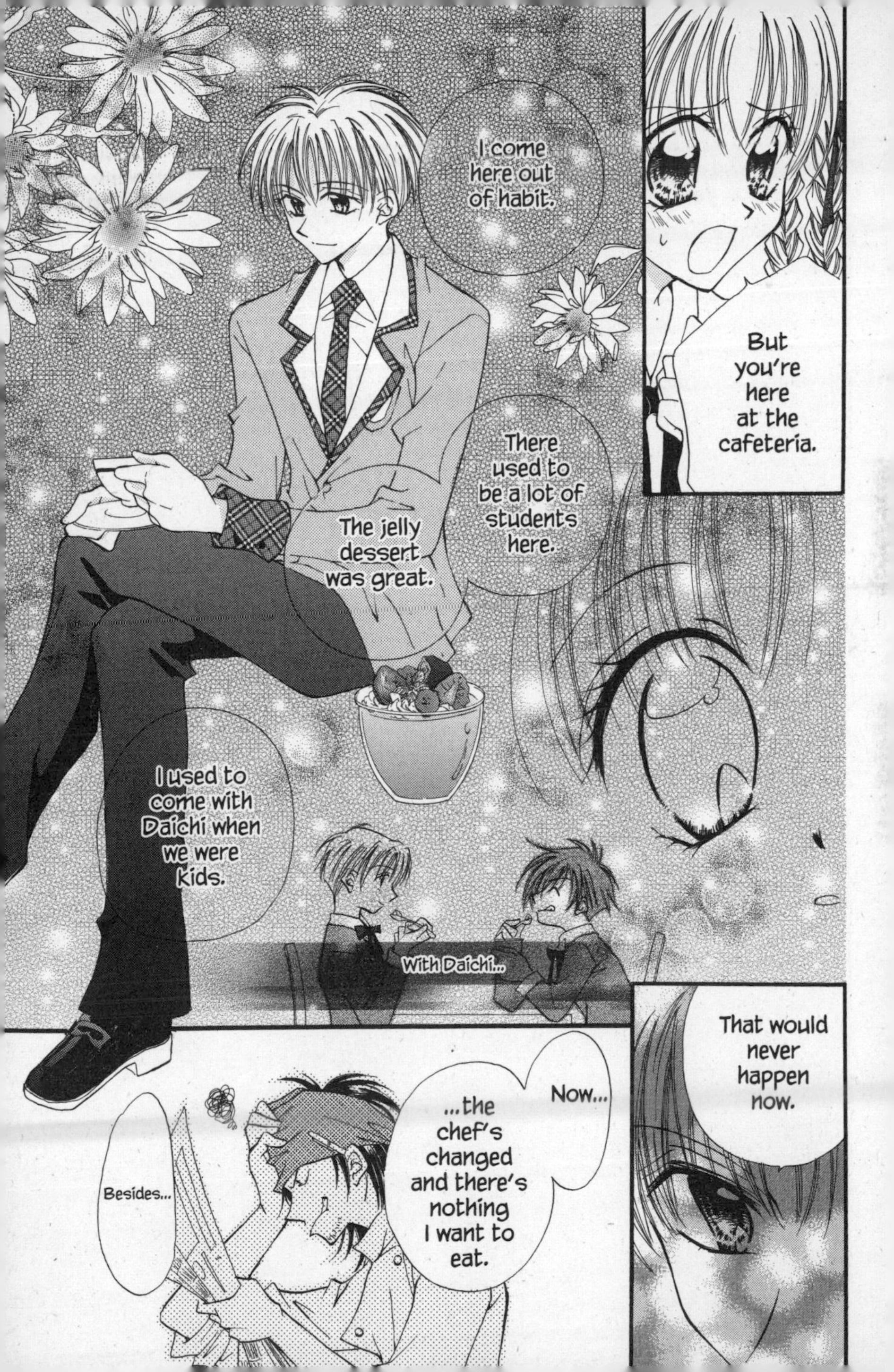

But you're here at the cafeteria.
I come here out of habit.
There used to be a lot of students here.
The jelly dessert was great.
I used to come with Daichi when we were kids.
With Daichi...
That would never happen now.
Now...
...the chef's changed and there's nothing I want to eat.
Besides...

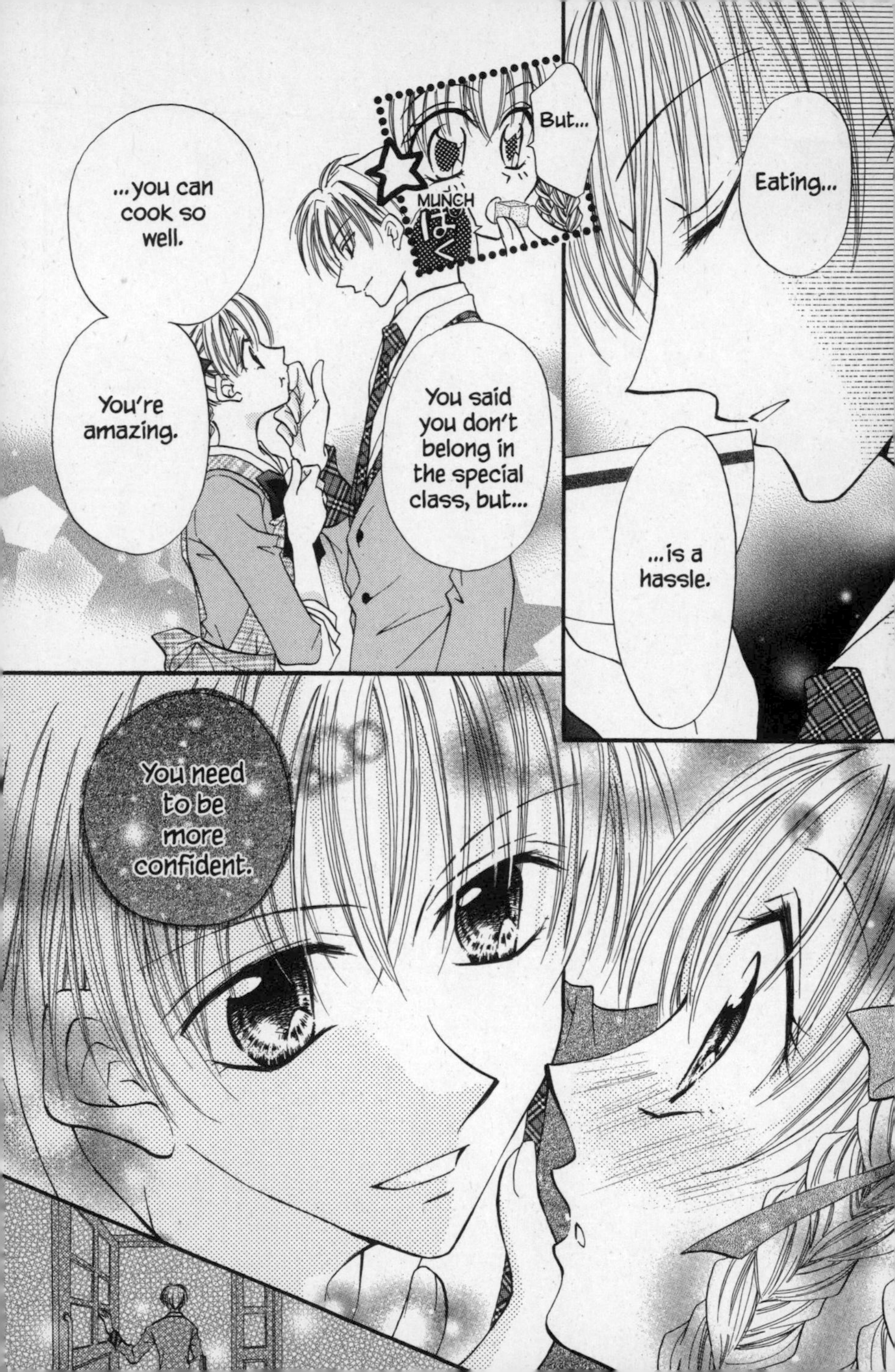
Eating...
...is a hassle.
But...
MUNCH
You said you don't belong in the special class, but...
...you can cook so well.
You're amazing.
You need to be more confident.

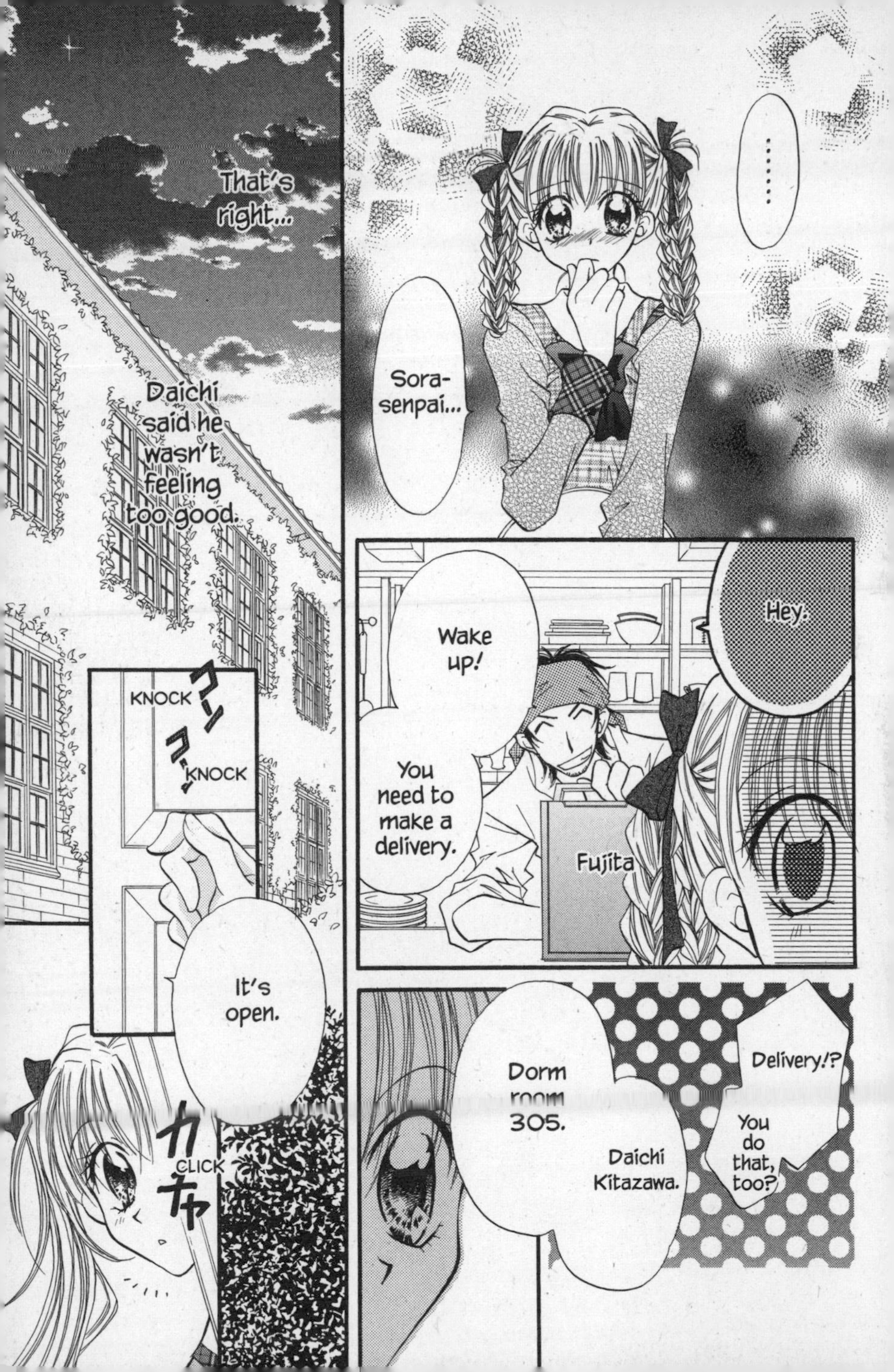

......
Sora-senpai...
Hey.
Wake up!
You need to make a delivery.
Fujita
Delivery!?
You do that, too?
Dorm room 305.
Daichi Kitazawa.
That's right...
Daichi said he wasn't feeling too good.
KNOCK
KNOCK
It's open.
CLICK

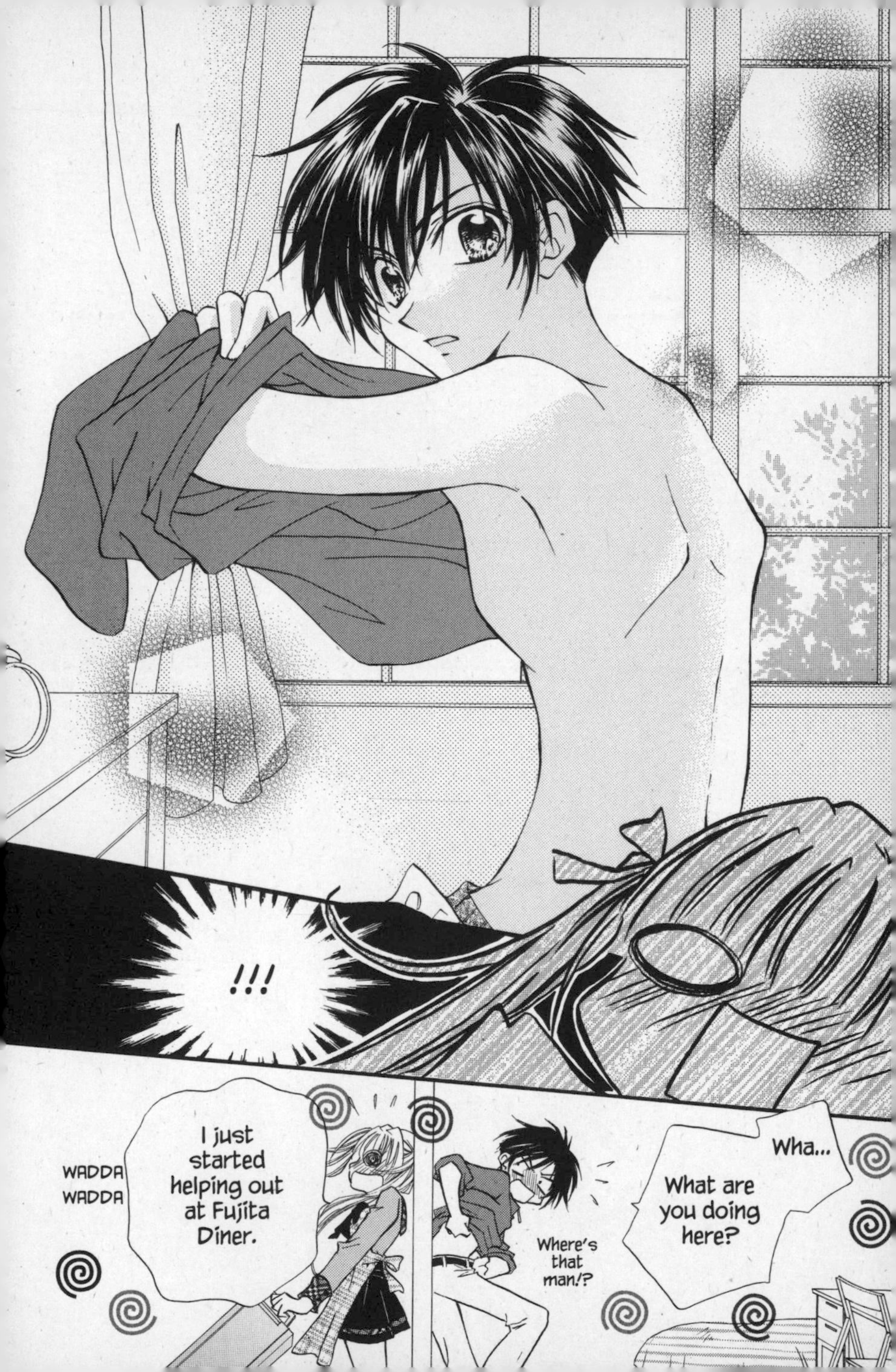
!!!
Wha...
What are you doing here?
Where's that man!?
I just started helping out at Fujita Diner.
WADDA WADDA

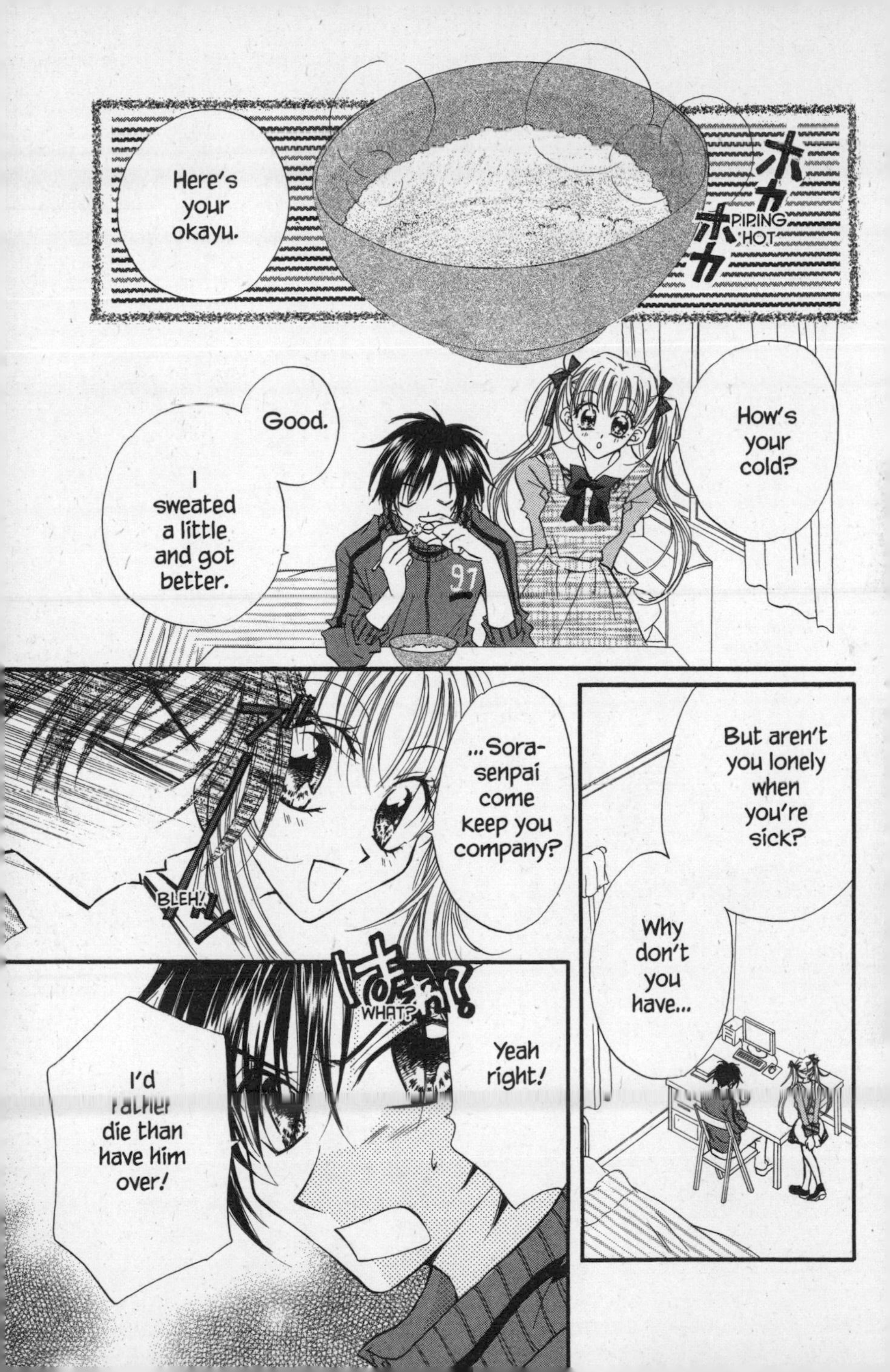
Here's your okayu.
PIPING HOT
How's your cold?
Good.
I sweated a little and got better.
But aren't you lonely when you're sick?
Why don't you have...
...Sora-senpai come keep you company?
BLEH!
WHAT?
Yeah right!
I'd rather die than have him over!

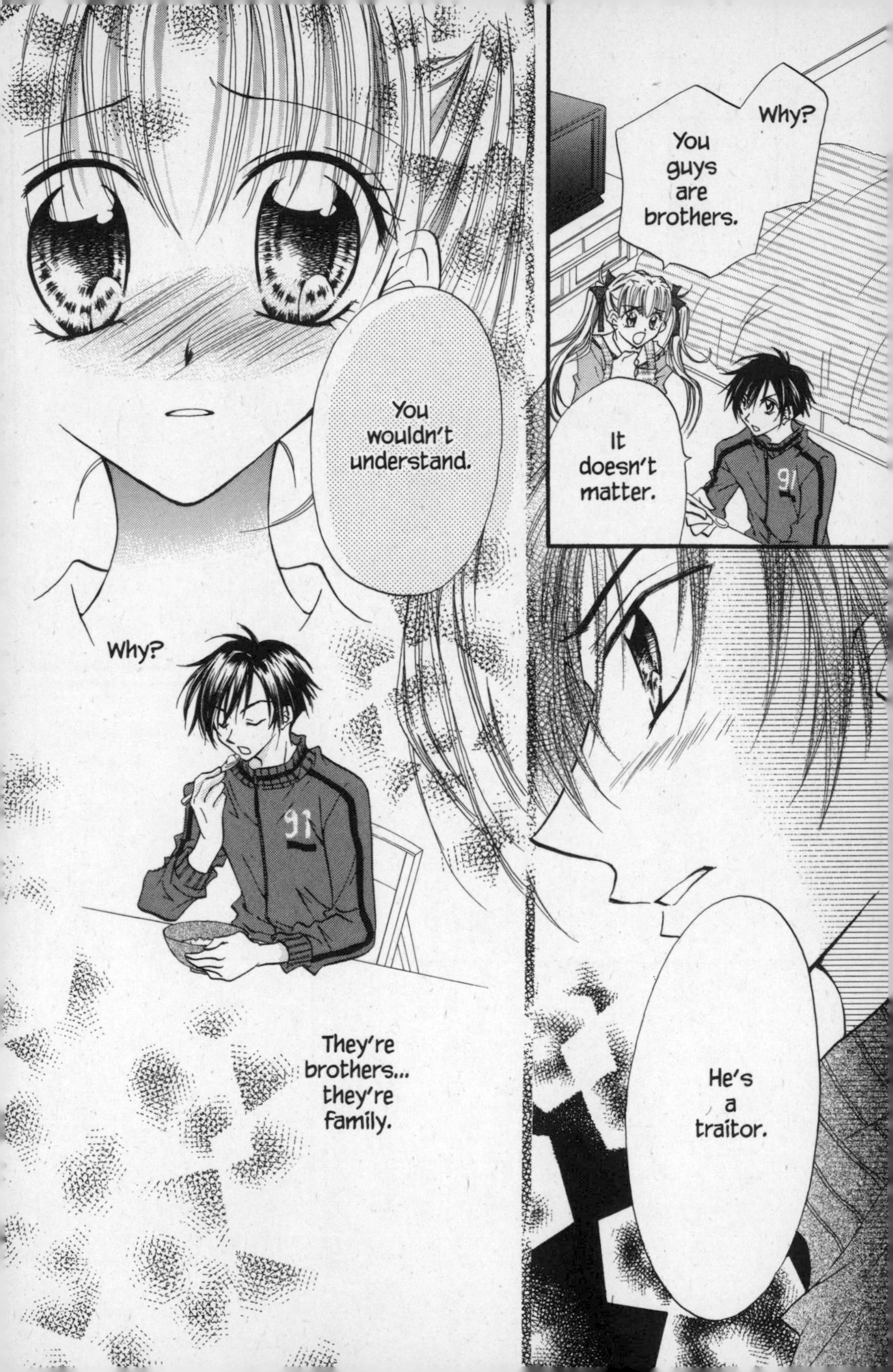
Why?
You guys are brothers.
It doesn't matter.
He's a traitor.
You wouldn't understand.
Why?
They're brothers... they're family.

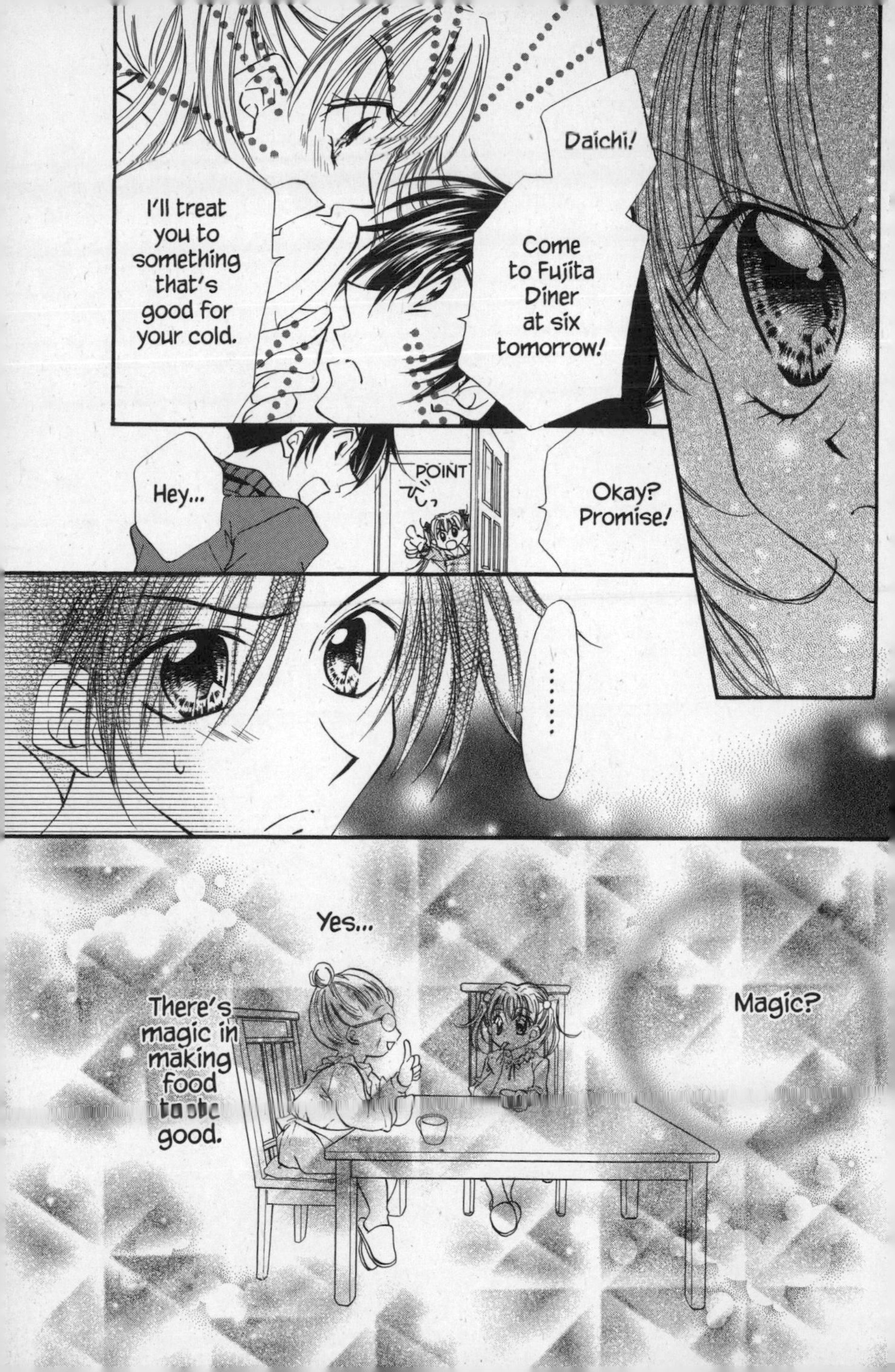
Daichi!
Come to Fujita Diner at six tomorrow!
I'll treat you to something that's good for your cold.
Okay? Promise!
POINT
Hey...
......
Magic?
Yes...
There's magic in making food taste good.

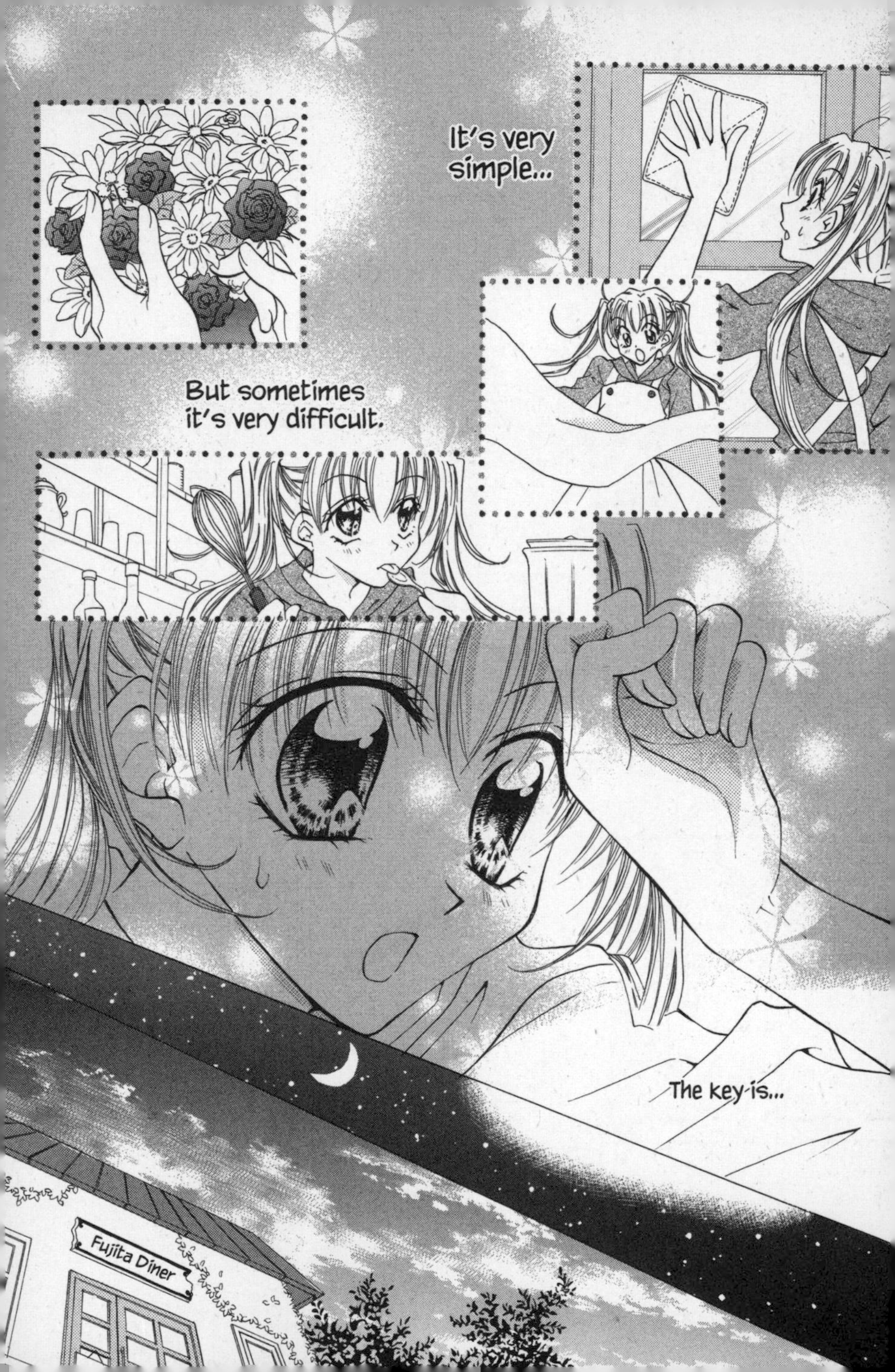
It's very simple...
But sometimes it's very difficult.
The key is...
Fujita Diner

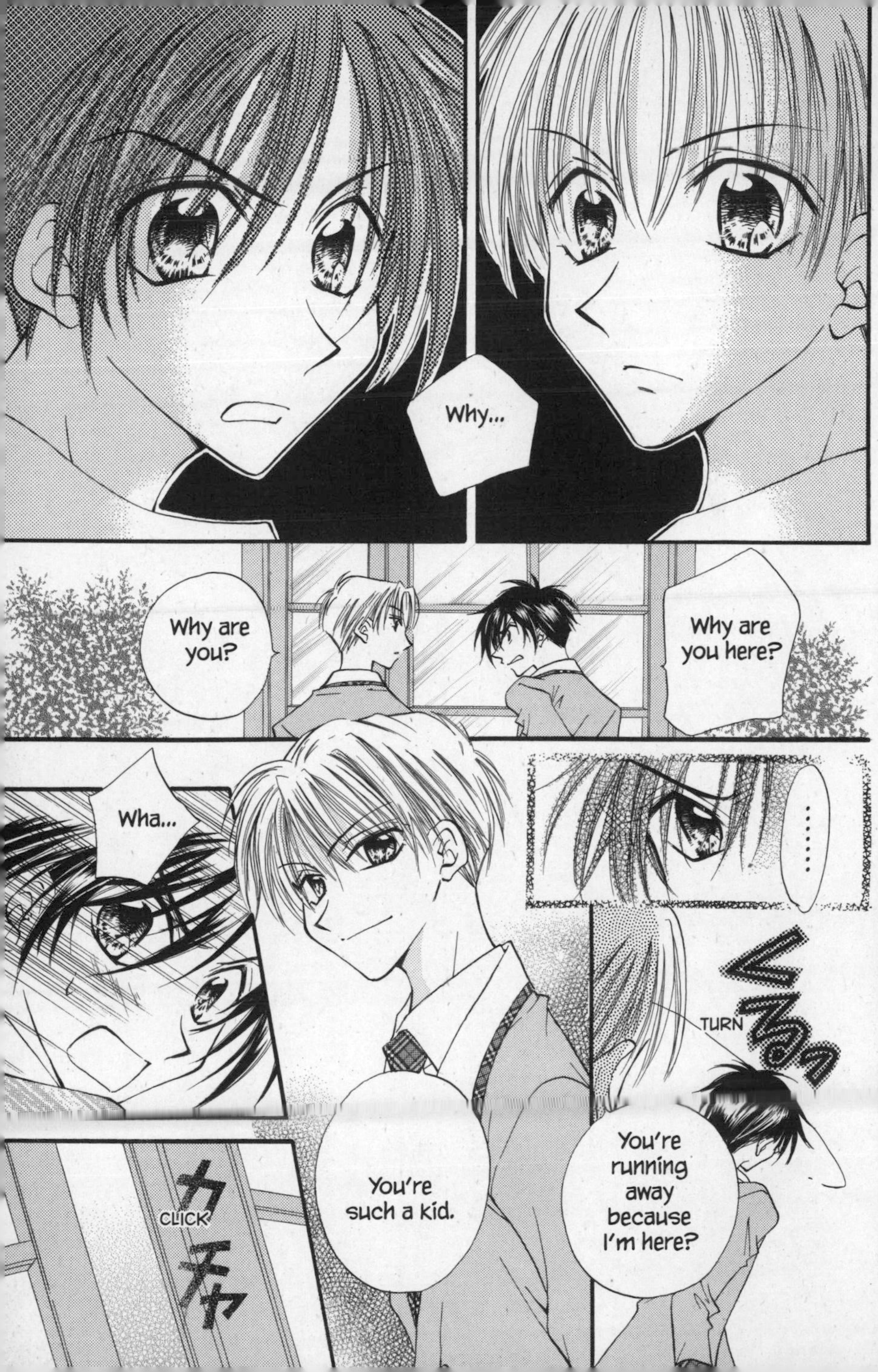

Why...
Why are you here?
Why are you?
......
TURN
You're running away because I'm here?
You're such a kid.
Wha...
カチャ
CLICK

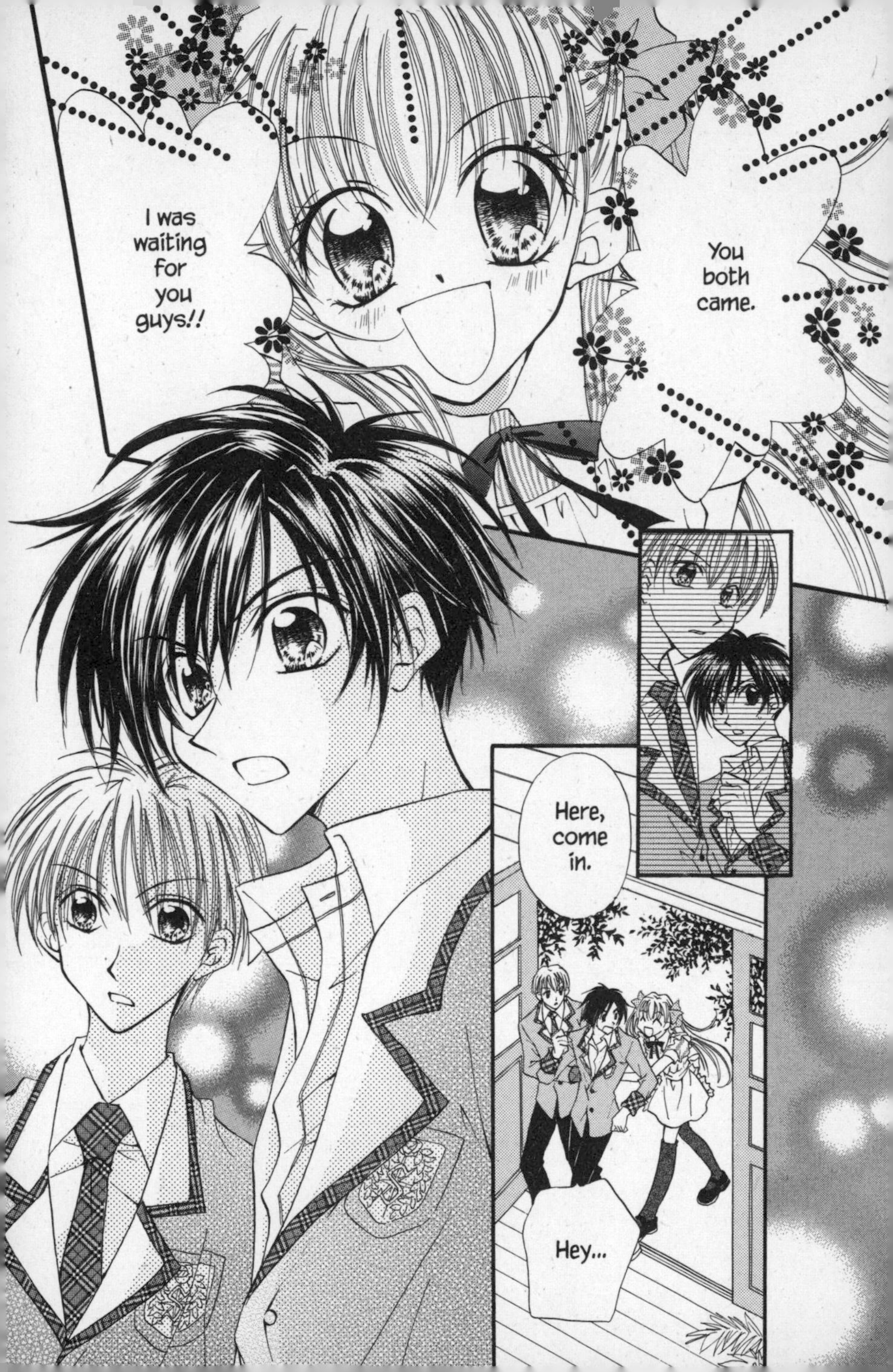
You both came.
I was waiting for you guys!!
Here, come in.
Hey...

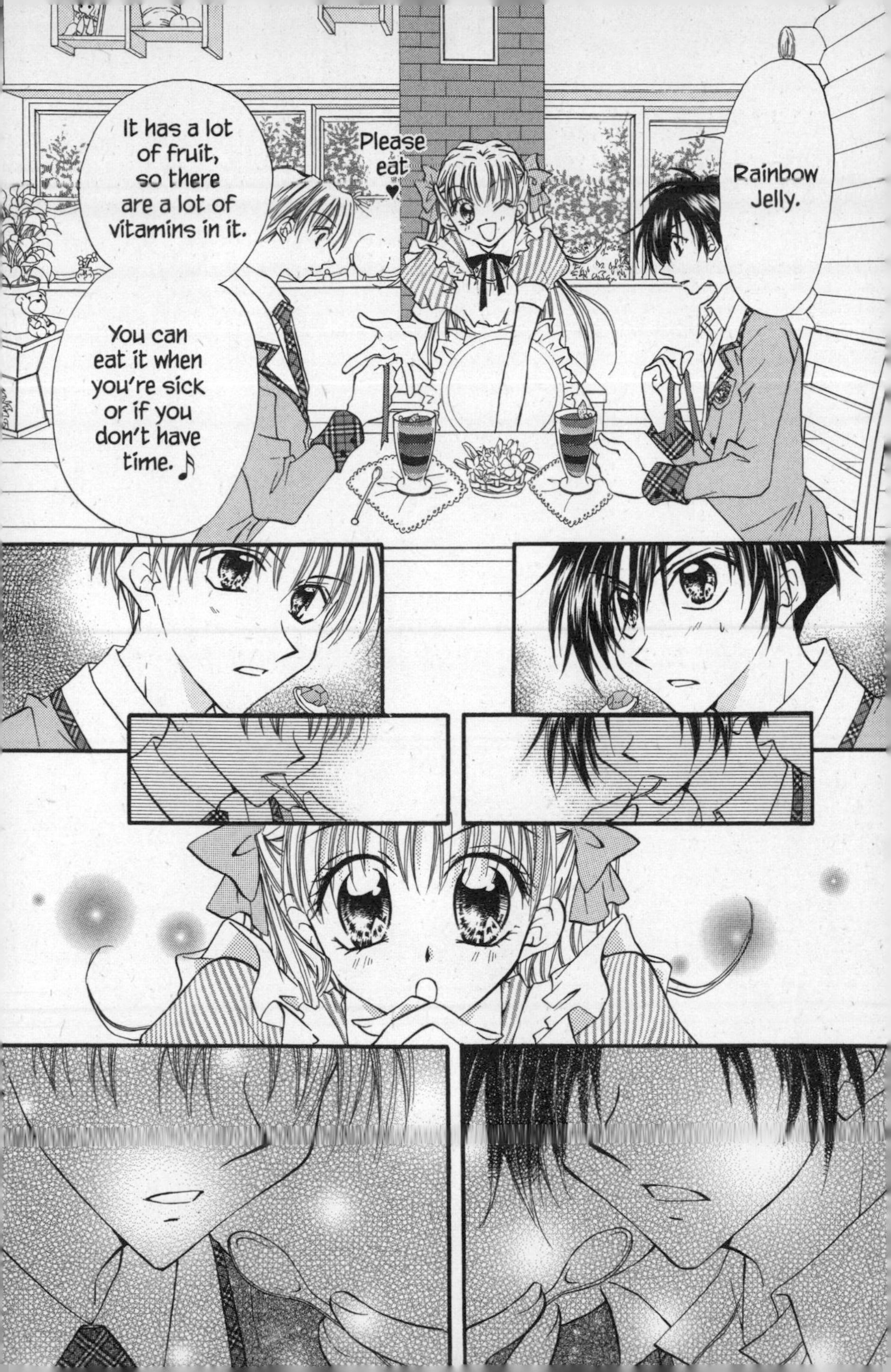
Rainbow Jelly.
Please eat ♥
It has a lot of fruit, so there are a lot of vitamins in it.
You can eat it when you're sick or if you don't have time. ♪

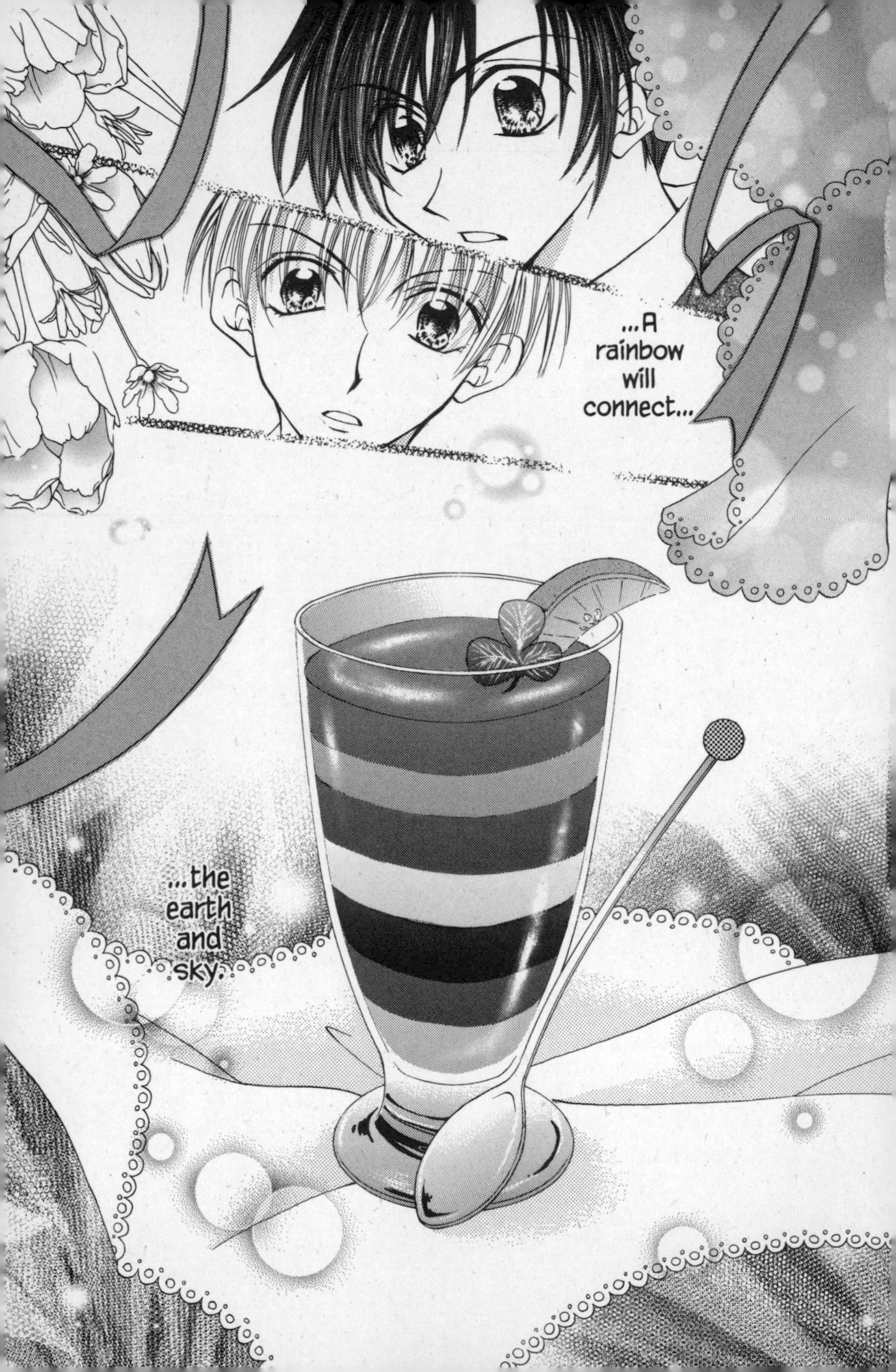
...A rainbow will connect...
...the earth and sky.

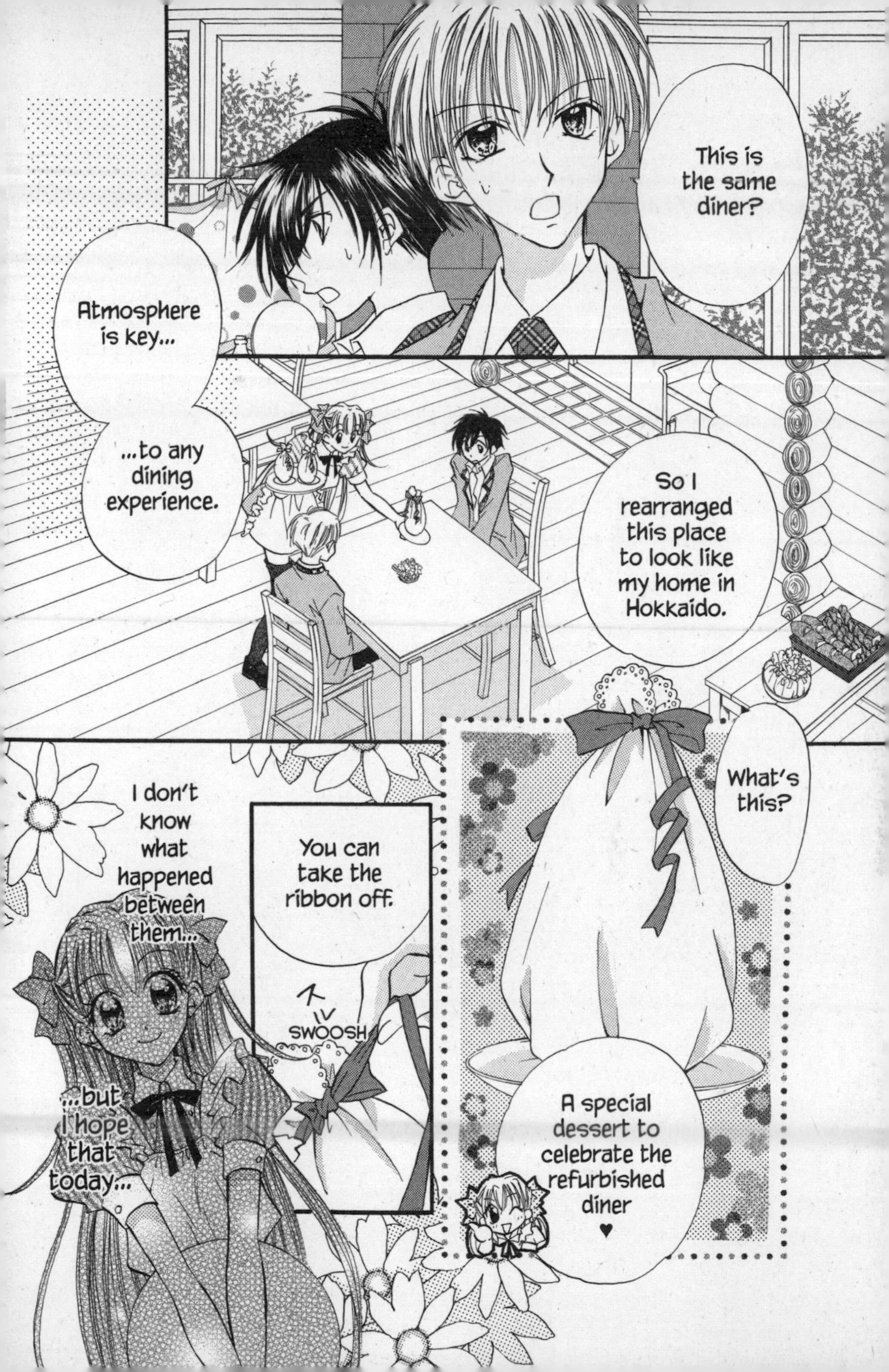
This is the same diner?
Atmosphere is key...
...to any dining experience.
So I rearranged this place to look like my home in Hokkaido.
What's this?
A special dessert to celebrate the refurbished diner ♥
You can take the ribbon off.
SWOOSH
I don't know what happened between them...
...but I hope that today...

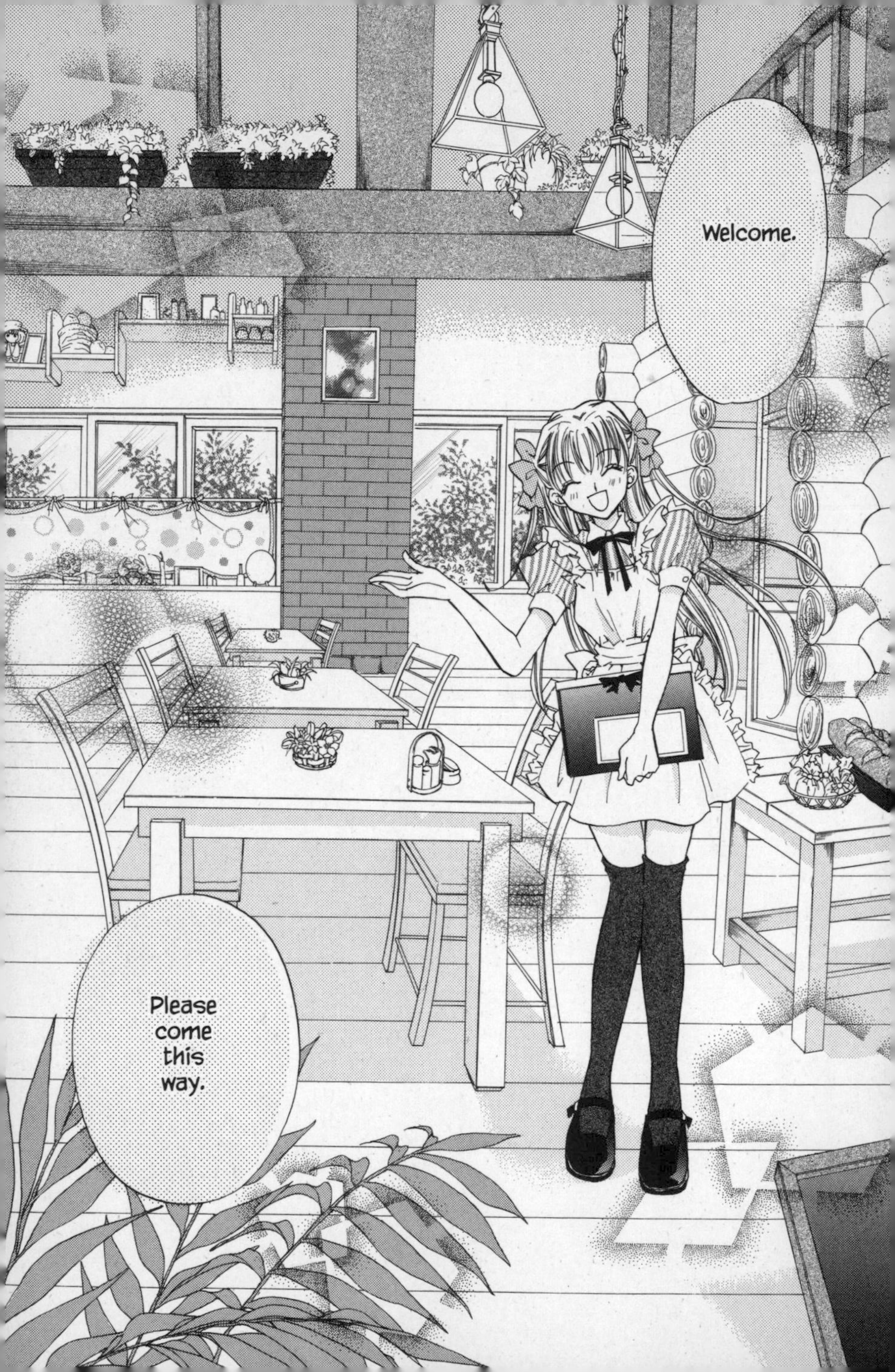
Welcome.
Please come this way.

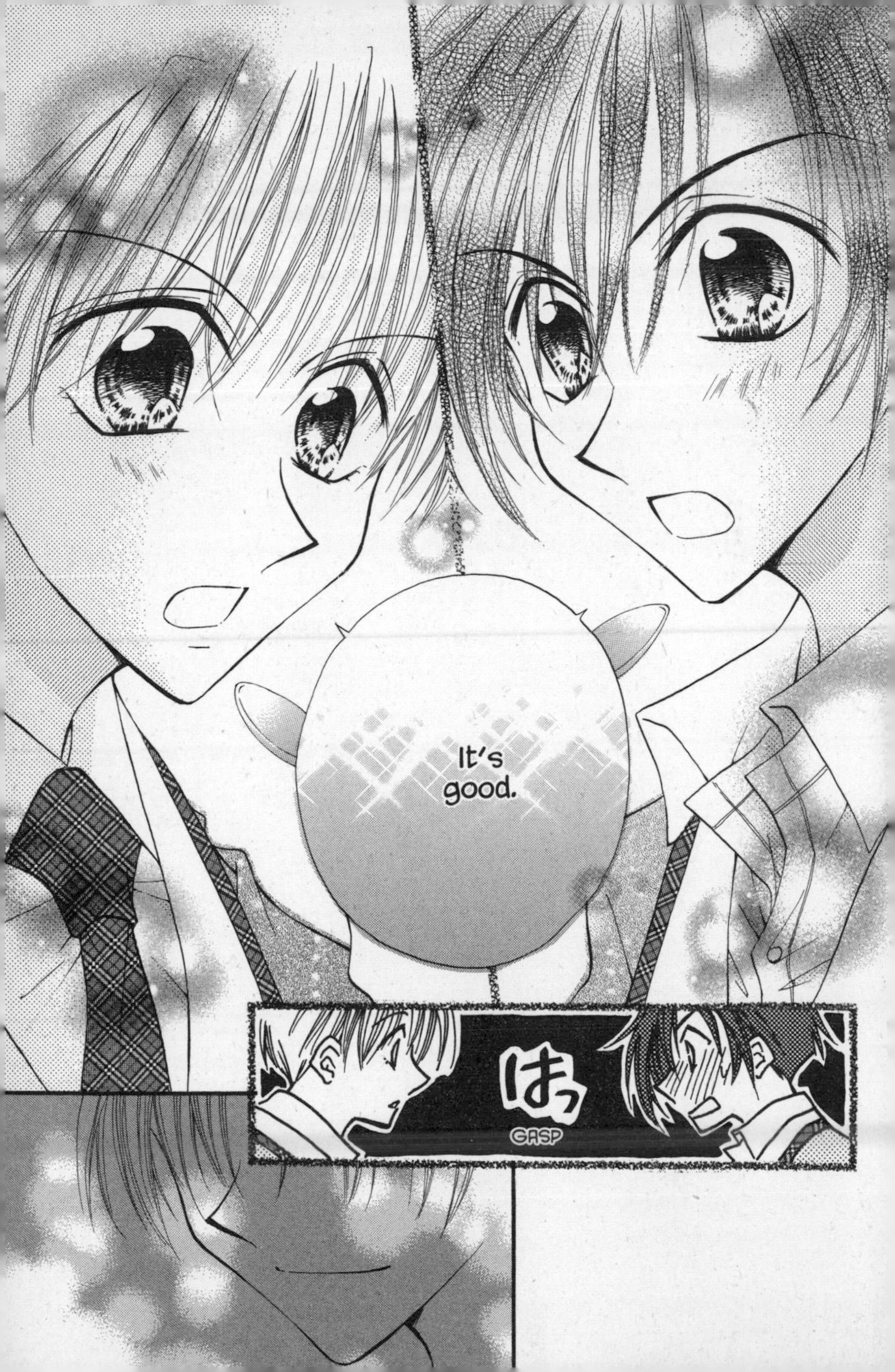
It's good.
はっ
GASP

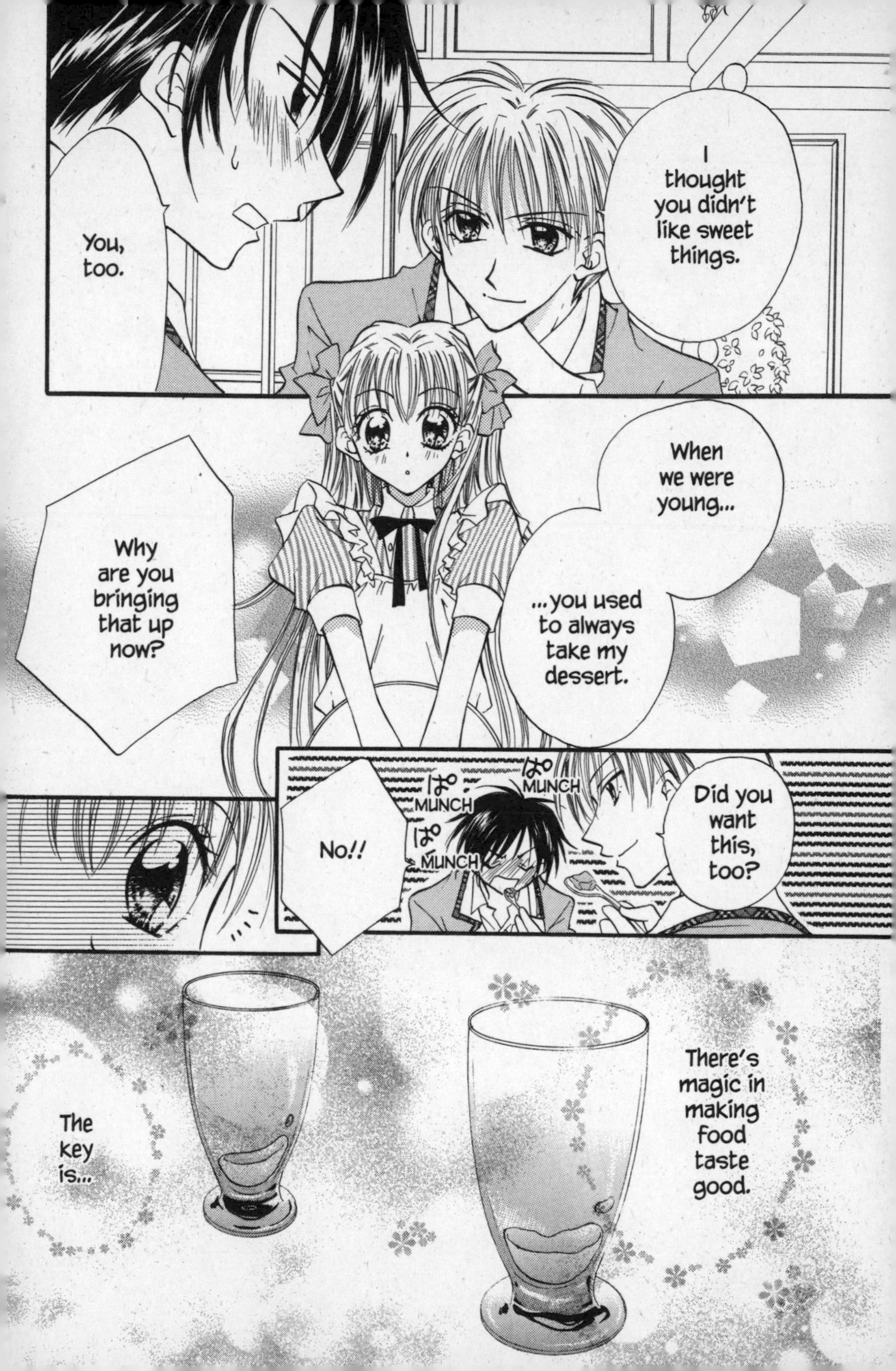
I thought you didn't like sweet things.
You, too.
When we were young...
...you used to always take my dessert.
Why are you bringing that up now?
Did you want this, too?
ぱ MUNCH
ぱ MUNCH
ぱ MUNCH
No!!
There's magic in making food taste good.
The key is...

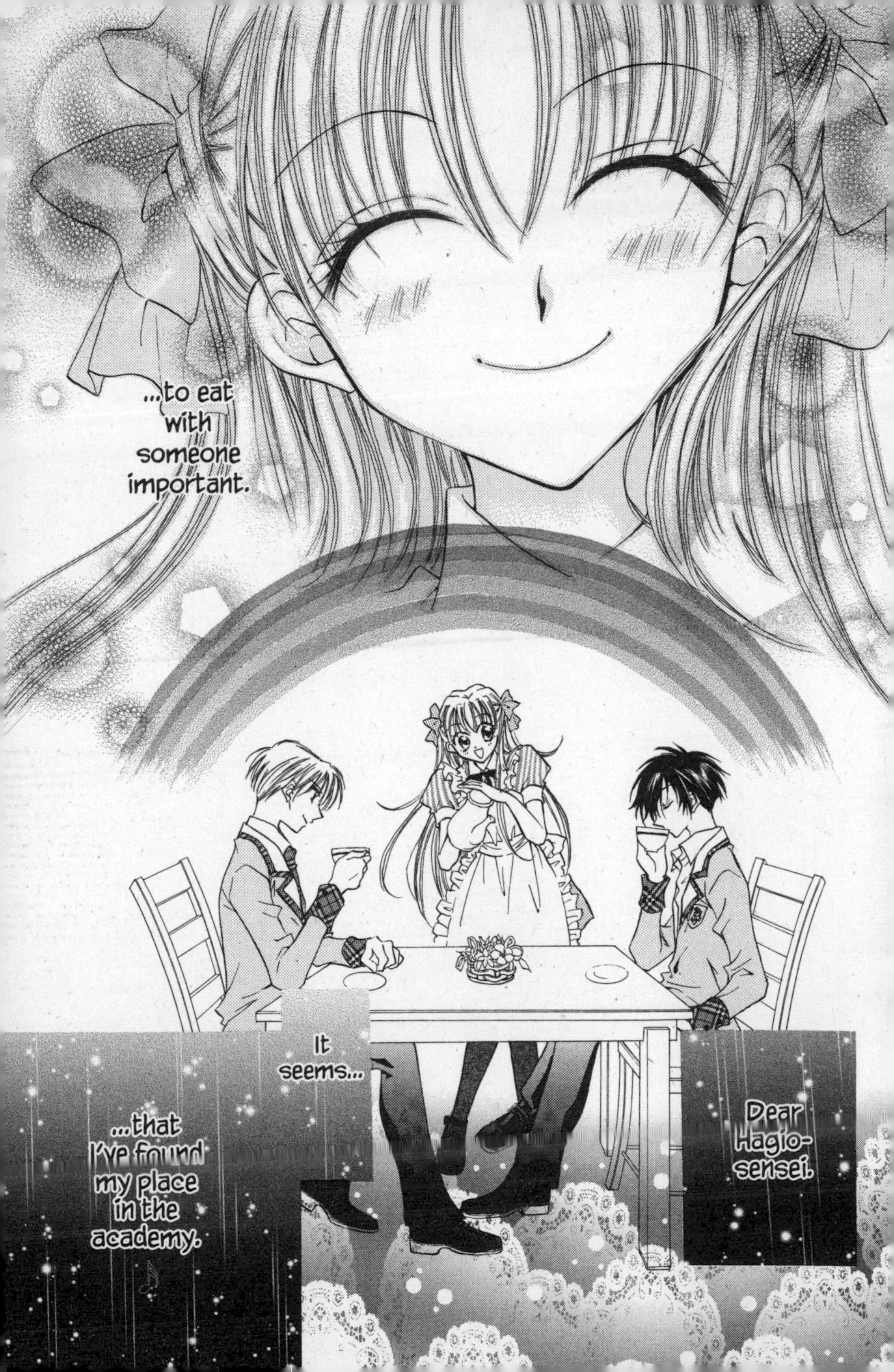
...to eat with someone important.
Dear Hagio-sensei.
It seems...
...that I've found my place in the academy.

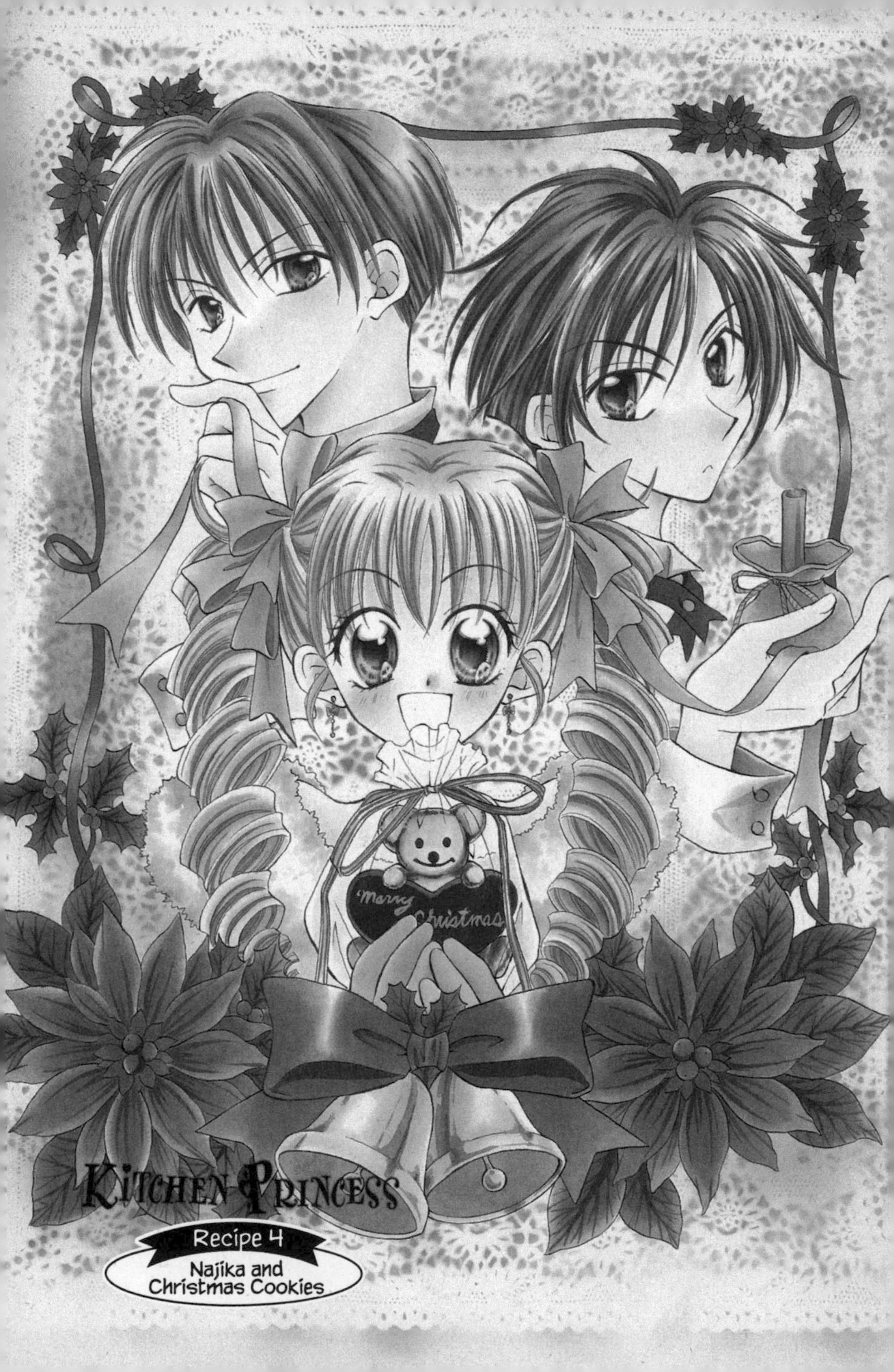
Merry Christmas
KITCHEN PRINCESS
Recipe 4
Najika and Christmas Cookies

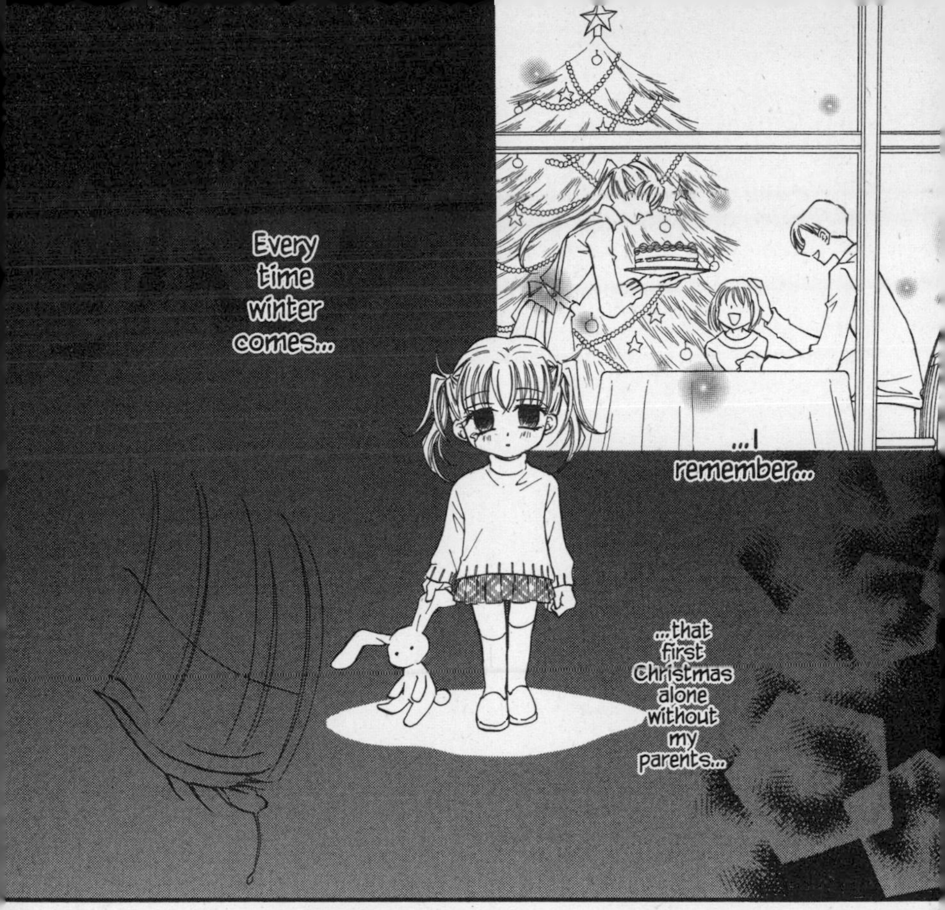
Every time winter comes...
...I remember...
...that first Christmas alone without my parents...

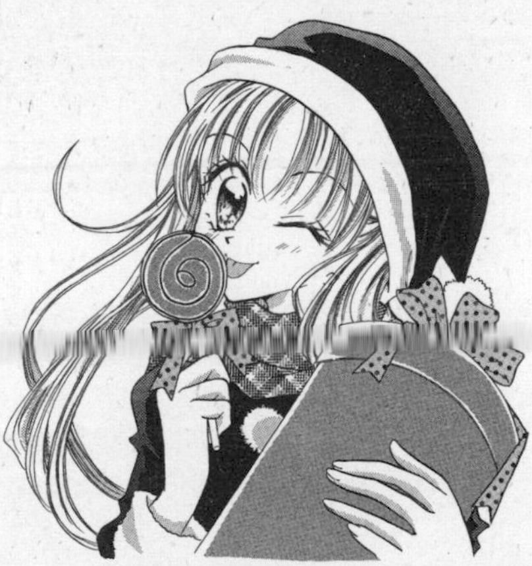

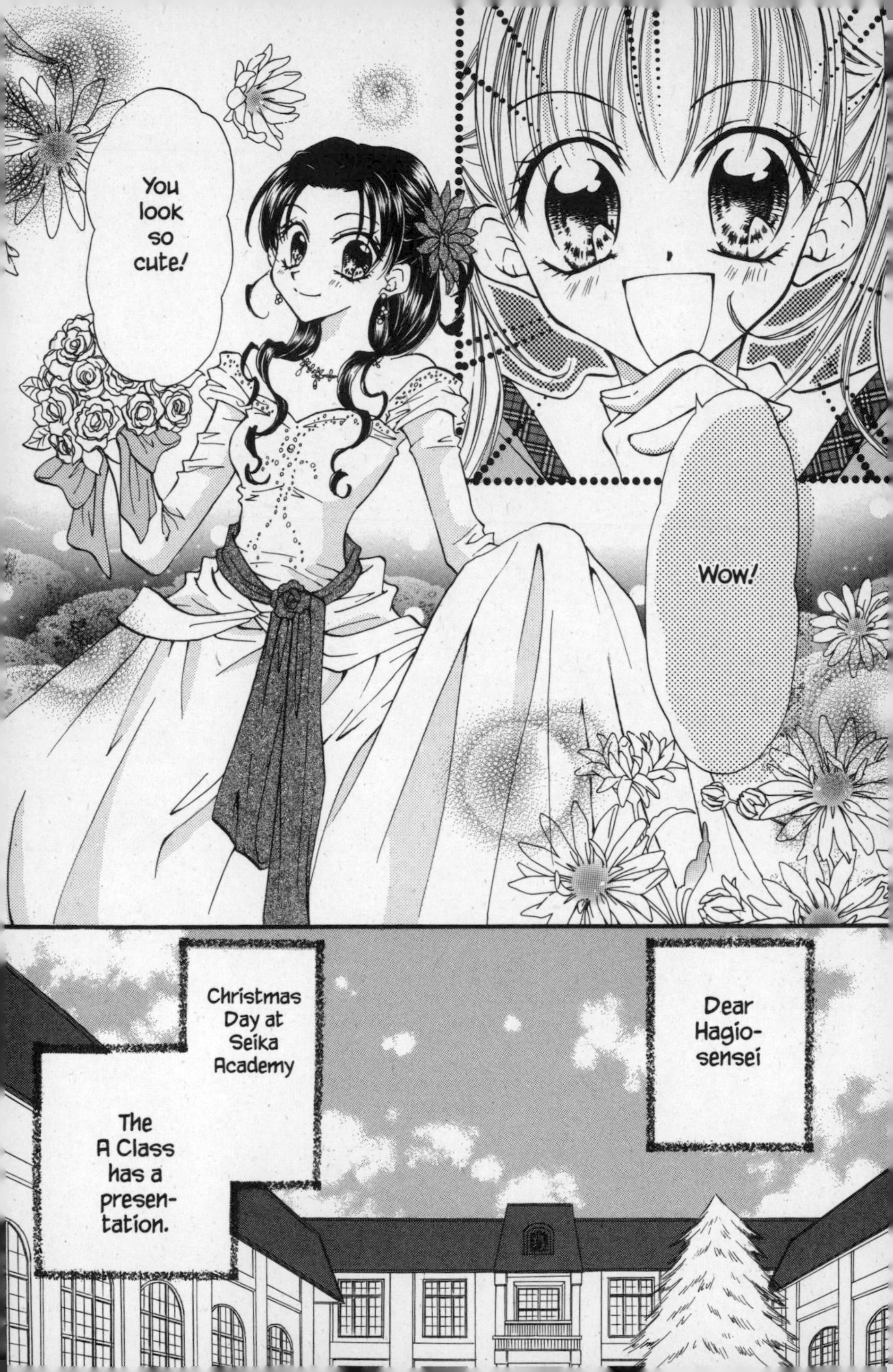
Wow!
You look so cute!
Dear Hagio-sensei
Christmas Day at Seika Academy
The A Class has a presentation.

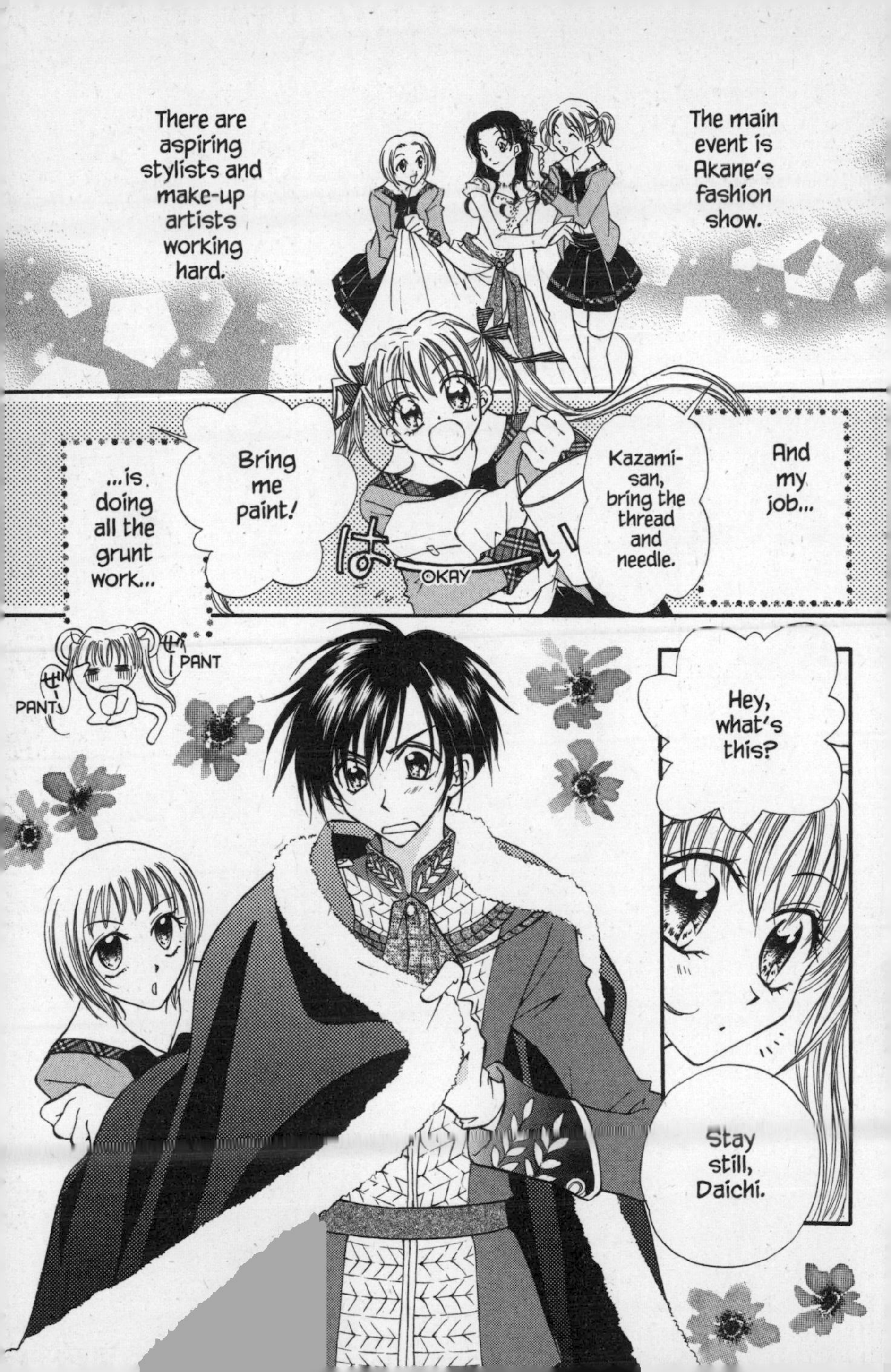
The main event is Akane's fashion show.
There are aspiring stylists and make-up artists working hard.
And my job...
Kazami-san, bring the thread and needle.
OKAY
Bring me paint!
...is doing all the grunt work...
Hey, what's this?
Stay still, Daichi.
PANT
PANT

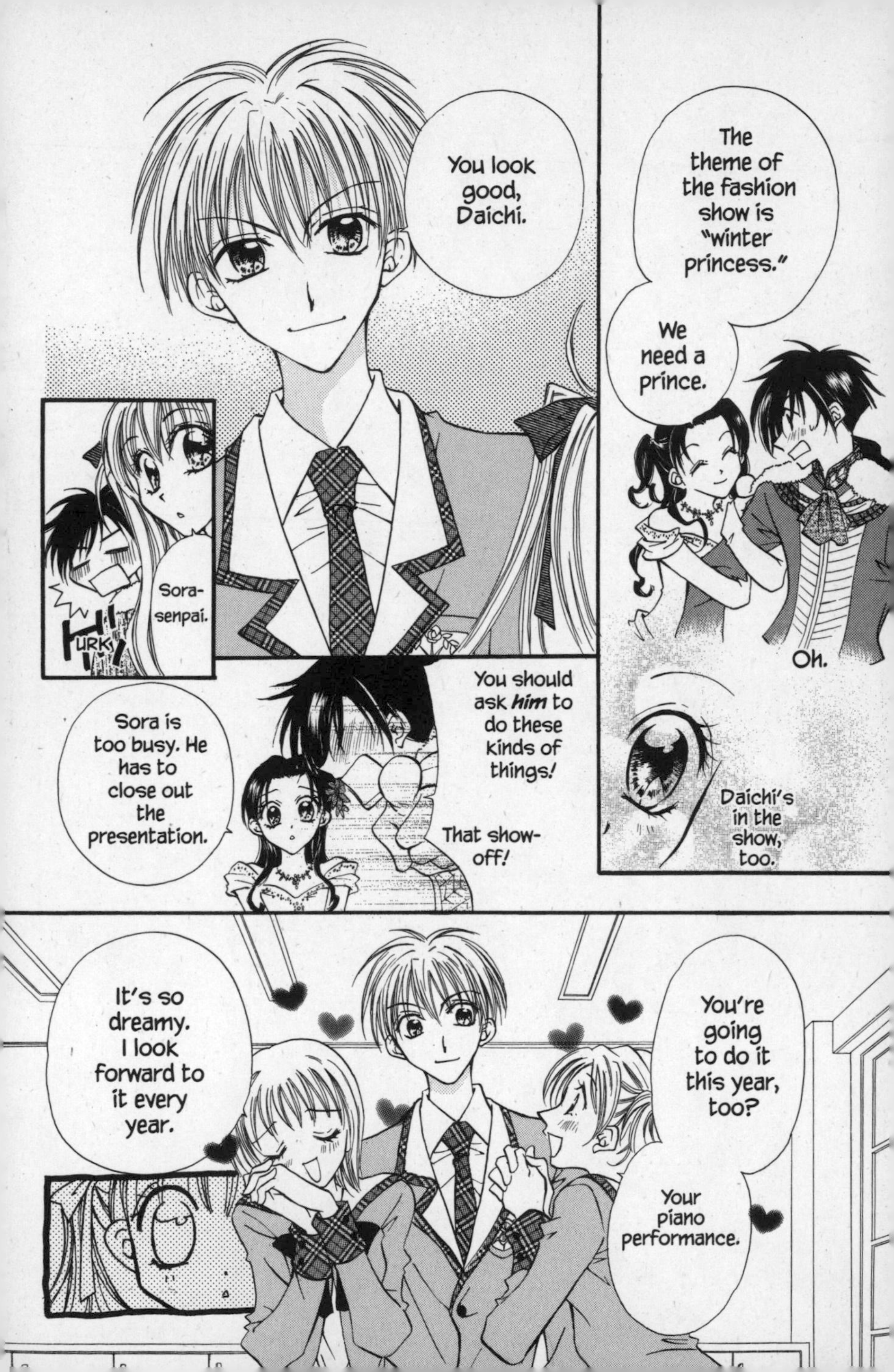
The theme of the fashion show is "winter princess."
We need a prince.
Oh.
You look good, Daichi.
Sora-senpai.
HURK
Daichi's in the show, too.
You should ask *him* to do these kinds of things!
That show-off!
Sora is too busy. He has to close out the presentation.
You're going to do it this year, too?
Your piano performance.
It's so dreamy. I look forward to it every year.

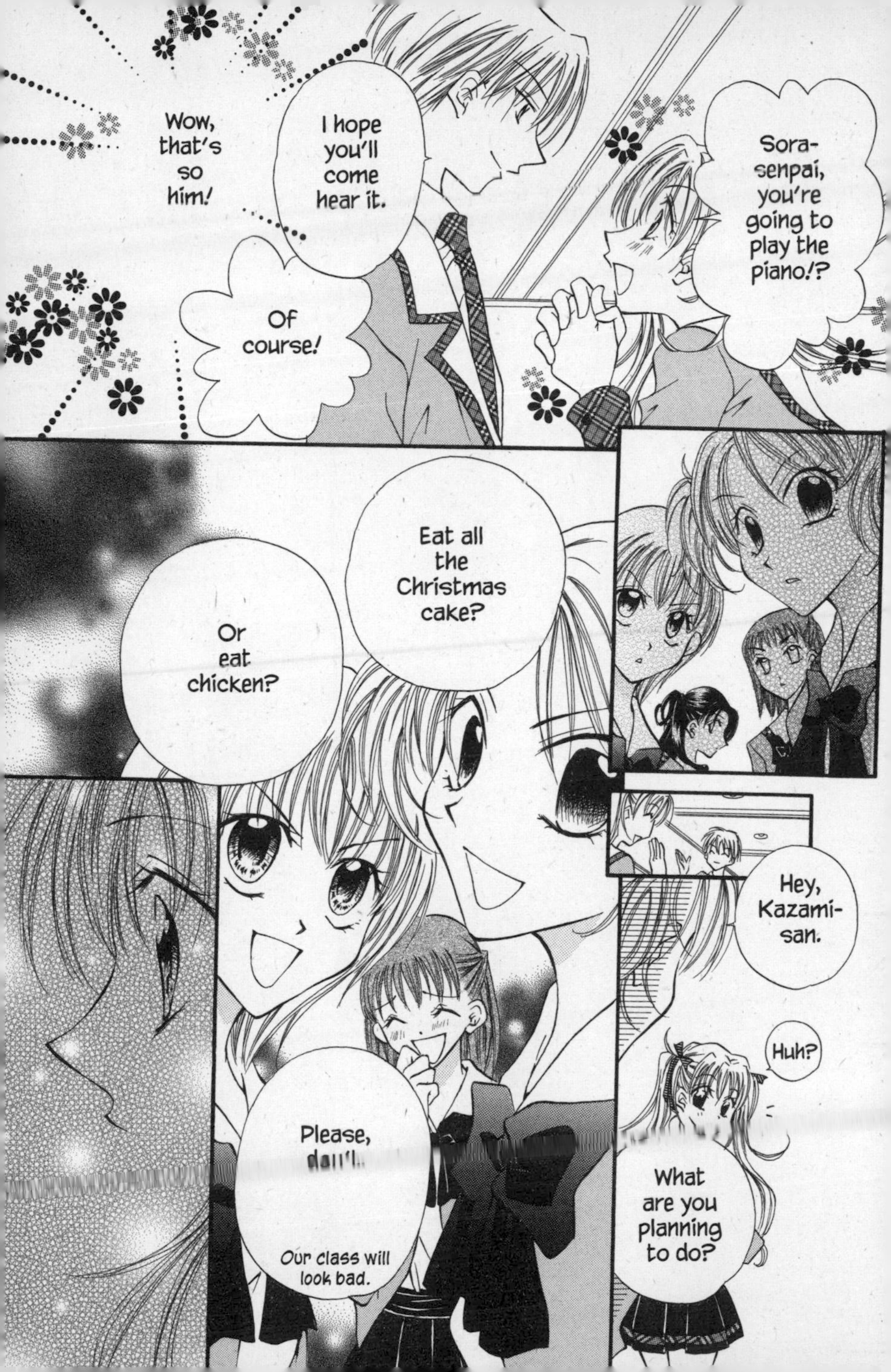
Sora-senpai, you're going to play the piano!?
I hope you'll come hear it.
Of course!
Wow, that's so him!
Hey, Kazami-san.
Huh?
What are you planning to do?
Eat all the Christmas cake?
Or eat chicken?
Please, don't.
Our class will look bad.

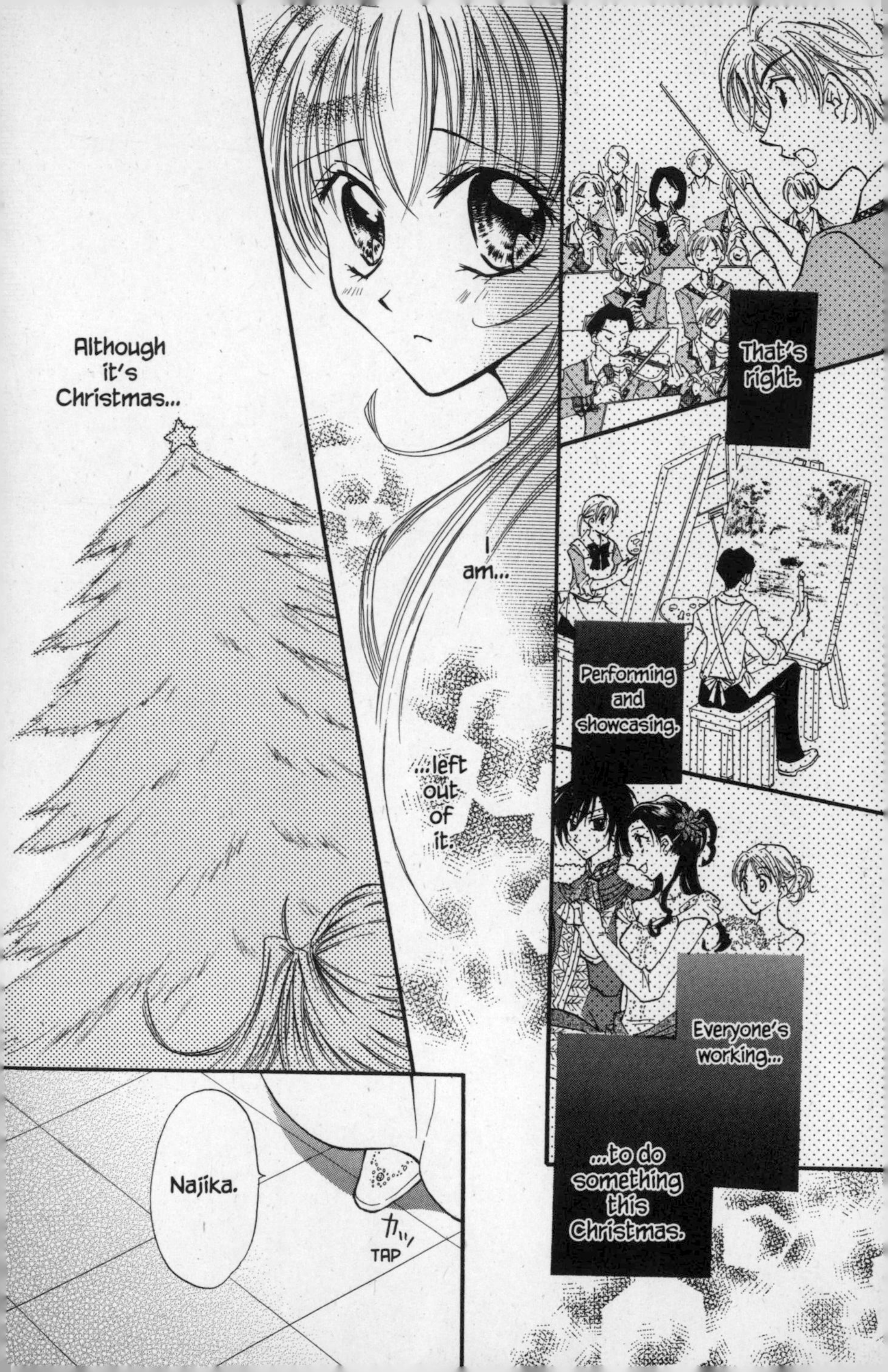
That's right.
Performing and showcasing.
Everyone's working...
...to do something this Christmas.
Although it's Christmas...
I am...
...left out of it.
Najika.
カッ
TAP

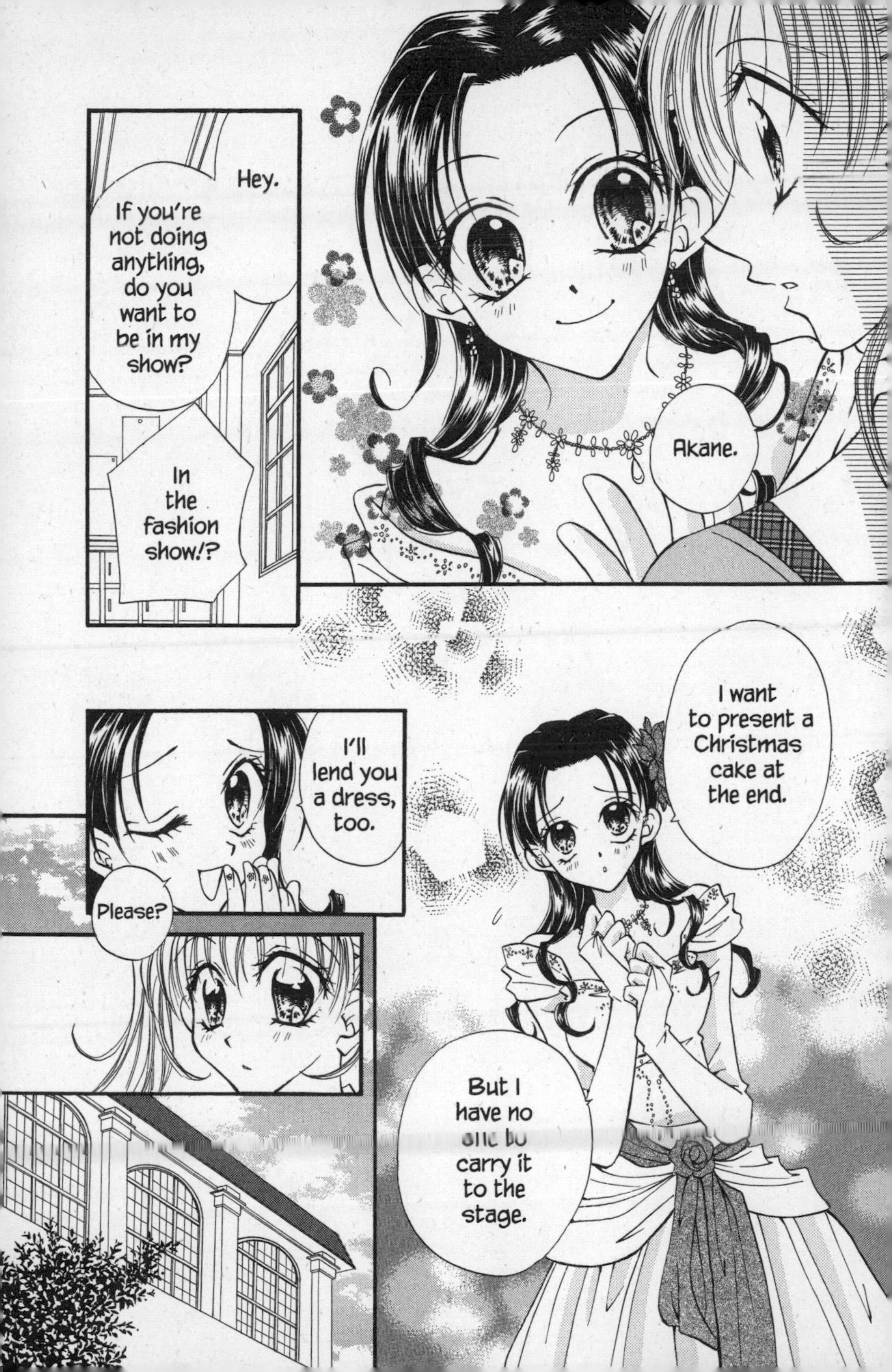
Akane.
Hey.
If you're not doing anything, do you want to be in my show?
In the fashion show!?
I want to present a Christmas cake at the end.
But I have no one to carry it to the stage.
I'll lend you a dress, too.
Please?

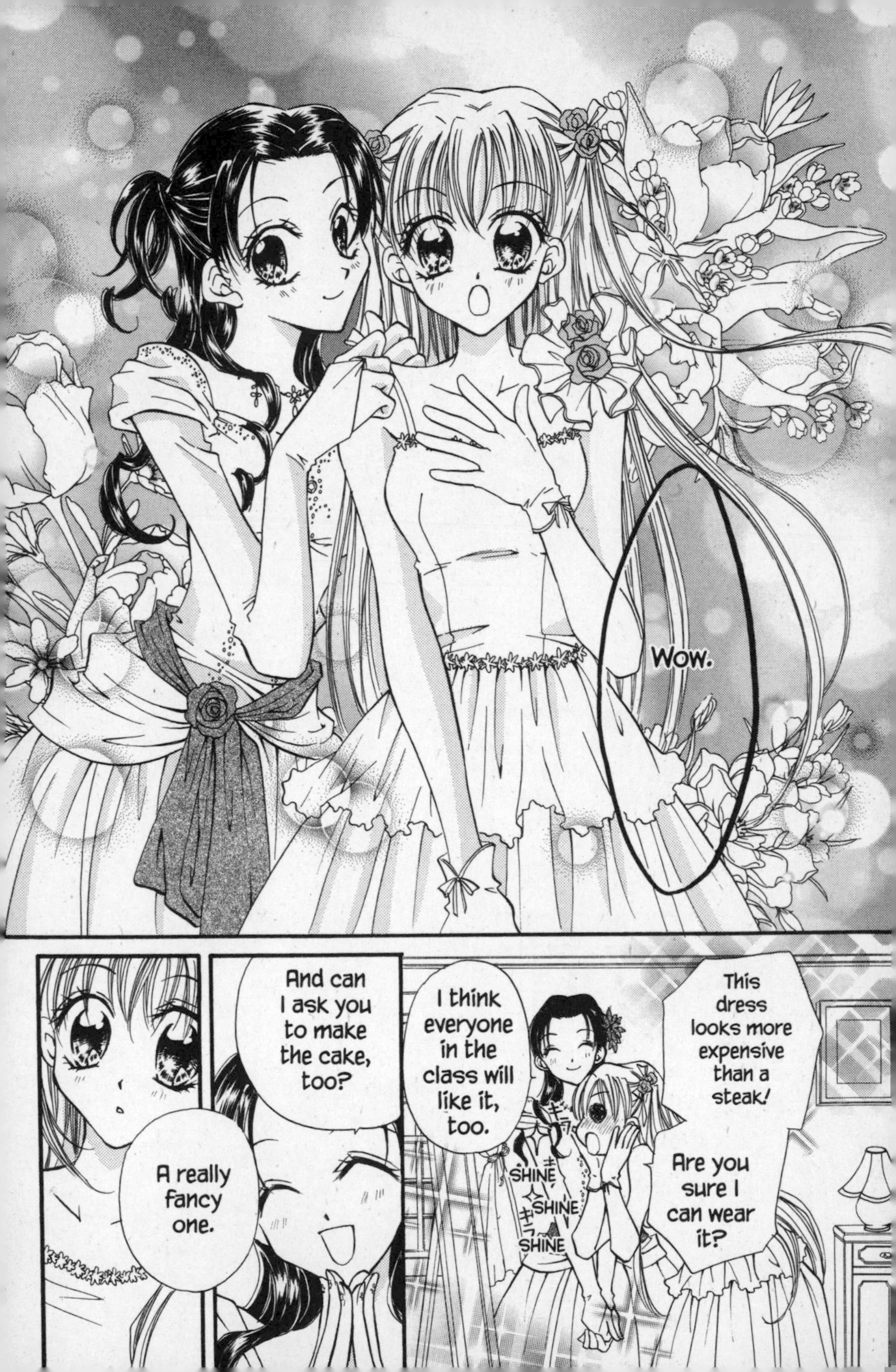

Wow.
This dress looks more expensive than a steak!
Are you sure I can wear it?
SHINE
SHINE
SHINE
I think everyone in the class will like it, too.
And can I ask you to make the cake, too?
A really fancy one.

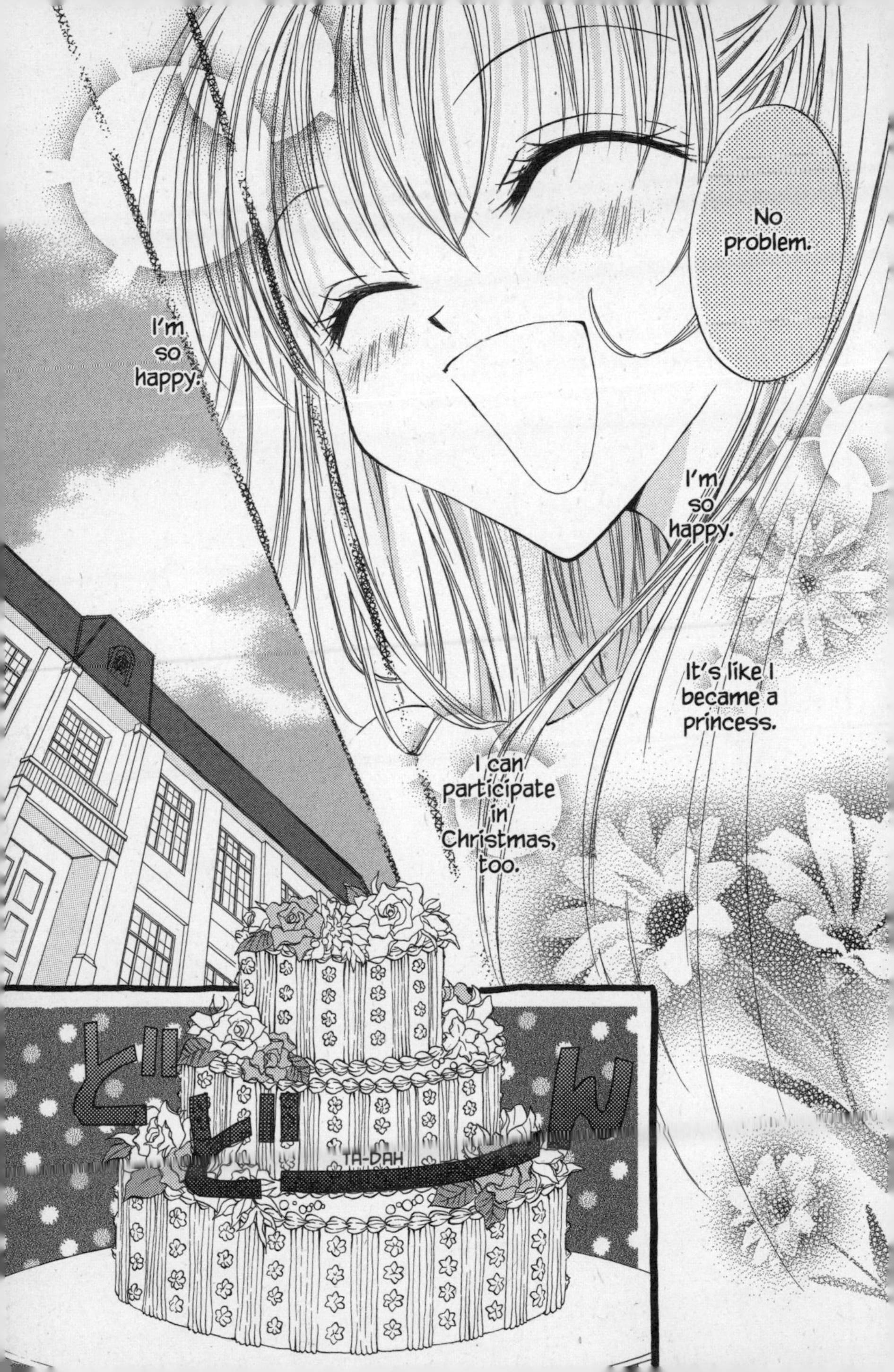
No problem.
I'm so happy.
I'm so happy.
It's like I became a princess.
I can participate in Christmas, too.
どどーん
TA-DAH

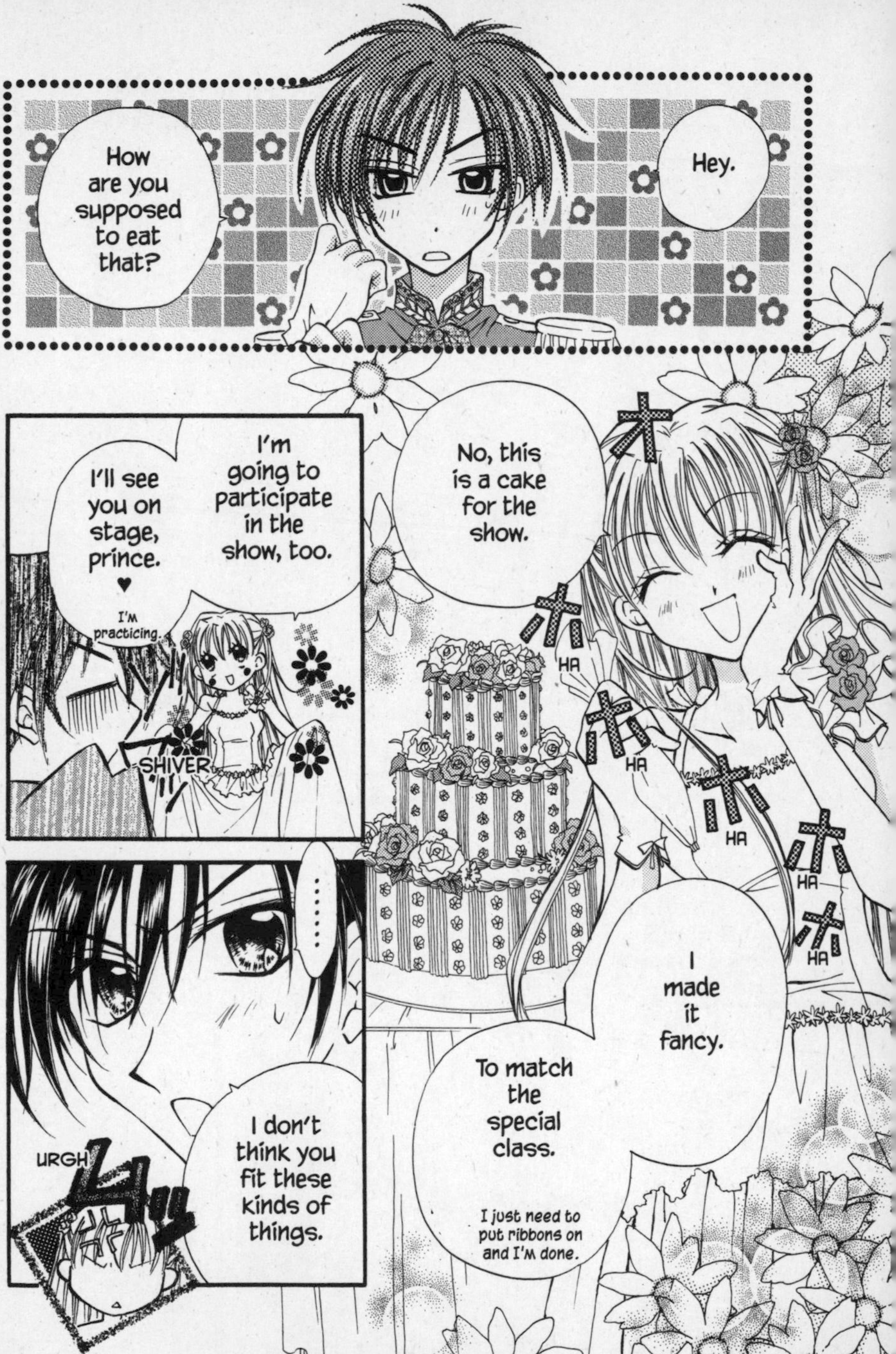
Hey.
How are you supposed to eat that?
No, this is a cake for the show.
HA HA HA HA HA
I made it fancy.
To match the special class.
I just need to put ribbons on and I'm done.
I'm going to participate in the show, too.
I'll see you on stage, prince. ♥
I'm practicing.
SHIVER
......
I don't think you fit these kinds of things.
URGH

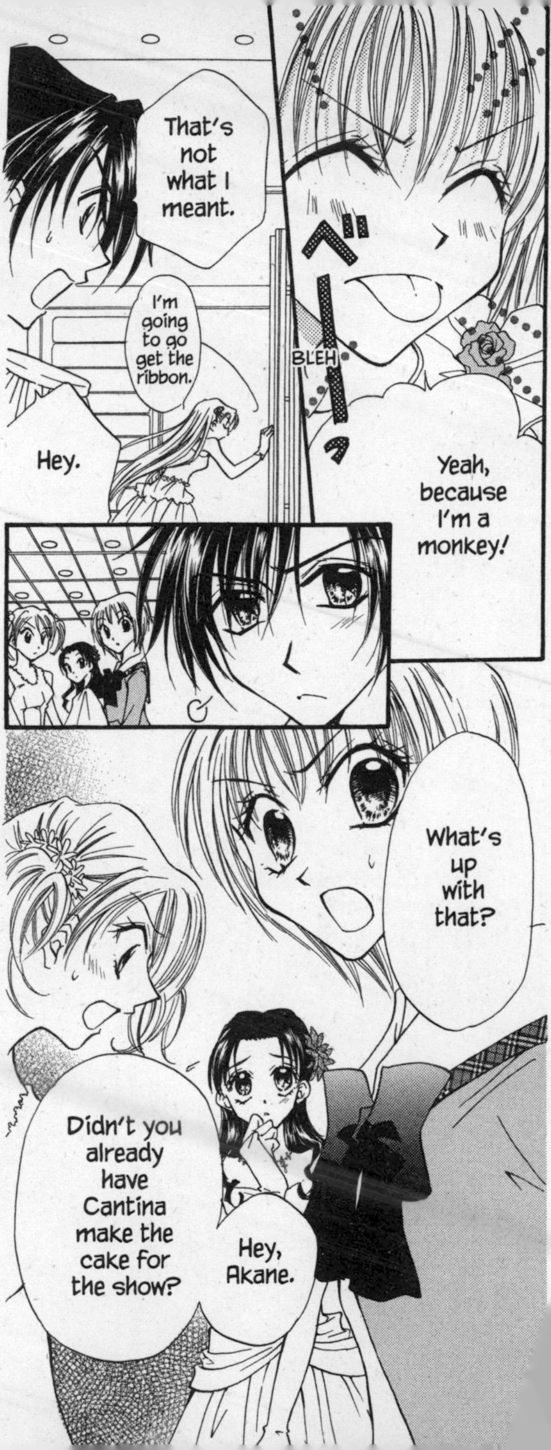
BLEH
Yeah, because I'm a monkey!
That's not what I meant.
I'm going to go get the ribbon.
Hey.
What's up with that?
Hey, Akane.
Didn't you already have Cantina make the cake for the show?

● All You Can Eat Buffet

I'm actually not good with this. I'm lazy, so I don't like to get up and go get the food. So what ends up happening is that I just sit around... I guess I'm a good customer for the restaurant!?

● A Popular Store with a Line Outside

The longest I waited to eat something was two and a half hours... It was at DisneySea, the curry buffet. When you get closer to the entrance, you can smell the curry and thirty minutes feels like an hour, and your empty stomach makes you only think of curry. It was torture. I was supposed to receive a pin, but by the time I got to my seat, I was so involved in eating that I lost the voucher...

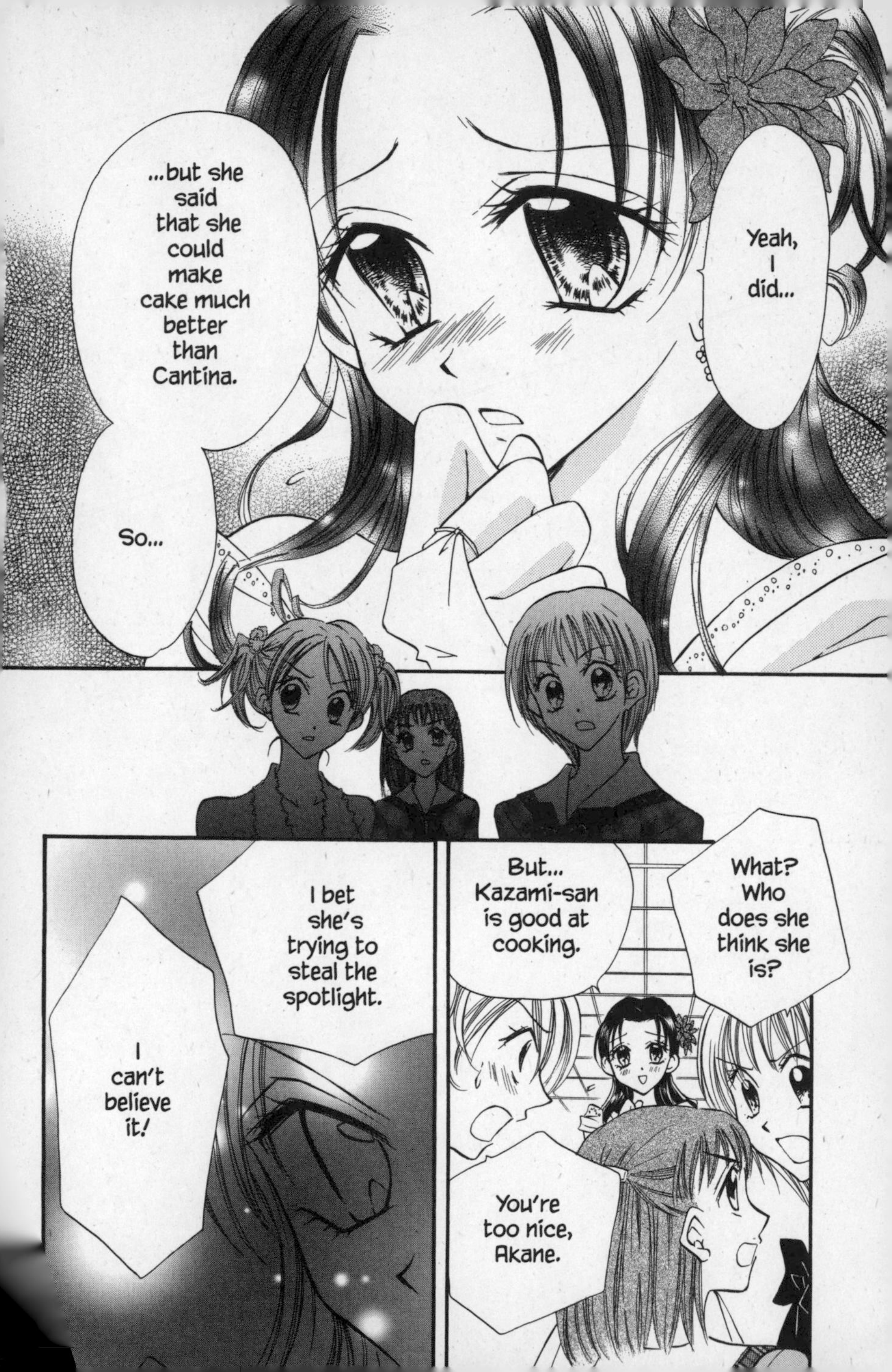
Yeah, I did...
...but she said that she could make cake much better than Cantina.
So...
What? Who does she think she is?
But... Kazami-san is good at cooking.
You're too nice, Akane.
I bet she's trying to steal the spotlight.
I can't believe it!

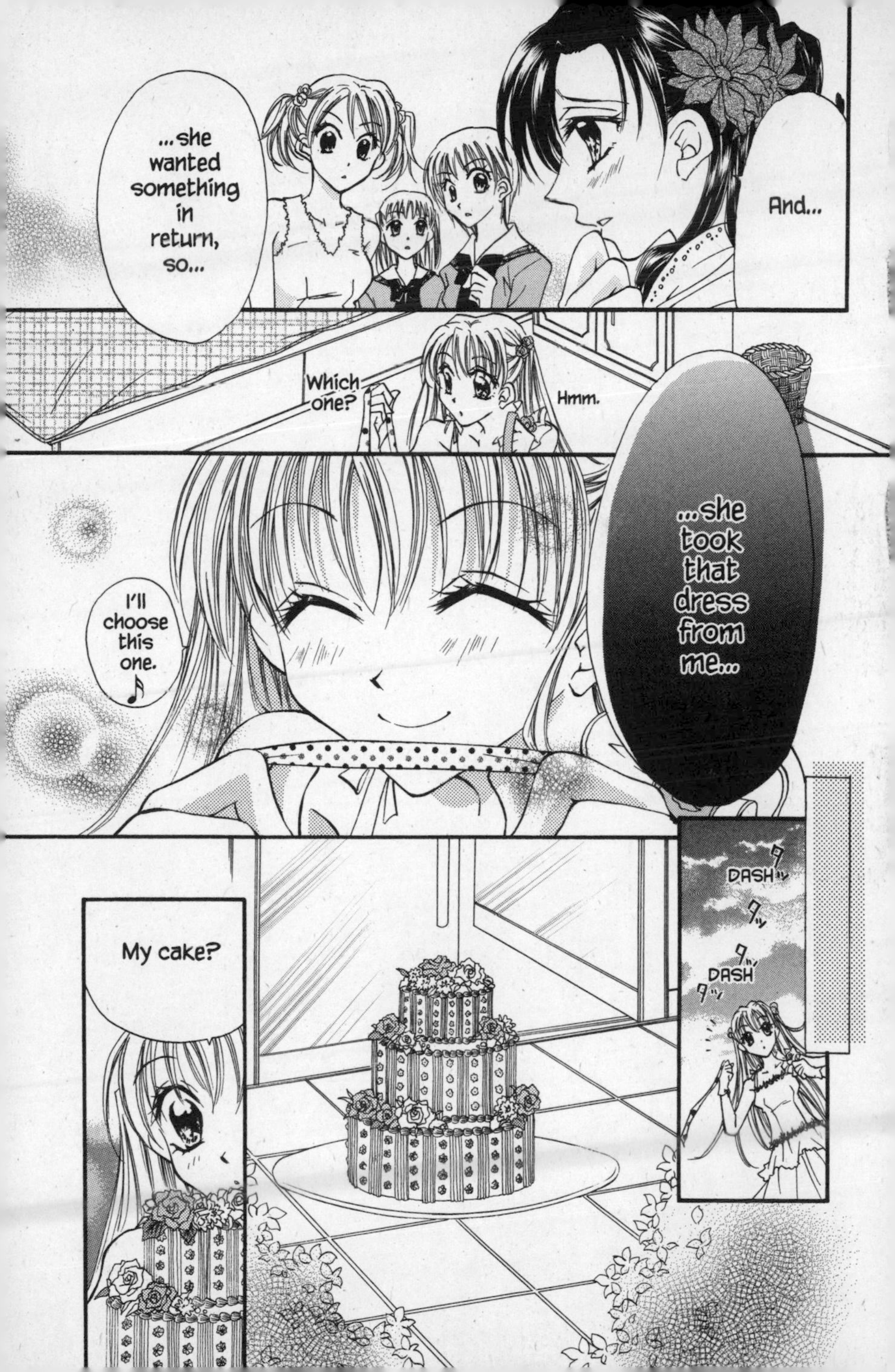
And...
...she wanted something in return, so...
...she took that dress from me...
Hmm.
Which one?
I'll choose this one. ♪
DASH
DASH
My cake?

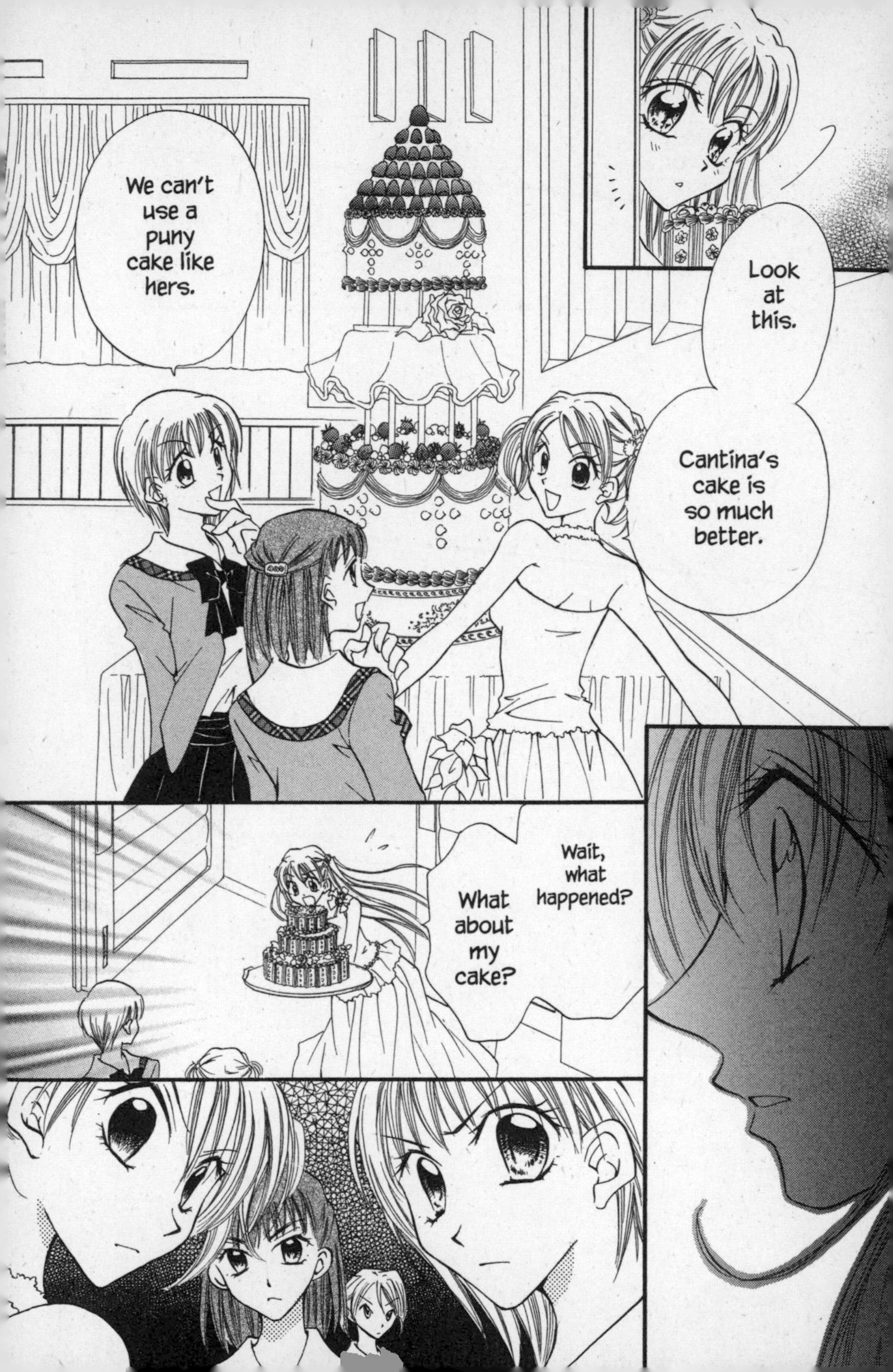
Look at this.
Cantina's cake is so much better.
We can't use a puny cake like hers.
Wait, what happened?
What about my cake?

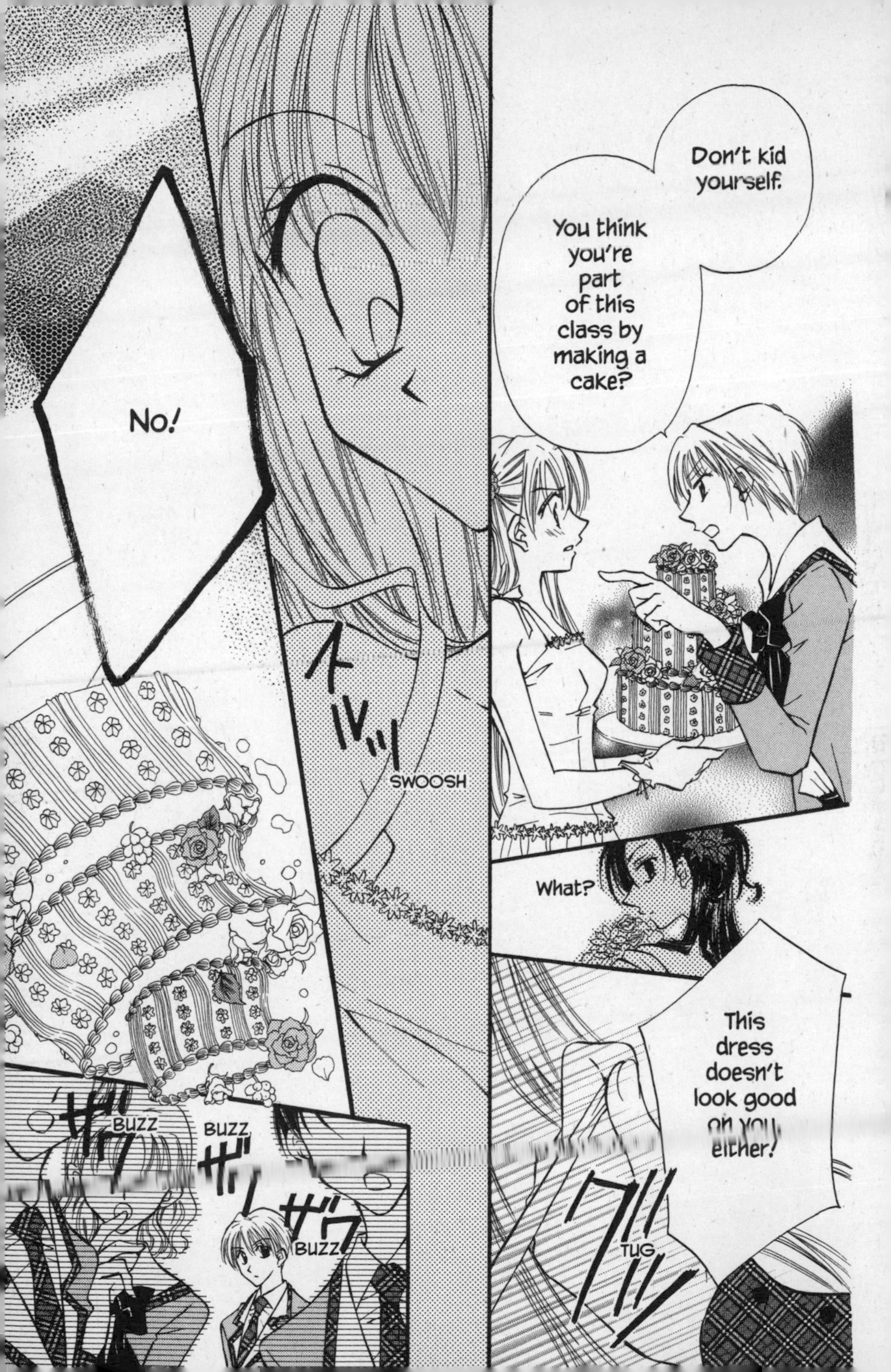

Don't kid yourself.
You think you're part of this class by making a cake?
What?
This dress doesn't look good on you, either!
TUG
No!
SWOOSH
BUZZ
BUZZ
BUZZ

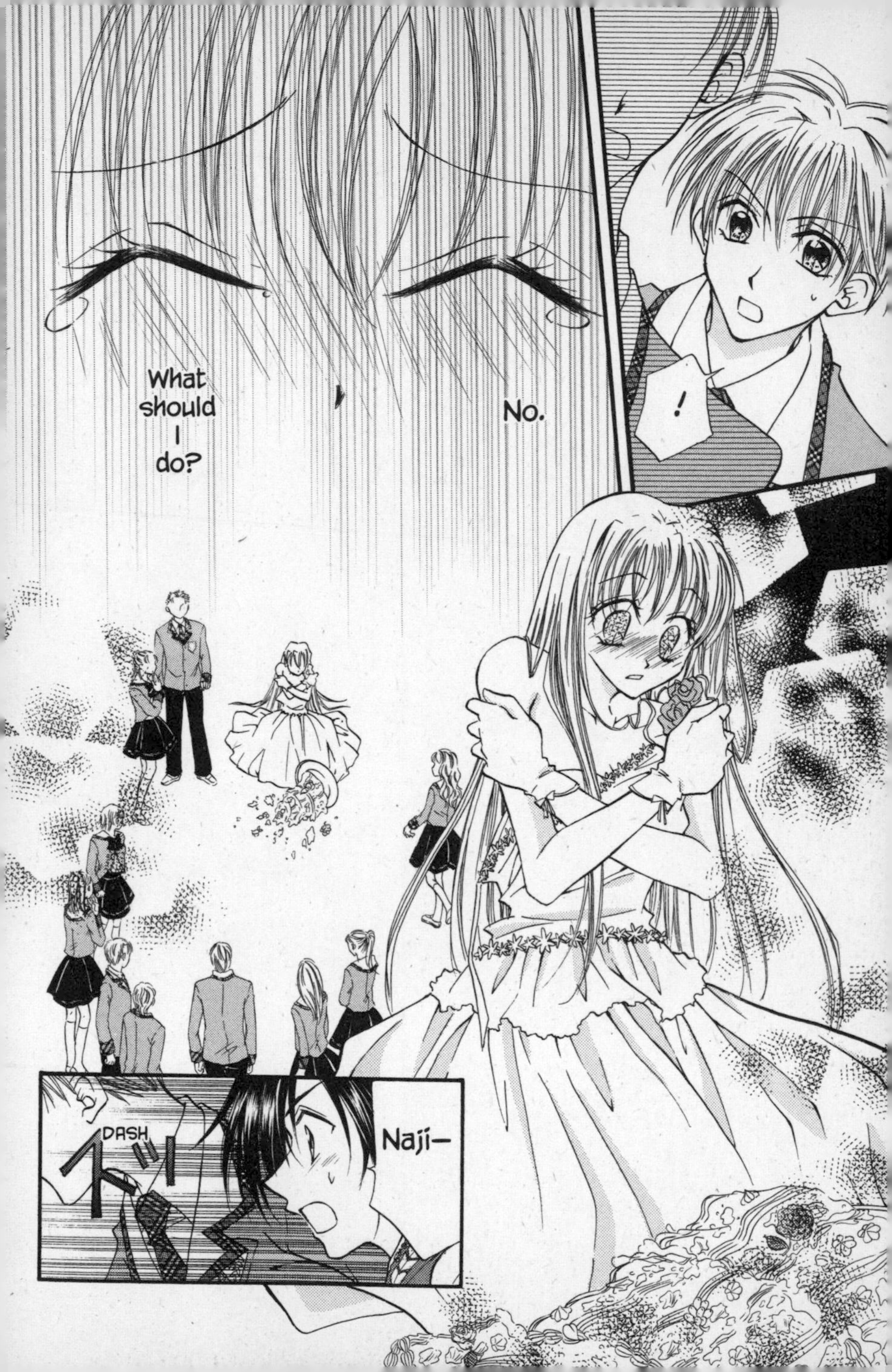

!
No.
What should I do?
Naji—
DASH

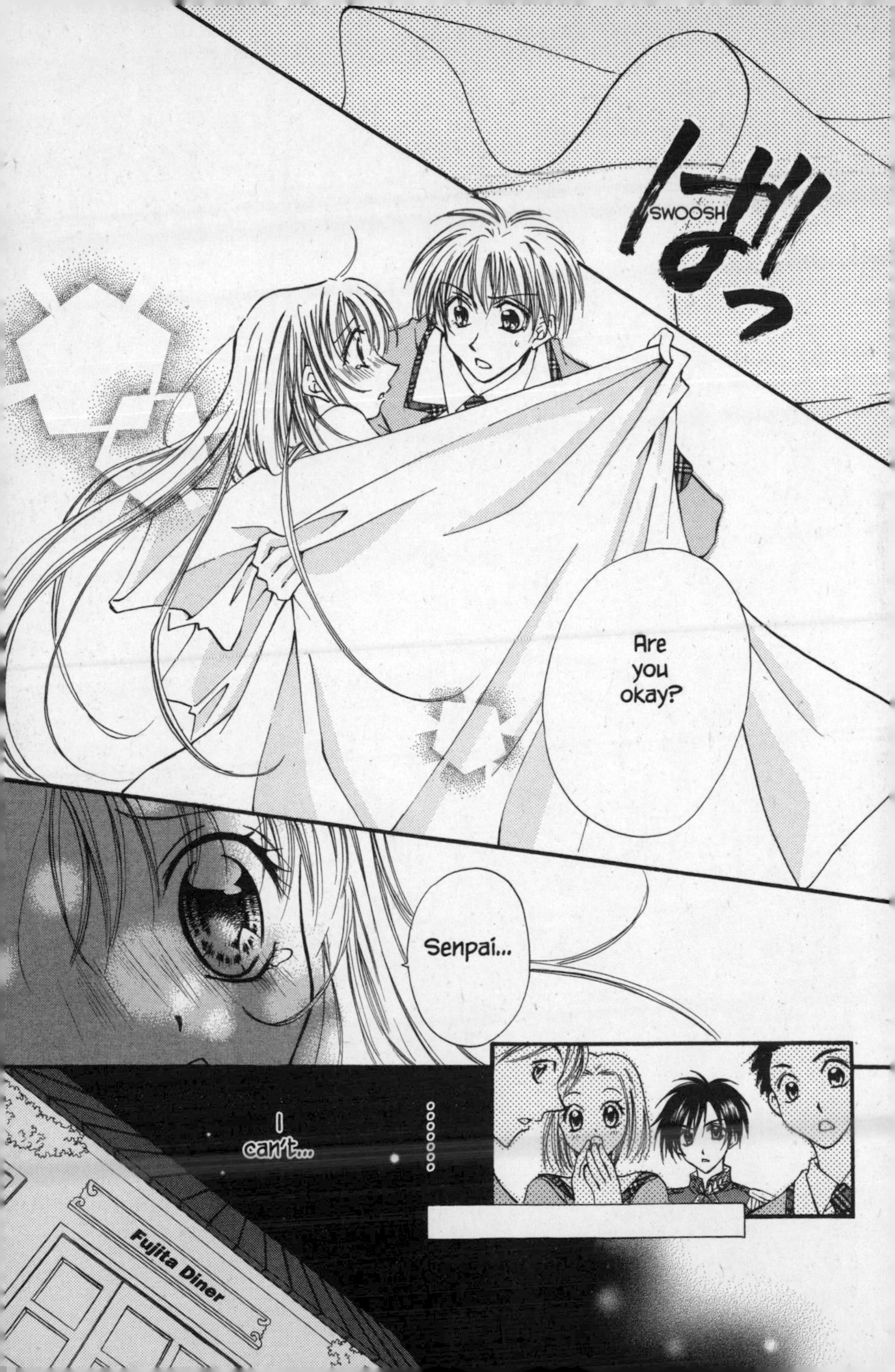
SWOOSH
Are you okay?
Senpai...
ooooooo
I can't...
Fujita Diner

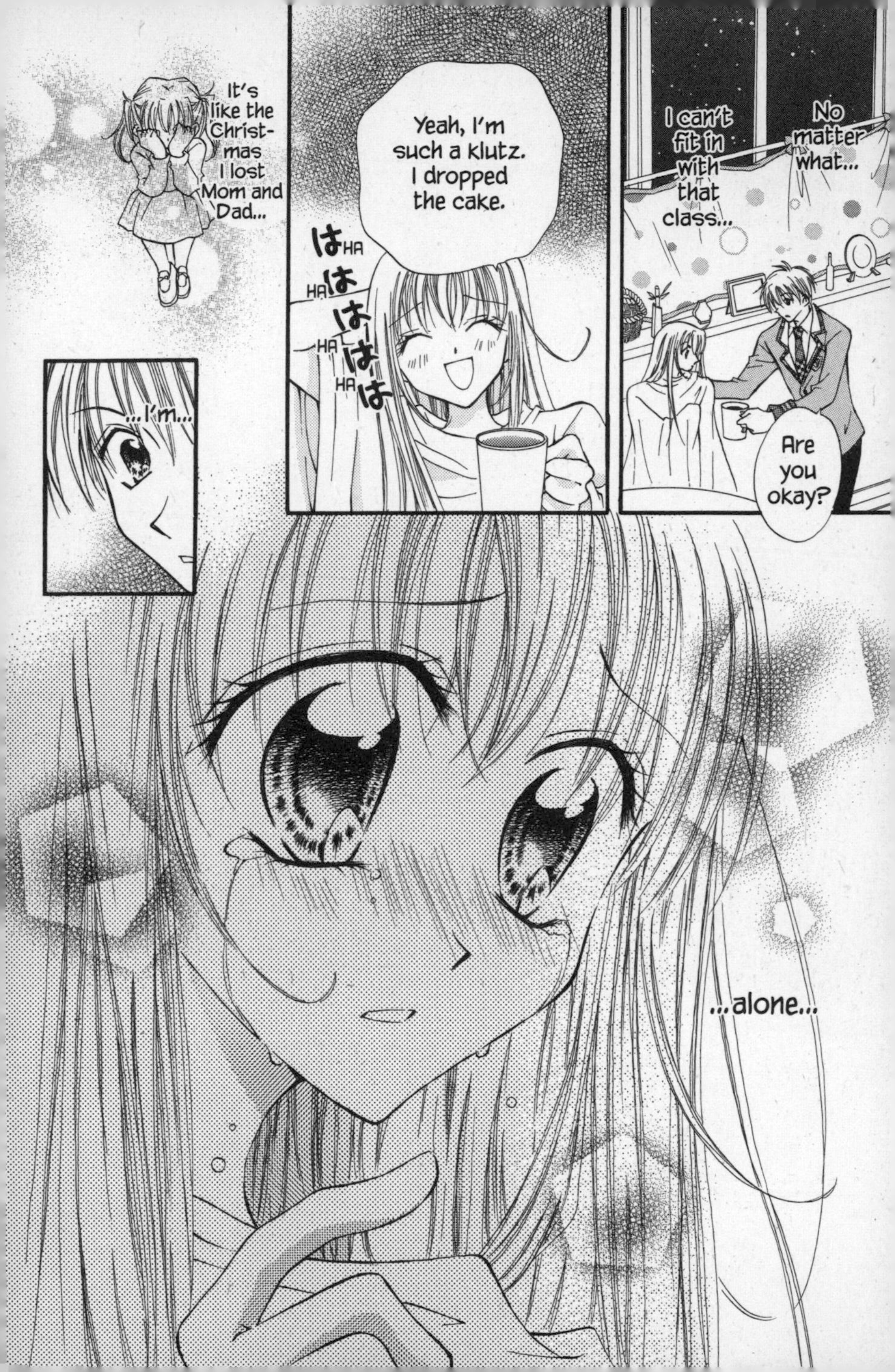
No matter what...
I can't fit in with that class...
Are you okay?
Yeah, I'm such a klutz. I dropped the cake.
は HA
HA は
HA は
HA は
は
It's like the Christmas I lost Mom and Dad...
...I'm...
...alone...

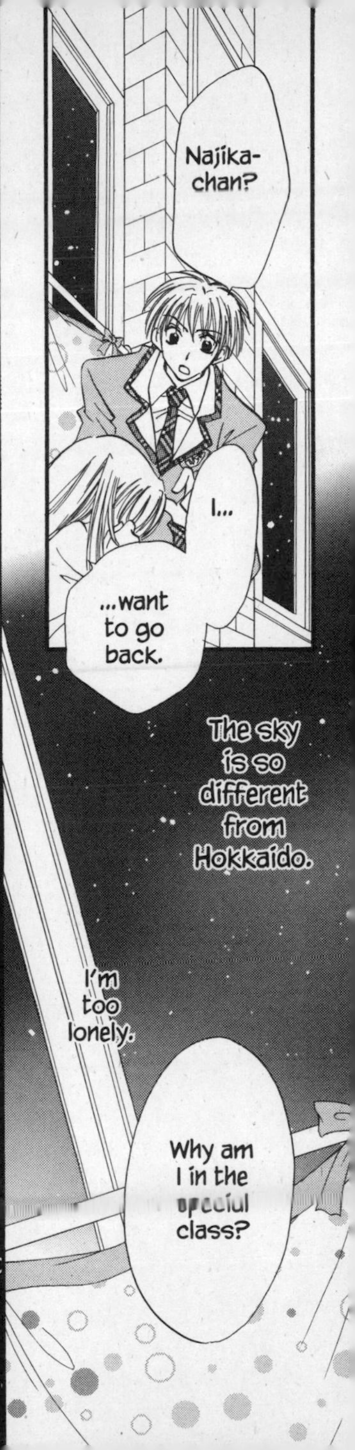
Najika-chan?
I...
...want to go back.
The sky is so different from Hokkaido.
I'm too lonely.
Why am I in the special class?
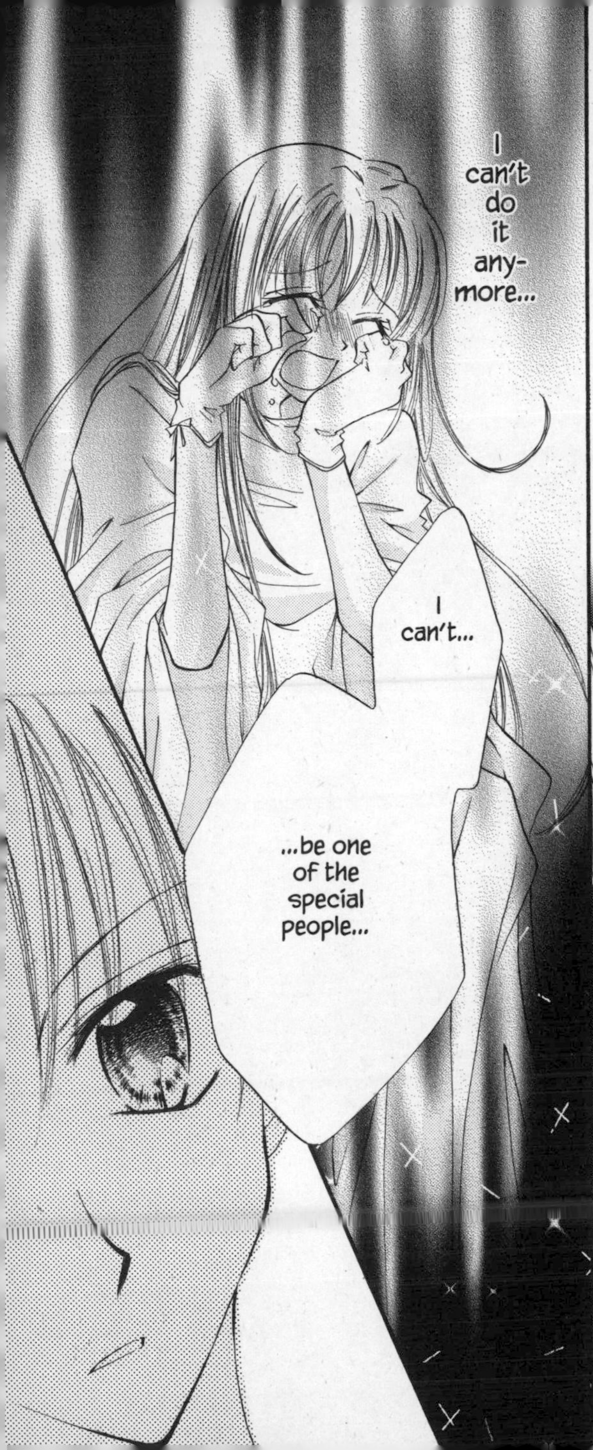
I can't do it anymore...
I can't...
...be one of the special people...

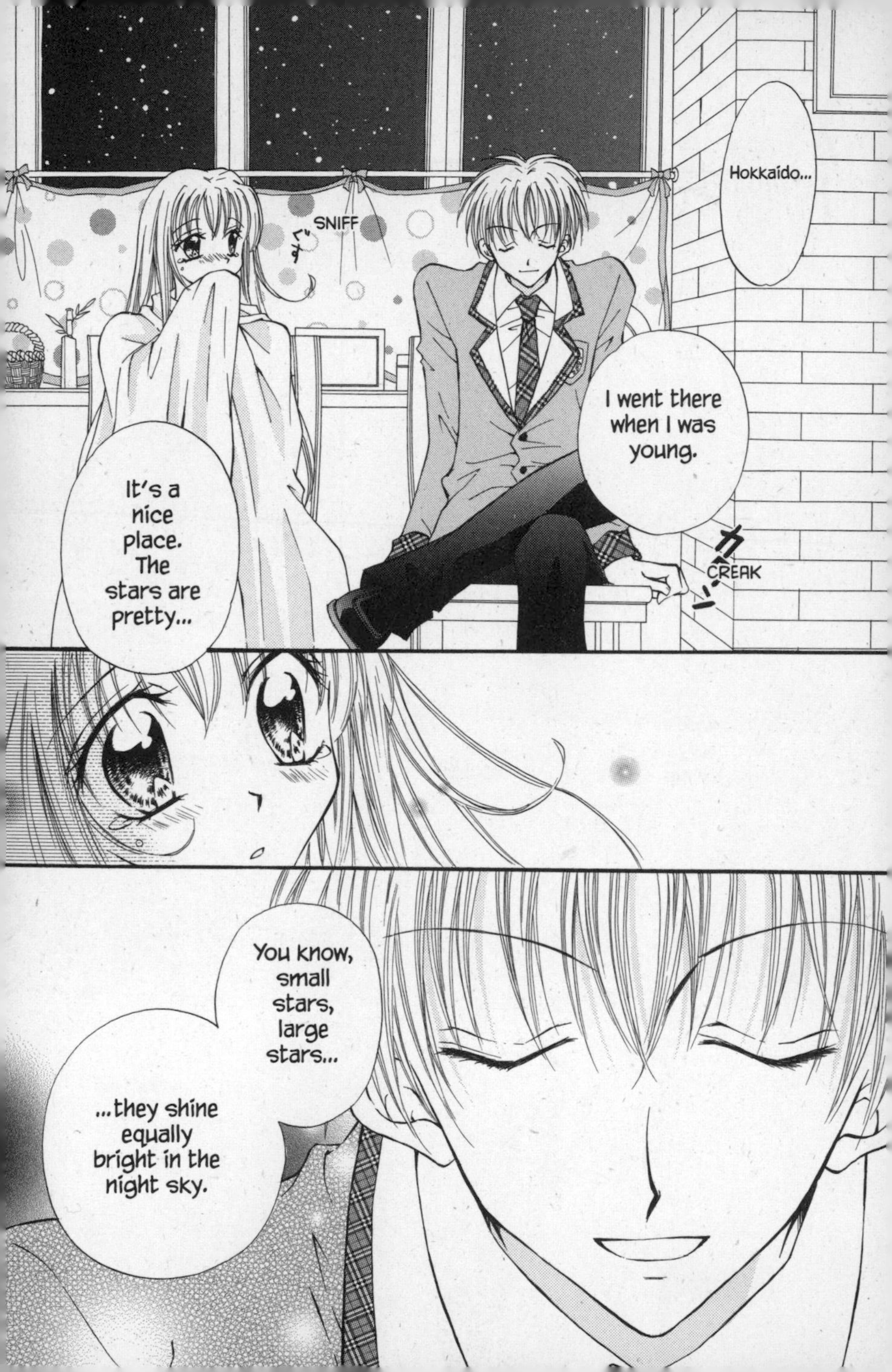
Hokkaido...
I went there when I was young.
SNIFF
CREAK
It's a nice place. The stars are pretty...
You know, small stars, large stars...
...they shine equally bright in the night sky.

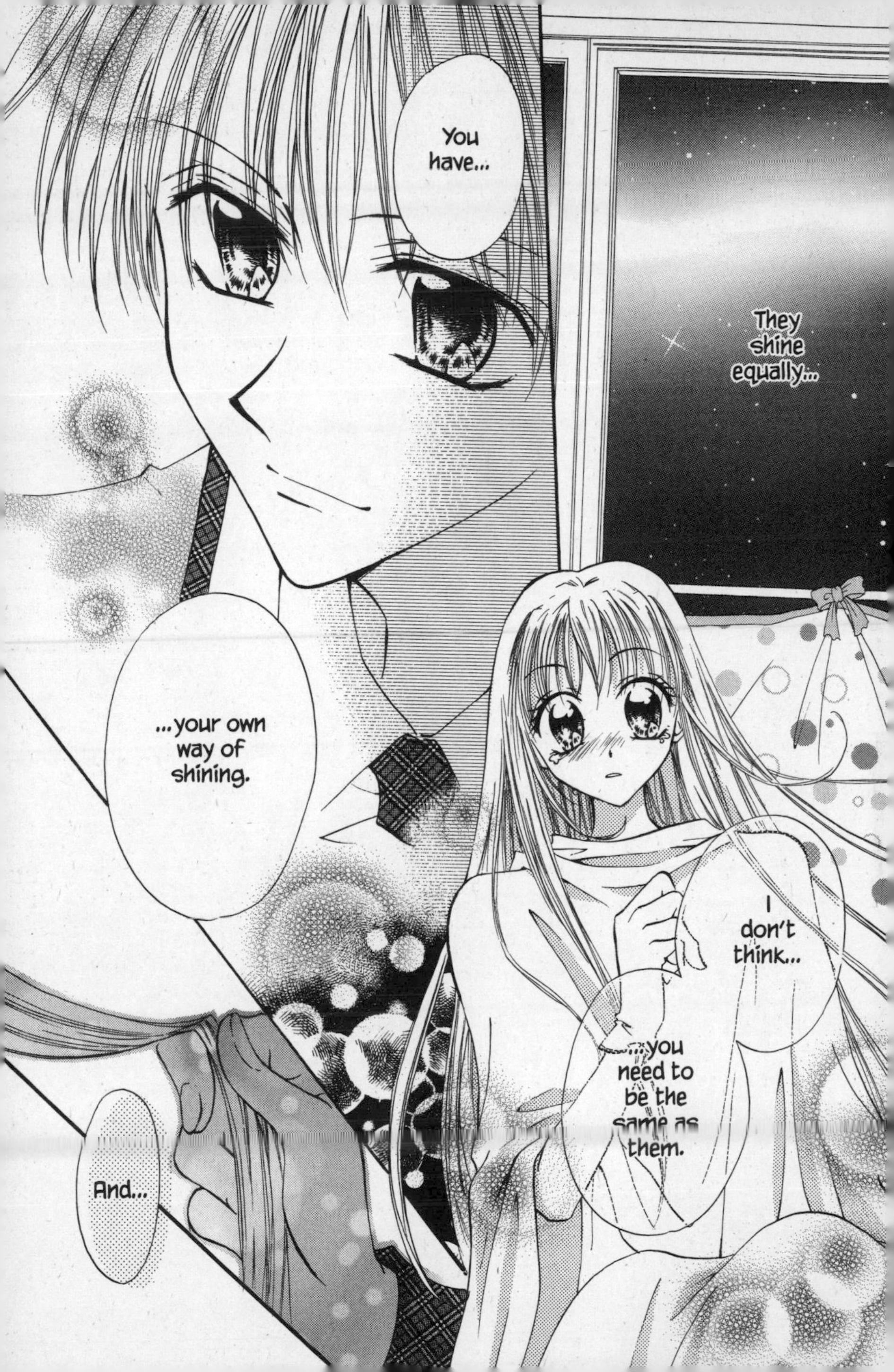
They shine equally...
You have...
...your own way of shining.
I don't think...
...you need to be the same as them.
And...

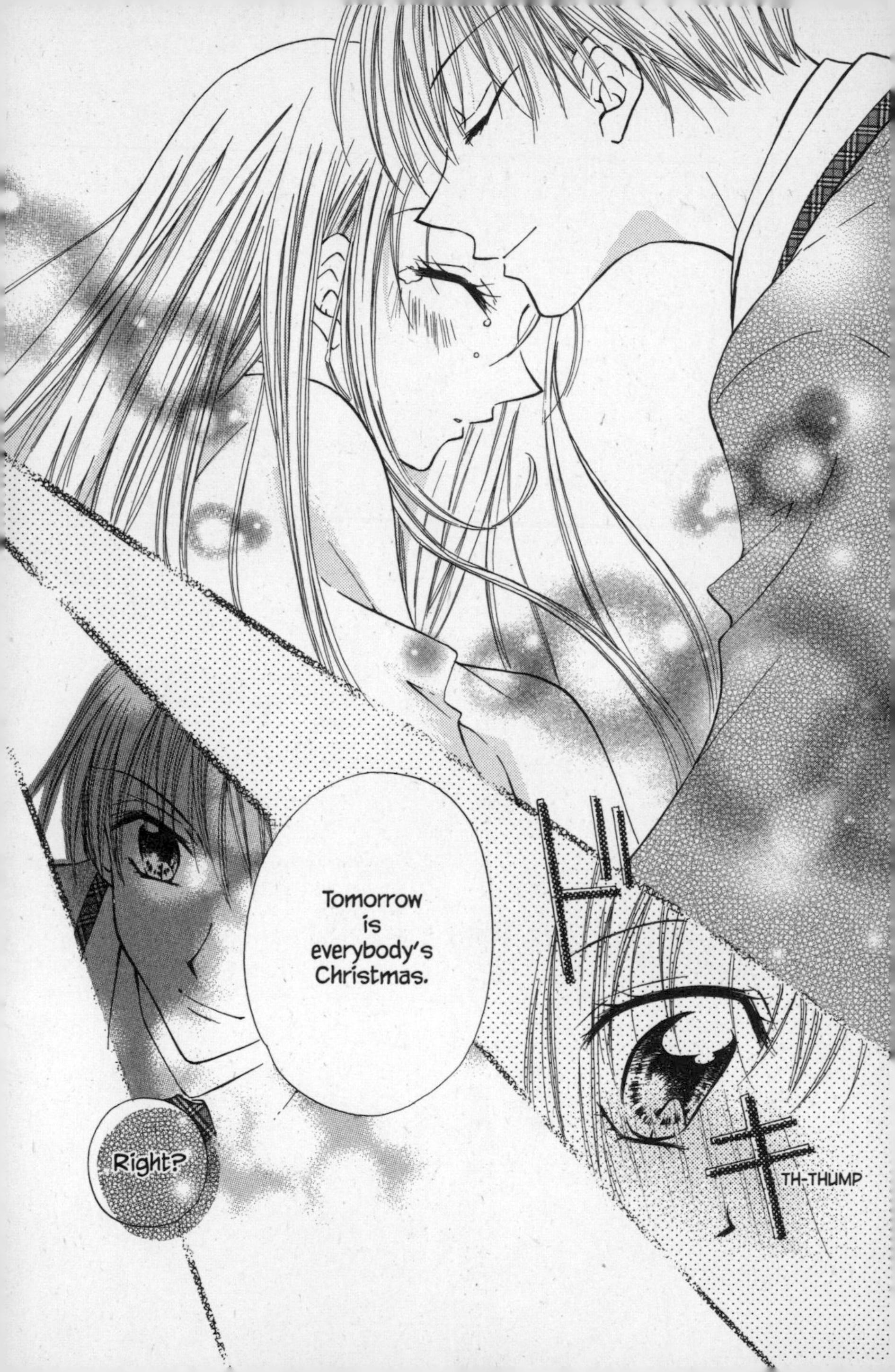
Tomorrow is everybody's Christmas.
TH-THUMP
Right?

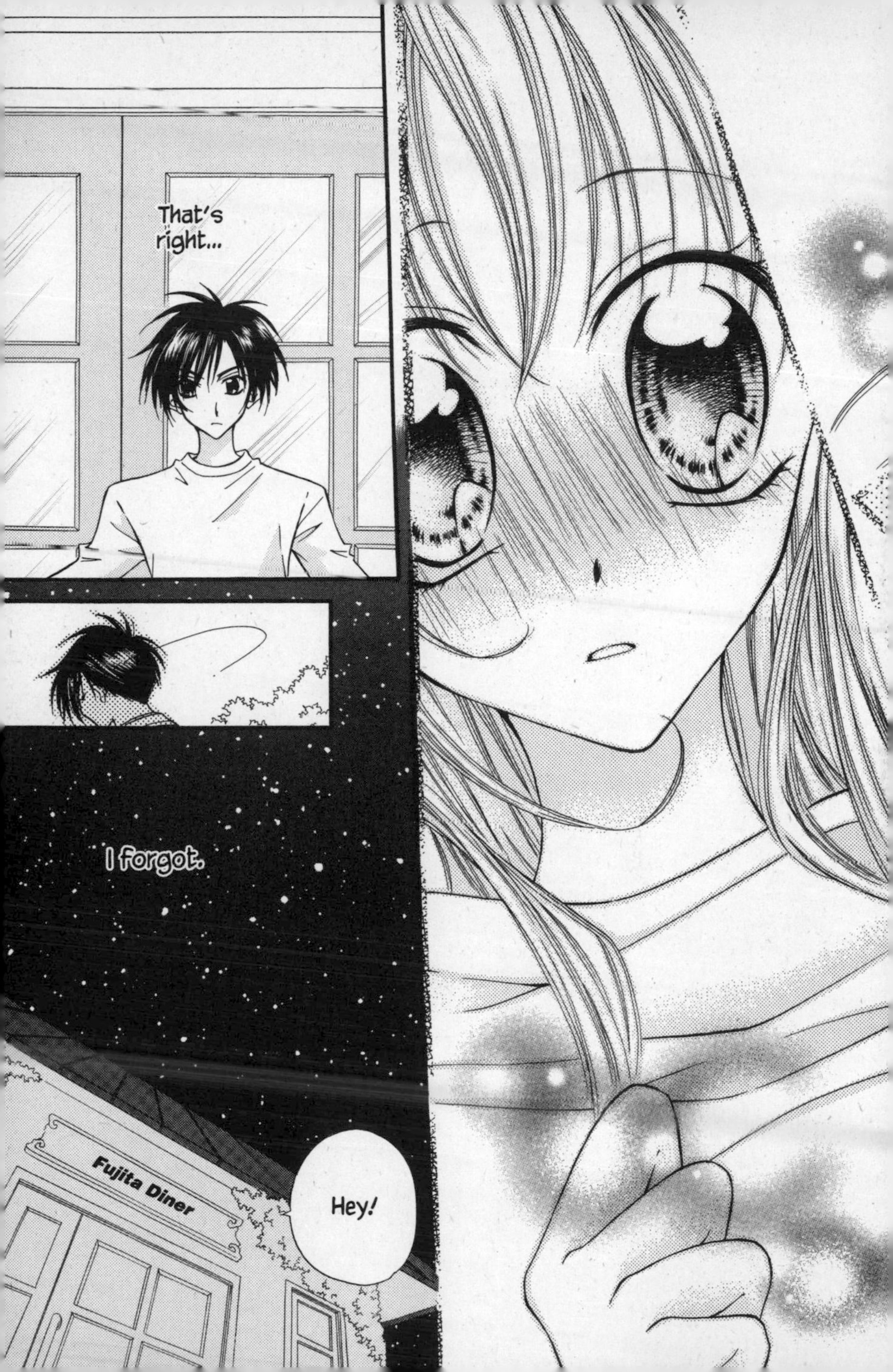
That's right...
I forgot.
Fujita Diner
Hey!

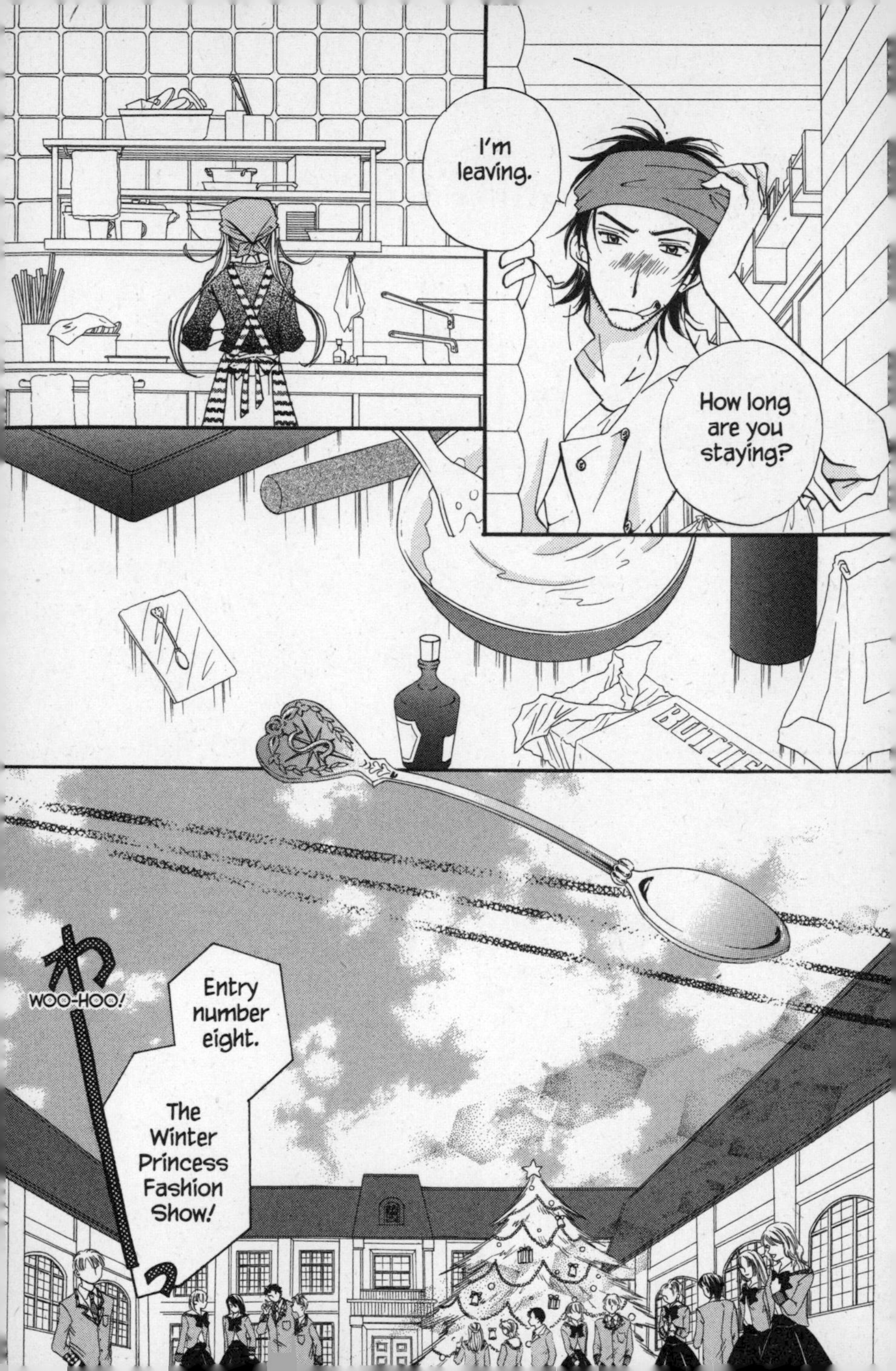
I'm leaving.
How long are you staying?
Entry number eight.
The Winter Princess Fashion Show!
WOO-HOO!

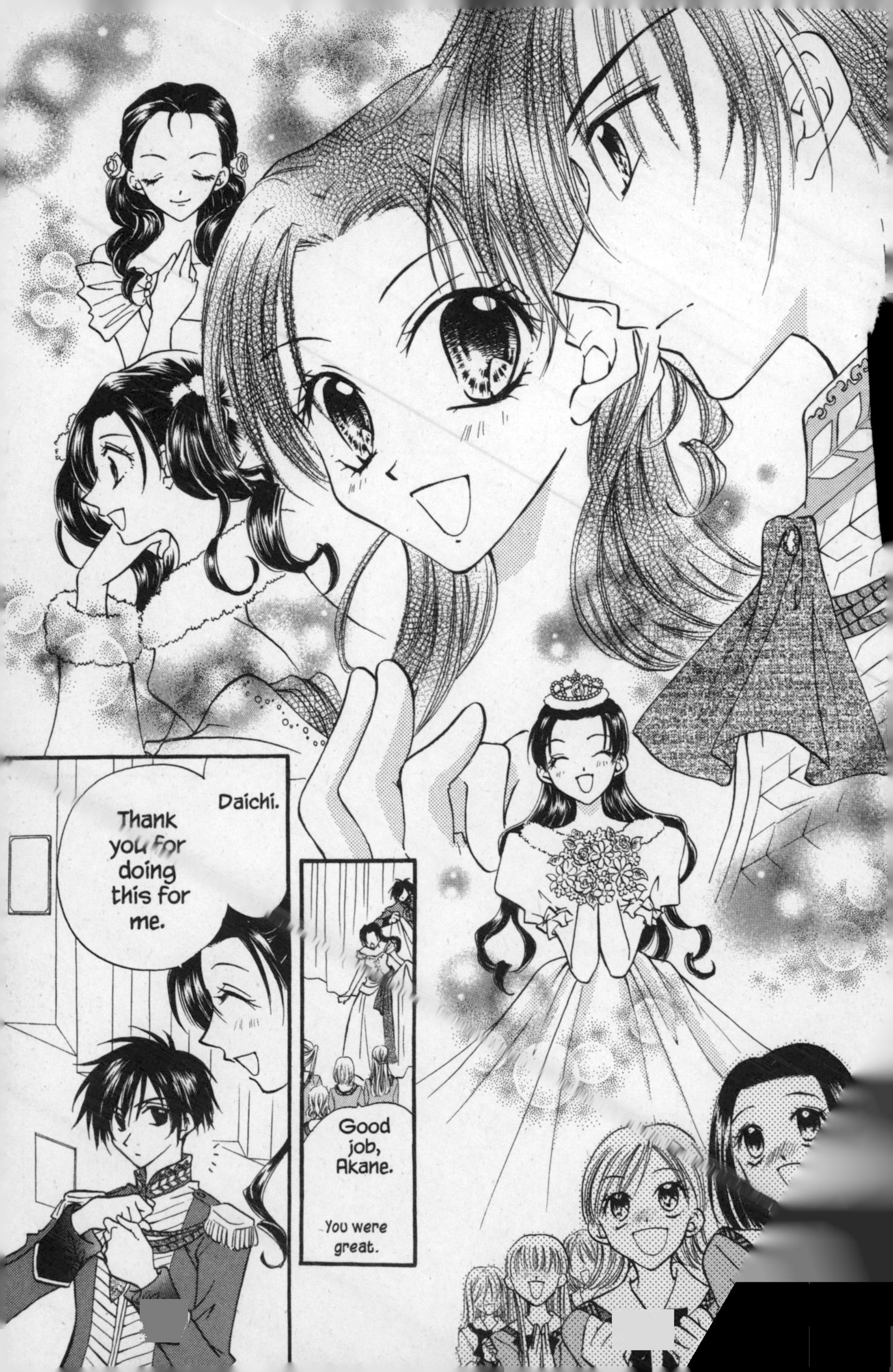
Good job, Akane.
You were great.
Daichi.
Thank you for doing this for me.

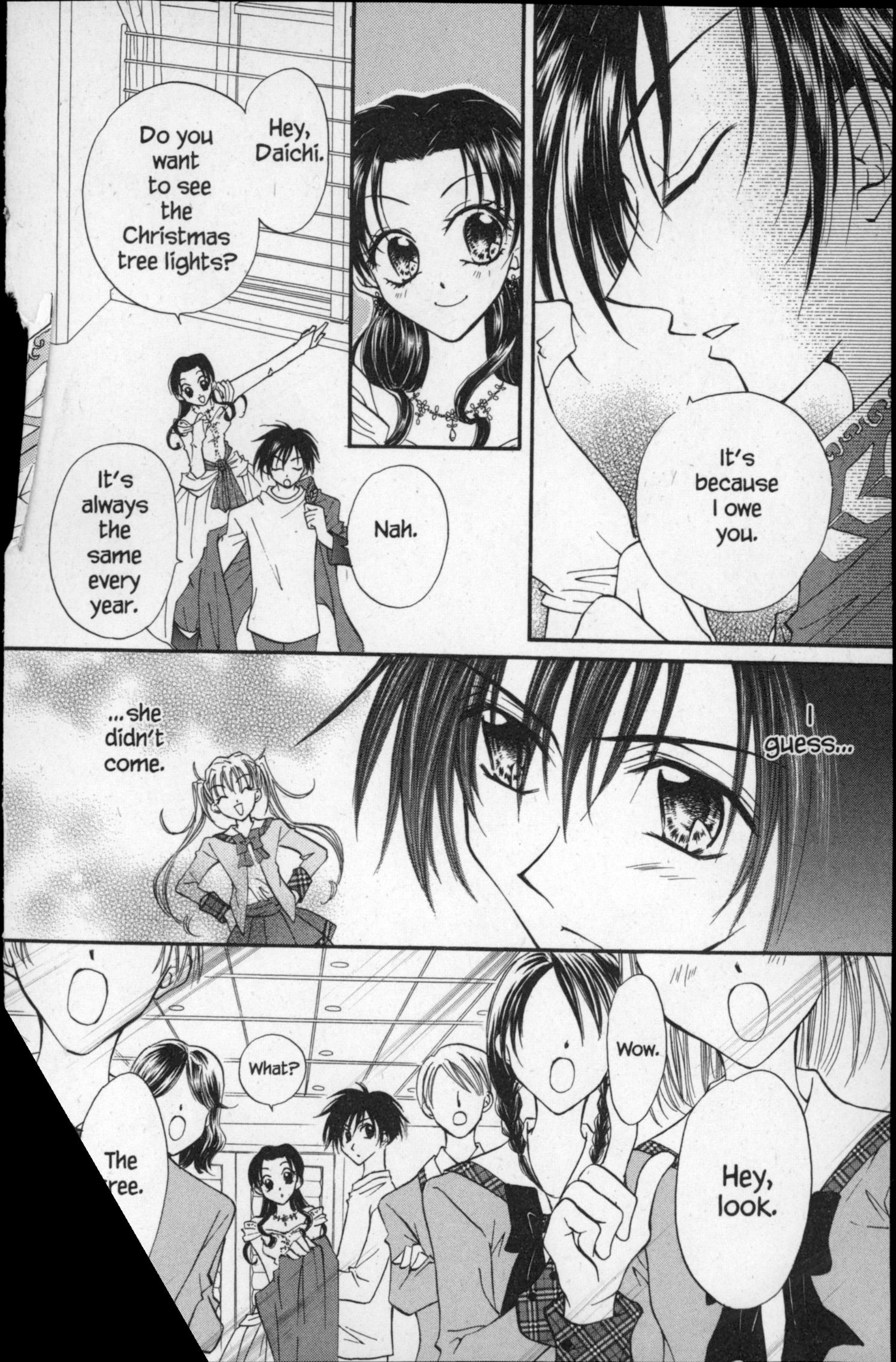
It's because I owe you.
Hey, Daichi.
Do you want to see the Christmas tree lights?
Nah.
It's always the same every year.
I guess...
...she didn't come.
Hey, look.
Wow.
What?
The ree.

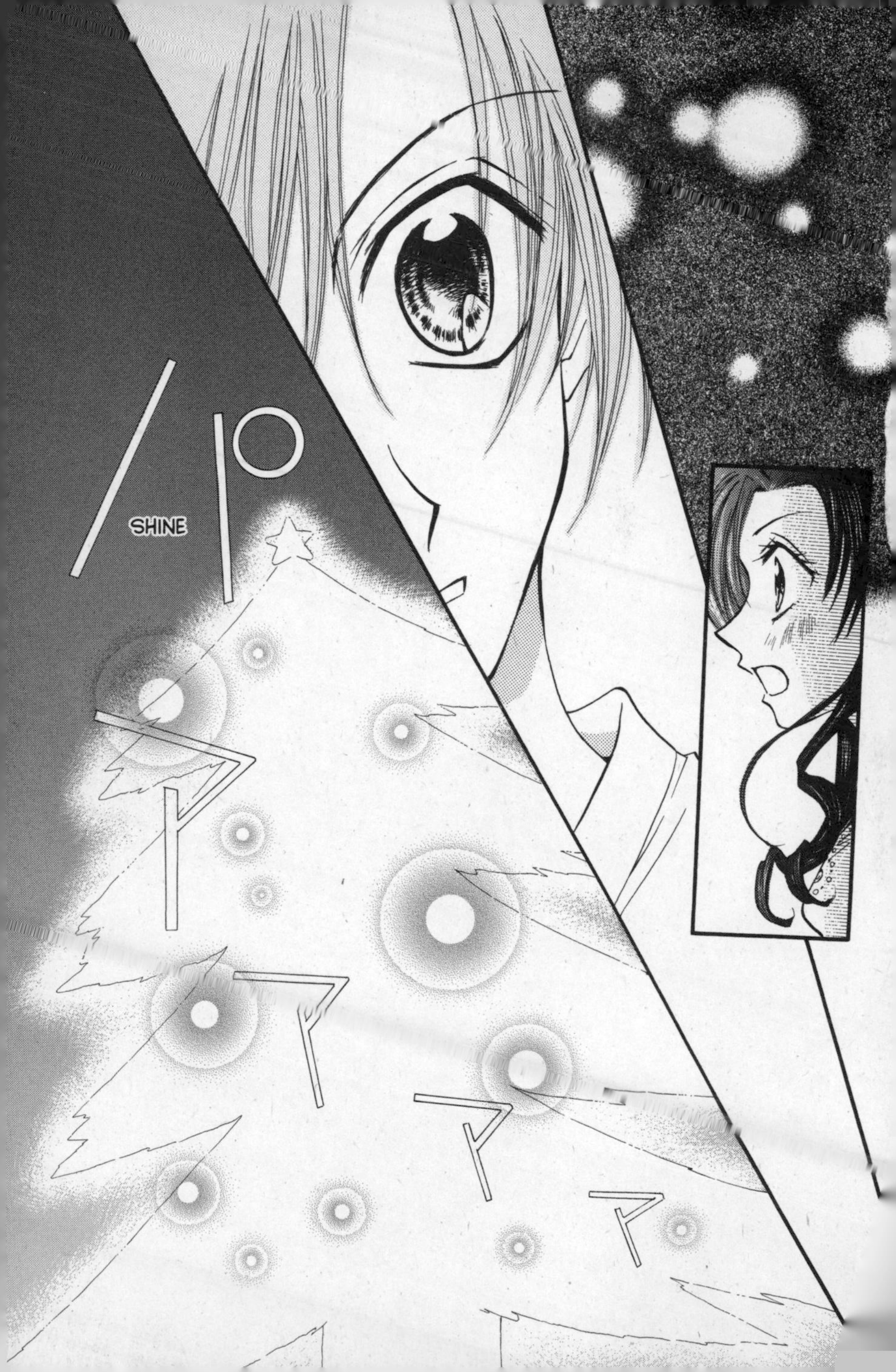
SHINE

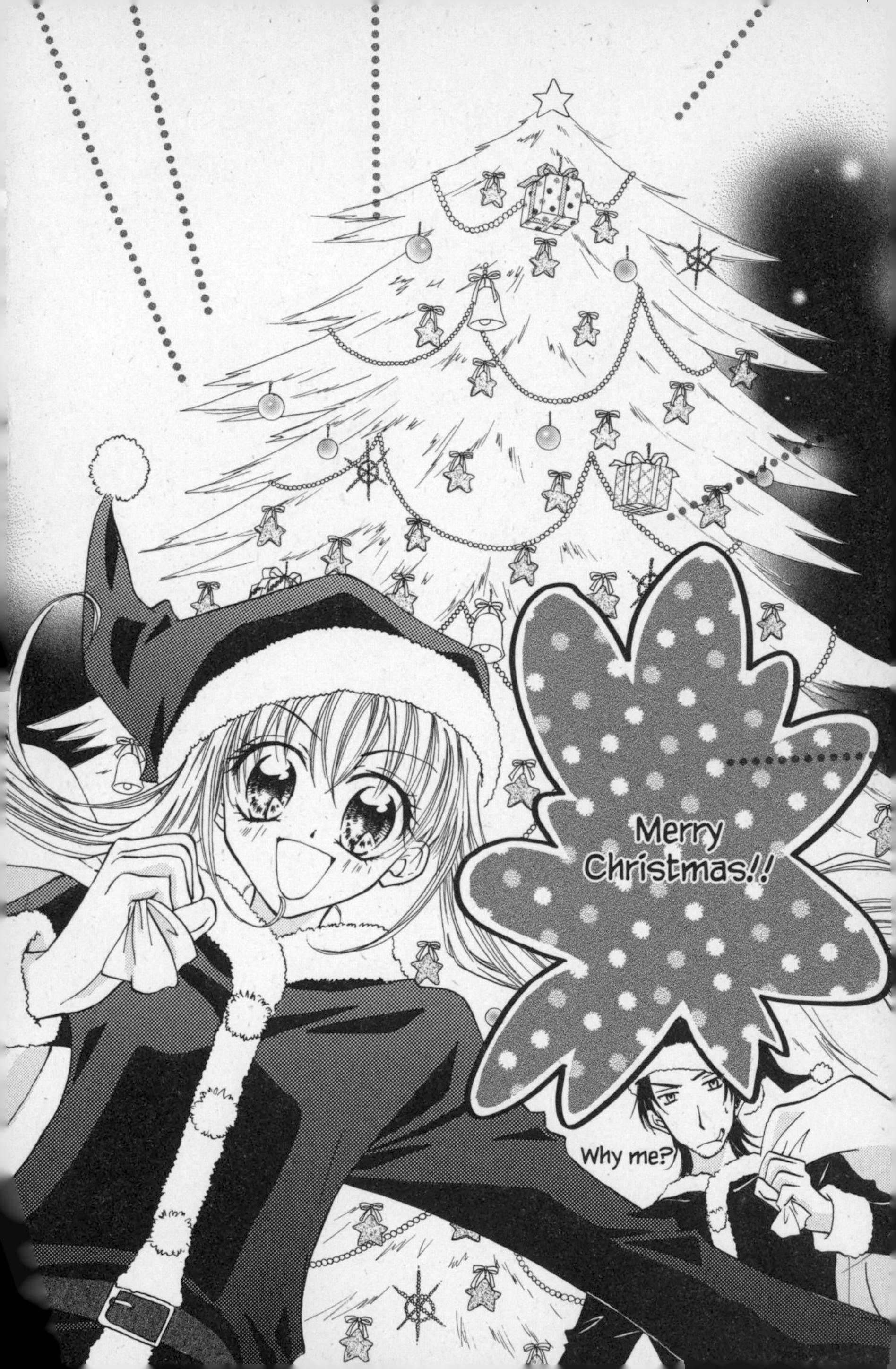
Merry Christmas!!
Why me?

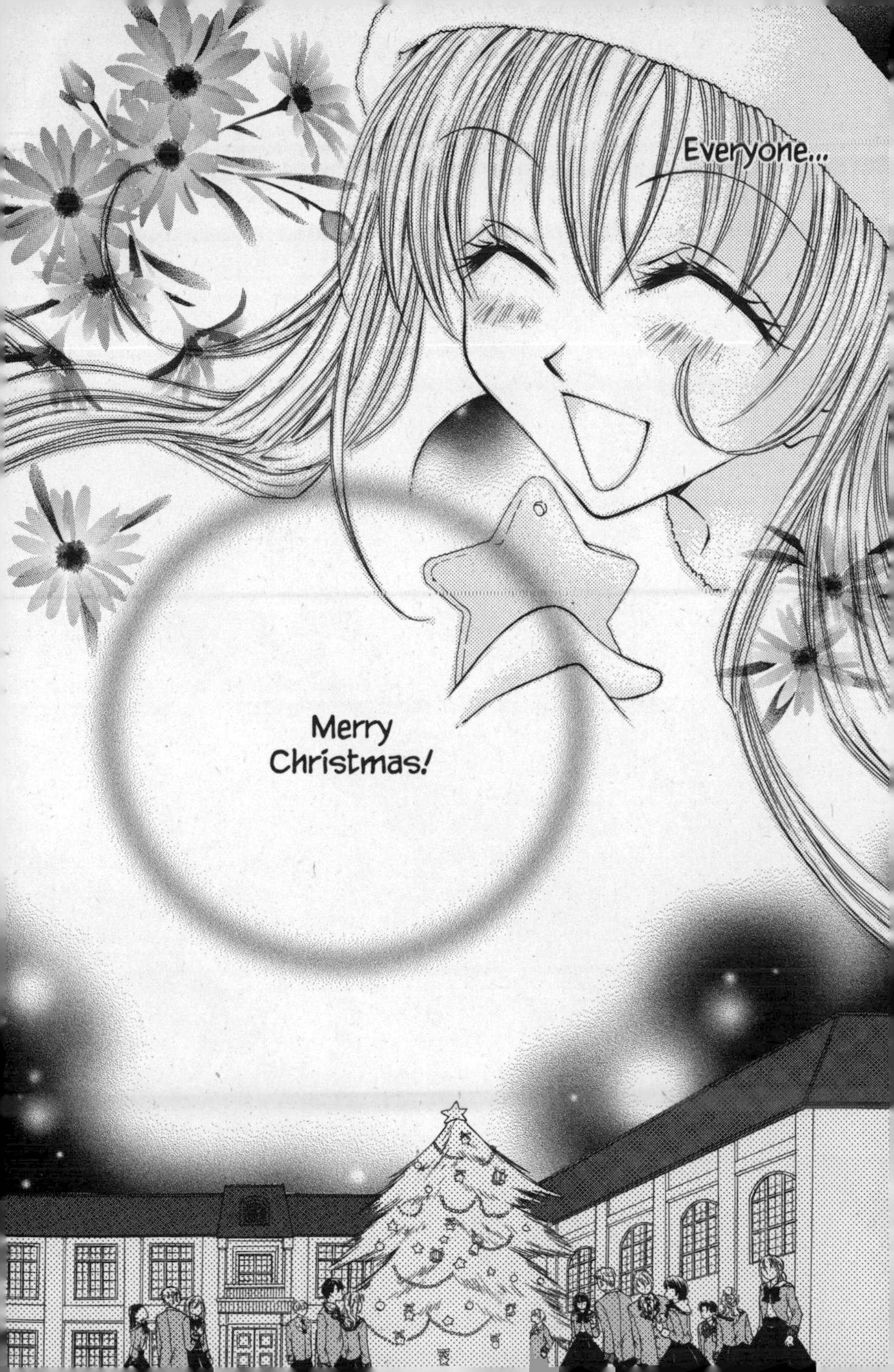
Everyone...
Merry Christmas!

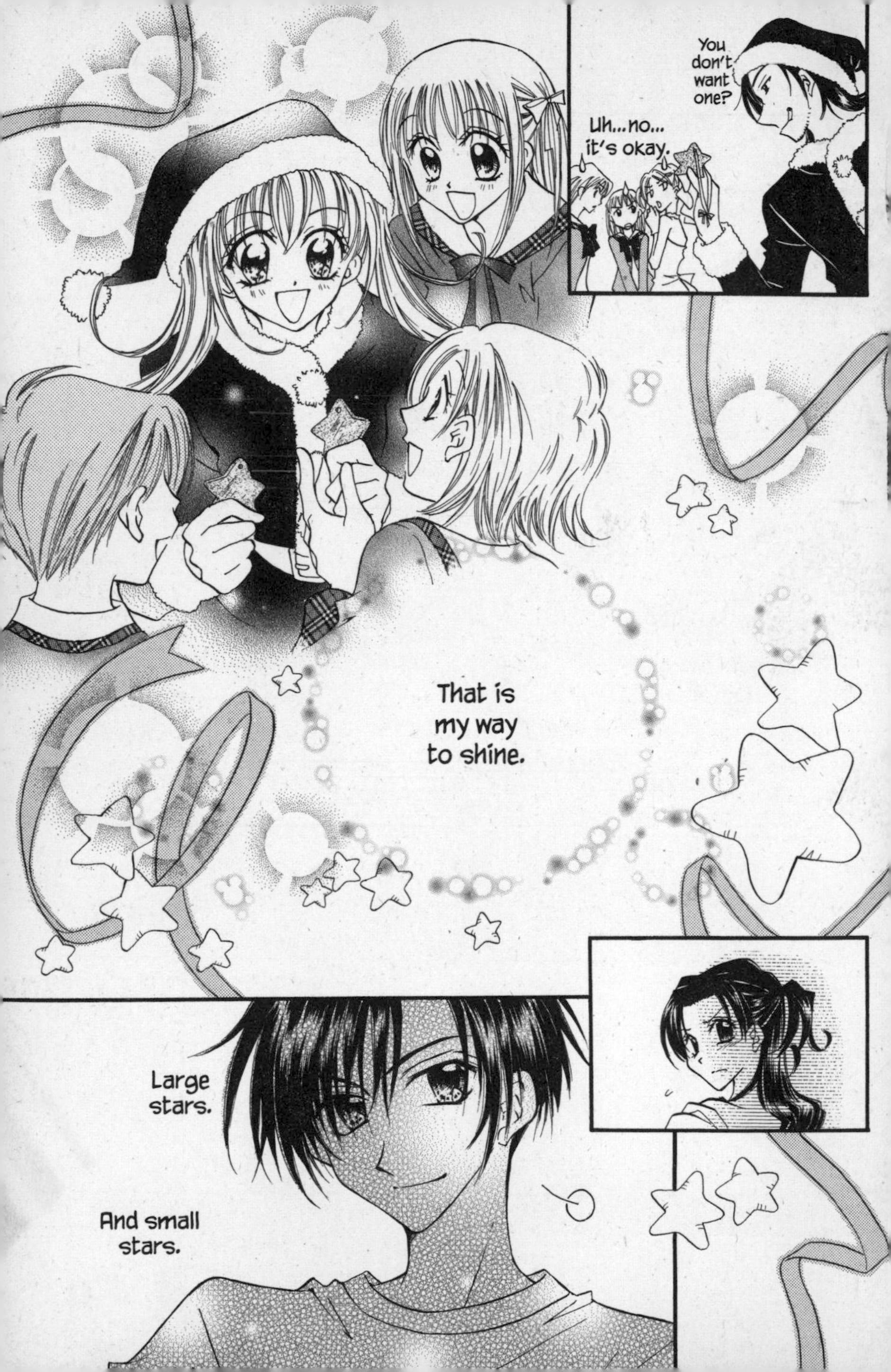
You don't want one?
Uh...no... it's okay.
That is my way to shine.
Large stars.
And small stars.

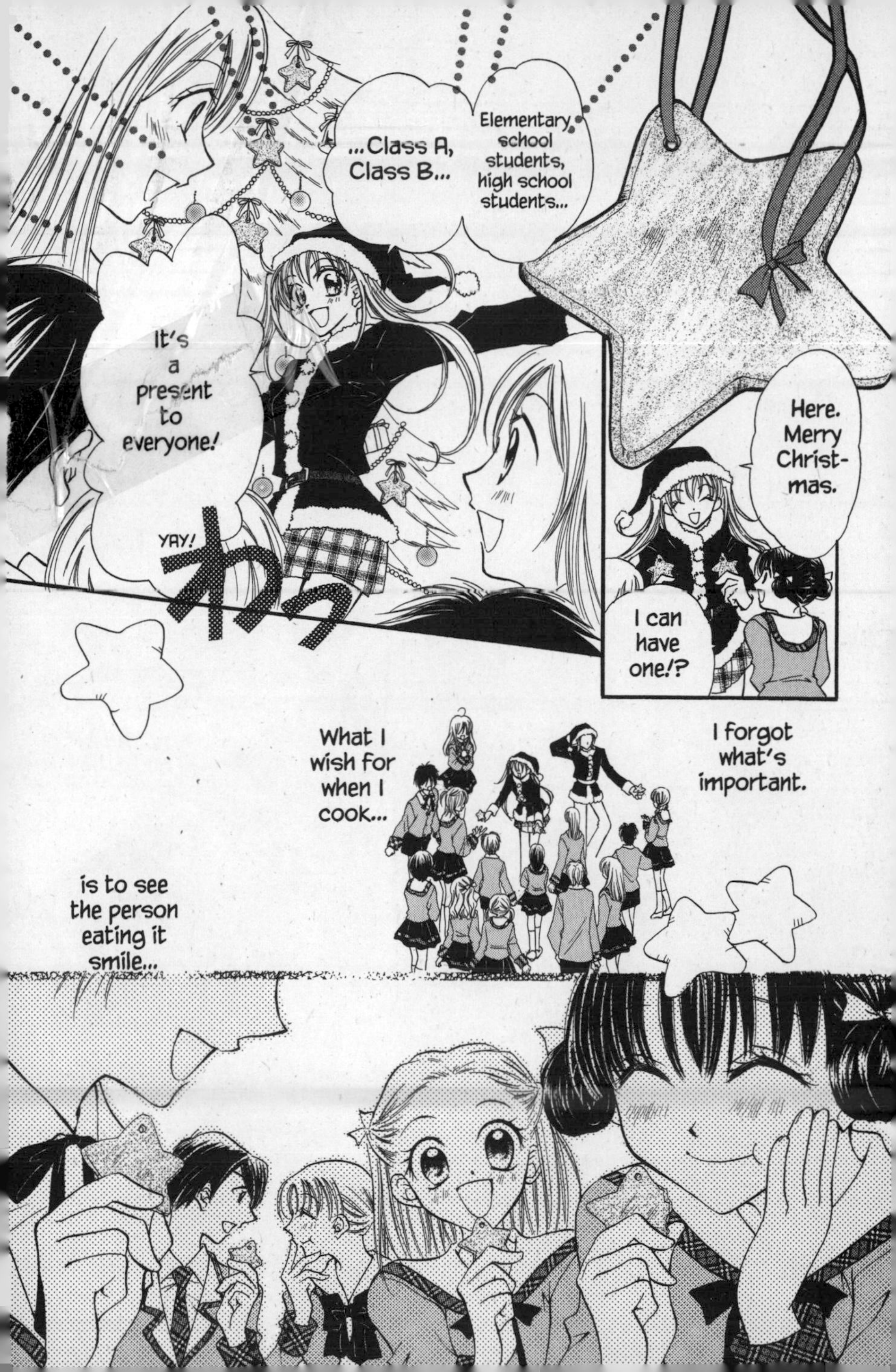
Elementary school students, high school students...
...Class A, Class B...
It's a present to everyone!
YAY!
わっ
Here. Merry Christmas.
I can have one!?
I forgot what's important.
What I wish for when I cook...
is to see the person eating it smile...

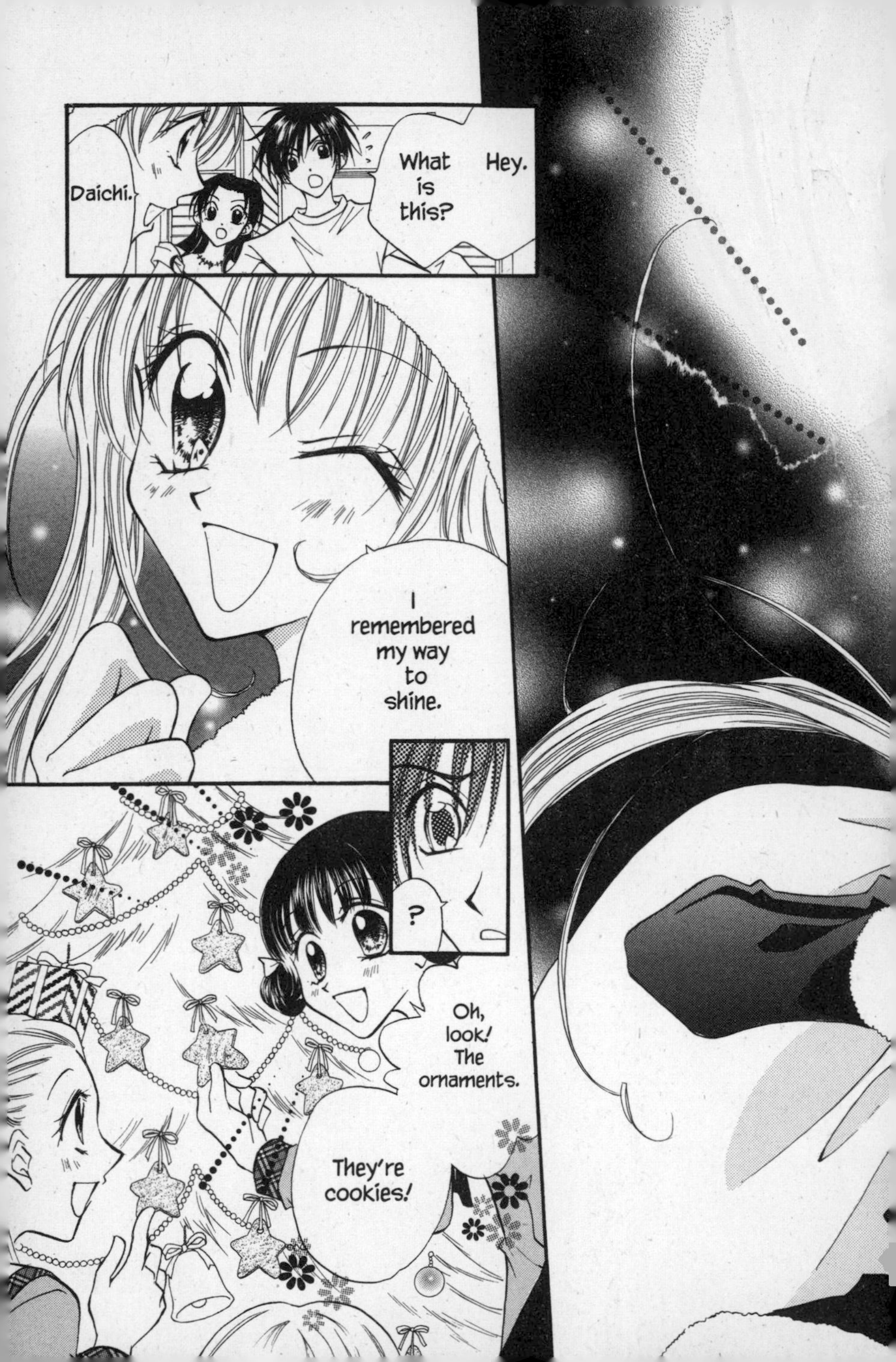

Hey.
What is this?
Daichi.
I remembered my way to shine.
?
Oh, look! The ornaments.
They're cookies!

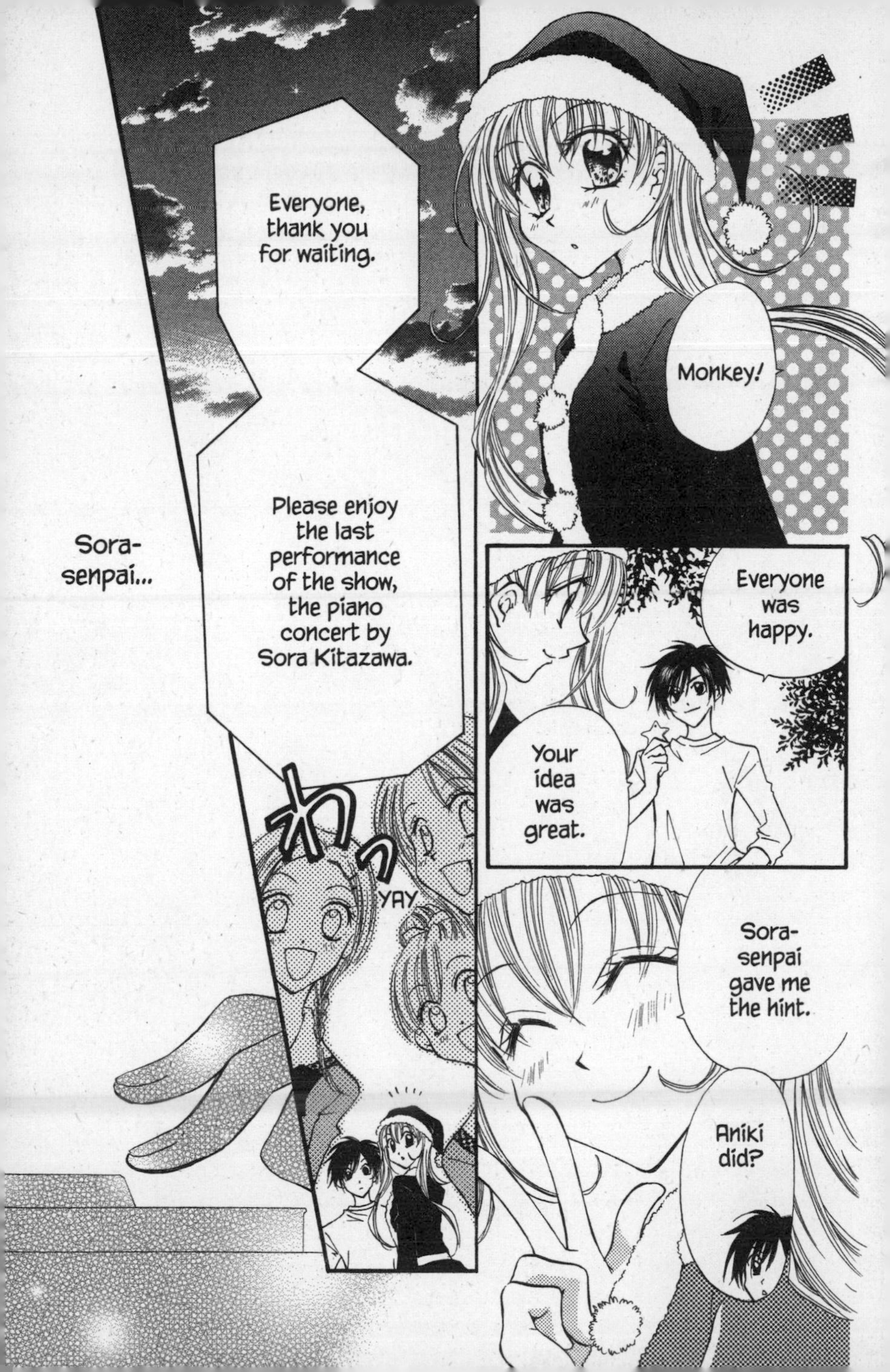
Monkey!
Everyone was happy.
Your idea was great.
Sora-senpai gave me the hint.
Aniki did?
Everyone, thank you for waiting.
Please enjoy the last performance of the show, the piano concert by Sora Kitazawa.
わっ
YAY
Sora-senpai...

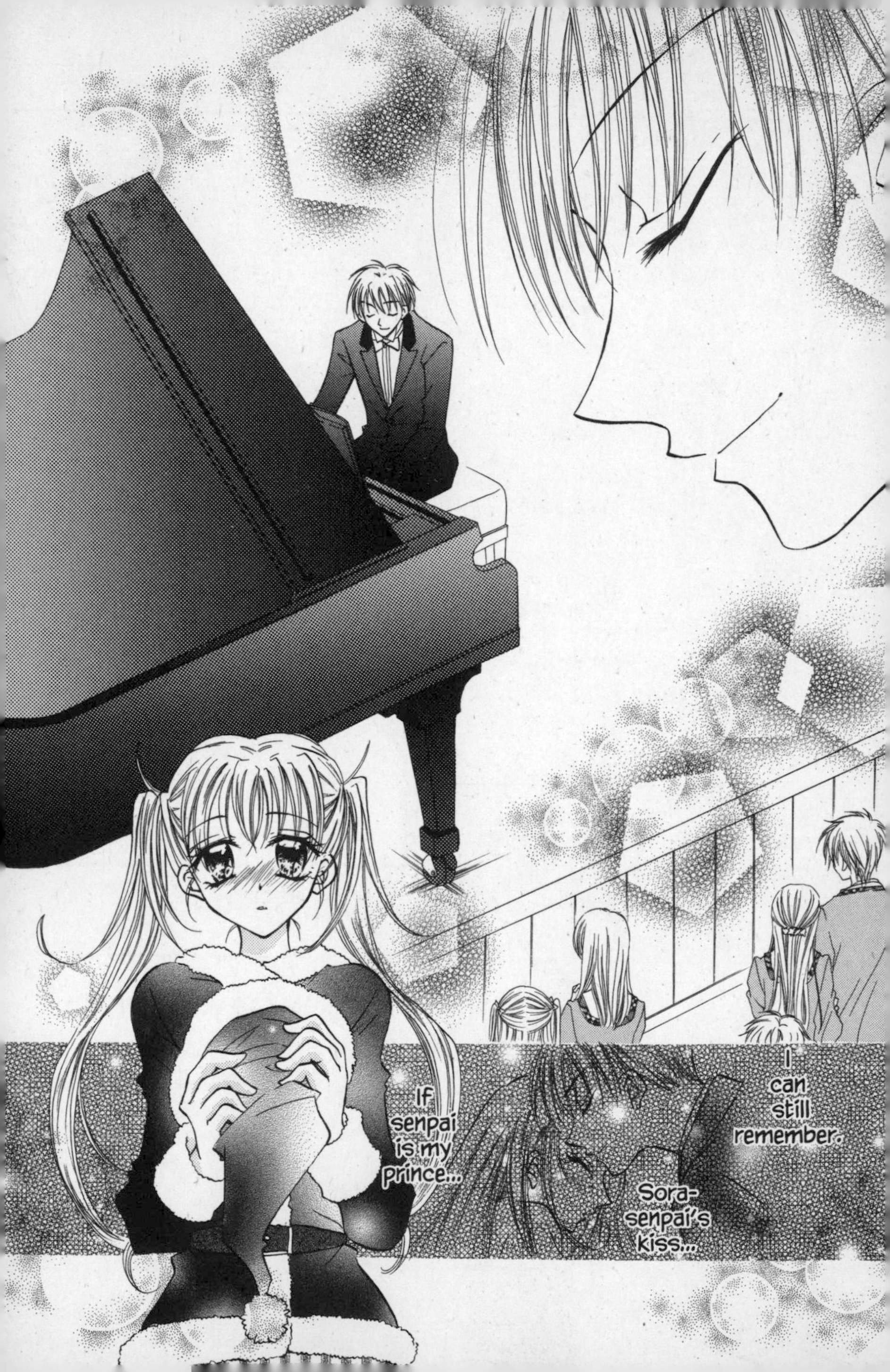
I can still remember.
Sora-senpai's kiss...
If senpai is my prince...

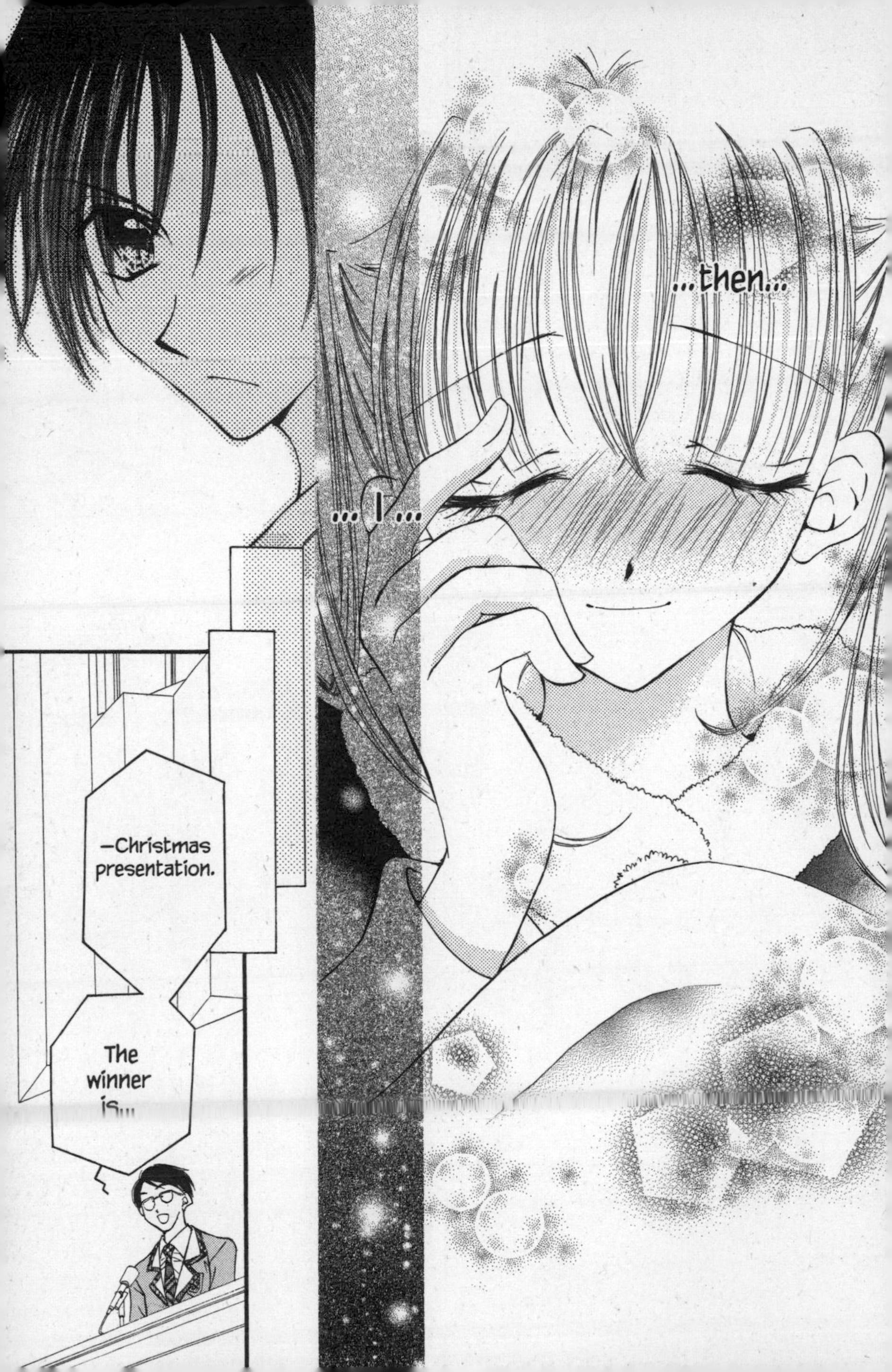

...then...
...I...
—Christmas presentation.
The winner is...

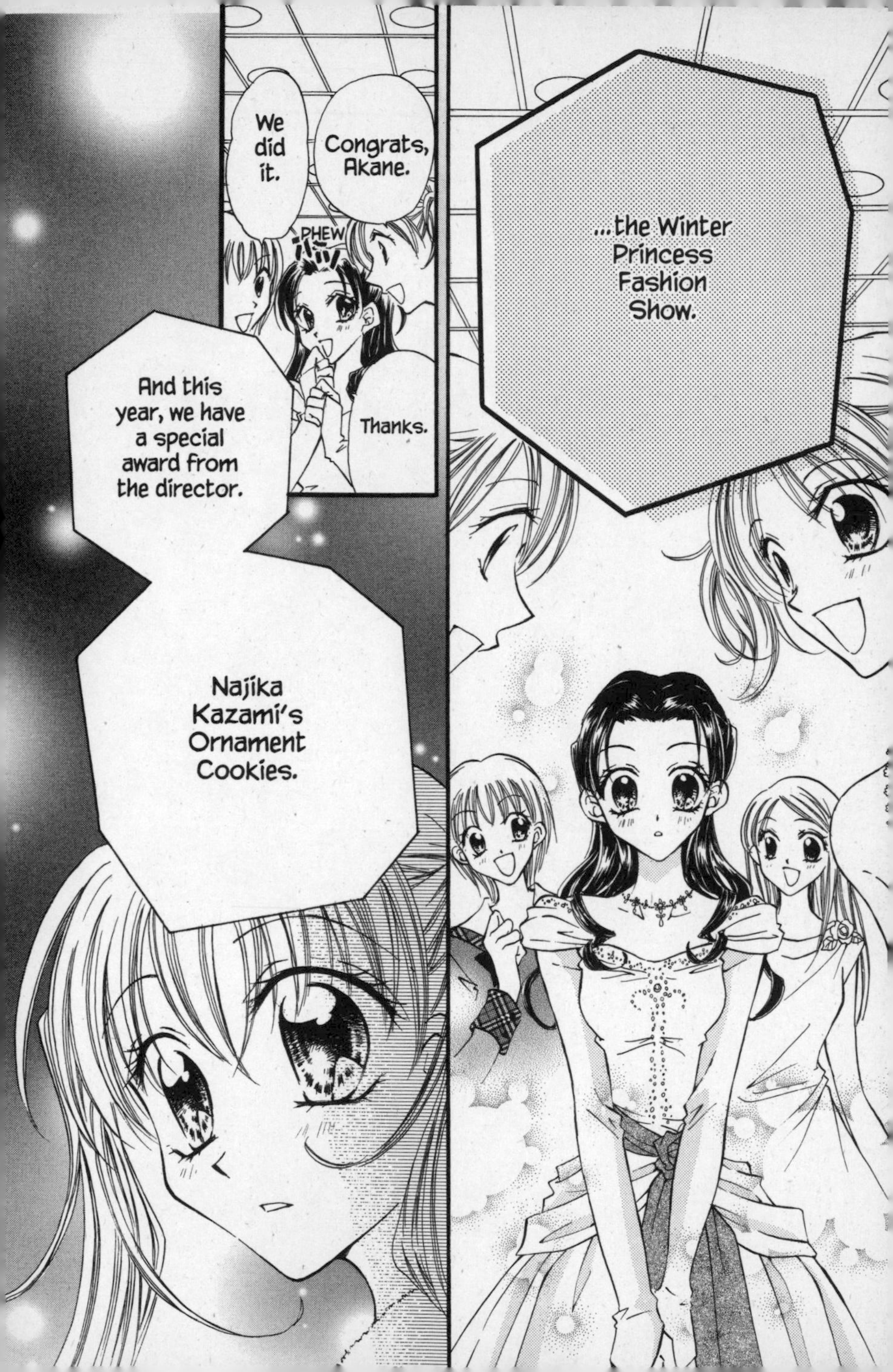
...the Winter Princess Fashion Show.
Congrats, Akane.
We did it.
PHEW
Thanks.
And this year, we have a special award from the director.
Najika Kazami's Ornament Cookies.

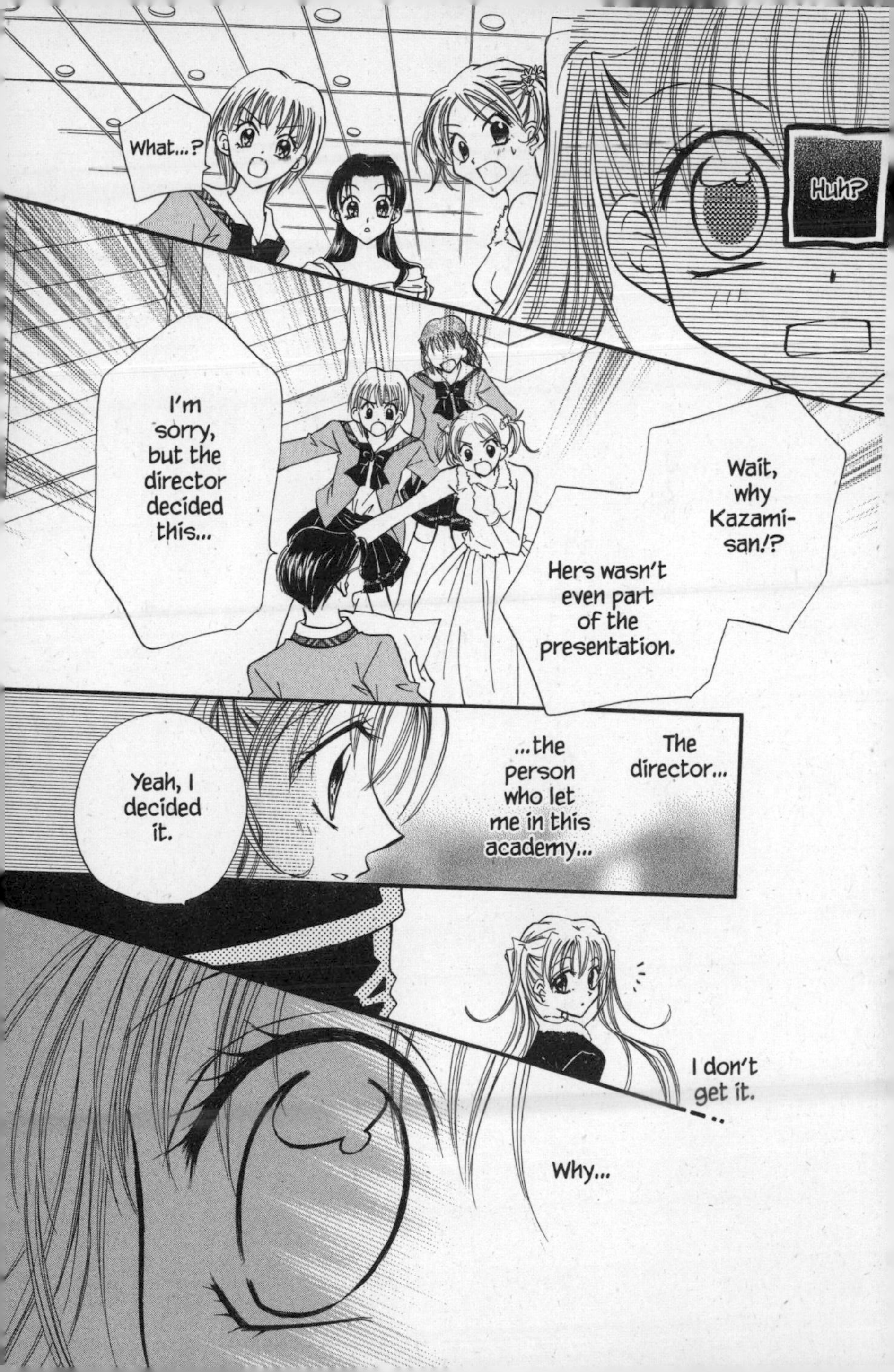
Huh?
What...?
Wait, why Kazami-san!?
Hers wasn't even part of the presentation.
I'm sorry, but the director decided this...
The director...
...the person who let me in this academy...
Yeah, I decided it.
I don't get it.
Why...

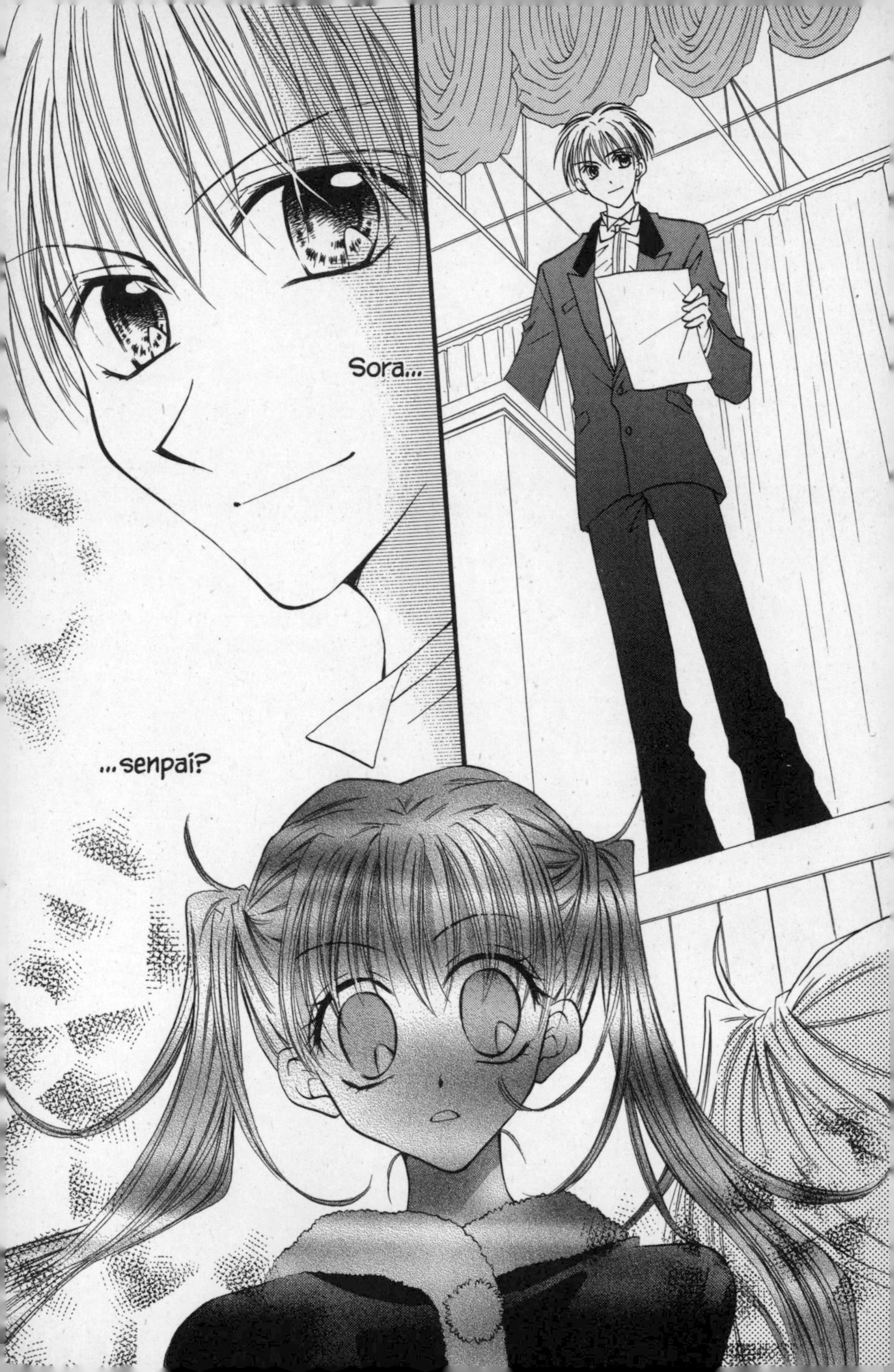
Sora...
...senpai?

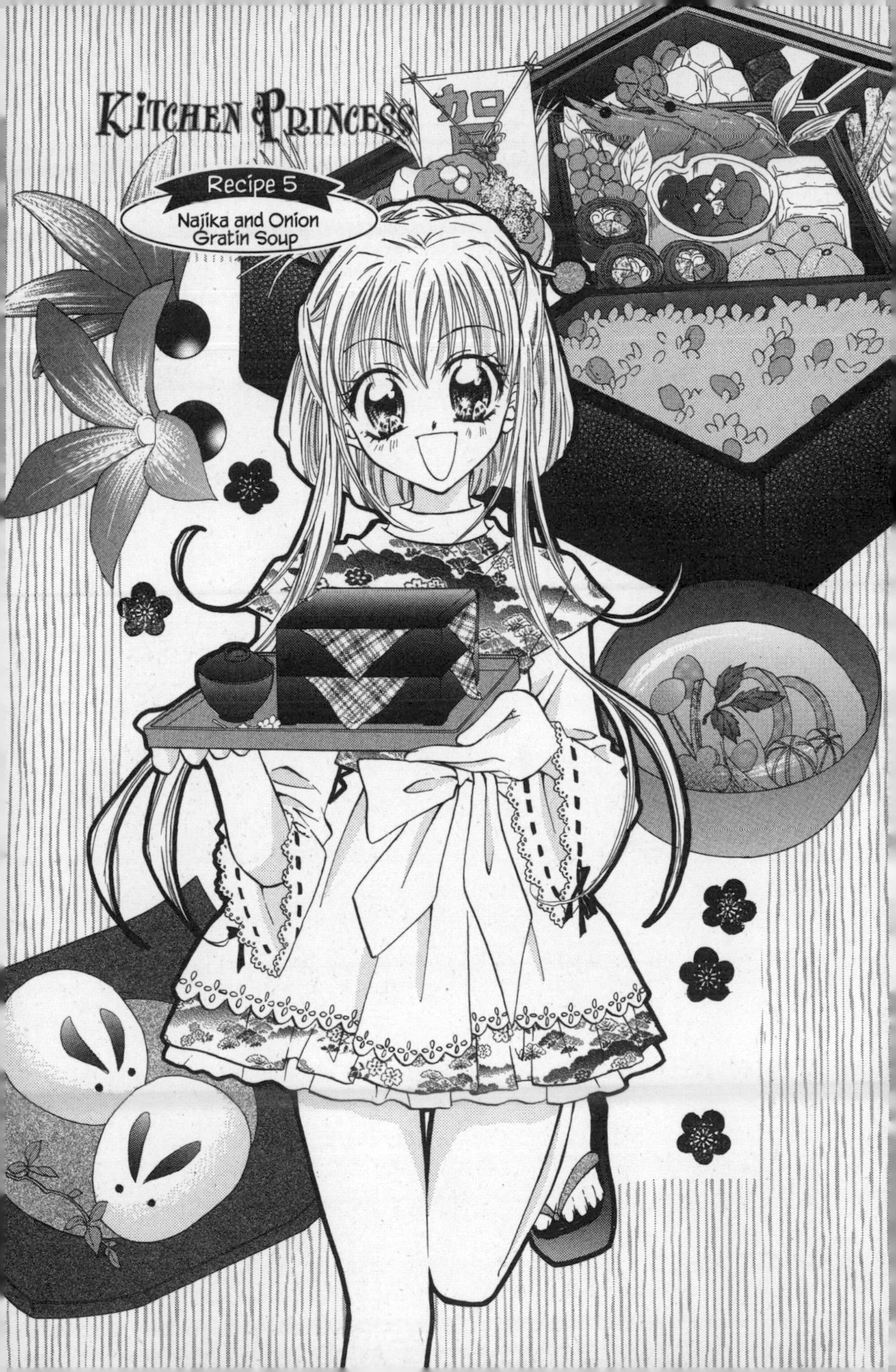
Kitchen Princess
Recipe 5
Najika and Onion Gratin Soup

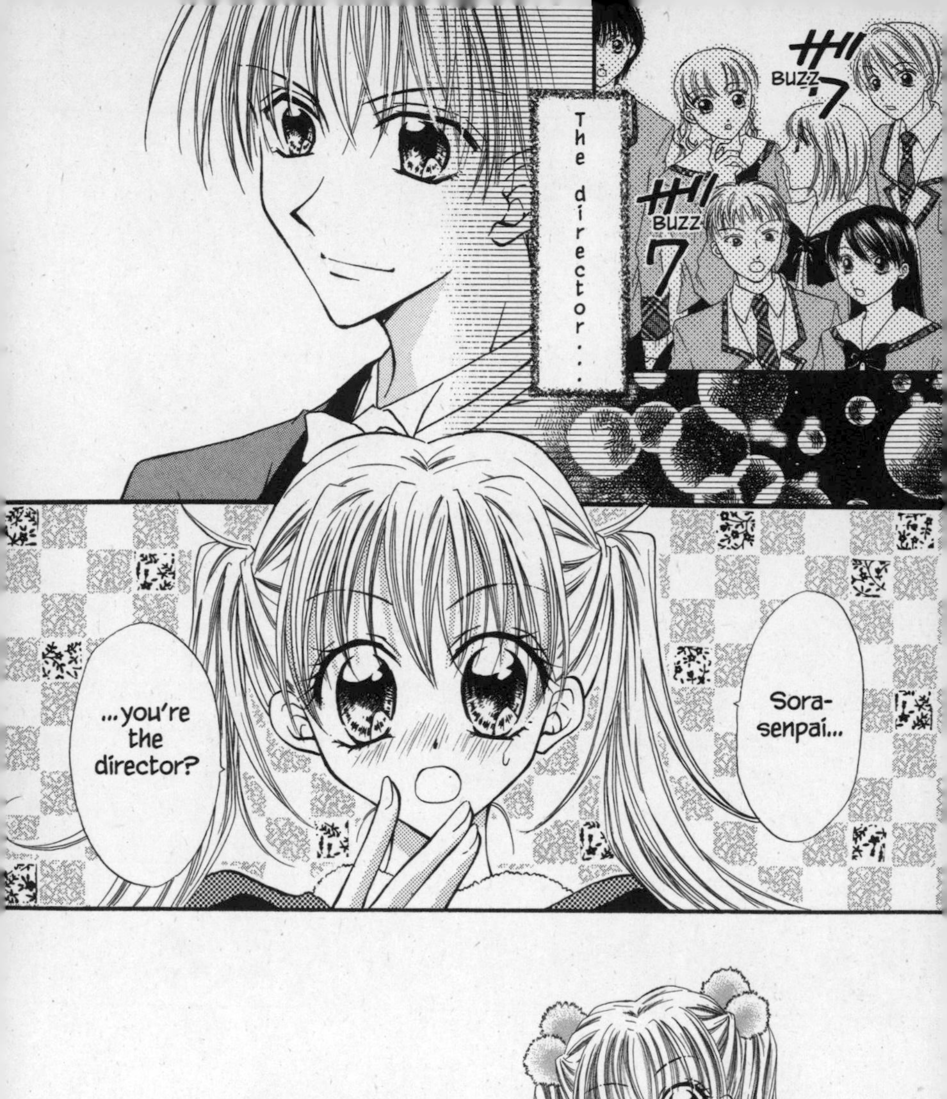
BUZZ
BUZZ
The director...
Sora-senpai...
...you're the director?
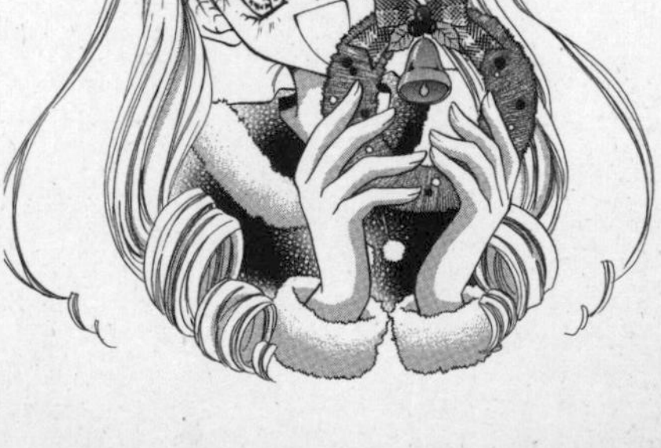

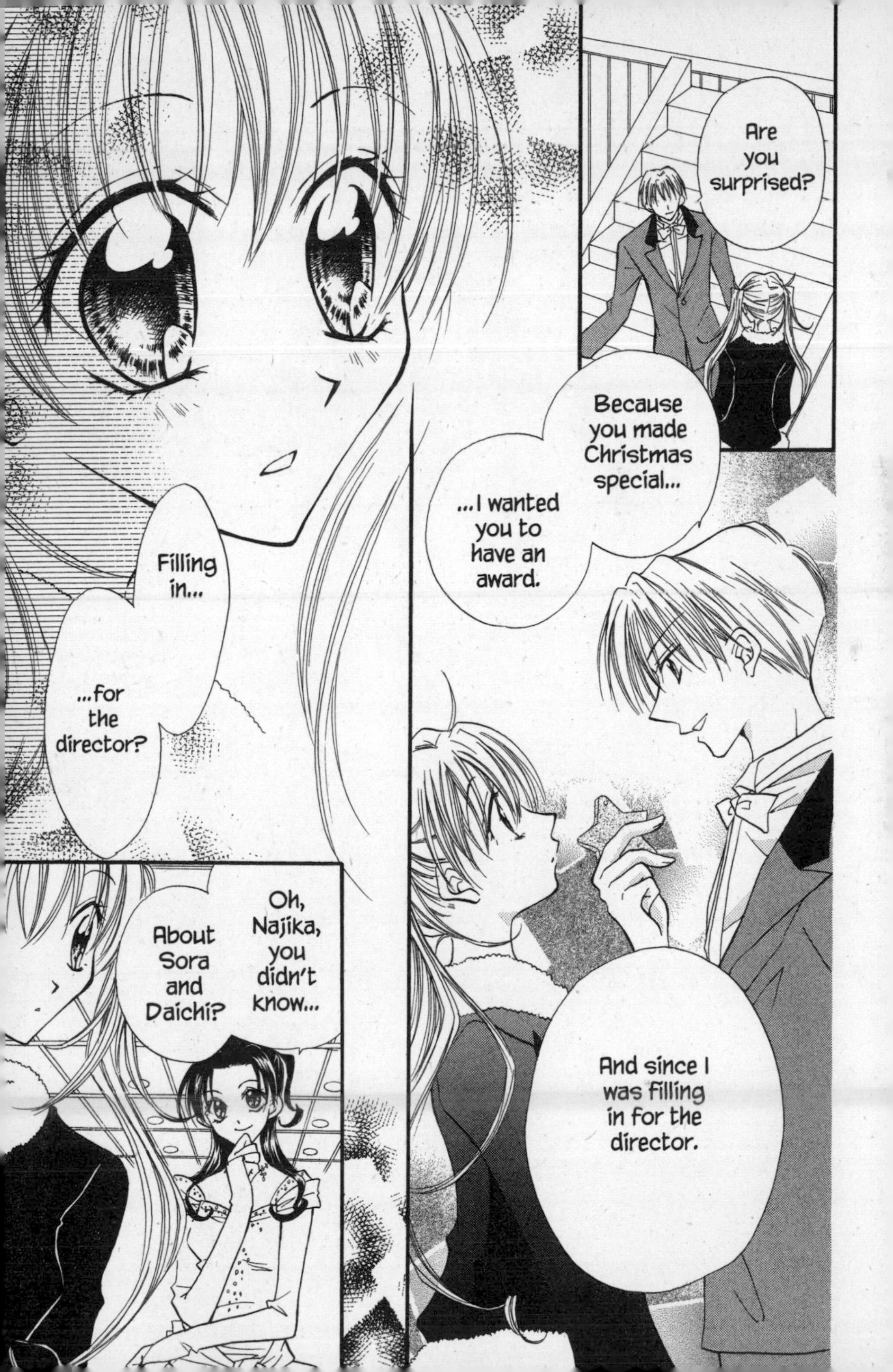
Are you surprised?
Because you made Christmas special...
...I wanted you to have an award.
And since I was filling in for the director.
Filling in...
...for the director?
Oh, Najika, you didn't know...
About Sora and Daichi?

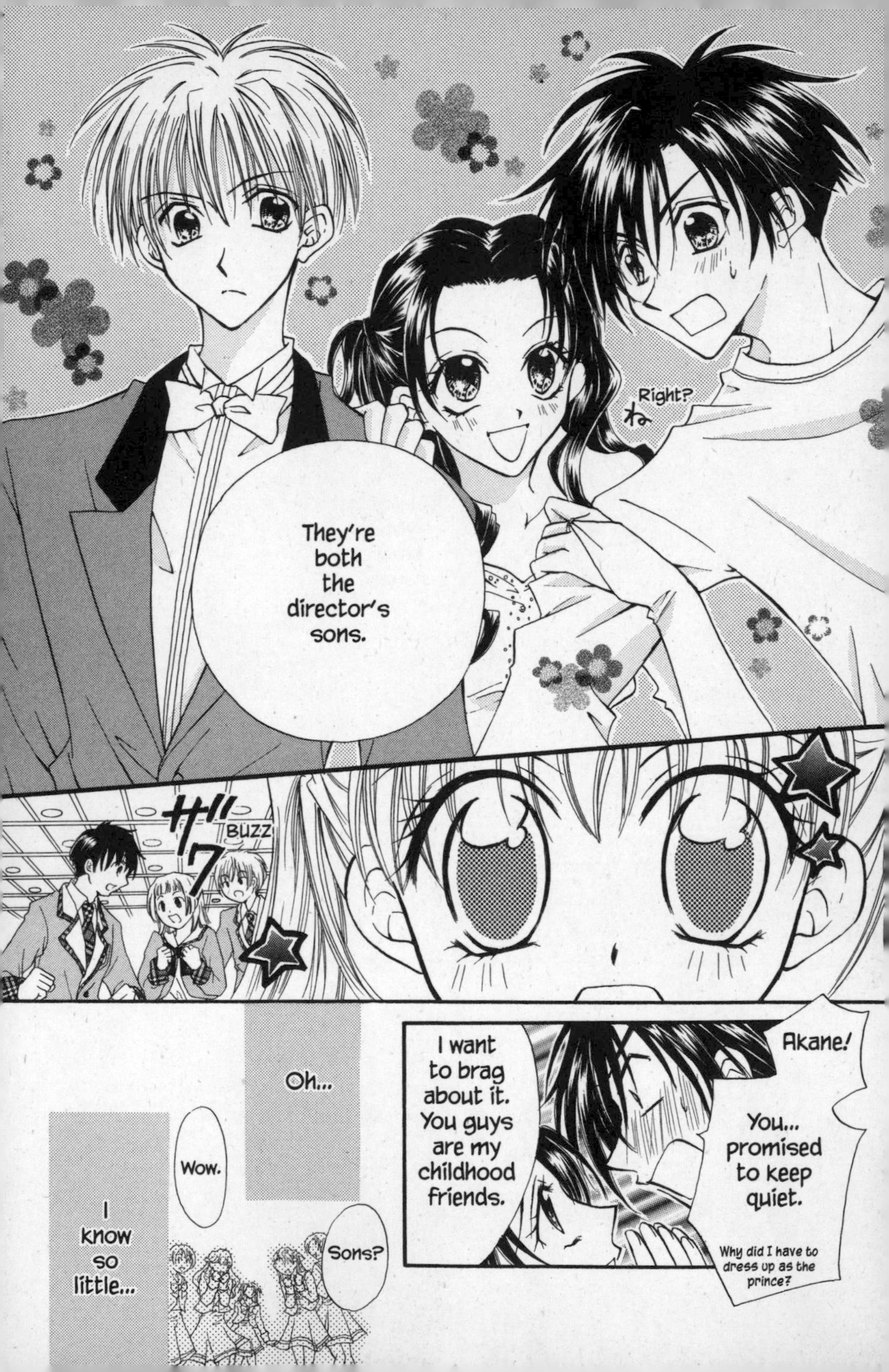
Right? ね
They're both the director's sons.
ザワ BUZZ
Akane!
You... promised to keep quiet.
I want to brag about it. You guys are my childhood friends.
Why did I have to dress up as the prince?
Oh...
Wow.
Sons?
I know so little...

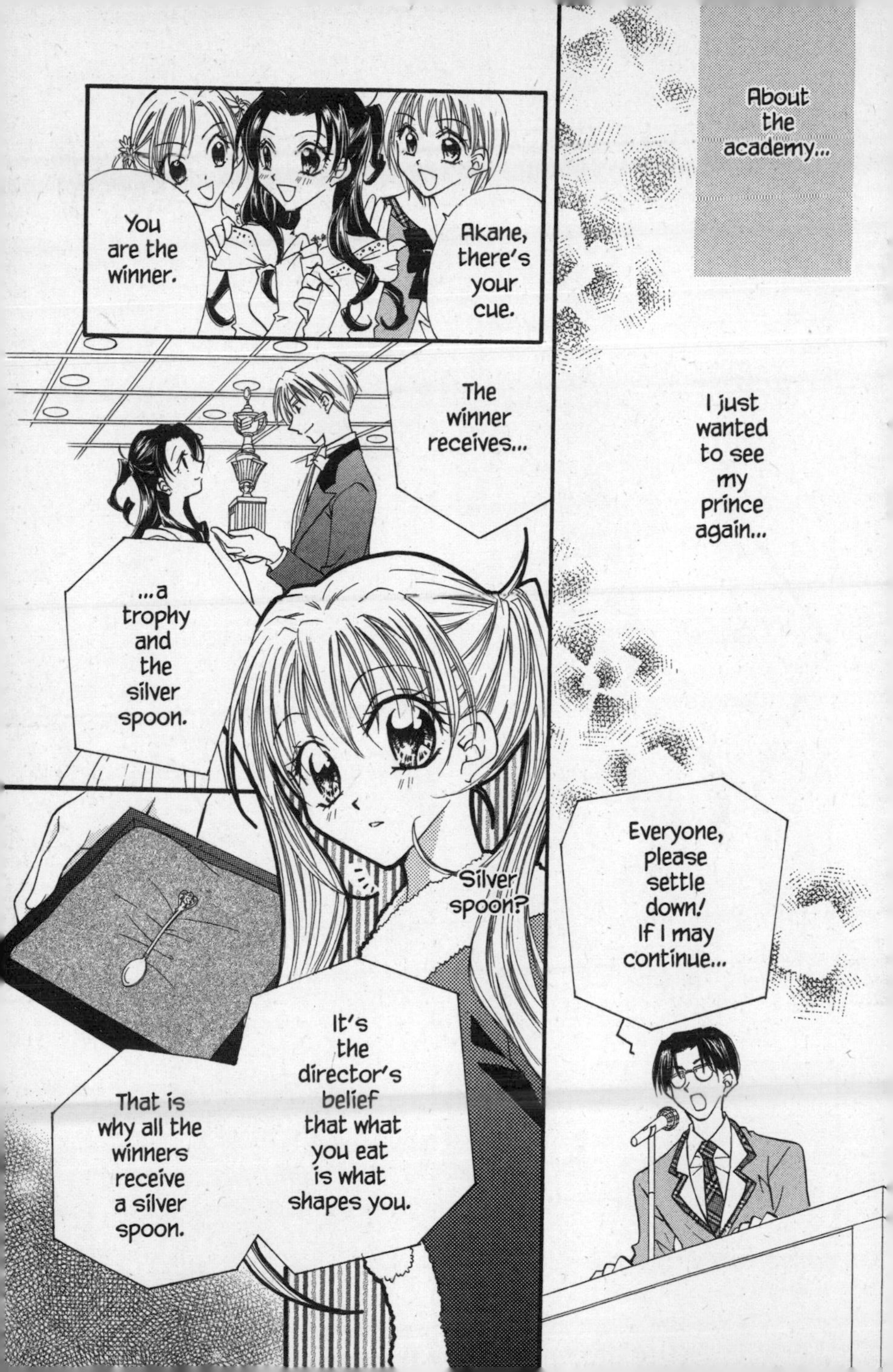
About the academy...
I just wanted to see my prince again...
Everyone, please settle down! If I may continue...
Akane, there's your cue.
You are the winner.
The winner receives...
...a trophy and the silver spoon.
Silver spoon?
It's the director's belief that what you eat is what shapes you.
That is why all the winners receive a silver spoon.

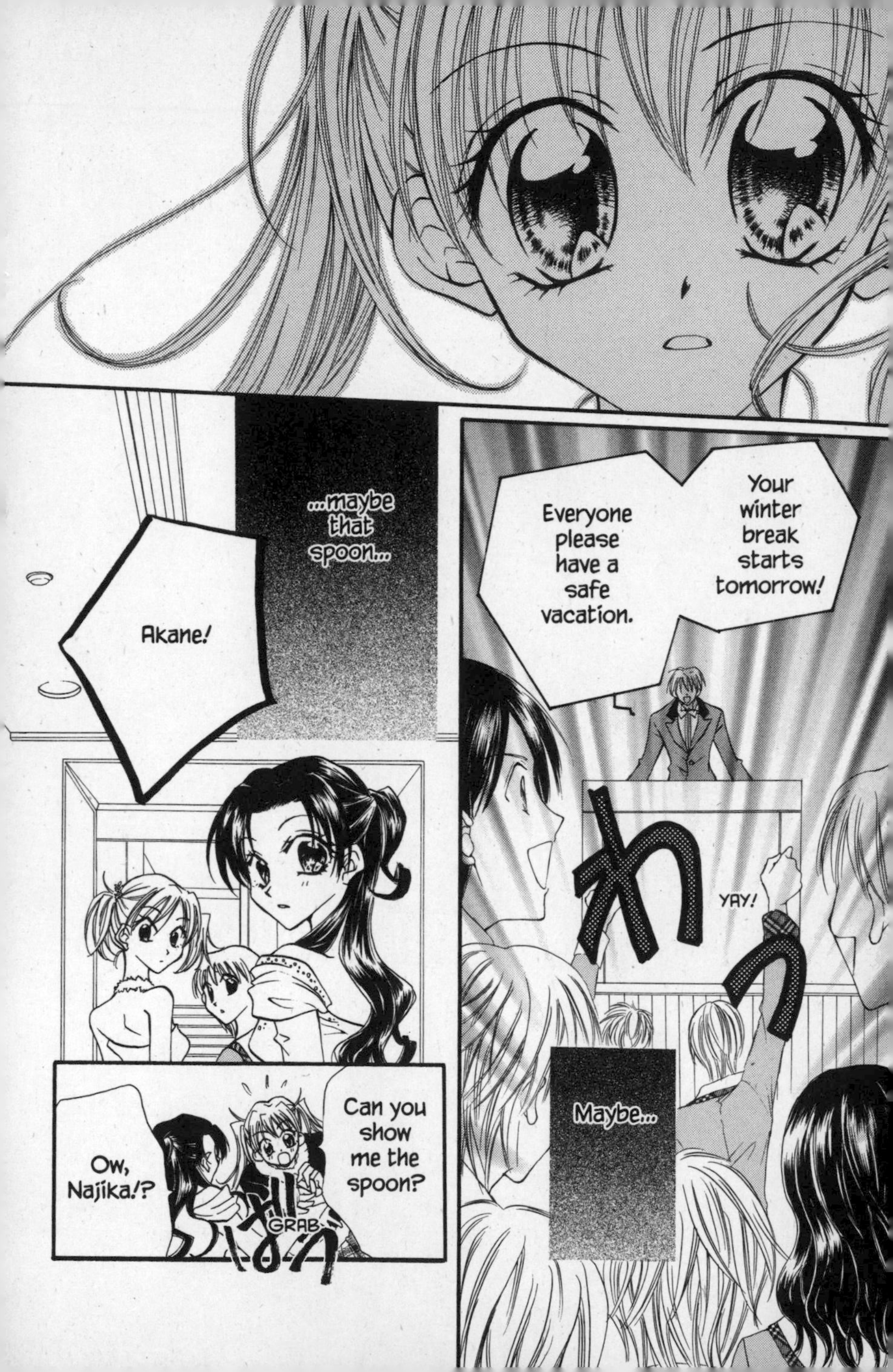
Your winter break starts tomorrow!
Everyone please have a safe vacation.
YAY!
Maybe...
...maybe that spoon...
Akane!
Can you show me the spoon?
GRAB
Ow, Najika!?

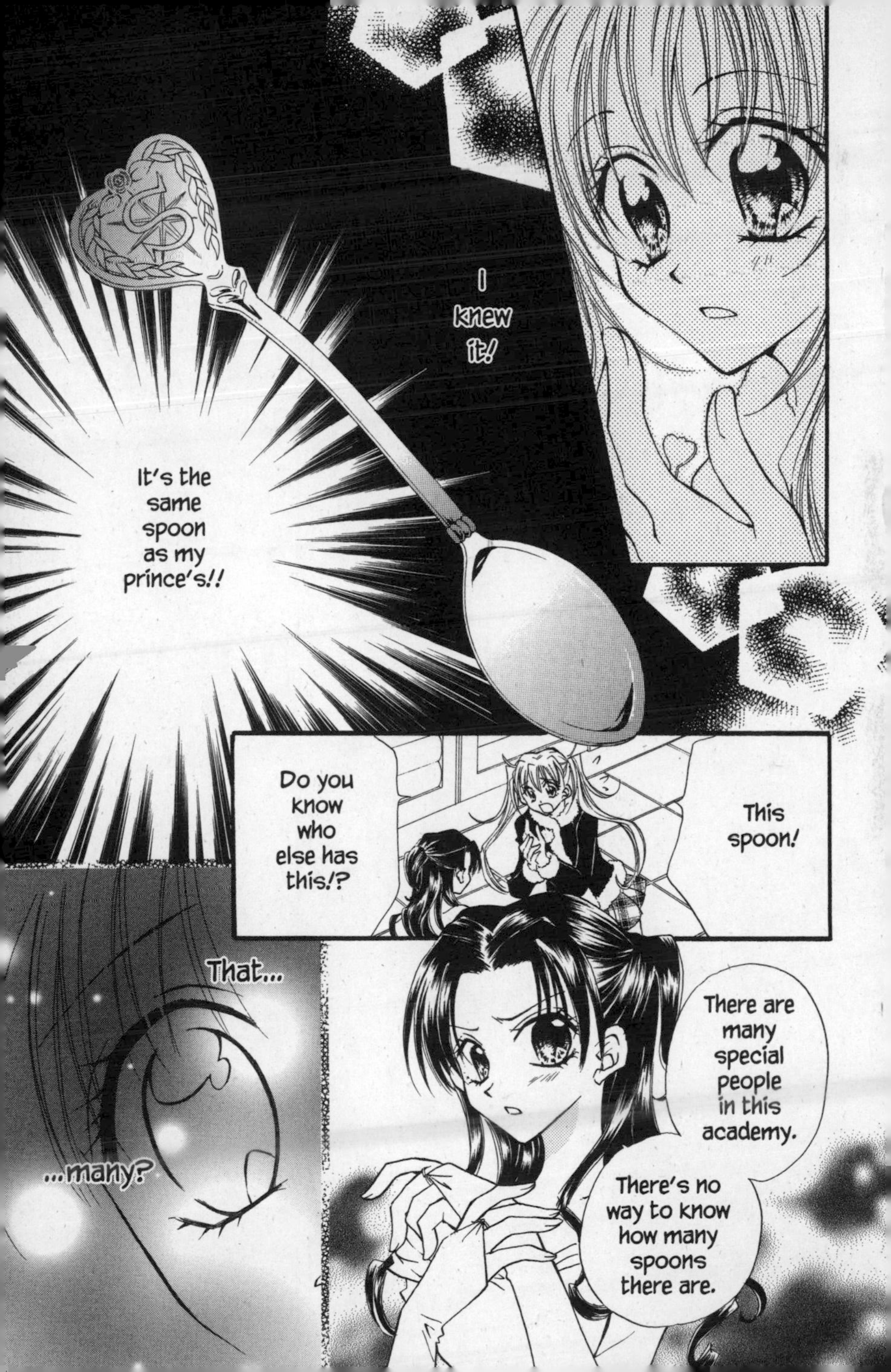
I knew it!
It's the same spoon as my prince's!!
This spoon!
Do you know who else has this!?
There are many special people in this academy.
There's no way to know how many spoons there are.
That...
...many?

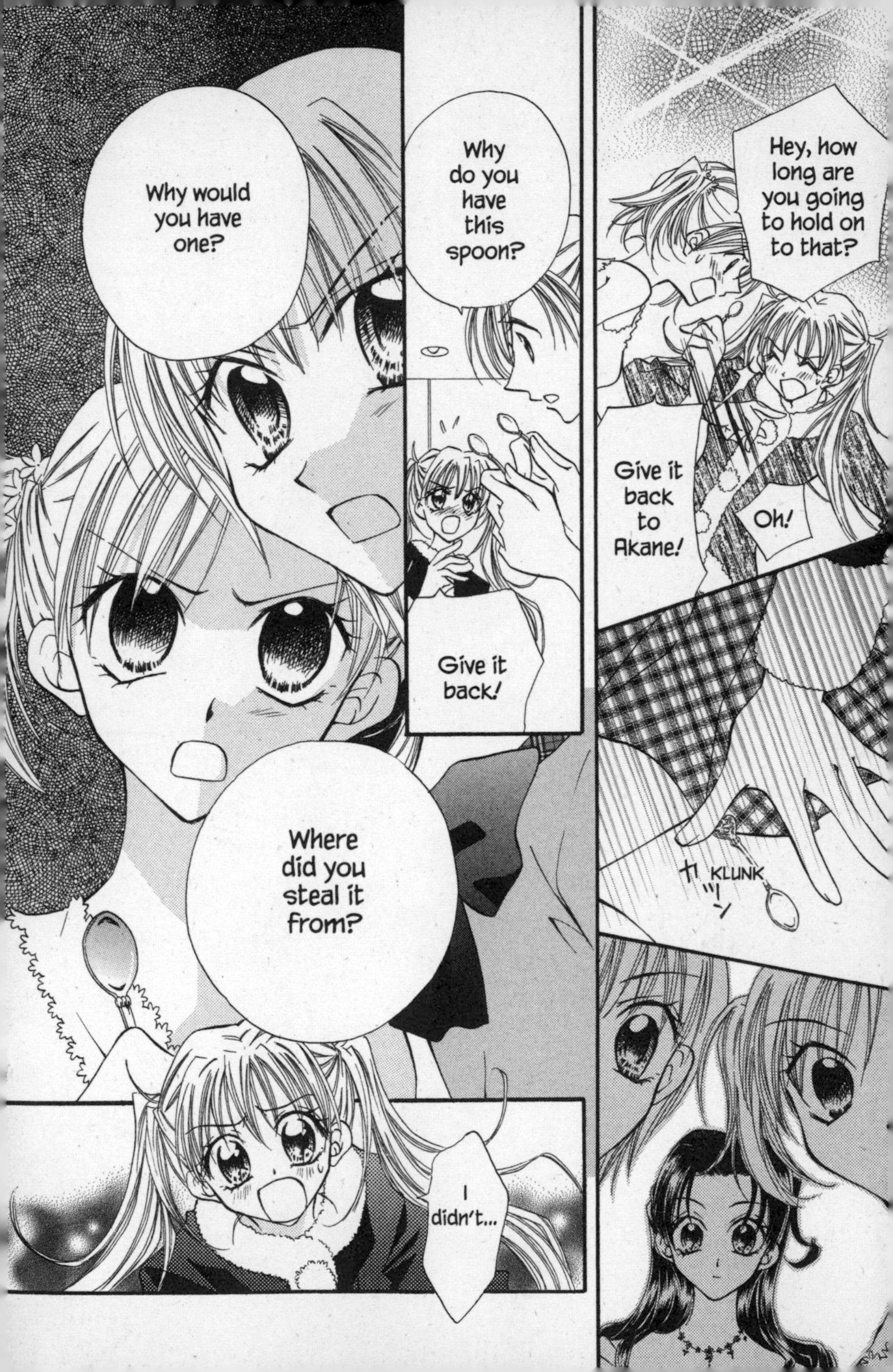
Hey, how long are you going to hold on to that?
Oh!
Give it back to Akane!
KLUNK
Why do you have this spoon?
Give it back!
Why would you have one?
Where did you steal it from?
I didn't...

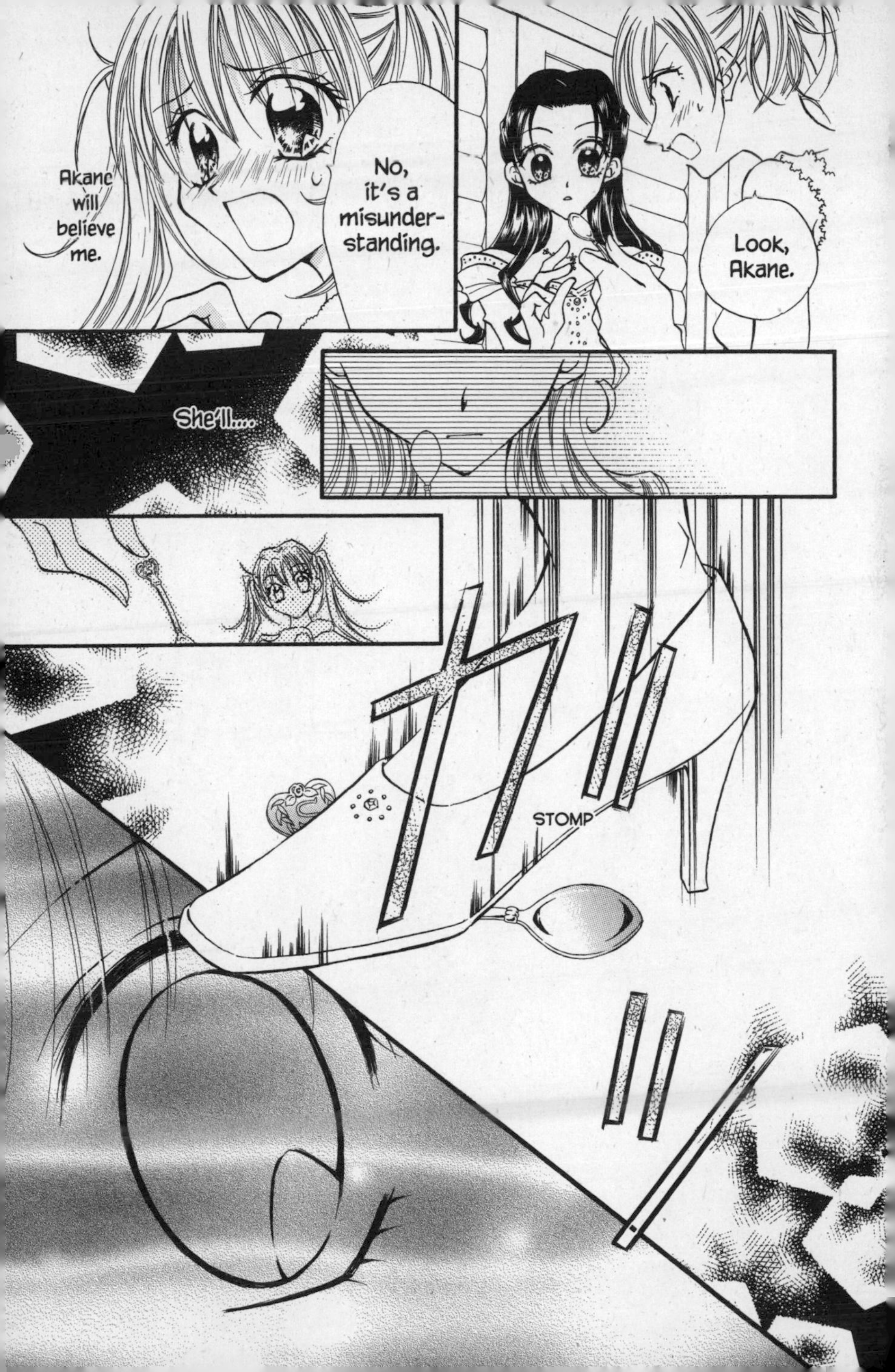
Look, Akane.
No, it's a misunderstanding.
Akane will believe me.
She'll...
STOMP

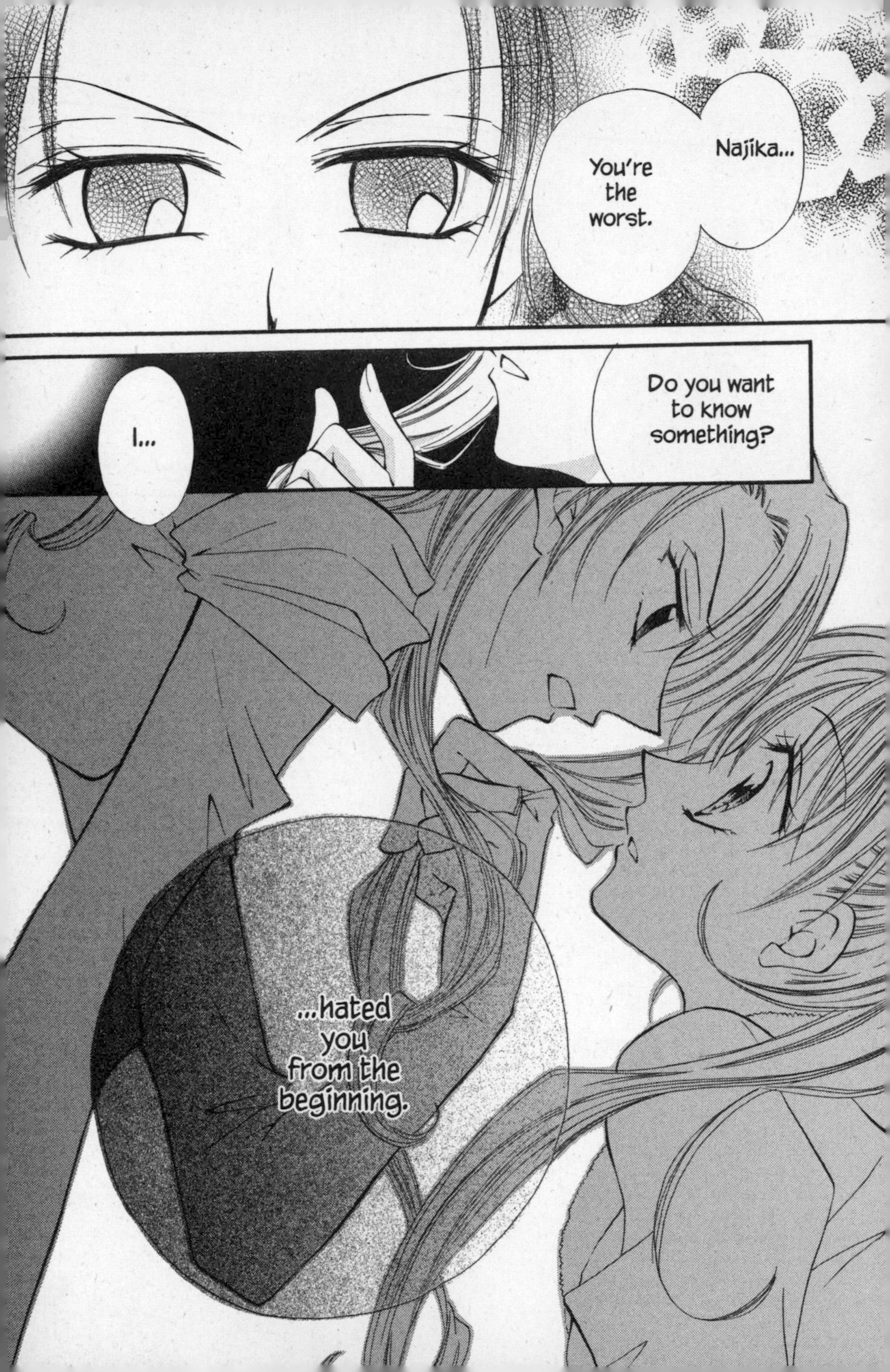
Najika...
You're the worst.
Do you want to know something?
I...
...hated you from the beginning.

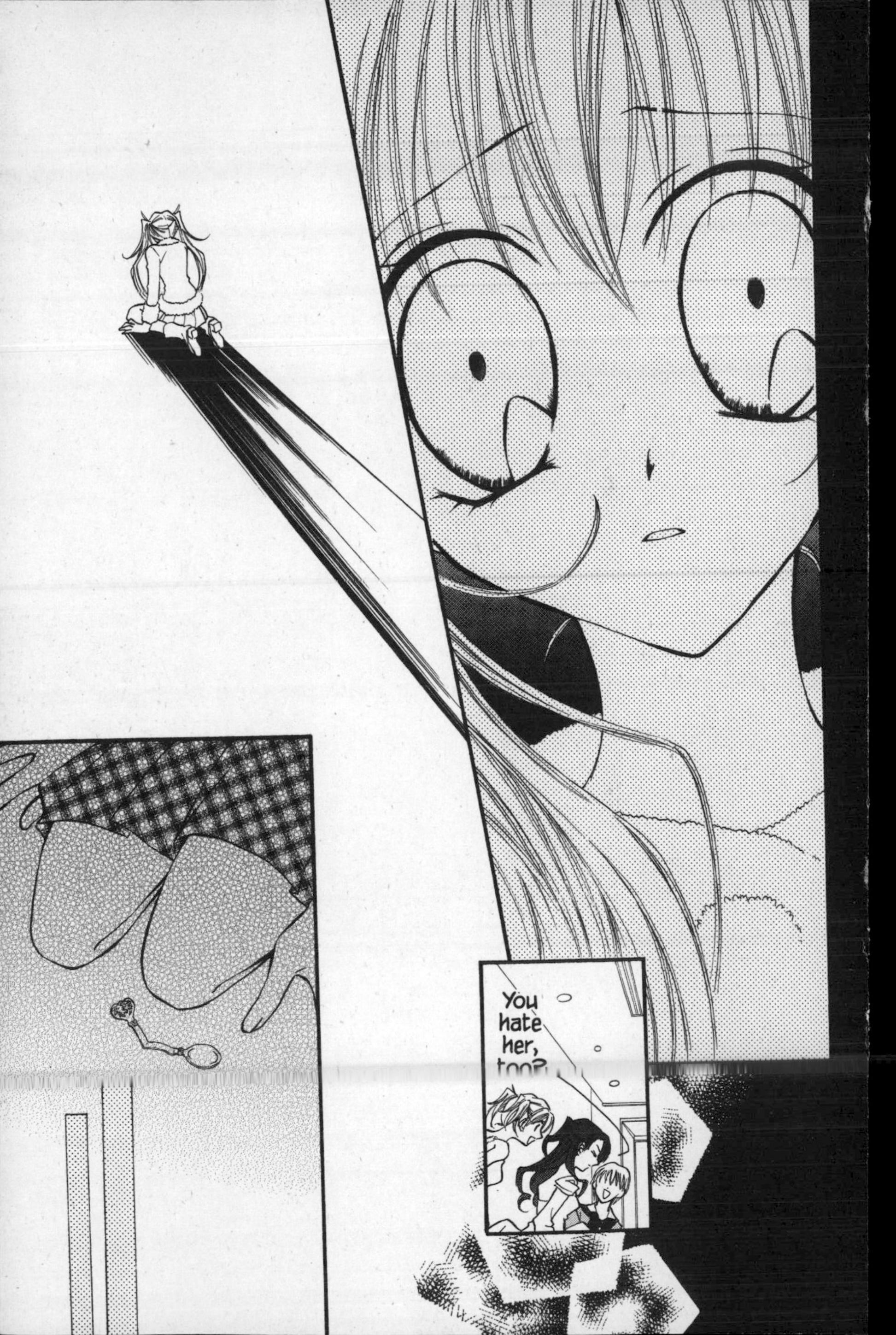
You hate her, too?

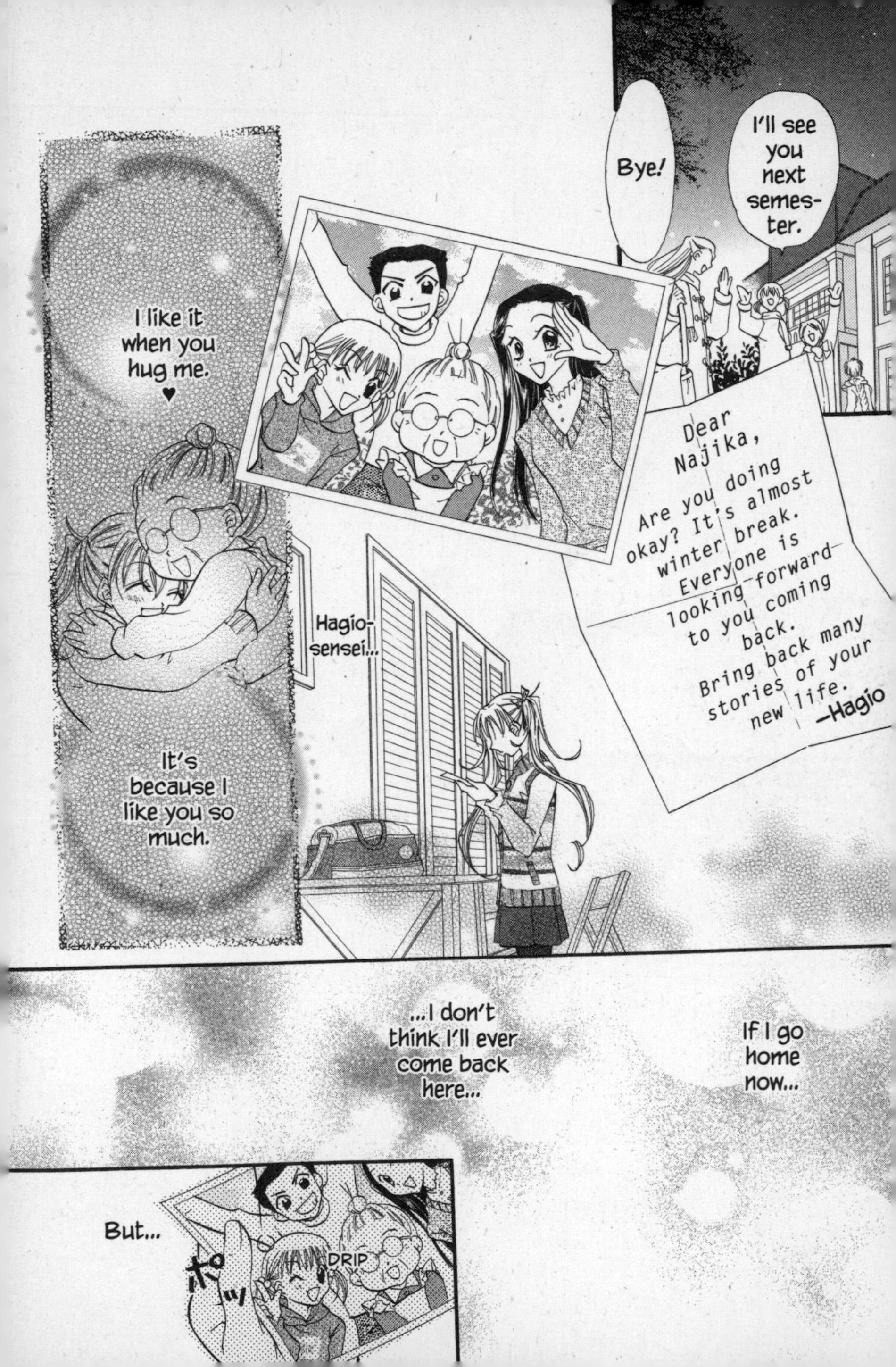

I'll see you next semester.
Bye!
Dear Najika,
Are you doing okay? It's almost winter break. Everyone is looking forward to you coming back.
Bring back many stories of your new life.
—Hagio
Hagio-sensei...
I like it when you hug me. ♥
It's because I like you so much.
If I go home now...
...I don't think I'll ever come back here...
But...
DRIP

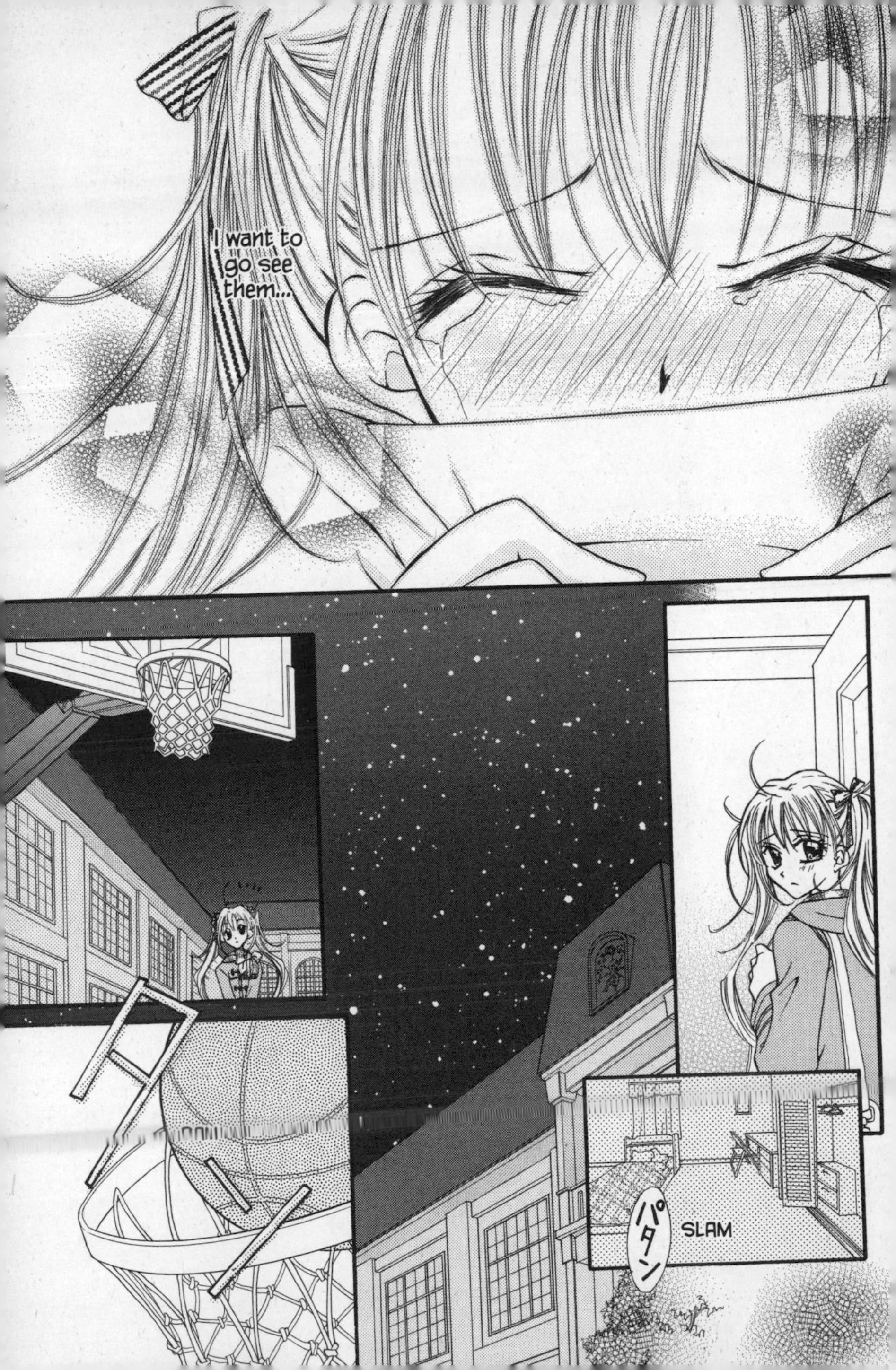
I want to go see them...
パタン
SLAM

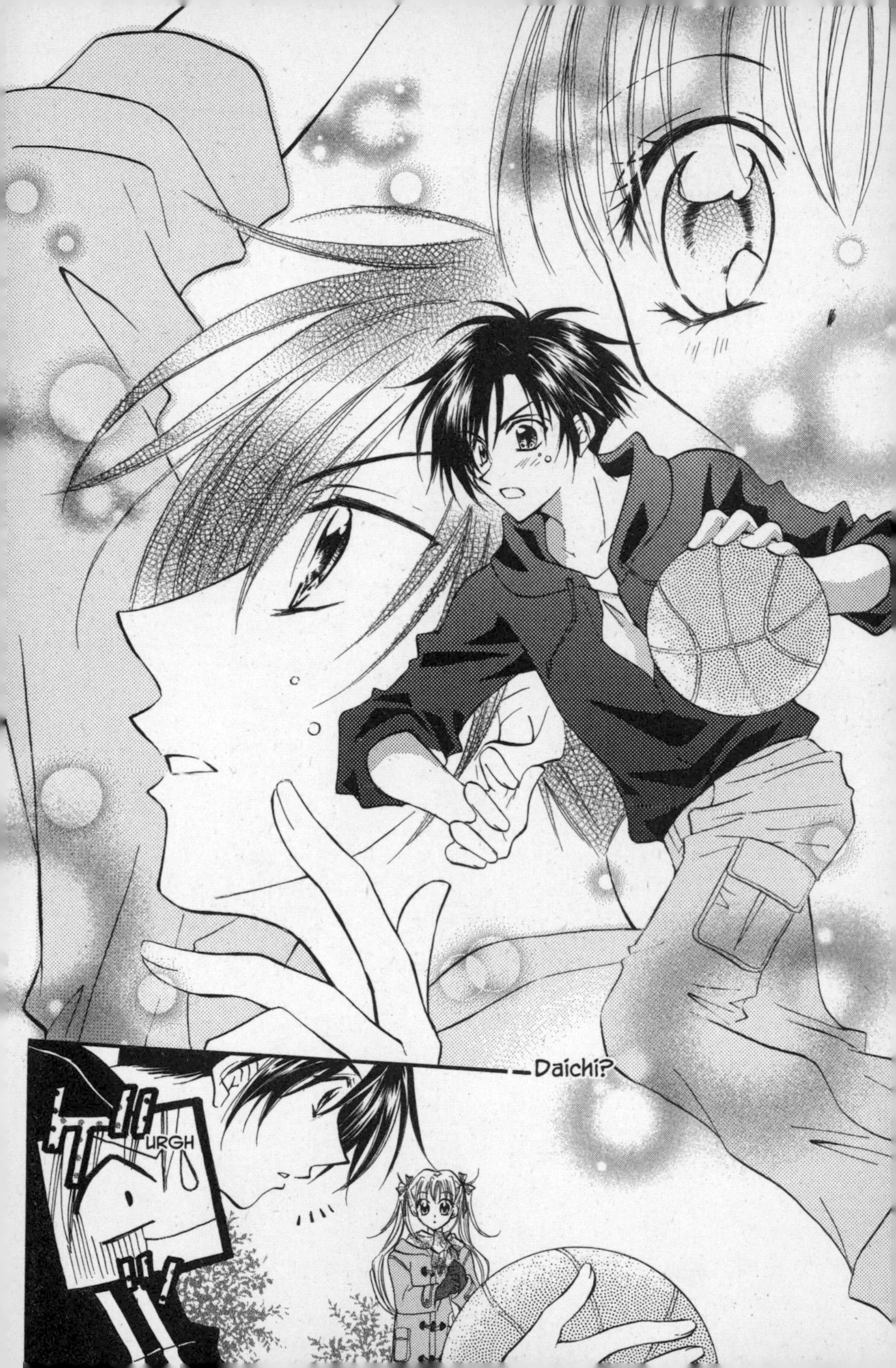
—Daichi?
URGH

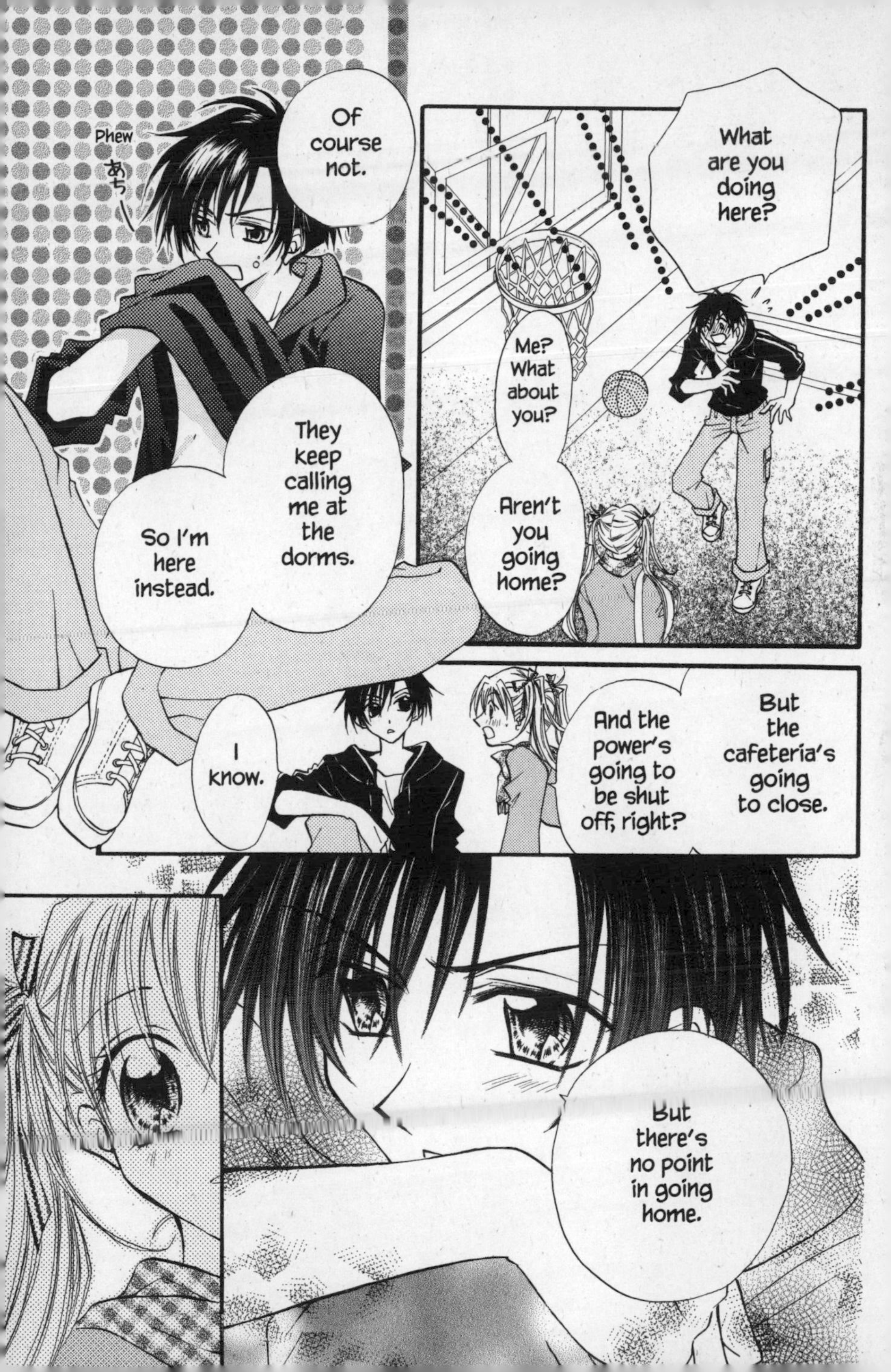
What are you doing here?
Me? What about you?
Aren't you going home?
Of course not.
Phew
あち
They keep calling me at the dorms.
So I'm here instead.
But the cafeteria's going to close.
And the power's going to be shut off, right?
I know.
But there's no point in going home.

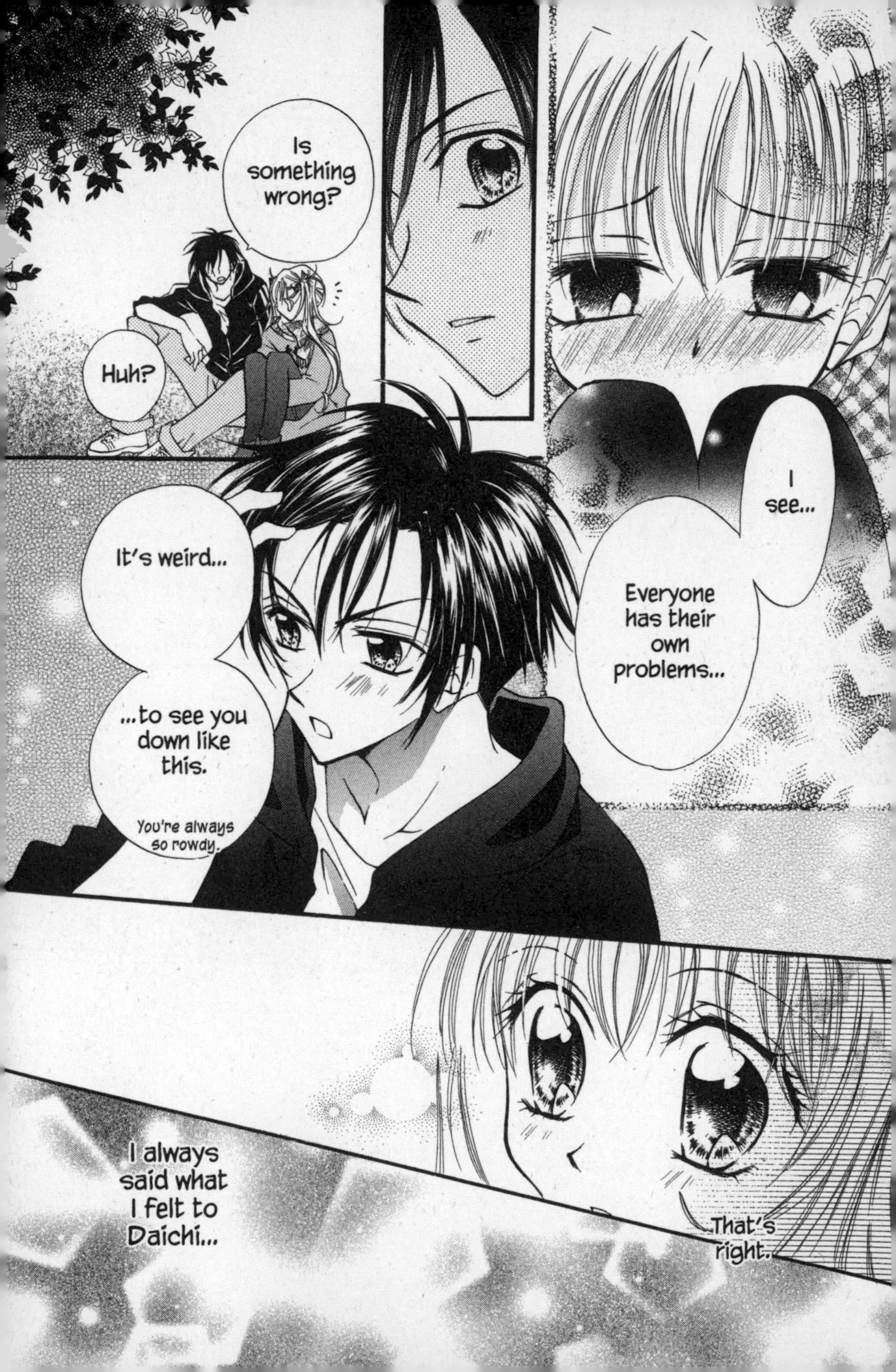
Is something wrong?
Huh?
I see...
Everyone has their own problems...
It's weird...
...to see you down like this.
You're always so rowdy.
That's right.
I always said what I felt to Daichi...

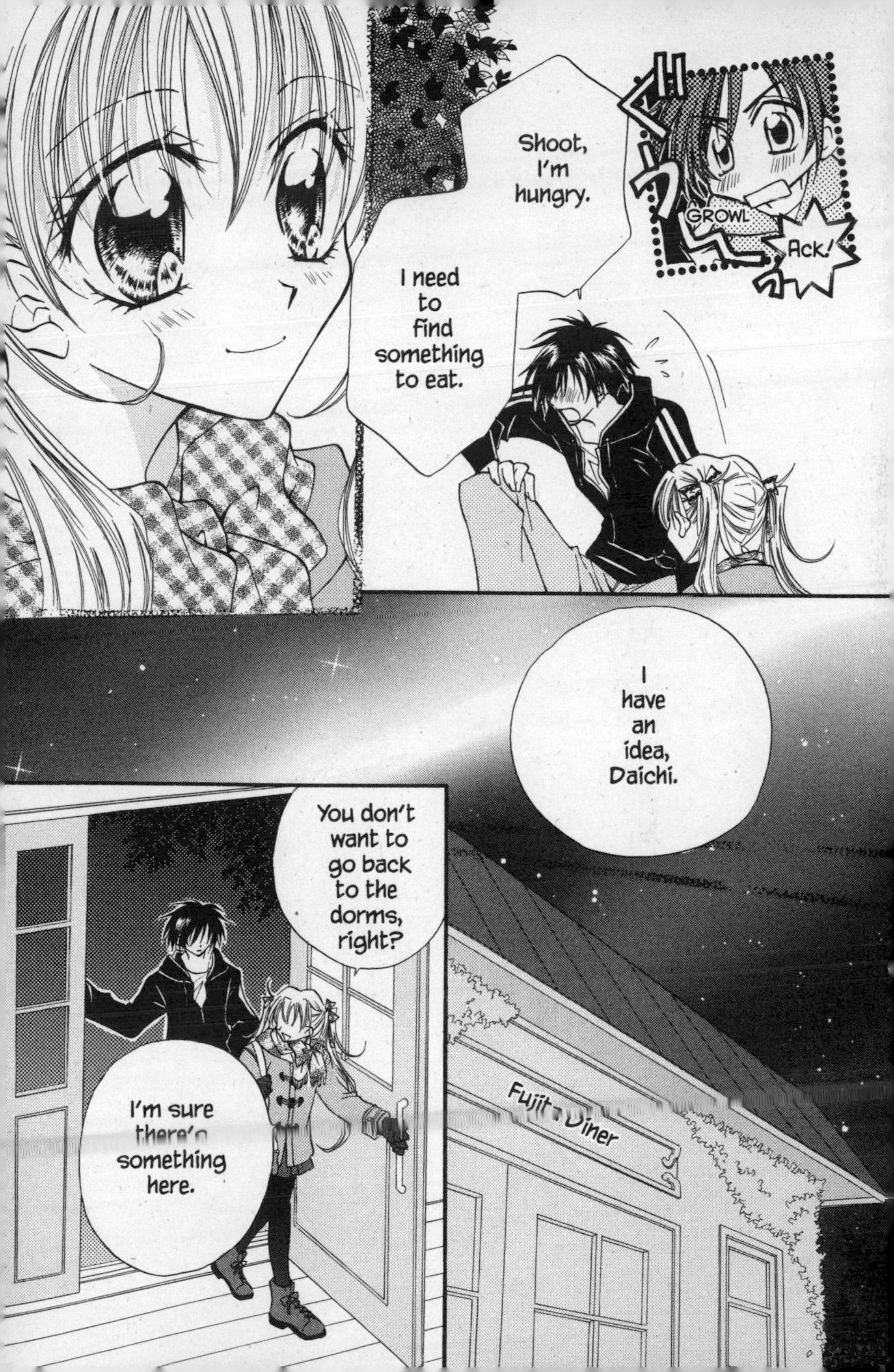
GROWL
Ack!
Shoot, I'm hungry.
I need to find something to eat.
I have an idea, Daichi.
You don't want to go back to the dorms, right?
I'm sure there's something here.
Diner

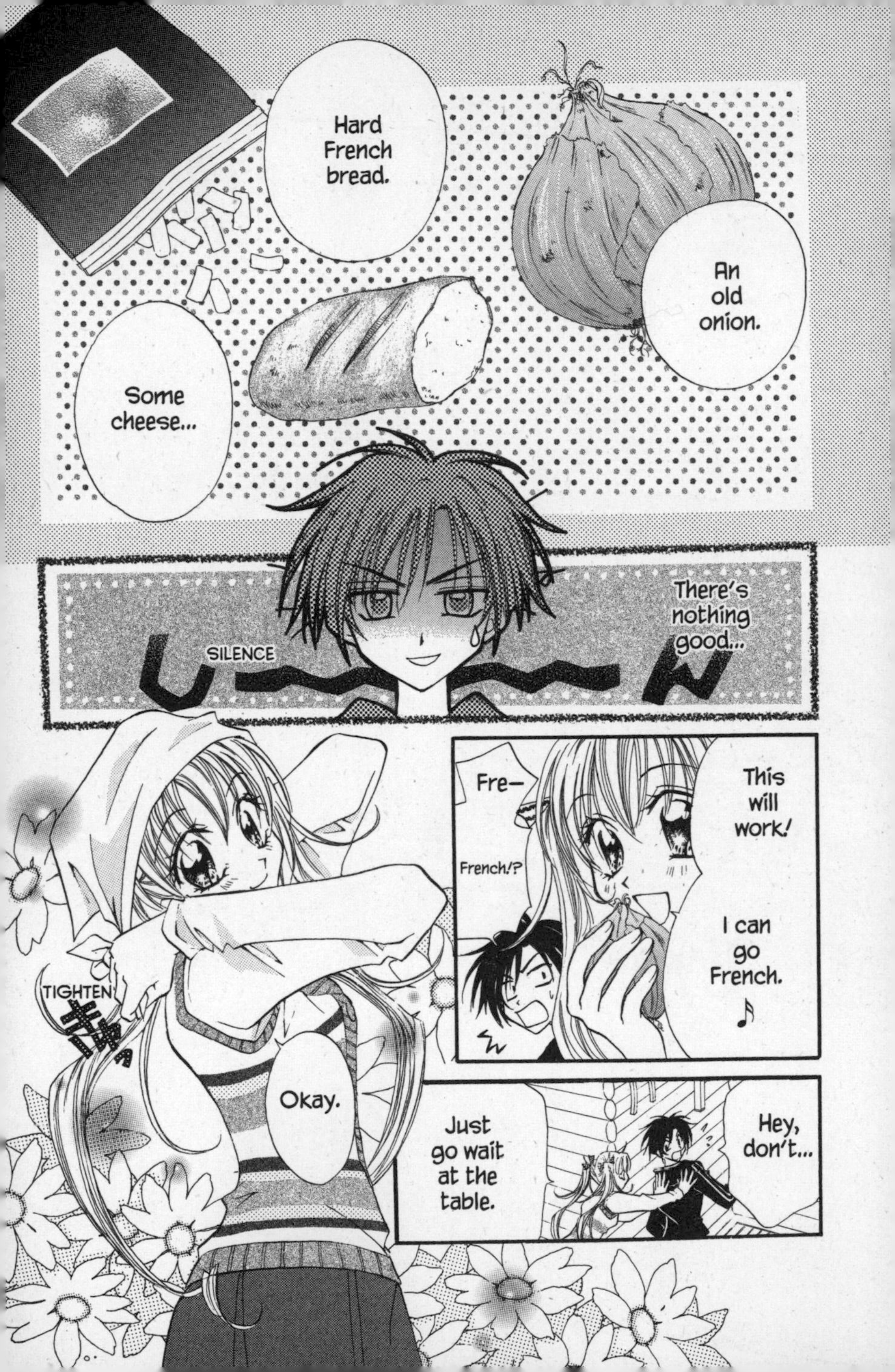
Hard French bread.
An old onion.
Some cheese...
There's nothing good...
SILENCE
U----N
This will work!
Fre—
French!?
I can go French. ♪
Hey, don't...
Just go wait at the table.
Okay.
TIGHTEN

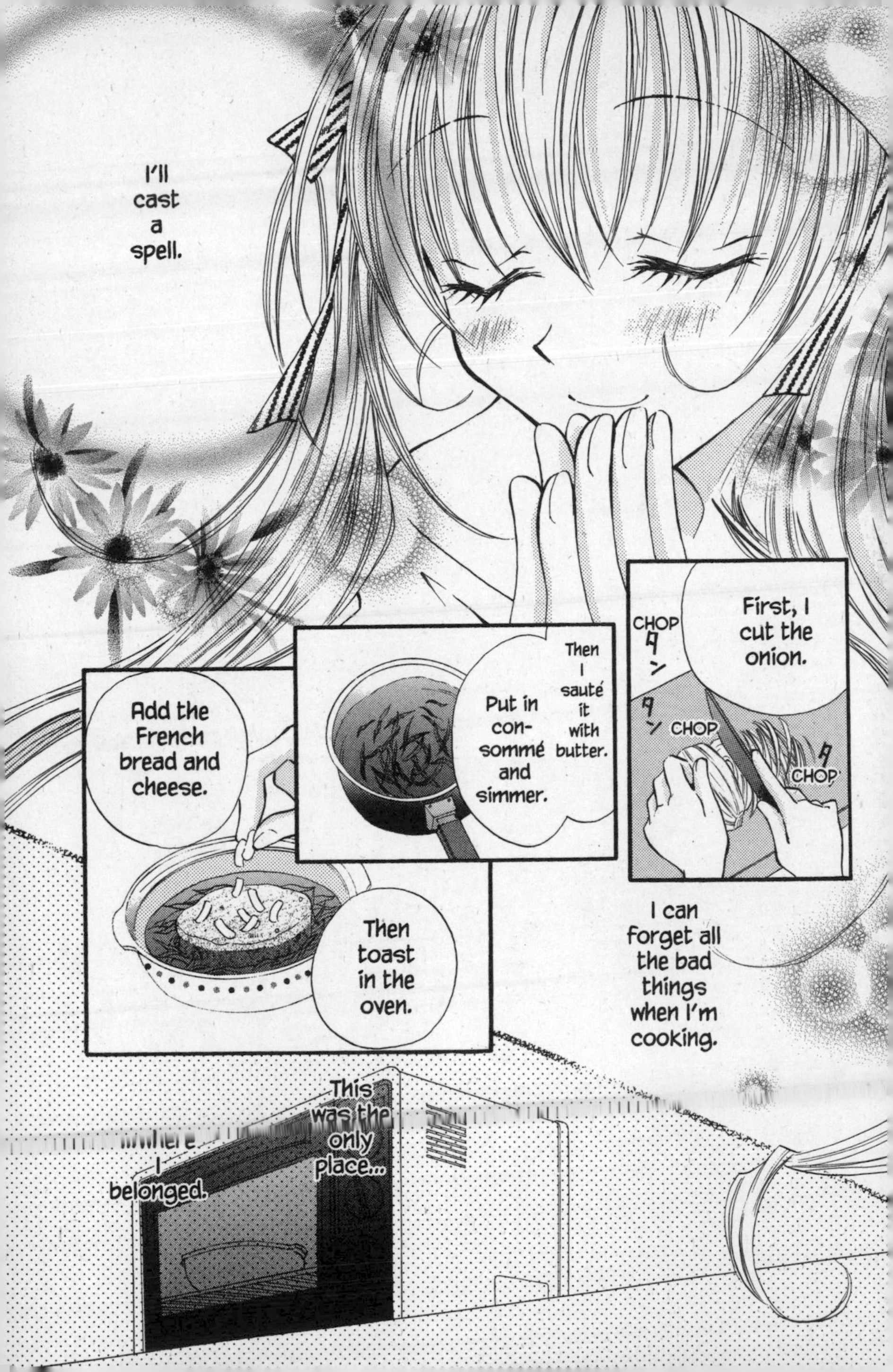
I'll cast a spell.
CHOP
First, I cut the onion.
CHOP
CHOP
Then I sauté it with butter.
Put in consommé and simmer.
Add the French bread and cheese.
Then toast in the oven.
I can forget all the bad things when I'm cooking.
This was the only place...
where I belonged.

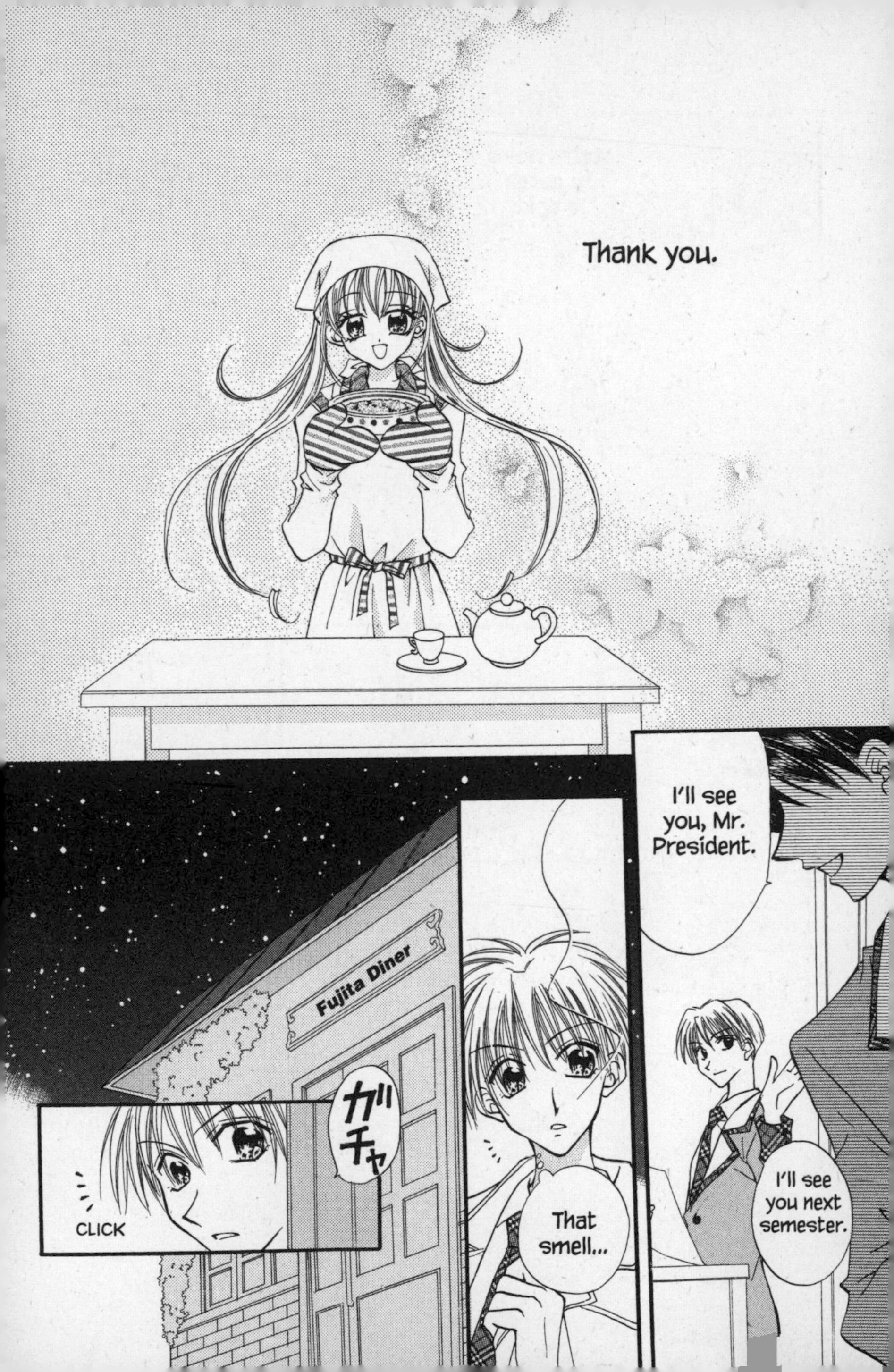
Thank you.
I'll see you, Mr. President.
I'll see you next semester.
That smell...
Fujita Diner
ガチャ
CLICK

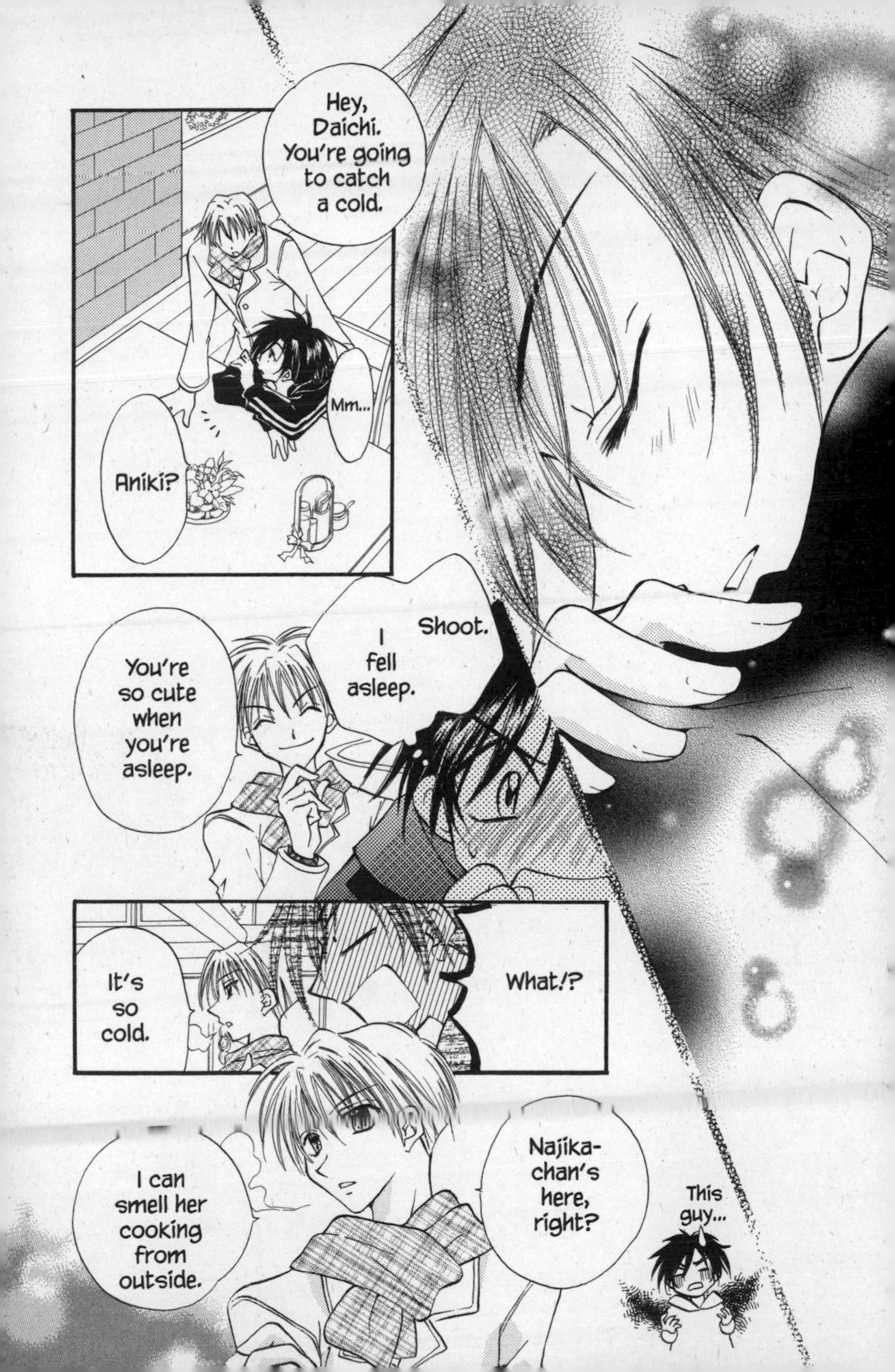

Hey, Daichi. You're going to catch a cold.
Mm...
Aniki?
Shoot.
I fell asleep.
You're so cute when you're asleep.
What!?
It's so cold.
Najika-chan's here, right?
I can smell her cooking from outside.
This guy...

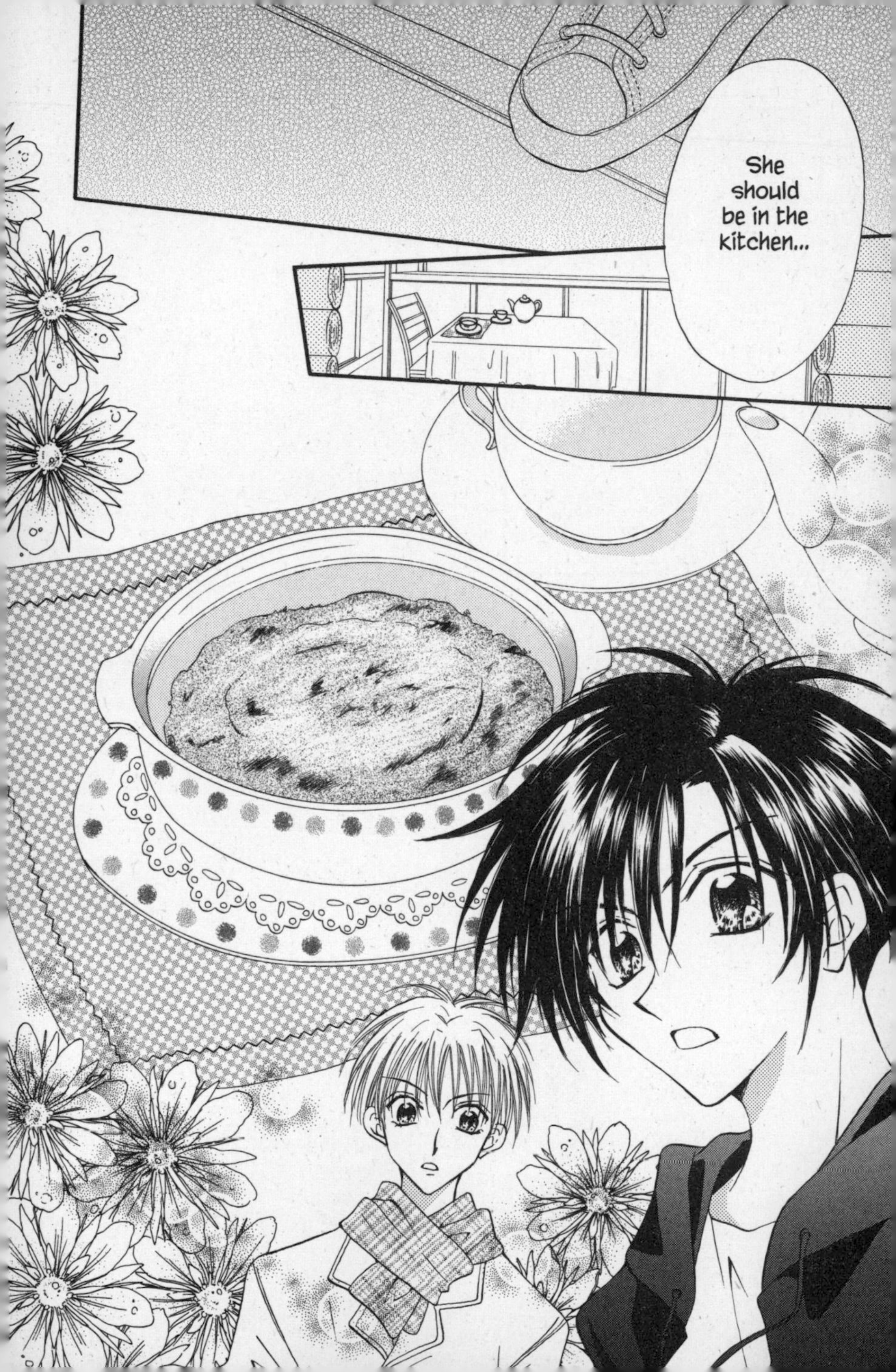
She should be in the kitchen...

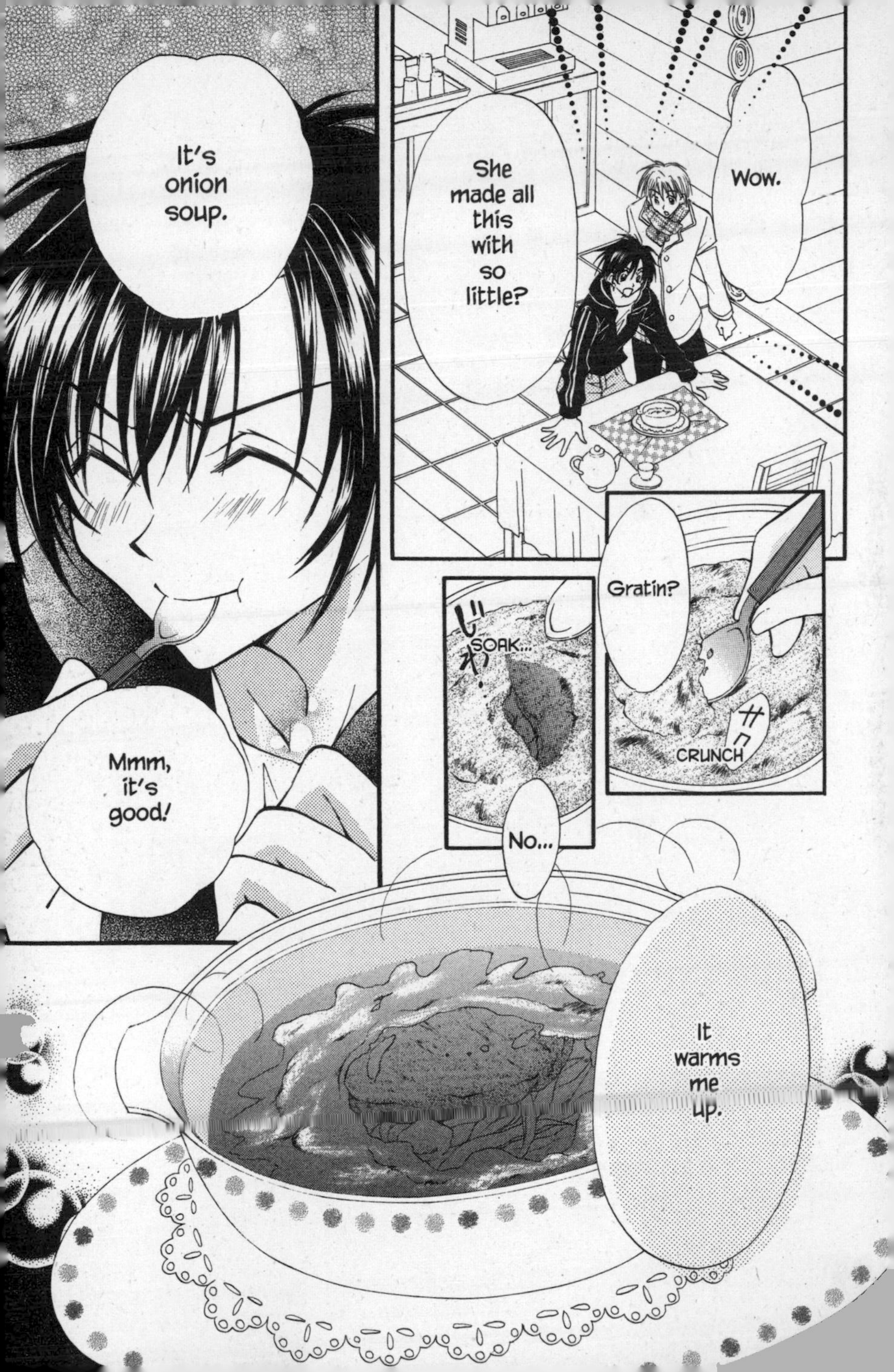

Wow.
She made all this with so little?
Gratin?
サク
CRUNCH
じわ
SOAK...
No...
It's onion soup.
Mmm, it's good!
It warms me up.

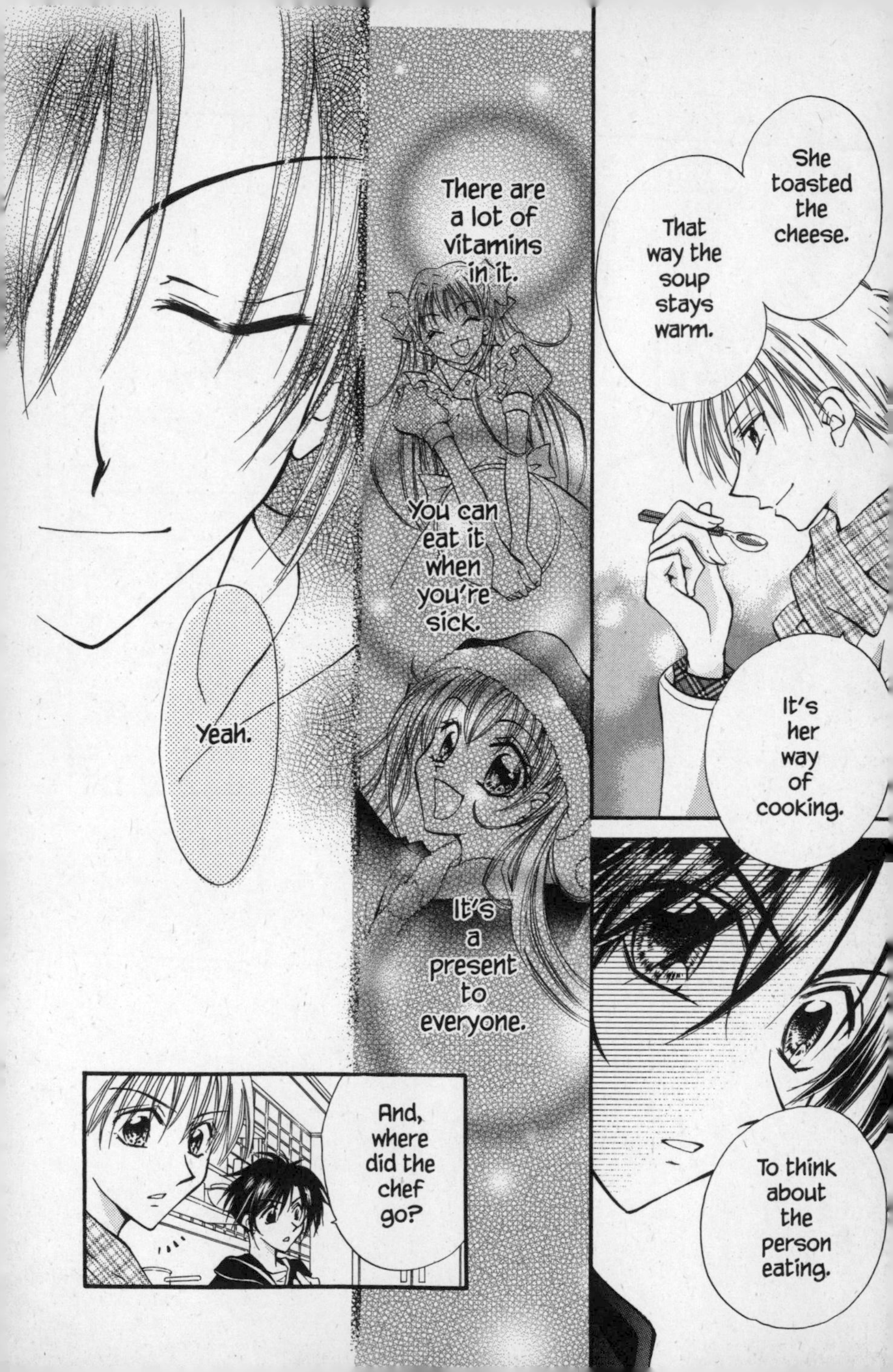
She toasted the cheese.
That way the soup stays warm.
It's her way of cooking.
To think about the person eating.
There are a lot of vitamins in it.
You can eat it when you're sick.
It's a present to everyone.
Yeah.
And, where did the chef go?

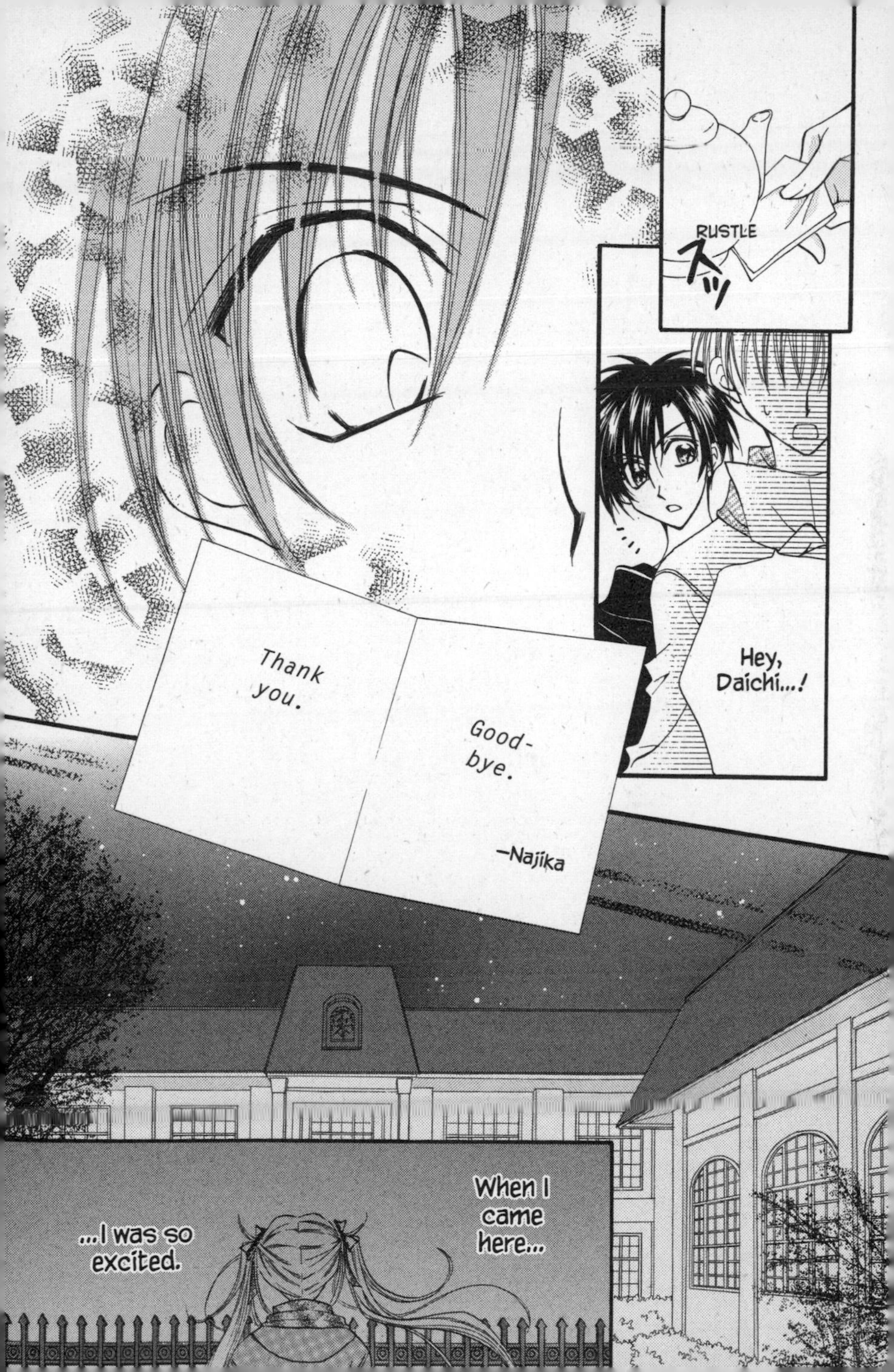
RUSTLE
スッ
Hey, Daichi...!
Thank you.
Good-bye.
—Najika
When I came here...
...I was so excited.

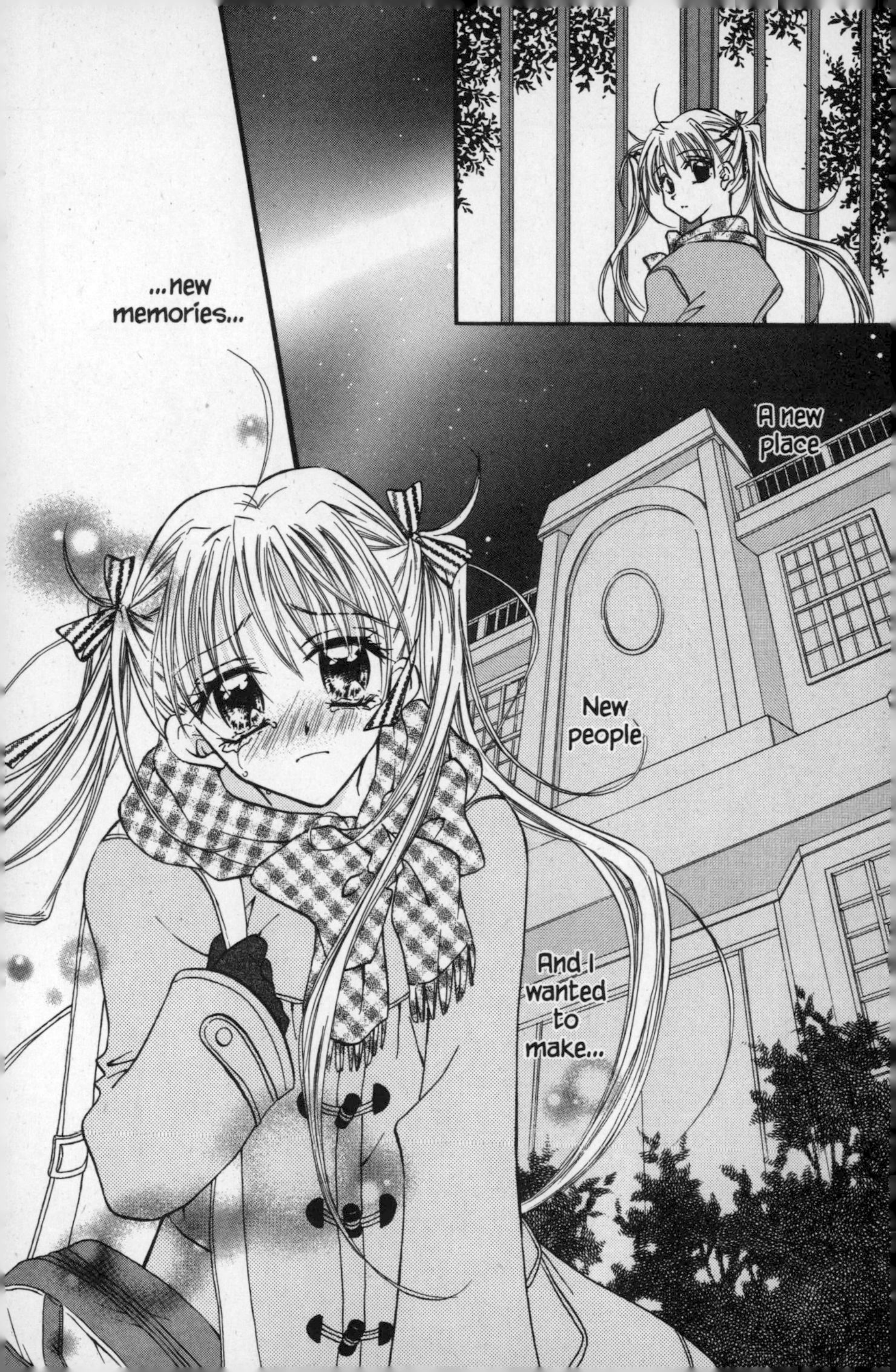
A new place
New people
And I wanted to make...
...new memories...

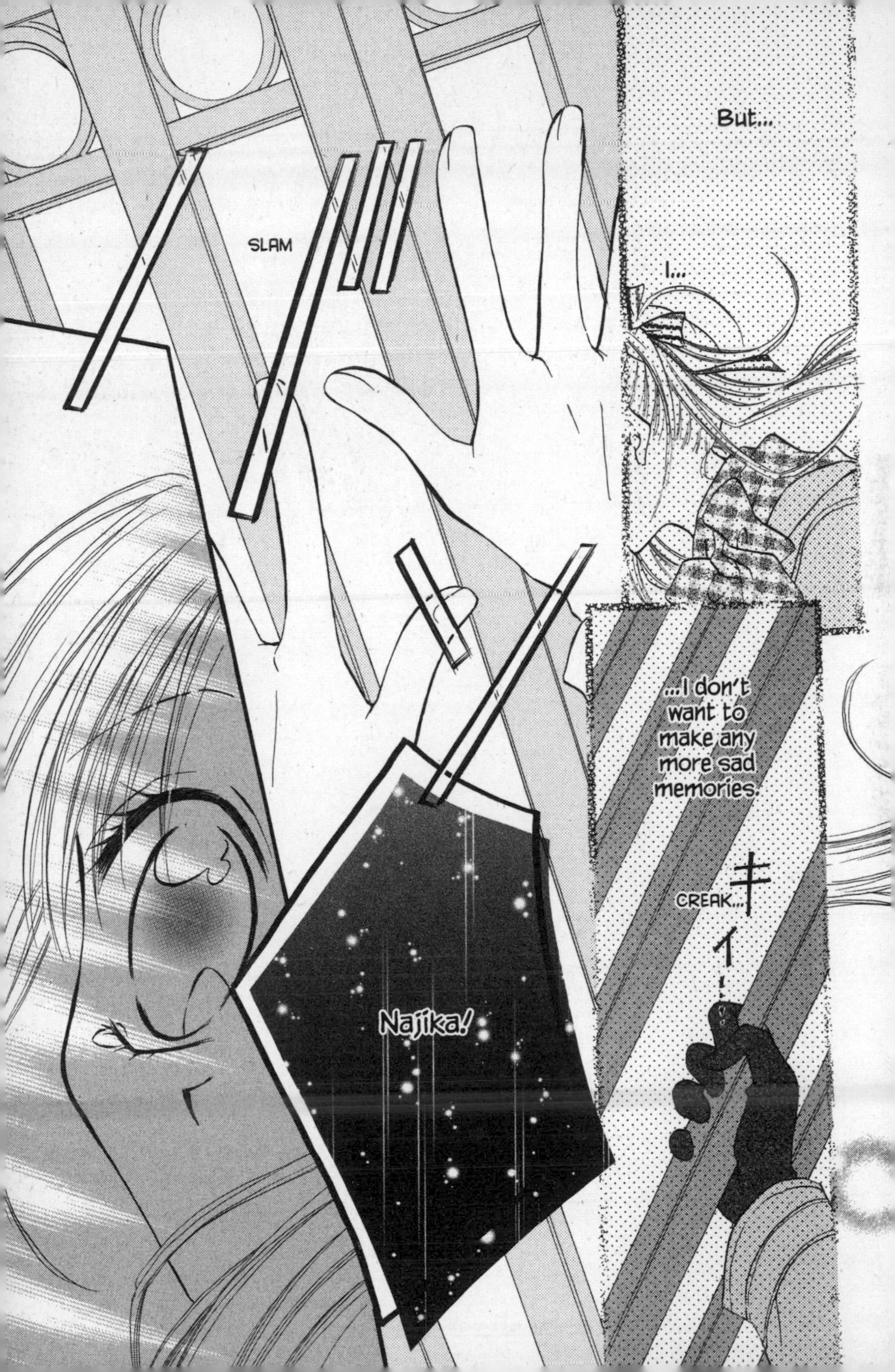

But...
I...
...I don't want to make any more sad memories.
CREAK...
キイ
SLAM
Najika!

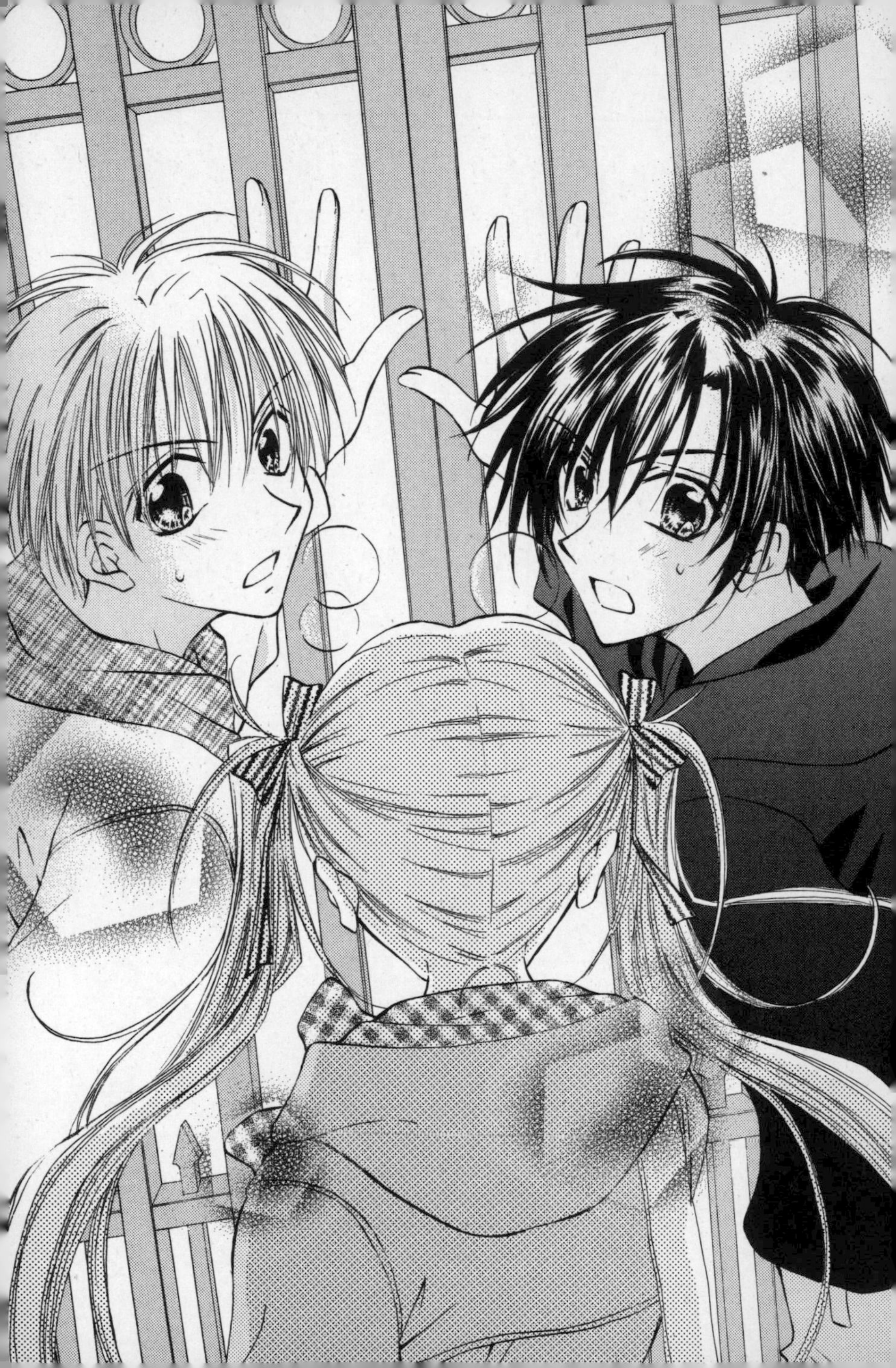

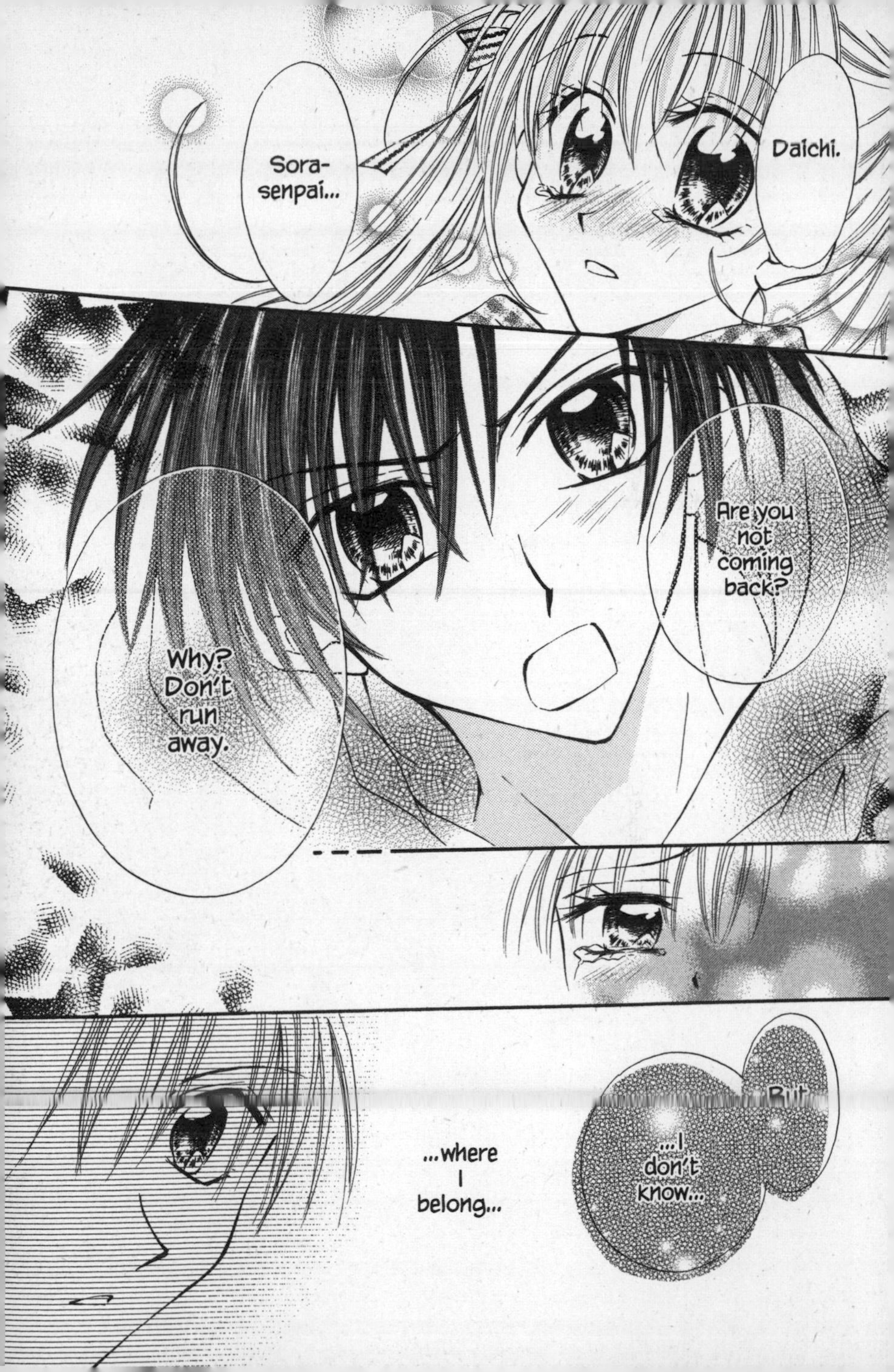
Daichi.
Sora-senpai...
Are you not coming back?
Why? Don't run away.
But
...I don't know...
...where I belong...

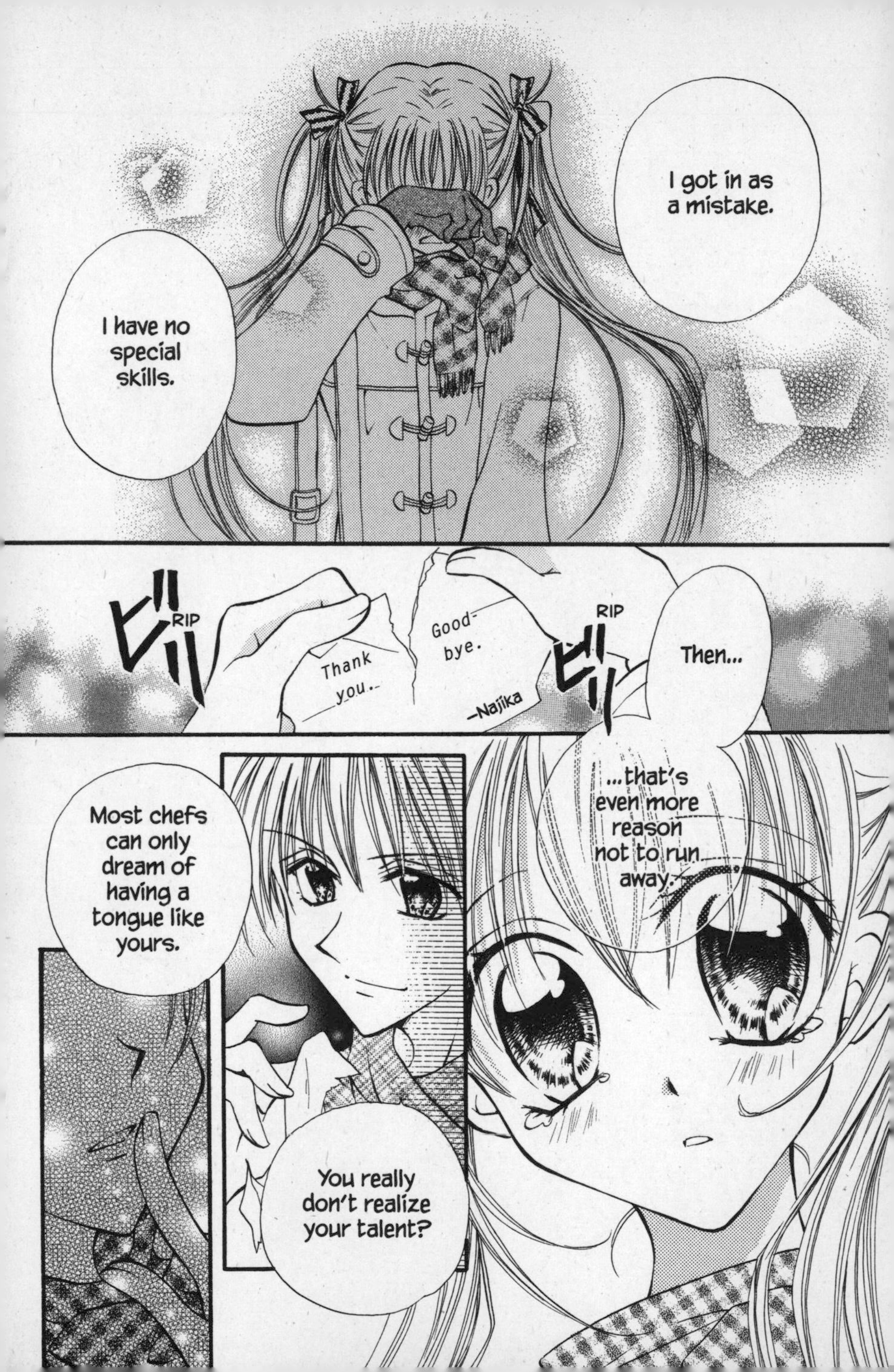
I got in as a mistake.
I have no special skills.
Then...
ビリ RIP
Thank you...
Good-bye.
—Najika
ビリ RIP
...that's even more reason not to run away.
Most chefs can only dream of having a tongue like yours.
You really don't realize your talent?

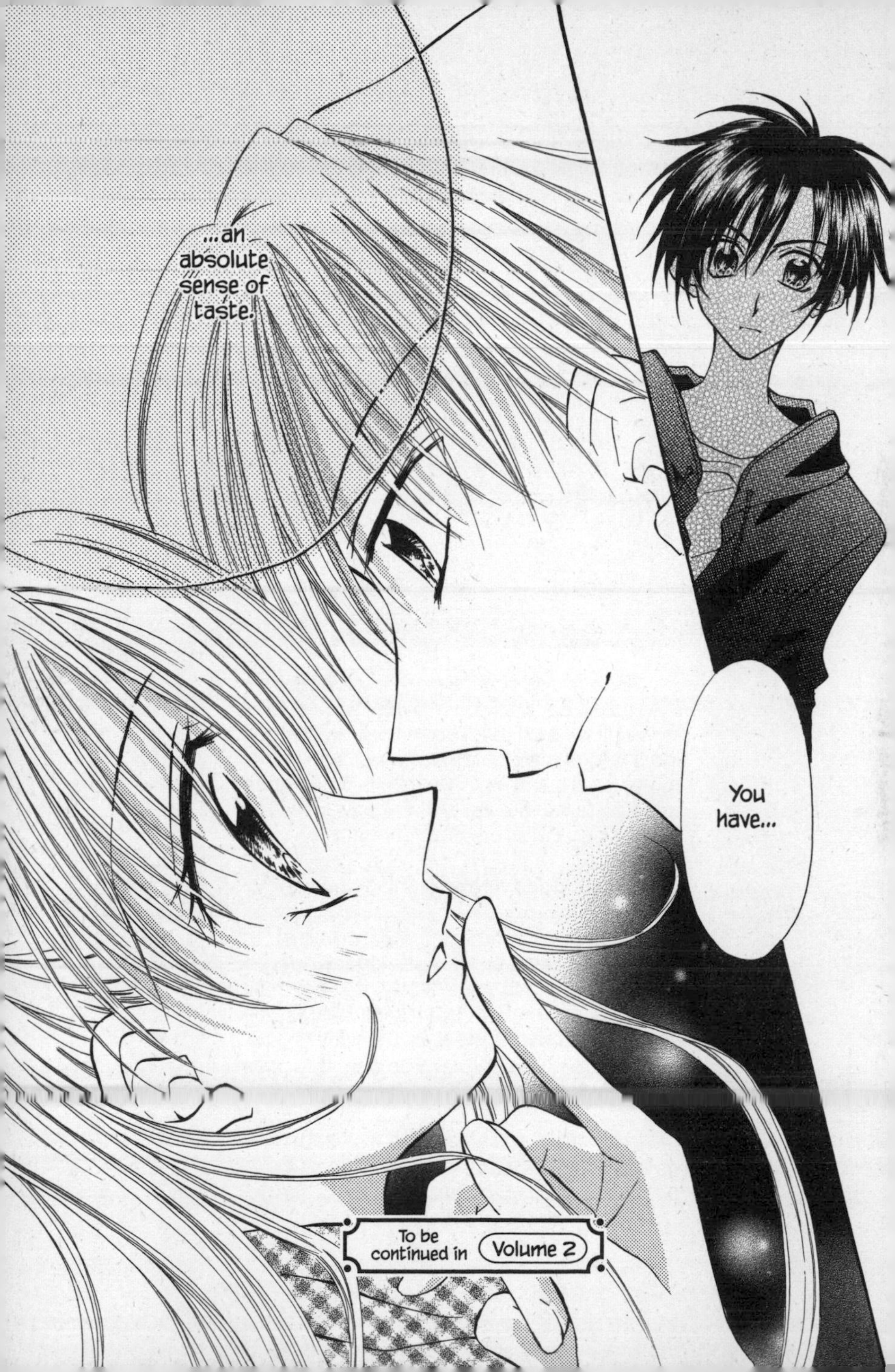
You have...
...an absolute sense of taste.
To be continued in Volume 2

Thank you
Maruyama-sama
Shobayashi-sama
Marimo-sama
Kishimoto-sama

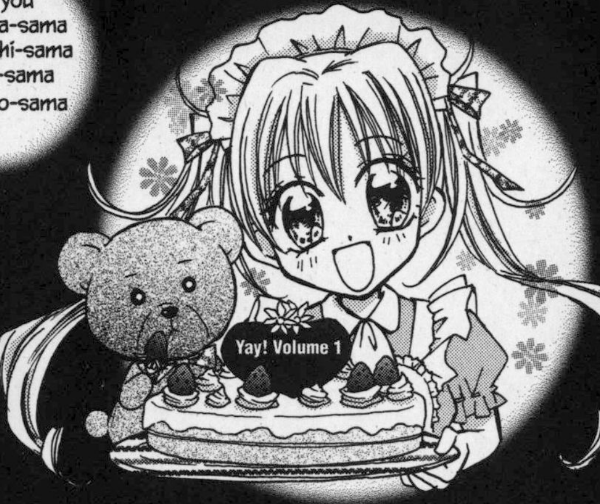
Yay! Volume 1

All the food that appears in Kitchen Princess comes from Miyuki-sensei, who sends pictures. I use those to draw the good food. It looks so delicious, I just want to run to her house and eat! The other day, I guess she heard my wishes, and I received the real thing (it comes in Volume 2 ♥).

It was so good, I finished it immediately.

It's my first time doing manga with a script, but Miyuki-sensei took my suggestions, too. Hagio-sensei being an old lady, and the design for the Diner chef (originally an old lady who looked like Hagio-sensei, but I made it into a rugged man) was all me. She was very open-minded, and I am so grateful for that.

And I'm also grateful to all my readers!! I am very, very behind in responding. But I will, so please don't give up on me. ♥ I'll see you again in Volume 2. ❀

Kitchen Palace

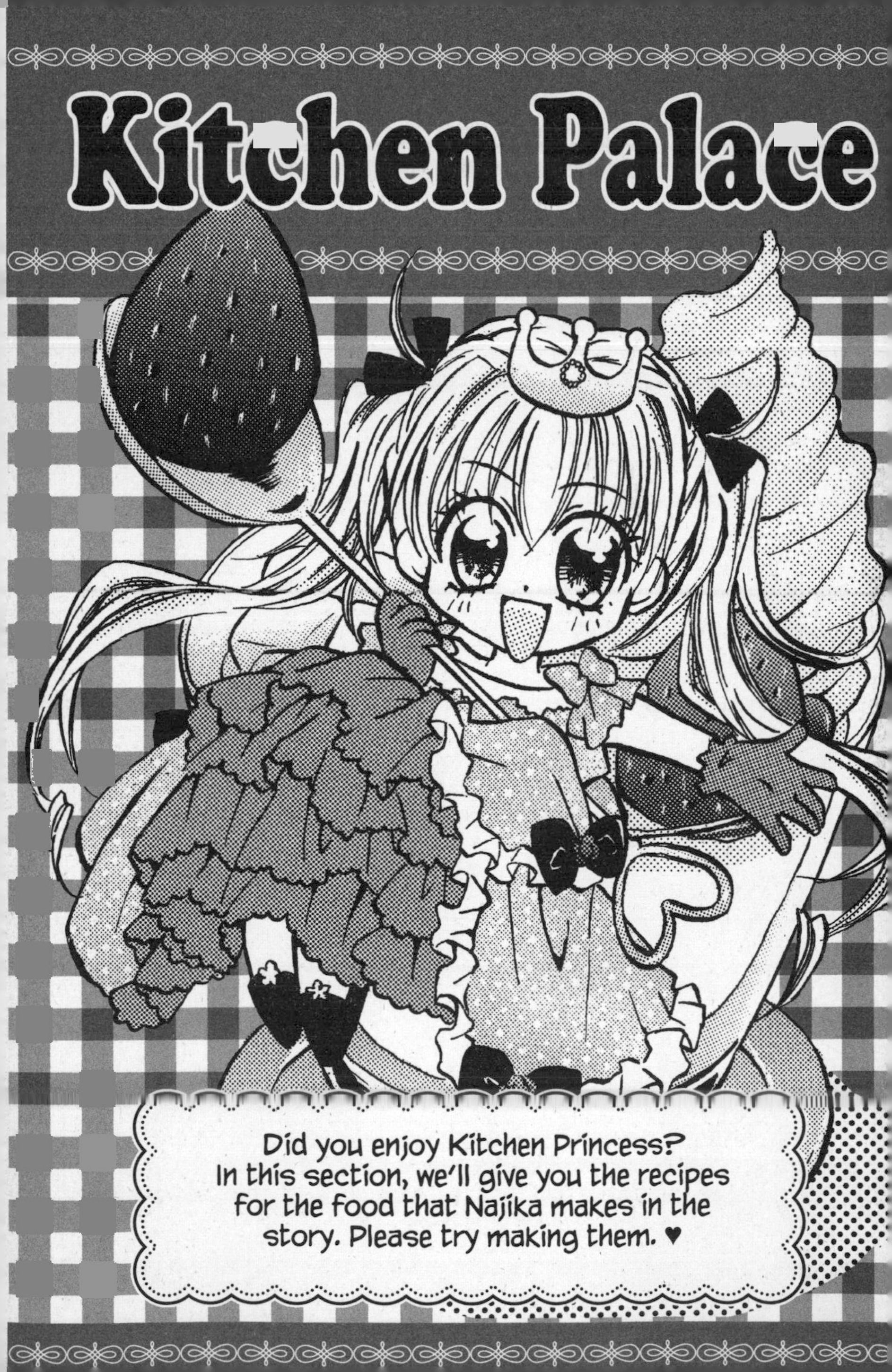

Did you enjoy Kitchen Princess?
In this section, we'll give you the recipes for the food that Najika makes in the story. Please try making them. ♥

Flan in a Cup

Najika's special flan is made by pouring it in a teacup. Metal flan cups conduct heat and are hard to manage. Making the flan in plastic is easier and it will come out prettier!

Tip from Najika.

Flan: Makes 4 cups of flan. 1¾ cups milk, 5 tablespoons sugar, 3 eggs, a little bit of vanilla. Caramel Sauce: 3 tablespoons sugar, 1 tablespoon water

How to make

1 Put milk on low heat and add sugar. Stir well and when the sugar melts, stop the heat and cool for a minute. Make sure you don't let the milk boil.

2 Break the eggs in a bowl and stir well.

3 Slowly pour the milk from step 1 into the bowl from step 2 and stir. Add some vanilla.

4 Pour the mix from step 3 through a strainer. This makes the flan smoother.

5 Make the caramel sauce in a small pot. Put the water and sugar in the pot and stir quickly over high heat. When it becomes brown, remove from heat and put it into four cups.

6 Pour the mix from step 4 into the cups over the caramel sauce.

7 Fill a pot with water and put a steamer above it. When the water starts steaming, stop the heat and put the cups in the steamer. Please be careful not to burn yourself. After 2 to 3 minutes on high heat, lower the heat and steam for another 13 to 15 minutes. When you put it on low heat, move the lid a little so some of the steam will escape. The point is to maintain it on low heat. If you put a towel under the lid, water won't get into the flan.

8 Poke a hole in the flan with a toothpick, and if juice doesn't come out, it's done. After it cools, put it in the refrigerator.

Done ♡

Top it with whipped cream or fruit and it'll be GOOD!!

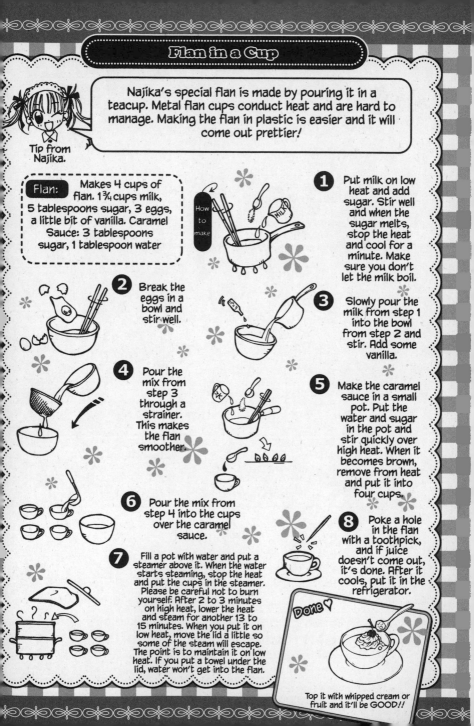

Taramasalata

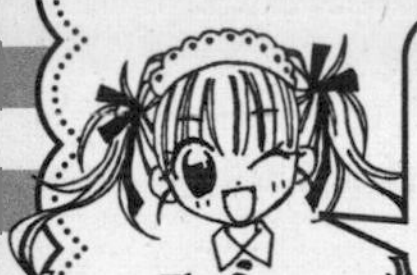

Tip from Najika.

This time we're making one of Greece's finest dishes, the taramasalata. It's good on sliced French bread or crackers. Depending on the saltiness of the roe, you can adjust the amount of salt used.

Taramasalata Serves two people.
1 medium-sized potato, 1 roe, 2 tablespoons mayonnaise, 1 teaspoon olive oil, 1 teaspoon lemon juice, some salt and pepper

How to make

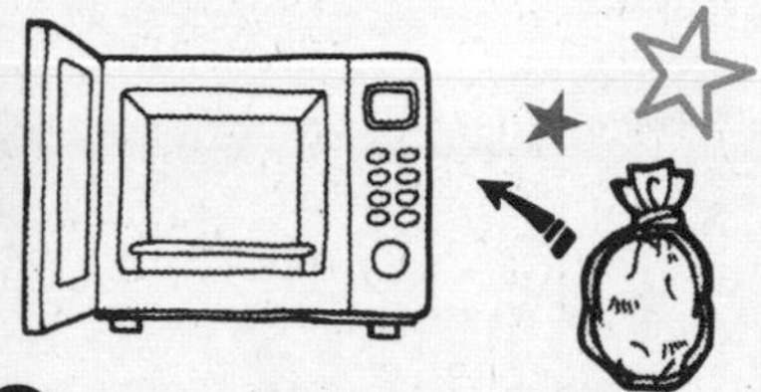

1. Wash the potato and wrap it in Saran Wrap. Microwave it for 5 minutes. It is ready when you can poke a bamboo stick through it.

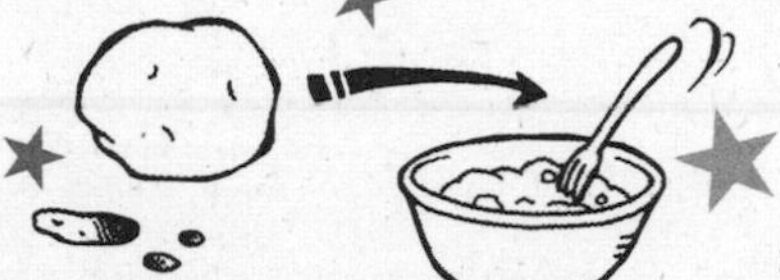

2. Peel the potato while it's still hot. Make sure you don't burn yourself! Put the potato in a bowl and crush it with a fork.

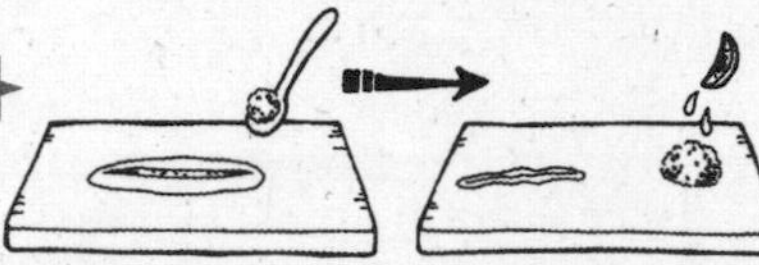

3. Cut a slit in the middle of the roe and scoop out the insides with a spoon. Pour lemon juice on it and throw away the roe skin. If you wrap the cutting board with Saran Wrap, it won't get dirty.

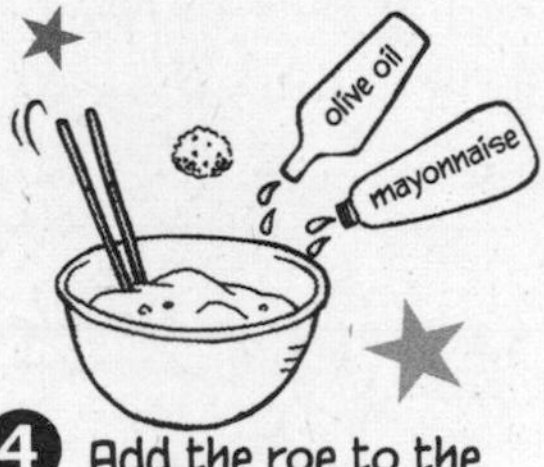

olive oil
mayonnaise

4. Add the roe to the bowl from step 2, along with the mayonnaise, olive oil, and pepper. Stir. Salt to taste, and then you're done!

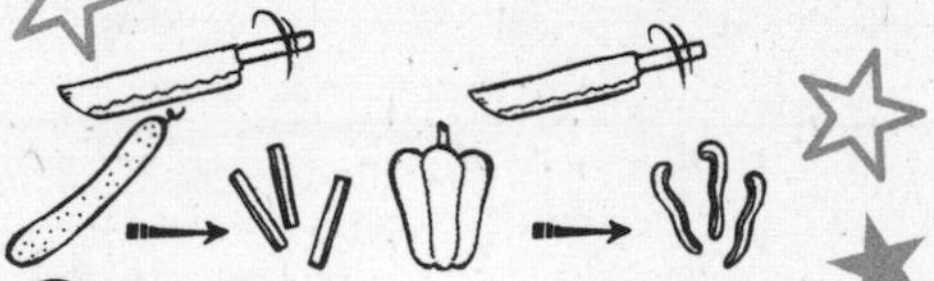

5. You can cut cucumbers or red peppers and lay them on a plate and put the taramasalata in the middle. Add basil or mint to make it pretty.

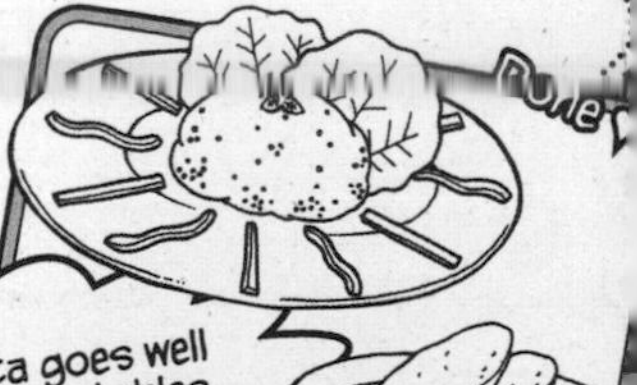

Taramasalata goes well with various vegetables. You can choose your favorite to eat with it!

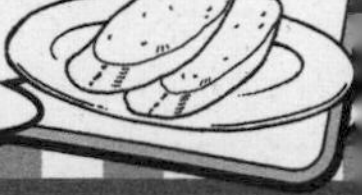

Rainbow Jelly

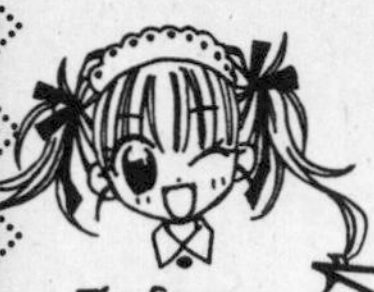

Tip from Najika.

This is jelly that you can enjoy in various flavors and colors. You can choose your favorite juices to use. It'll be delicious if you top it with fruit, too. ♥

Rainbow Jelly Makes eight glasses. 1 cup each of five different juices (grape, orange, melon, grapefruit, etc). *Try to choose different-colored juices. 5 bags gelatin, 2 teaspoons granulated sugar for each juice. *Adjust the sugar according to the sweetness of the juice

How to make

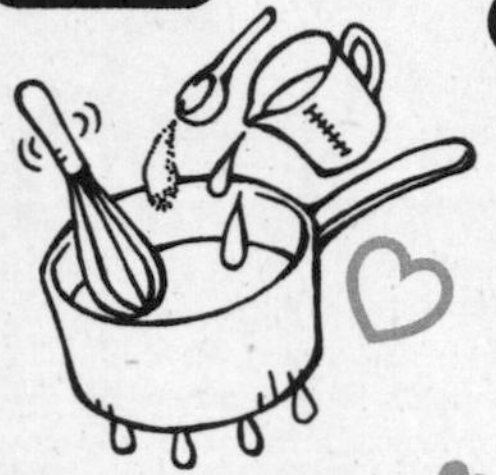

1. In a small pot, add 1 cup juice over low heat. When it warms up, add the granulated sugar and stir. When the sugar melts, stop the heat. Make sure you don't let the mix boil.

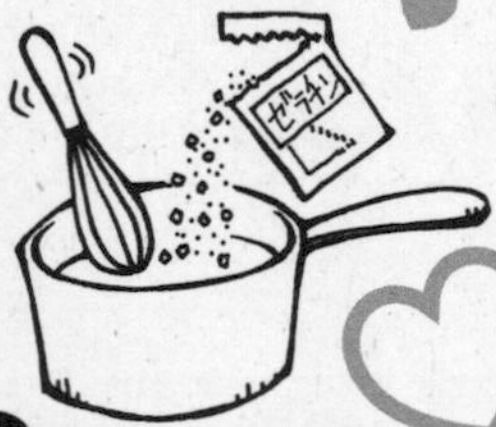

2. Put gelatin in the pot and stir until it is completely melted.

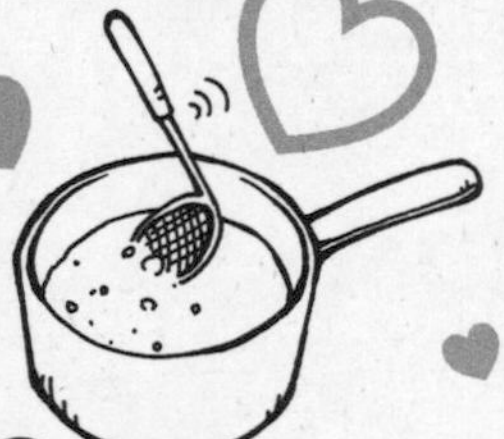

3. When you stir it, white foam will form, so remove it with a ladle. The jelly becomes smoother with this step.

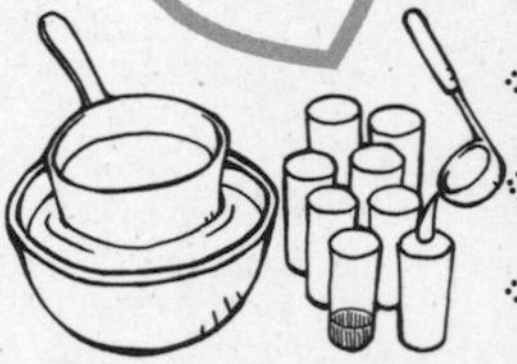

4. Put the pot from step 3 in a bowl filled with ice to cool. When the mix is cool, pour it into eight glasses.

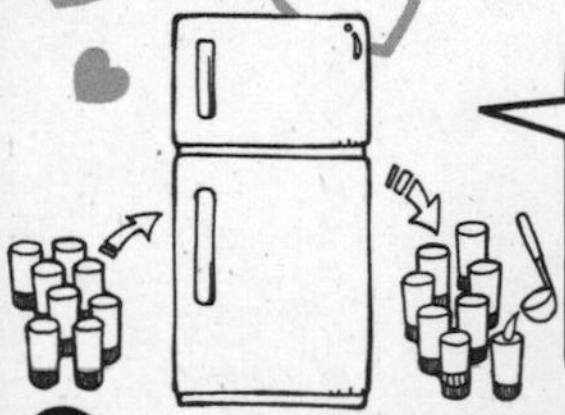

5. Put the glasses in the refrigerator and leave them in for about an hour. When the jelly hardens, you repeat the steps and add the different juices one at a time in the glass.

If you repeat the steps, you'll get a colorful jelly in your glass. If you want to make less, you can make each jelly with half the ingredients.

A rainbow is seven colors, but we made it with five colors this time for simplicity. If you get better at it, please try seven jelly colors!

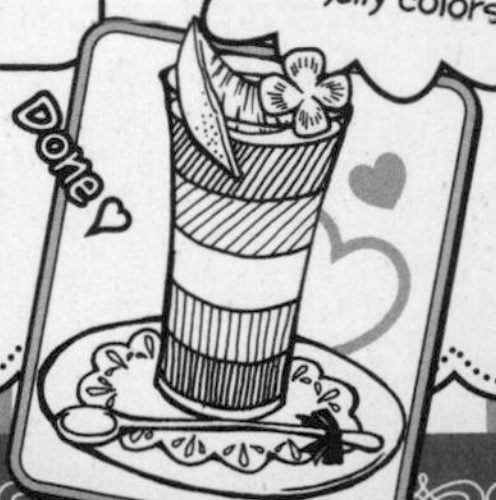
Done♥

Christmas Cookies

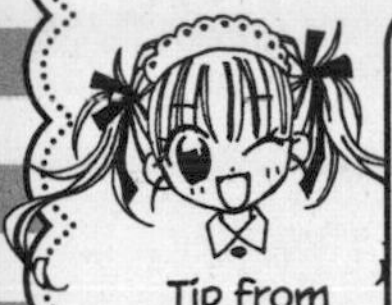

Tip from Najika.

Try making cookies! You can make them into ornaments like I did. If you put frosting on the cookies, they become colorful and pretty!

Christmas Cookies

Makes about 20 cookies.
½ cup soft flour,
½ cup sugar, 1 small egg,
7 tablespoons butter

How to make

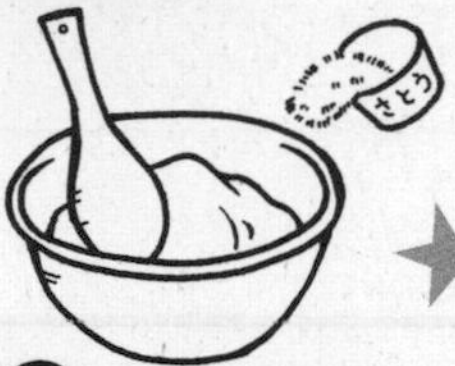

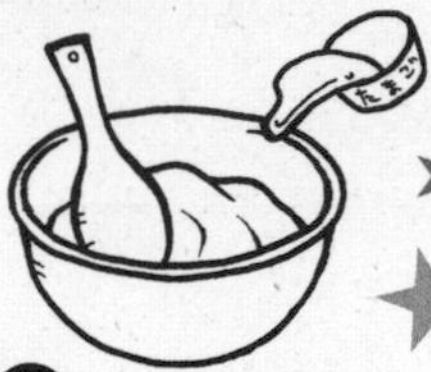

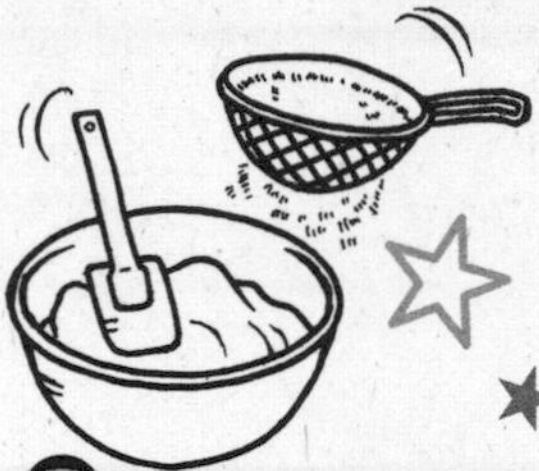

1. Soften the butter at room temperature and crush it in a bowl with a wooden spoon. Add sugar and stir more.
2. Add the egg and mix.
3. Sieve the flour into the mix and stir. It is ready when the white flour chunks are gone.

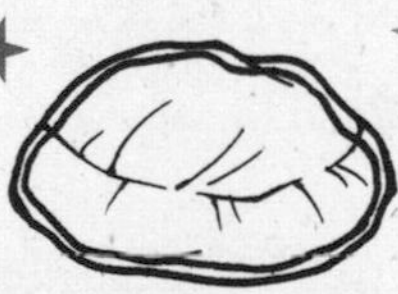

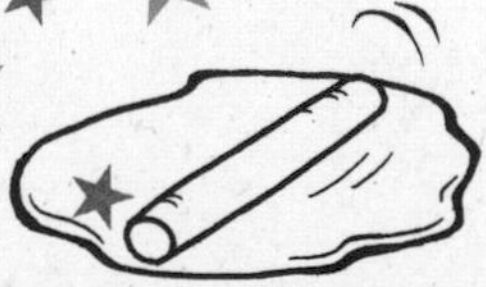

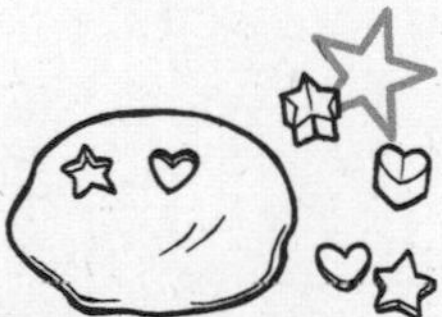

4. Wrap the mix in saran wrap and put it in the refrigerator for over 30 minutes.
5. Pour some flour on the board and put the mix from step 4 onto it and flatten it with a rolling pin.
6. Cut out pieces using cookie cutters.

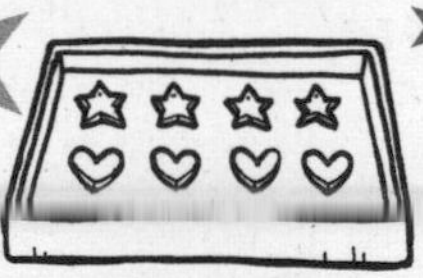

Done♡

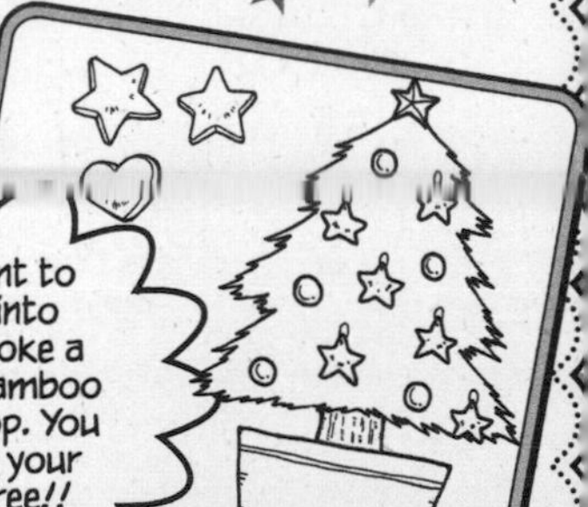

7. Lay out the pieces on a cookie sheet covered with wax paper and bake in the oven at 180 degrees Celsius (approx. 350 F) for 12 to 13 minutes. After it is baked, let cool.

When you want to make them into ornaments, poke a hole using a bamboo stick at the top. You can decorate your Christmas tree!!

Onion Gratin Soup

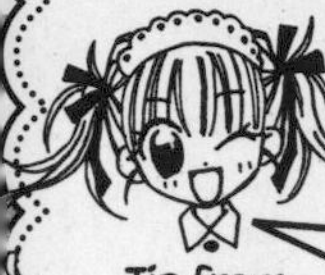

Tip from Najika.

You can make it Japanese style by using mochi instead of French bread. You can eat it New Year's Day.

Onion Gratin Soup

Serves two people. 1 large onion, 1 ½ tablespoons butter, 1¾ cups consommé soup (uses 1 block of consommé), ½ cup shredded cheese, 2 teaspoons grated cheese, 2 slices French bread, some salt and pepper

How to make

1. Boil 1¾ cups water and add 1 block consommé. Set the soup aside.

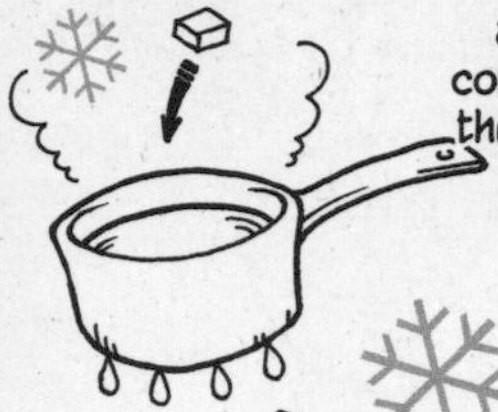

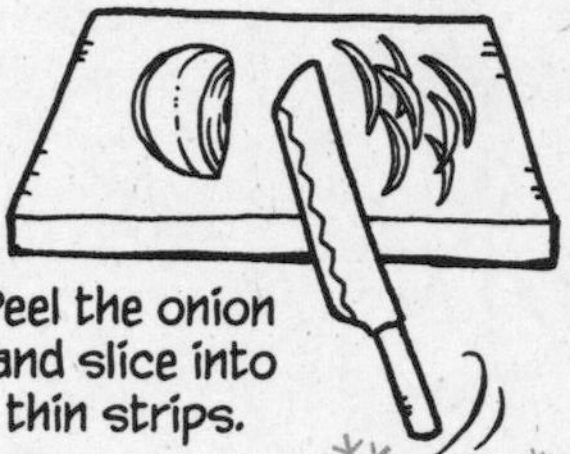

2. Peel the onion and slice into thin strips.

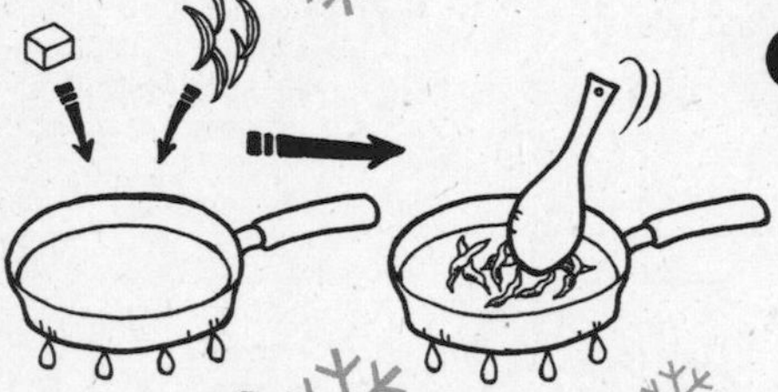

3. Heat the butter on medium in a frying pan. Be careful not to burn the butter. Put the onion in the butter and sauté until the onion turns a dark yellow color. Stir well with a wooden spoon so it won't burn. Sautéing it well here makes the sweetness come out of the onion!

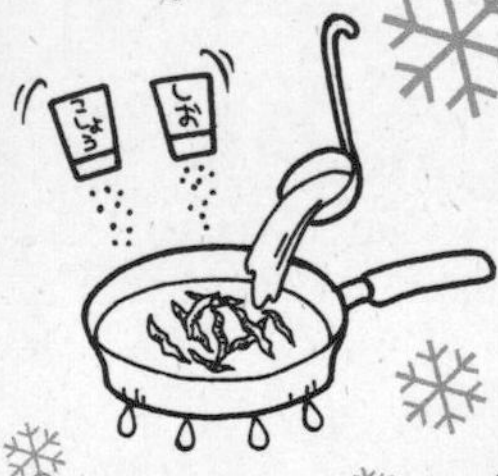

4. Add the consommé soup to the frying pan and stir. Add salt and pepper to taste.

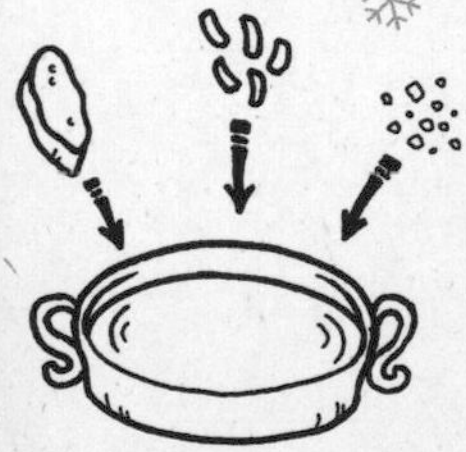

5. Put the soup into a heat-resistant bowl or cup. Put the French bread and shredded cheese on top, and shake some grated cheese on top of that. Put it in an oven toaster and toast for about 4 to 5 minutes. When it turns golden brown, it's done!

This is a classic French dish that can be made out of simple ingredients. Eat it while it's hot!

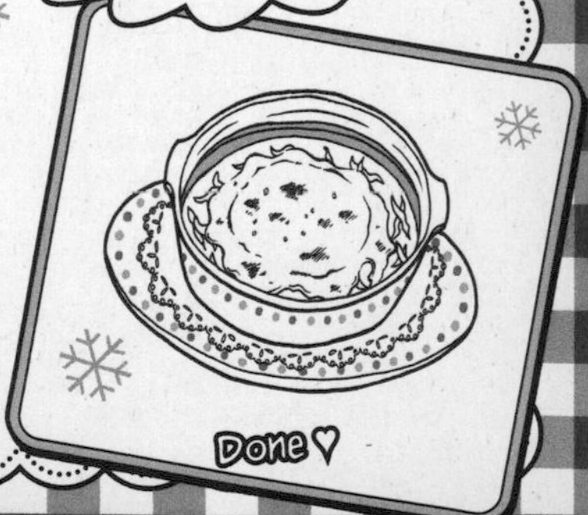
Done♥

Kitchen Princess

From the Writer

Thank you for reading Volume 1 of Kitchen Princess! I am the writer, Miyuki Kobayashi. Usually I write novels for teen girls under the Kodansha X Bunko Teen's Heart label. There are over 100 volumes under this label, so please look for them in bookstores and the library! You might find something you like.

But back to *Kitchen Princess*. I usually think of the character's name first, and then the story. I really like Najika's name! It's ethnically ambiguous and the seven colors of the rainbow make it very nature-like. It's the perfect weird name for a mysterious new student. And then I made the two boys' names to match hers, by naming them "Daichi" and "Sora." I wanted Najika to connect the two boys. Please tell me which one you like...earth or sky? I'll be waiting for your letters!

Finally, I would like to thank Ando-sensei, my editor Kishimoto-san, and my publisher Nouchi-san. Thank you so much! I'll see you in Volume 2!

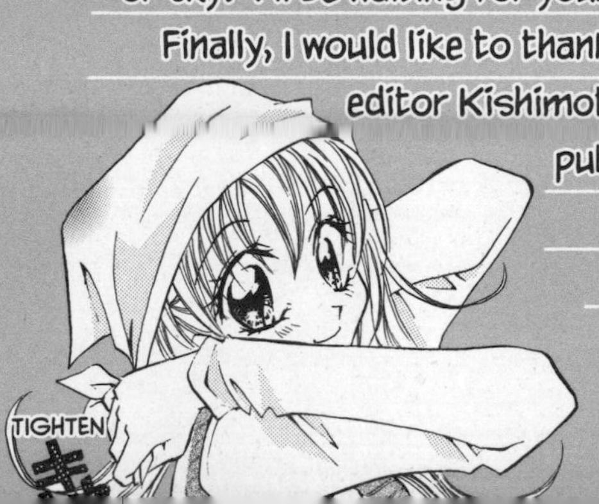
TIGHTEN

About the Creator

Natsumi Ando

She was born on January 27th in Aichi prefecture. She won the 19th Nakayoshi Rookie Award in 1994 and debuted as a manga artist. The title she drew was *Headstrong Cinderella*. Some of her other known works are Zodiac P.I. and Wild Heart. Her hobbies include reading, watching movies, and eating delicious food.

Translation Notes

Japanese is a tricky language for most Westerners, and translation is often more art than science. For your edification and reading pleasure, here are notes on some of the places where we could have gone in a different direction in our translation of the work, or where a Japanese cultural reference is used.

Hokkaido, page 6

Hokkaido is located in the northern part of Japan. It is the second largest island and the biggest prefecture.

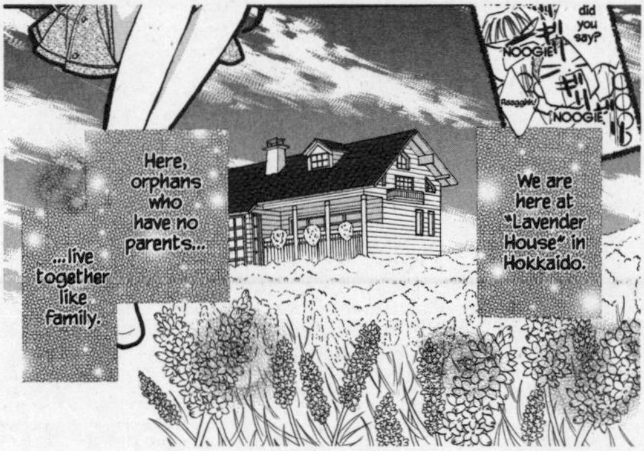
did you say?
NOOGIE
NOOGIE
We are here at "Lavender House" in Hokkaido.
Here, orphans who have no parents...
...live together like family.

Hacchou Miso, page 33

Hacchou miso is a special type of red miso made with soybeans only, without using bacteria. It is manufactured in Aichi prefecture and is known for its rich taste. The name comes from the village, Hacchou, where it is manufactured.

Nagoya, page 33

Nagoya is the capital of Aichi prefecture, and one of the bigger cities in Japan. It is located just between Tokyo and Kyoto on the eastern side of Japan.

Tempura, page 33

Tempura is a Japanese dish that consists of seafood or vegetables dipped in a batter and deep-fried.

Aniki, page 75

Aniki is a term for "older brother," usually used by boys (or girls who are tomboys) in their younger teens. It is less honorific than "onee-chan" and "onee-san."

Good.
Aniki.

Okayu, page 97

Okayu is the Japanese word for "rice porridge." Because it is easy to digest and because it makes your body warm, it is a common thing to eat when one is sick.

Here s your okayu.
PIPING HOT

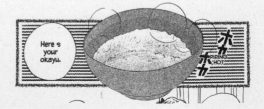

...A rainbow will connect...

Rainbow, earth, and sky, page 105

Najika's name, in Japanese characters, contains the character for "rainbow." That is why there are several references to rainbows in the manga. Daichi's name means "earth," and Sora's name means "sky." In this panel, Najika wants to be the rainbow that connects the earth and sky.

DisneySea, page 121

DisneySea is part of the Tokyo Disney Resort, located right next to Tokyo Disneyland. It is more adult-oriented than Disney and has a water theme.

Mochi, page 186

Mochi is the Japanese word for "rice cake," and it is usually eaten on New Year's Day. It is very sticky and elderly people often choke on it.

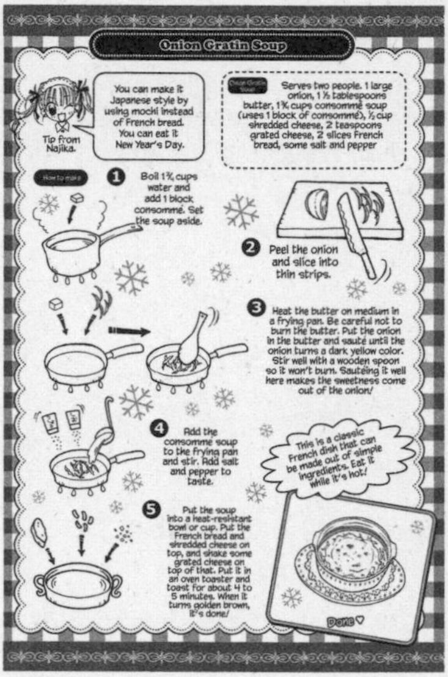
Onion Gratin Soup
Tip from Najika.
You can make it Japanese style by using mochi instead of French bread. You can eat it New Year's Day.
Serves two people. 1 large onion, 1 ½ tablespoons butter, 1¾ cups consommé soup (uses 1 block of consommé), ½ cup shredded cheese, 2 teaspoons grated cheese, 2 slices French bread, some salt and pepper
1 Boil 1¾ cups water and add 1 block consommé. Set the soup aside.
2 Peel the onion and slice into thin strips.
3 Heat the butter on medium in a frying pan. Be careful not to burn the butter. Put the onion in the butter and saute until the onion turns a dark yellow color. Stir well with a wooden spoon so it won't burn. Sauteing it well here makes the sweetness come out of the onion!
4 Add the consommé soup to the frying pan and stir. Add salt and pepper to taste.
5 Put the soup into a heat-resistant bowl or cup. Put the French bread and shredded cheese on top, and shake some grated cheese on top of that. Put it in an oven toaster and toast for about 4 to 5 minutes. When it turns golden brown, it's done!
This is a classic French dish that can be made out of simple ingredients. Eat it while it's hot!
Done ♡

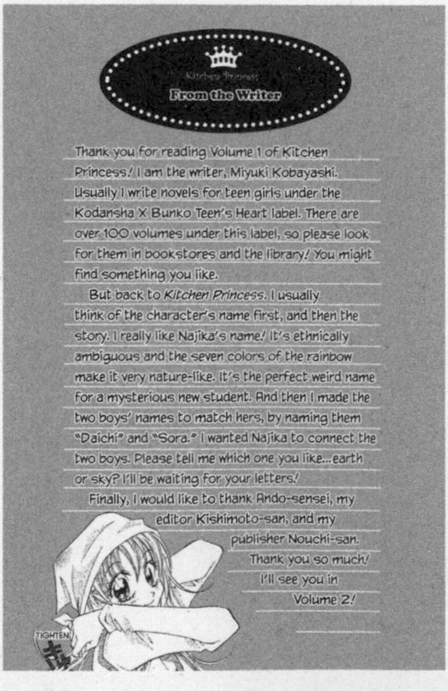
From the Writer
Thank you for reading Volume 1 of Kitchen Princess! I am the writer, Miyuki Kobayashi. Usually I write novels for teen girls under the Kodansha X Bunko Teen's Heart label. There are over 100 volumes under this label, so please look for them in bookstores and the library! You might find something you like.
But back to *Kitchen Princess*. I usually think of the character's name first, and then the story. I really like Najika's name! It's ethnically ambiguous and the seven colors of the rainbow make it very nature-like. It's the perfect weird name for a mysterious new student. And then I made the two boys' names to match hers, by naming them "Daichi" and "Sora." I wanted Najika to connect the two boys. Please tell me which one you like...earth or sky? I'll be waiting for your letters!
Finally, I would like to thank Ando-sensei, my editor Kishimoto-san, and my publisher Nouchi-san.
Thank you so much!
I'll see you in Volume 2!
TIGHTEN

Najika's name, page 187

Najika's name is a combination of the characters for "seven," "rainbow," and "fragrance."

Preview of Volume 2

We are pleased to present to you a preview from the next volume of *Kitchen Princess*. This volume is available in English now!

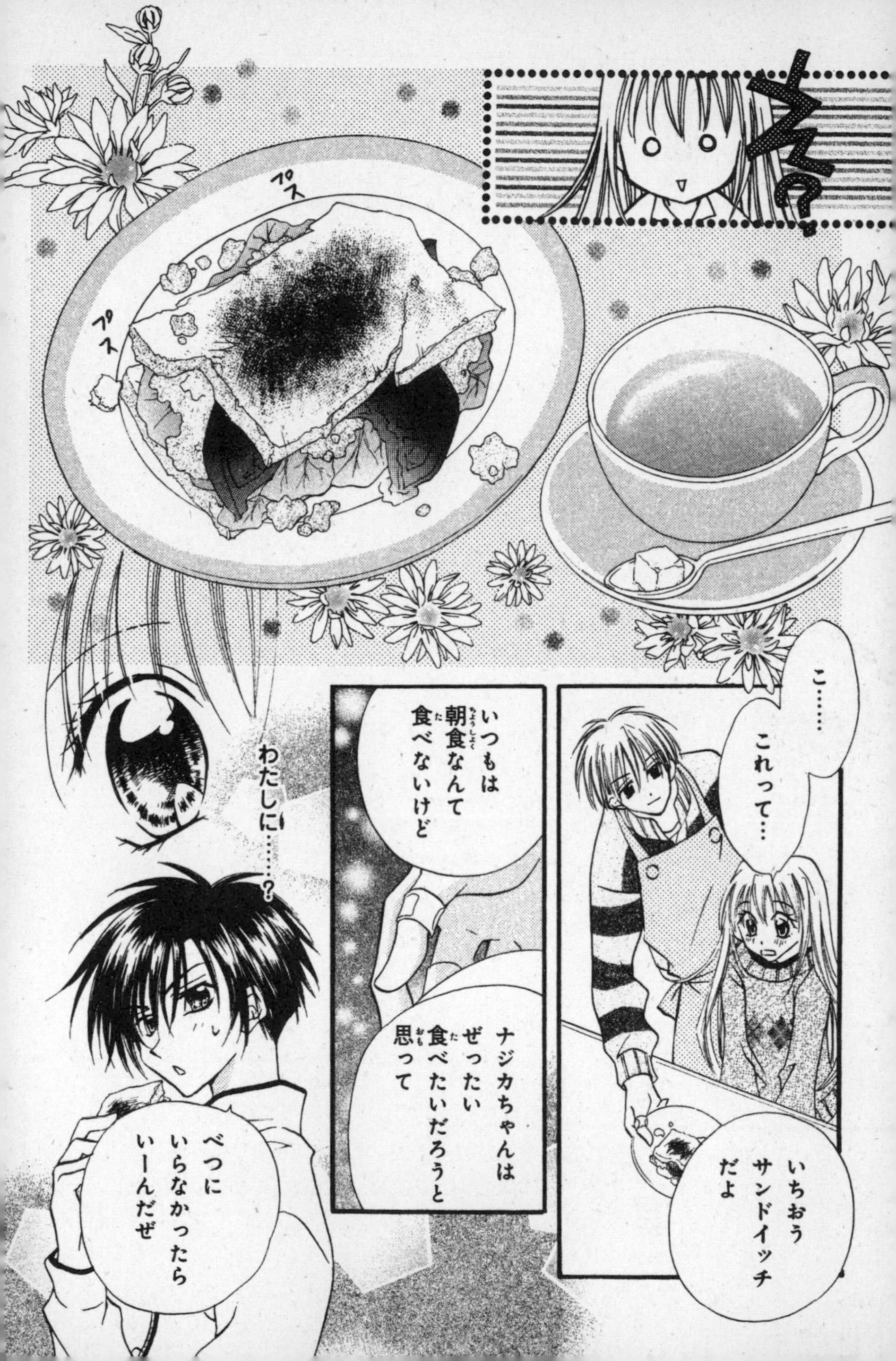

プス
プス
こ……
これって…
いちおう
サンドイッチ
だよ
いつもは朝食なんて食べないけど
ナジカちゃんはぜったい食べたいだろうと思って
わたしに……?
べつにいらなかったらいーんだぜ

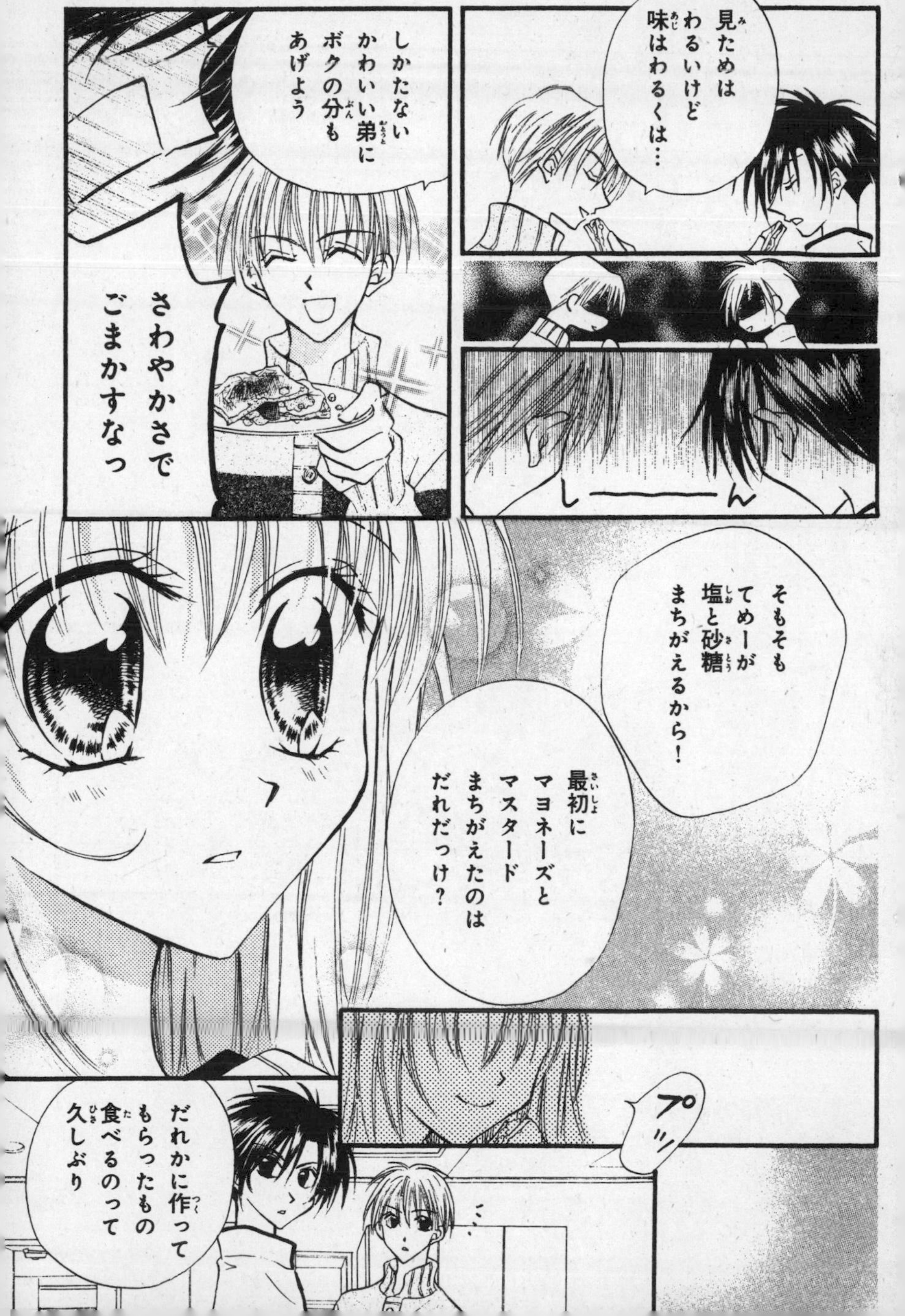
見ためはわるいけど味はわるくは…
しーーーーん
しかたないかわいい弟にボクの分もあげよう
さわやかさでごまかすなっ
そもそもてめーが塩と砂糖まちがえるから!
最初にマヨネーズとマスタードまちがえたのはだれだっけ?
プッ
だれかに作ってもらったもの食べるのって久しぶり

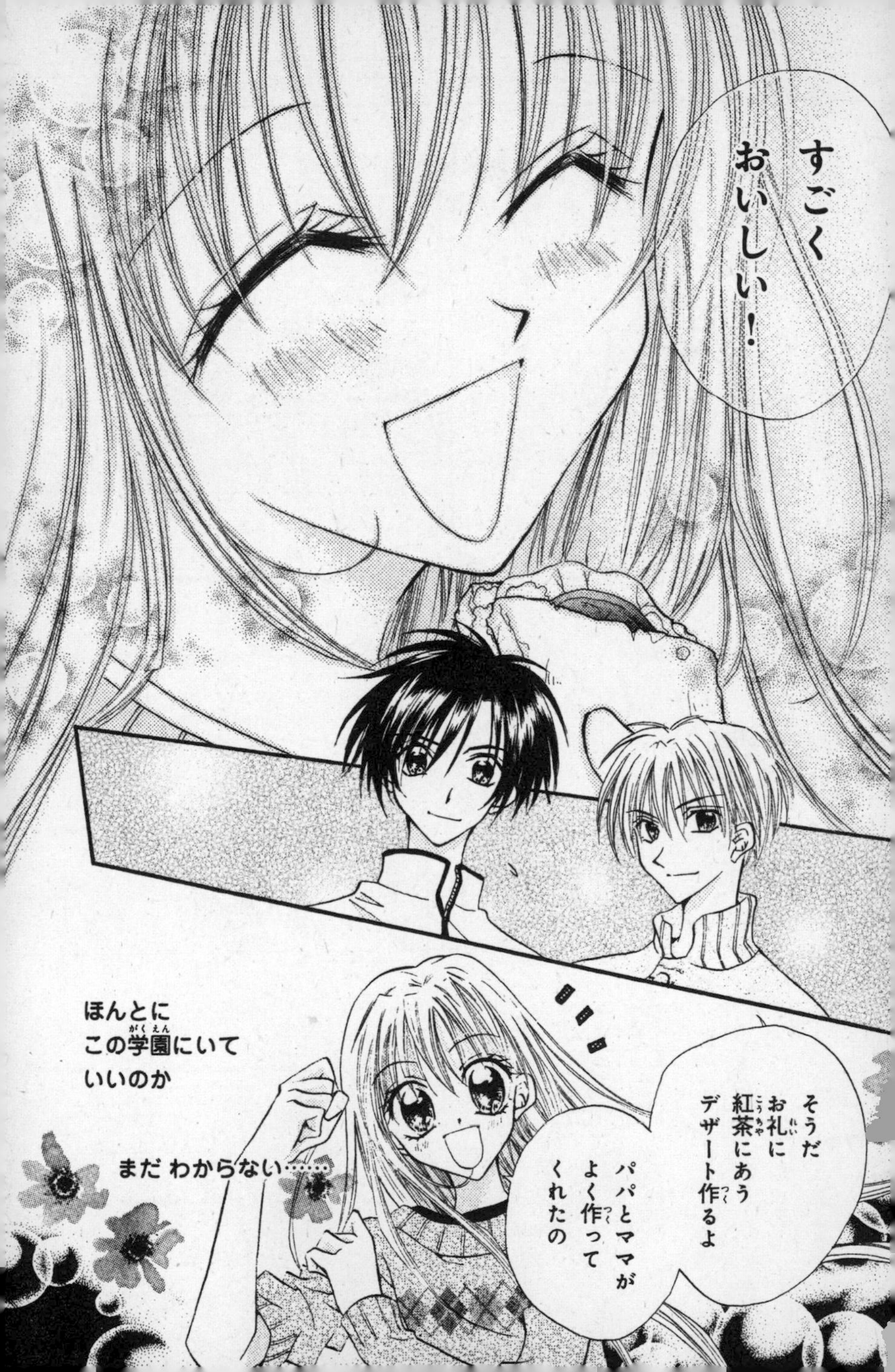
すごくおいしい！
そうだお礼に紅茶にあうデザート作るよ
パパとママがよく作ってくれたの
ほんとにこの学園にいていいのか
まだ わからない……

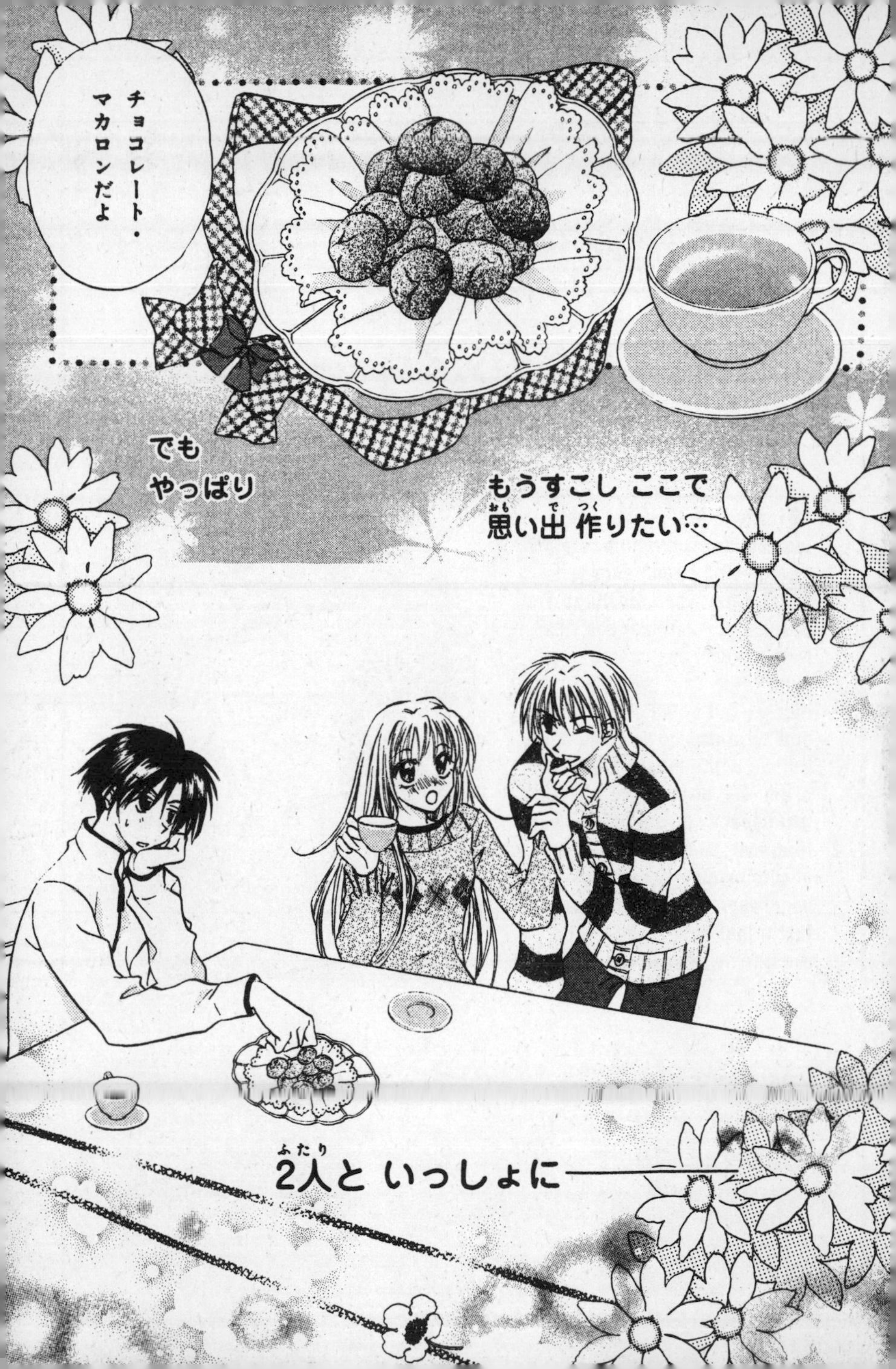
チョコレート・マカロンだよ
でも やっぱり
もうすこし ここで 思い出 作りたい…
2人と いっしょに——

Mamotte! LOLLIPOP

MICHIYO KIKUTA

BOY CRAZY

Junior high schooler Nina is ready to fall in love. She's looking for a boy who's cute and sweet—and strong enough to support her when the chips are down. But what happens when Nina's dream comes true . . . twice? One day, two cute boys literally fall from the sky. They're both wizards who've come to the Human World to take the Magic Exam. The boys' success on this test depends on protecting Nina from evil, so now Nina has a pair of cute magical boys chasing her everywhere! One of these wizards just might be the boy of her dreams . . . but which one?

Michiyo Kikuta
1
Mamotte! LOLLIPOP

Special extras in each volume! Read them all!

VISIT WWW.DELREYMANGA.COM TO:
- Read sample pages
- View release date calendars for upcoming volumes
- Sign up for Del Rey's free manga e-newsletter
- Find out the latest about new Del Rey Manga series

RATING T AGES 13+

DEL REY MANGA デルレイ

The Otaku's Choice

BY JIN KOBAYASHI

SUBTLETY IS FOR WIMPS!

S he . . . is a second-year high school student with a single all-consuming question: Will the boy she likes ever really notice her?

He . . . is the school's most notorious juvenile delinquent, and he's suddenly come to a shocking realization: He's got a huge crush, and now he must tell her how he feels.

Life-changing obsessions, colossal foul-ups, grand schemes, deep-seated anxieties, and raging hormones—School Rumble portrays high school as it really is: over-the-top comedy!

Ages: 16 +

Special extras in each volume! Read them all!

TOMARE!

止まれ

[STOP!]

You're going the wrong way!

Manga is a completely different
type of reading experience.

To start at the *beginning,*
go to the end!

That's right! Authentic manga is read the traditional Japanese way—
from right to left. Exactly the *opposite* of how American books are
read. It's easy to follow: Just go to the other end of the book, and read
each page—and each panel—from right side to left side, starting at
the top right. Now you're experiencing manga as it was meant to be!